Music Business Research

Music business research is a new multidisciplinary field that puts a number of different analytical approaches into mutual dialogue. It is located at the intersection of economic, artistic, musical, cultural, social, legal, and technological understandings of this cultural industry and it aims to generate a better understanding of the creation, distribution and consumption of music as a cultural good. As a field it is therefore characterised by methodological diversity and involves linking academic research with music business practices. The book series welcomes monographs and edited volumes that feature groundbreaking research into this dynamic and exciting field.

More information about this series at http://www.springer.com/series/15800

Phil Graham

Music, Management, Marketing, and Law

Interviews Across the Music Business Value Chain

Springer

Phil Graham
School of Communication and Creative Industries
University of the Sunshine Coast
Sunshine Coast, QLD, Australia

ISSN 2522-0829 ISSN 2522-0837 (electronic)
Music Business Research
ISBN 978-3-030-02142-9 ISBN 978-3-030-02143-6 (eBook)
https://doi.org/10.1007/978-3-030-02143-6

Library of Congress Control Number: 2019930071

This Springer imprint is published by the registered company Springer Nature Switzerland AG
The registered company address is: Gewerbestrasse 11, 6330 Cham, Switzerland

Acknowledgements

I offer my deepest thanks to Michael Smellie and Stuart Rubin whose idea was to teach in such a way as to preserve an invaluable historical record and share the experience of an era with those who could most benefit from it. They organised the interviews, managed the schedule, and accompanied each of the speakers from various parts of the country to conduct the events. I was left with the fun part: speaking with history-making individuals about their experiences and, more so, their insights into what the music world was, is, and might become. I thank Queensland University of Technology (QUT) for their support in running the classes the way we did, and in innovating across multiple levels to help deliver what was a series of very unique pedagogical events. I thank QUT music staff, Creative Industries staff, students, and the many members of the public whose involvement made the series of interviews special. I hope you get as much from them as I did. I also thank the University of the Sunshine Coast who supported the finalisation of this project. Most of all I thank our interviewees, each of whom gave so generously of their time and experience to make invaluable contributions to the future of music by telling us about their past.

University of the Sunshine Coast, May 2018 Phil Graham

Contents

Chapter 1
Introduction

Abstract This chapter contextualises the book, which centres around a series of public interviews designed to capture the implications of a pivotal moment in the global recorded music business and record a wealth of professional knowledge and perspectives that extend from the late 1960s through to late 2012 when the interviews were held. It positions the author and interviewer in the flow of events, introduces the interviewees, and gives an overview of their contributions to the global music industry. It has long been argued and demonstrated that music is a "canary in the coal mine" of broader political economic changes. This chapter re-emphasises that perspective and backgrounds the political economic perspective informing the questions asked and answered in the book.

This book centres around a series of public interviews designed to capture the implications of a pivotal moment in the global recorded music business, and to record a wealth of professional knowledge and perspectives that extend from the late 1960s through to late 2012 when the interviews were held. The idea for the series and its presentation came from discussions with Michael Smellie and Stuart Rubin during 2010 and 2011. We were concerned with understanding changes in the production, distribution, and exploitation of commercial recorded music associated with digital technologies, and how it related to past practices and experiences of industry professionals. It has long been argued and demonstrated that music is a "canary in the coal mine" of broader political economic changes. As Jacques Attali puts it: 'Music: herald of the future' (1985/2009, p. 144; see also, Graham, Dezuanni, Arthurs, & Hearn, 2015; Mumford, 1934/1962, pp. 202–203; Pacey, 2001, chap. 1). It pays to keep in mind that the term "music industry" is almost entirely misleading. The term suggests that there is some coherent and stable set of entities that persists among what is, at any given time, a complex and chaotic combination of characters, institutions, organisations, technologies, trends, relationships, cultures, sectors, business models, and so on, *ad infinitum* (Graham, 2016). To grasp the diverse elements that go together to make up what is commonly called "the music industry", and to understand the dynamics of change that this book deals with, I have found Veblen (1923) and Marx (1976, 1981) to be of conceptual help. From Veblen I make as clear a distinction as possible between business and industry, with

P. Graham, *Music, Management, Marketing, and Law*, Music Business Research,
https://doi.org/10.1007/978-3-030-02143-6_1

industry being the making and doing of useful things (production) and business being the buying and selling of those things to make money (exchange). In some cases there are clear distinctions, with music composition, production, and performance clearly being industry in Veblen's definition because it is that part of the complex that makes new music. Publishers are most clearly on the business end of the chain because their sole function is to exploit copyrights. The major recording labels have historically had a foot in each camp, sometimes owning and operating large studio complexes, commissioning and overseeing the creation of new works, while also being involved in the marketing, distribution, mass replication, and sale of original recordings (Tschmuck, 2012; Wikström, 2013). In more recent times, the major labels have to significant degree moved away from activities associated with industry in favour of business, having divested themselves of stakes in large studio complexes, in line with overall trends in political economy (cf. Graham & Luke, 2011; Tschmuck, 2012, p. 262; Wikström, 2013, pp. 190–206).

More bizarre relationships enter into consideration when we take the historical role of mass media in commercial music into account. They neither make, buy, nor sell music. Their business model is based on what Dallas Smythe (1981) calls 'audience labour', the process by which audiences work on cultural material to "sell" things to themselves. Mass media companies such as commercial radio stations harness specific types of programming (music is our case in point here) to motivate audience labour on a mass scale and build audiences that they can then sell to advertisers (1981, p. 4). And because they are not directly involved in the production or exploitation of music media companies are therefore easily understood as either music industry or business. Yet promotion of music through mass mediation greatly increases demand for recorded music, is an essential aspect of copyright exploitation, and has formed the bedrock of the mass market for commercial recorded music since at least the mid 1930s (Tschmuck, 2012, chap. 5; Wikström, 2013). Marx's (1981, chap. 48) theorising of circulation, including transport and communication as moments in the process of exchange, is useful here, especially when we note the essential role of promotion in the exploitation of ephemeral cultural goods of which music is a primary exemplar (Attali, 1985/2009, p. 57). Cultural commodities operate with an inverse logic to that of more materially bound commodities (Graham, 2006). That is especially evident when we consider three elements that are inherent in the recorded musical work: (1) any recorded musical work can be reproduced without limit and, with the advent of digital, by means of reproduction that are almost universally of high fidelity; (2) unlike material commodities which are defined as undifferentiated and therefore substitutable for one another (Pine & Gilmore, 2011), each new musical commodity is necessarily unique, even when it is a "cover" or "copy" of another; (3) unlike material commodities, recorded musical works, and the musicians that make them, increase in cultural and commercial value as the commodities are used more, regardless of whether they are purchased or simply played in environments that are susceptible to promotion and public performance rights generation.

Here is where Marx's elaboration of Adam Smith's (1776/1997) labour theory of value becomes useful. It is helpful to focus on the kinds of "work" involved at each stage of the value chain, without which the grounds of industrial transformation get obscured. Peter Tschmuck (2012, p. 253) identifies 'Artist & Repertoire (A&R) management', 'music production and ... physically manufacturing phonograms', 'music marketing and promotion', and 'phonogram distribution' as 'the most important processes of action' for analytical focus on innovations in the value chain of commercial recorded music. The interviews collected here address all those and more, heralding in some cases, an almost total reorientation of relationships among and between the various aspects of labour in the face of digital technologies (Wikström, 2013, chap. 3). Such changes are especially evident in the interview with Kate Miller-Heidke and Keir Nuttall which took place just as Kate was on the verge of moving from being a "signed" to a major label to becoming entirely independent.

There is much discussion throughout the interviews about digital challenges to copyright, new kinds of contracts, and the vastly changed relationships between major record labels and mass media, especially commercial radio and television. The interviews of course contain much about the effects and affordances of digital technologies right across the value chain. In some cases there are claims that there is not much about digital that is very new given the long history of technological innovations, associated *faux pas*, and outright pratfalls in the history of recorded music (Tschmuck, 2012). We must keep in mind that new technologies are simply innovations in the way we do things (White, 1940) rather than necessarily being innovations in the things we do. The temptation to see technology as incidental beckons to the latter perspective. Again, I find Marx helpful in understanding the role of technological change, noting that the development of the means of production (that is, historical changes in the way we make and do things) is always shaped by prevailing conditions, regardless of whether those developments accord with or react to those conditions (Marx, 1976, chap. 15).

This is perhaps an overly complex web of theory to foist upon the reader given the largely concrete character of the interviews presented here. But I think those perspectives can help us understand the nature of the changes addressed throughout the interviews, why they are important well beyond the sphere of commercial recorded music, and why this collection is important in helping us understand those changes, both practically and theoretically. I should also be clear and honest about my own position in all of this because, as becomes evident throughout the interviews, one's place in the chaotic changes of the commercial music landscape profoundly shapes the way one perceives the challenges the sector continues to face. My own experience of commercial music certainly shaped the questions I asked. I wanted to know why musicians' share of recording revenues had dropped. I wanted to know how musicians could make a better living in future. I wanted to know how experts and professionals from different parts of the music value chain understood the changes that had taken place during their careers and what they meant for the future of musical careers. I wanted to know how they thought about new technologies and new kinds of commercial relationships that had begun to develop since digital distribution had made such a public impact on perceptions of what it meant to be a professional in the recorded music business and industries.

My perspective, and hence my questions, are those of a musical labourer, a part of what was once Australia's "musical middle class", which today no longer exists. I spent well over two decades making music for all kinds of commercial purposes, beginning as a busker on the streets of Sydney's red light district, moving into theatre; then into band, duo, and solo work in every manner of venue, from restaurants to large rock venues. I later moved into advertising, film, documentary, and television work as a session musician, composer, recording engineer, and producer. I worked for publishing and record companies, owned and operated studios, and made music for almost anyone who would pay me to do so.

My sensitivity to the technical comes from direct experience. I began my recording career in the early 1980s when a professional studio cost several million to establish and upwards of two thousand dollars a day to hire. By the time I made the permanent move to academia some 20 years later, the cost of establishing a broadcast quality studio had dropped to the order of tens of thousands of dollars, PC-based digital recording had become feasible to integrate into high turnover commercial workflows, and SMPTE and MIDI Time Code standards had become universally established as languages for controlling and sequencing digital equipment and locking it to tape and video. Tape was still essential, but vastly cheaper half-inch formats had achieved broadcast quality and digital equipment had achieved rapidly lowered costs, making commercial quality recording widely affordable. Production fees were dropping as more people became music producers.

As far as popular music was concerned it had become clear to my colleagues and I by 1991 that the last barrier to independent operators was distribution: access to large audiences, both in terms of producing and distributing mass runs of physical media (cassettes, CD, and vinyl), and of gaining the attention of audiences who would buy music. Composers and performers still needed the support of large recording companies, mass media corporations (especially radio), advertising agencies, or publishing companies to be successful. Musicians therefore needed to be part of a network that was global in reach and scale, long before the term "globalisation" entered common parlance. The major labels dominated distribution and promotion of commercially recorded product the world over. Television and radio dominated national and local markets. To be outside those systems was to be hopelessly "firewalled" from success in any kind of mass market.

By the mid-1990s, just as hard disk recording started to become widely available and affordable, live performance work in Australia had started to disappear, or at least to yield rapidly diminishing revenues to musicians (Johnson & Homan, 2003). Depending on whose version of events one accepts, the causes included drink driving laws, noise restrictions associated with inner-city gentrification, the introduction of gambling machines into venues, smoking laws, fire regulations, and licensing laws among numerous others (APRA, 2011; Deloitte Access Economics, 2011; Hoegh-Guldberg, 2012; Johnson & Homan, 2003). From the perspective of a working musician, it was clear that "computerised" solo and duo acts that could sound like a band were driving live revenues down (ask any working drummer from that period) while ever cheaper studio technologies continued to drive down recorded commercial revenues as more people entered a once highly restricted market. In Australia and elsewhere, free trade agreements about cultural imports almost overnight eroded income streams from advertising and television, major staples of session work for musicians. For the musical middle class, the combination of reduced opportunities for performance income combined with an almost total drop in session work led to a rapid hollowing out of the market and revenues for musical labour and therefore of the musical middle class itself. It reached the point for me in late 1996 that the pressures of a young family drove me to seek a future elsewhere. From the perspective of a musical labourer from a once-thriving musical middle-class in Australia, music had become a non-viable career by the mid 1990s, thanks in no small part to the strange impacts of digital technologies on music production and performance.

The Visibility and Effects of Digital Distribution

It was not until the distribution issues associated with the internet came to the fore with Napster in the late 1990s that the effects of the digital revolution in music became a high-profile issue of popular, industry, and academic concern. Popular interest was piqued by early litigation threats from the major record labels aimed at universities whose students were the first to innovate with distribution platforms because of access to high speed internet connections (Latonero, 2001). The first high-profile study of online music distribution was conducted out of the Annenberg School of Communication at UCLA by Mark Latonero (2001; see also New York Times, 2000). The study followed closely on the heels of UCLA's ban on Napster 'amid speculation of widespread copyright violations and threatening litigation' (Latonero, 2001, p. 1). It showed what would later become fairly predictable patterns of perception and preference among users more generally: that music was overwhelmingly either important or very important in people's day to day lives; that people who downloaded music were happy to, and more likely to, pay for music; that they felt copyright holders should be remunerated for downloads; and that CDs were overpriced (Latonero, 2001, p. 3).

Despite those early findings, and given Napster's express willingness to 'find a structure that works with everybody and respects copyrights', the Recording Industry Association of America (RIAA) began legal action against Napster the same year, the result of which was to force the closure of the service by July, 2001 (The Guardian, 2001) with its total liquidation happening by September 2002, despite a pending sale and partnership deal with Bertelsmann (Pyyny, 2002). The rapid chain of events that marked Napster's (first) rise and fall began in June 1999 and ended in liquidation by September 2002. It had a verified 26.4 million users by February 2001. The Napster episode set the pattern for years to come, with record companies, publishers, and collecting agencies pursuing litigation, first against platforms, then against universities, later against internet service providers (ISPs), still later against individuals, with new digital distribution platforms proliferating almost weekly.

The third point at which digital became an issue for music also happened well before internet distribution of music became possible. The Compact Disc (CD) was a massive windfall for the major labels. Michael Smellie tells the story of the CD in his interview, and is indeed one of the central characters its success as a distribution format, so I won't rehearse the details here. However it is worth recognising the role of the CD as a benchmark in discussions about the rise and fall of revenues for recorded music, and about the Janus-faced nature of digital production and distribution of music. It is a commonplace for current revenues for major labels to be compared with the height of CD sales in 1999 (see, for comparison, Degusta, 2011; IFPI, 2013). However, as Michael Smellie and Stu Rubin tell us, the level of revenues from CD was historically unprecedented, being the first time in history that entire catalogues were re-issued and re-bought in a new format by audiences the world over. And although the CD was still what Attali (1985/2009, p. 96) describes as a kind of "semi commodity", requiring a separate commodity to be used to hear it, it was still digital, and probably the first digital mass commodity. In any case, the CD revenue "bubble" transformed the recorded music business from a global network of what Michael Smellie describes as "cottage industries" into a small number of massive global corporations reaping unprecedented revenues. Thus a prior digital "revolution" underpins the most typical perceptions of how digital distribution has so negatively affected revenue flows for major record companies.

So to briefly recap the earliest days of digital and its impacts on various moments in the commercial music value chain: first, it becomes part of production, affecting the way people made music. Then it becomes part of organisation, affecting the way people configured themselves in music making groups, with smaller numbers of people required to make audibly "massive" sounds whether in live performance or in the recording studio. Thereafter it quickly becomes an influence on revenues, negatively in respect of certain classes of music makers as various musical functions were automated or synthesised, positively for the major labels in respect of the explosion of revenues associated with CD sales. Digital technologies also transformed plant and equipment, with the cost of equipment for commercial quality production dropping from millions in the early 1980s, to under two hundred thousand in the late 1980s, to almost zero by the early twenty-first century (Graham, 2006). Finally the recorded musical commodity slips its physical bonds in the late 1990s as more efficient compression algorithms combine with higher network speeds to make Napster possible. Distribution of music gives way to pure circulation at this point; binary code becomes simultaneous player of music, music played, means of circulation, and means of promotion.

At no time since the first incursions of digital technologies into the commercial music value chain have the trends affecting all aspects of that chain slowed or become any less problematic. By the time the interviews in this book were collected, recording technologies had become not only free but arguably (very arguably) better quality than those used in the multi-million dollar studio era. Music making technologies, such as synthesisers and sequencers, had become devastatingly complex, sophisticated, compact, and cheap. Organisation of labour and production has become a matter of global proportion and complexity, with collaborative applications being built into the most basic production software, thus allowing musicians to work together across the globe, if not in "real time" then in the most efficient asynchronous terms possible given the speed of light and computer processing efficiency. Relationships between musical labour and multinational record labels were changing rapidly. In attempts to recover revenues lost to internet distribution, the majors began confecting "360°" contracts with artists; no longer signing artists to merely collect shares of recording revenues, but now also revenues from merchandise, live touring, publishing, and synchronisation (broadcast soundtrack) revenues. The distribution landscape was continuing to produce innovation, litigation, and business disruption in equal proportions, with music makers coming off worst in the fight for revenues from new and popular platforms such as Spotify, Apple Music, and YouTube. The legal landscape was also changing rapidly, with new kinds of relationships being constructed between artists, their music, and the corporate entities controlling massive collections of commercial copyrights. In Australia, legal battles were breaking out between copyright holders, commercial broadcasters, and collection agencies. Mass media advertising revenues had started to dwindle rapidly as more and more people were moving online for their entertainment. Netflix had just started producing its own audiovisual offerings, but the writing had been on the wall for free-to-air television and radio since 2004 when, for the first time in the history of mass media, consumers paid more for access to media than advertisers (Graham, 2006). Spotify had only just registered its first million users after 4 years of operation. Such was the situation at the time we held the interviews.

About the Interviews

In developing the interview series, Smellie, Rubin, and I aimed to involve as wide a possible spread of professions and experiences, from the working artist through to the global record executive, to capture the character and quality of changes across as much of the industry as possible. While most of the interviewees are Australian, and much of the context refers to the Australian "scene", each of the interviewees has contributed in ways that have been influential on both international and global scales. The interviews were very public, conducted as weekly classes that were open to music, music industry, and entertainment industry students at the Queensland University of Technology. As well as having the series open to multiple classes of students, we also opened it to interested members of the local industry and the public, advertising it through Queensland's peak contemporary music organisation, Q-Music, and through the university's publicity channels. The underlying aims of the series were (a) to develop an engaging, timely, and relevant pedagogy for students that addressed the most pressing issues facing their future livelihood and (b) to capture the experiences of people whose careers helped to shape a global business that was quickly passing into history and transforming into something entirely new, often because of technical developments the interviewees themselves had been directly involved in implementing.

Like many books of interviews, the authorship of this collection is highly ambiguous and I recognise the role of the interviewees in "writing" it (Ong, 1977). It is what Walter Ong once called 'a talked book' and he is worth quoting at length on this important definition:

> I was recently interviewed for such a talked book. The supervisor of the book, as we might style him, or the production manager—he is not the author nor am I; there is no author in any earlier sense of the word—called me first in St. Louis by telephone from New York to arrange an interview with me in Bethlehem, Pennsylvania. He brought a tape recorder to the interview and taped my answers to questions which he put to me. Then he slept on the tape in Bethlehem hotel and came back the next morning with supplementary questions for a fill-in interview, which he also taped. He took all the tape back to Brooklyn and had it transcribed. Of course the stenographer edited the tape in transcribing it. The supervisor of production manager edited the transcription some more, after which he sent it to me for further editing. [. . .] When the book comes out, what do we have? The "book" is presented as an interview, with his questions and my responses. But in fact the total is something that neither of us said and that neither of us ever wrote. We have no term or readily available concept for this sort of thing. Perhaps we should call the end result a "presentation" or "production". (Ong, 1977, pp. 83–84).

The interviews were indeed produced for presentation and I find myself in the role of a producer and presenter of expert discourse on music industry and business. From the outset, the series was developed to be an enduring public record, spoken to be written and heard "live" by students and the public, and then subject to numerous stages of refinement for publication in print. The interviews were filmed and recorded for transcription, with all of us being aware that the series was to be recorded, filmed, and later published. I developed the questions in collaboration with each speaker after researching their professional lives as extensively as possible. About 2 weeks prior to the event, speakers were given proposed questions. In each case, the questions were developed with a view towards two things: (a) identifying the most relevant ways in which each speaker could contribute to what might best be described as "a history of the present" with a view to future action, especially for people relatively new to the business, and (b) to draw out the principles that each of the interviewees had developed as a professional over decades of high level practice. The interviews are presented here in logical order rather than in the order in which they were conducted, but there are of course many ways they could be framed and presented. The material covered is extensive, and includes the aesthetic, artistic, technical, commercial, legal, and strategic aspects of the industry and the challenges it faces. There are also many ways these interviews could be analysed, but the themes in each are strong and clear enough to stand on their own.

Of course we would have liked to present the collection sooner, but many factors intervened to slow the process, none of which need bore you here. In any case, the interviews literally speak for themselves, and the general nature of what is said is timeless in terms of its historical significance for the music business and in its relevance for people wanting to understand the dynamics of ongoing changes in the commercial music landscape. In research terms this collection could be seen as a book of "raw" data. As a 'talked book', the transcripts have gone through many stages of refinement in collaboration with the interviewees. Much of the interaction between interviewer and interviewee that was specific to the context of the "classroom" (the location was in fact a very large lecture theatre with a capacity of around 500) has been removed to improve the flow of things for the reader. Other than that, they are fairly much what happened on the day. All that remains is to provide some context for each of the interview participants and to briefly summarise their individual contributions.

Michael Smellie is Australia's most successful major label record executive. From his beginnings as an accountant in the publishing business he became Chief Operations Officer for Sony BMG (Global) and led the company through what was to prove an historic merger. His time with Sony coincided with the advent of the CD and the subsequent explosion in revenues for the major record labels. Michael also played a major part in funding and conceptualising one of the most exciting and successful independent record labels in the history of Australian music, Rooart Records, the many achievements of which include the international success of INXS. An accountant by training, Michael brought a new management ethos and radical financial logic to the music business. The interview covers expansive ground, including Rooart; Warner BMG (the merger that almost happened prior to Sony BMG); the relationship between sport and music; and commentary on the nature and quality of management in the major labels sector of the music industry.

Peter Colby is our technological and logistics voice in the collection. Peter began his career as a recordist for the ABC, Australia's national broadcaster, and was in 2012 Global President of Sony DADC, the company's digital production arm. Peter has been responsible for the development and implementation of numerous new music media and platforms for mass and niche markets and has overseen the building of massive plant and equipment for both the production and distribution stages of commercial recorded music, including the legendary Armstrong Studios in Melbourne, Australia. Peter details the history of production technologies used in both the recording and distribution phases of the record business through his experience as a professional involved in practically every aspect of commercial music and video production. Peter's grasp of the complexities and tensions inherent in commercial media forms is unique. His is a perspective based in quality, and in numerous places he foregrounds the many complex, sensitive, and often paradoxical balances between convenience and quality, fidelity and finance, consumer lifestyle and consumption formats, and digital security and system interoperability. What becomes clear is Peter's dedication both to the art and science of presenting cultural material to a mass audience, and to a deep understanding of how people actually prefer to experience those materials. As far as this series goes, Peter presents the most comprehensive grasp of logistics across the entire value chain of both pre- and post-streaming eras of commercial music.

John Watson is widely recognised as being one of Australia's most successful and innovative artist managers. His career in music began in a Townsville record store during his teenage years, then moved through playing bass for an indie rock band called *The Spliffs*, music journalism, and music publicist. In 1991 John became A&R

manager of Sony Australia and in 1994 became the company's Director of International Marketing. He began his management career with Silverchair in 1995, helping to sell 6 million albums for the band. In 2000 he established Eleven: A Music Company and took up the management of Silverchair once the band had finalised its contract with Sony. The company manages a small but influential roster of artists that includes Gotye, Missy Higgins, Cold Chisel, The Presets, and Birds of Tokyo. Eleven was in many ways a pioneer for a new music business model. It combines the functions of a label with the functions of management and has been widely emulated, at least throughout the Australian industry. What becomes clear reading John's interview is how thoroughly systematic he is in thinking about what he does. Some parts of the interview could quite easily be framed as a philosophy of music management. Like others in this series, John's interview reveals a broad and deep knowledge about the details of the industry well beyond the concerns of management.

Michael Taylor is today joint managing director of Universal Music Group, Australia. At the time of the interview he was Australian VP of A&R for Universal and head of Island Records, a Universal imprint. Michael's career began at Clark University where he booked nationally and internationally significant acts as President of the Student Entertainment Committee. He also toured the US as a drummer for The Vangos. His first music business job was at the William Morris Agency in New York. He then became an A&R scout for Columbia Records and went on to be A&R Manager at Madonna's label, Maverick, and Senior A&R Director at Epic Records. In the mid-1990s Michael founded the Go Big label, a project that fused music licensing with lifestyle sports, which he ran with a flatmate out of his kitchen in New York. In 2001 Michael moved to Australia to head up A&R at Sony Music. In 2008 he established Island Records Australia as General Manager. Michael was promoted to Executive VP of A&R Universal Music Australia in 2013 and in 2014 became co-Managing Director of the company. Michael's interview shows how the A&R function extends well beyond the mere discovery of talent. In fact, Michael's approach combines science, intuition, experience, and a general knowledge of the industry to deliver the artists vision. Once again we see in this interview the character of success in a business that relies on bringing together new ideas, new talent, new audiences in configurations that are specific to each new act. We also see how intensely personal this business can be. The interview highlights an interesting point of difference with Michael Smellie, at least where their conceptions of sport and music are compared.

At the height of his career, *Stuart Rubin* was Senior VP of Worldwide Marketing for Sony BMG. Stuart's career in music started in New Zealand in 1976 with PolyGram. He "crossed the ditch" and held a number of senior marketing roles in PolyGram and BMG in Australia before moving to Hong Kong in the 1990s where he became BMG's VP of International Marketing for the Asia-Pacific region. In 2001 he moved to New York, becoming Senior VP International for BMG. Following the merger with Sony 3 years later, Stuart was made Senior VP International of Commercial Marketing. Stuart's interview reveals a person fascinated with people, whether they are artists or music lovers. His long experience in selling music to a global market, and as an A&R professional, gives him a unique perspective on the industry. One of Stuart's unique contributions to this series is his analysis of the "prefab" phenomenon that has been a topic of discussion where the majors are concerned for years. In some ways, Stuart concludes that, yes, with enough experience, and a sense of what works in which genres, and of course with enough money, you can actually plan a campaign for a release with reasonably predictable outcomes. On the other hand, it remains the case that marketing in general, and music in particular, is still as much an art as it is a science.

Shane Simpson (AM) is Australia's best-known copyright lawyer. He set up his practice in 1986 and has since acted from many of the leading artists in Australia and elsewhere. He began his career in more conventional areas of the law, coming to the bar in New Zealand in 1973, in New South Wales in 1978, and stepping down in 1986 to pursue his work in the arts. While he is perhaps best known for his work in the music business, Shane's experience and influence extends far beyond. His first work in copyright, and an enduring area of personal interest, was in visual arts. He has extended that work into areas such as museum law, media law, information technology law, and of course music. His contributions to the Arts in general include the establishment of Australia's first Arts Law Centre, a free service for artists who could not afford legal advice. The most striking aspect of interviewing Shane was the historical depth and detail of his legal and business knowledge. He takes us back to 1403 to frame the issues of the current era, and does so with a degree of ease and felicity that presents any current problems as being typical of new technologies rather than anything especially unusual or frightening. With the same depth of knowledge and experience, Shane explains the detail of what it takes to be successful as an artist—an obsession with perfection, a well developed sense of personal responsibility, and a willingness to take control of the things that matter.

At the time of the interview *Shaun James* was head of XYZ Music and centrally involved in the direction of Foxtel's music channels, V, V Hits, Max, and CMC. He has since moved on to front Presto, Foxtel's streaming video on demand (VOD) service. Shaun's industry history includes being CEO of Warner Music (Australia and New Zealand) during a time of massive market growth for that label, Chief Marketing Officer of the national TEN television network, and Vice Chairman of ARIA. Shaun's experience across television, digital, and major music labels gives him yet another distinct and unusual perspective on the past and future of the music business. Shaun's is the mind of a technology business strategist. He sees the technology, the rules, the signal flows, the money flows, and the way value gets created across multiple platforms and the connections among them. In that sense, this interview reveals a sophisticated sense of value ecologies for music that is both futuristic and paradoxical in its implications. As in many of the other interviews presented here, Shaun points to the idea that the present state of business is a form of interregnum, a pregnant pause in power dynamics between one dominant regime that has faded and another that is still emerging.

Toby Creswell is one of the Australia's most influential music journalists. He edited *Rolling Stone* (Australia) and was founding editor of *Juice* magazine. He has written numerous books, articles for multiple publications both national and international, and has also worked extensively in television and publishing. Toby's interview shows a more classically critical mind at work than we have become used to from younger music critics. There is a sense of ecology when it comes to understanding what makes music good or bad, a sense of conditions, collaborations, and contexts. The worst appraisal from Toby is one of mediocrity, of being part of the "sludge". A song needs a story to be worth listening to or worth writing about. It needs to be a unique contribution to culture.

The critic sits in a strange relation to music. The new media have challenged the role of the music critic as fundamentally as it has the role of the musician and composer. But there is no sense of nostalgia for a lost profession here. Rather Toby has a sense of opportunity and optimism about the future of criticism not, though, for the future of popular music whose golden age he sees as being well in the past. We hear again a critique of the establishment major music businesses whose personnel missed the significance of digital media, even while the evidence was directly in front of them.

In introducing him to our audience, I described *Harley Medcalfe* as the most famous person I'd never heard of. Of course Harley is well known by all at the "top end" of entertainment but he is all but invisible to the public he has served so well for over 40 years. Harley began life as a tour manager and played a major part in setting up a national touring grid in Australia. Details of Harley's credits would by themselves take up a large book. A few highlights will suffice. Harley managed every Elton John tour ever brought to Australia; was Barry Humphries' (Dame Edna Everage) manager for decades; toured Marlene Dietrich, Frank Sinatra, and Queen to Australia; globally tour-managed Formula One racing; and started (against all advice and music industry ridicule) the globally successful *Burn The Floor* series of shows after discovering an enthusiasm for Ballroom Dancing.

Harley is an innovator and an eternal pioneer. He shows us, again, the importance of paying attention to detail. In fact it could be said that this is Harley's method—minute attention to detail at every stage. It is a lesson learned from costly mistakes, including one small mistake with limousines and airline schedules that unfolded into the spectacular 1974 debacle involving Frank Sinatra, the Australian Journalists Association, some indiscriminate security guards, a national union black ban, and a consequent worldwide media scandal. Harley's innovations are all the more remarkable for the fact that they have been made in the oldest quarters of the entertainment industries: live performance, whether in music, theatre, dance, or sport. It is at the level of the personal and contractual that he is most interesting. His interest in and love of people shines through, as does his almost total mistrust of them.

He successfully toured Dame Edna in the Middle East. He helped to successfully revive Tap and Ballroom dancing. He has toured acts of all kinds in over 300 cities, world-wide. He has worked with the very best in the business. Yet he has remained all but invisible to the public eye. He makes clear in the interview that this is because he is a promoter. For Harley, promoters should promote artists, not themselves.

Kate Miller-Heidke and *Keir Nuttall* represent "ground zero" of the music industry for the series: the artists, the creative labourers who make the music that makes money for them and everybody else in the business. Kate and Keir are partners in life and music, and in that sense they are a rare combination. Kate's creative repertoire spans indie-alternative, pop, heavy metal, musical theatre, and Opera. The couple is quite obviously on a journey of continual renewal at every level: as artists, musicians, and business people. The interview makes clear, I think, that Kate and Keir are new kinds of artists who are emblematic of the music business's digital interregnum. Kate benefited from early involvement in a major label system with Keir deliberately staying outside so that he could get paid rather than having to wait for any financial returns to be written off against recoupable advances of one sort and another. Shortly after the interview, Kate would leave her label and the pair would become entirely independent, with both beginning solo ventures in areas as diverse as comedy, musical theatre, and opera, as well as continuing their professional collaboration.

This interview is perhaps the most raw of the whole series. At times we can see the relationship between the two working itself out in front of the audience, never too seriously, and always with a razor wit and self-conscious personal insights that seem to be typical of the couple's approach. There is nothing to say talent and intelligence are two attributes of the same syndrome. Often, in fact, the opposite seems to be the case. Kate and Keir have both. Their grasp of circumstances, creative process, and changing potentials are astute and acute. The interview covers everything from the psychology of drama in song composition to the composition of the industry and its changing demands.

There could be much more by way of analysis and commentary in this introduction, but I think that would do our interviewees an injustice. The interview process was exhausting and, at many points, as fiercely intense as any performance in which I have been involved. I have read over the series many times during its editorial processes since late 2012, and the insights, humour, intelligence, and great willingness to pass valuable insights on to the future of music become more evident with each reading. Thus any further analysis on my part would be unbecoming, incomplete, and for its own sake. I can say, though, that a common theme throughout the interviews is a love of music evident in every line. Everyone involved began their careers as fans. There are layers and layers of wisdom, intelligence, and good advice to be had from these lines and I am pleased to have the opportunity to present them to you.

References

Attali, J. (1985/2009). *Noise: The political economy of music*. Minneapolis: University of Minnesota Press.

Australasian Performing Right Association (APRA). (2011). *Economic contribution of the venue-based live music industry in Australia*. Sydney: APRA.

Degusta, M. (2011). The REAL death of the music industry. *Business Insider Australia*. Available at: https://www.businessinsider.com.au/these-charts-explain-the-real-death-of-the-music-industry-2011-2

Deloitte Access Economics. (2011). *The economic, social and cultural contribution of venue-based live music in Victoria*. Melbourne: Arts Victoria.
Graham, P. (2006). Monopoly, monopsony, and the value of culture in a digital age: An axiology of two multimedia resource repositories. In C. Kapitzke & B. C. Bruce (Eds.), *Libr@ries: Changing information space and practice* (pp. 253–270). New Jersey: Lawrence Erlbaum.
Graham, P. (2016). Paradigmatic considerations for creative practice in Creative Industries research: The case of Australia's Indie 100. *Creative Industries Journal, 9*(1), 47–65.
Graham, P., & Luke, A. (2011). Critical discourse analysis and political economy of communication. *Cultural Politics, 7*(1), 103–132.
Graham, P., Dezuanni, M., Arthurs, A., & Hearn, G. (2015). A Deweyan experience economy for higher education: The case of the Australian Indie 100 Music Event. *Cultural Politics, 11*(1), 111–124.
Hoegh-Guldberg, H. (2012). Casual music workforce. *Music in Australia knowledge base*. Sydney: The Music Trust. Retrieved from http://musicinaustralia.org.au/index.php?title=Casual_Music_Workforce
IFPI. (2013). *IFPI digital music report 2013: Engine of a digital world*. Available at: https://www.ifpi.org/downloads/dmr2013-full-report_english.pdf
Johnson, B., & Homan, S. (2003). *Vanishing acts: An inquiry into the state of live popular music opportunities in New South Wales*. Sydney: Australia Council and the NSW Ministry for the Arts.
Latonero, M. (2001). *Survey of MP3 usage: Report on a University Consumption Community*. Los Angeles: The Norman Lear Center, USC.
Marx, K. (1976). *Capital: A critique of political economy (Vol. 1),* (trans: Fowkes, B.). London: Penguin.
Marx, K. (1981). *Capital: A critique of political economy (Vol. 3)*, (trans: Fernbach, D.). London: Penguin.
Mumford, L. (1934/1962). Technics and civilization. New York: Harcourt Brace & Co.
New York Times. (2000, June 24). Napster eyes new business models while preparing defense. *The New York Times*. Retrieved from http://www.nytimes.com/2000/06/24/technology/napster-eyes-new-business-models-while-preparing-defense.html
Ong, W. J. (1977). *Interfaces of the word: Studies in the evolution of consciousness and culture*. Ithaca: Cornell University Press.
Pacey, A. (2001). *Meaning in technology*. Cambridge, MA: The MIT Press.
Pine, J., & Gilmore, J. (2011). *The experience economy* (updated ed.). Boston: Harvard Business Review Press.
Pyyny, P. (2002, September 4). Napster to liquidate. *After Dawn*. Retrieved from http://www.afterdawn.com/news/article.cfm/2002/09/04/napster_to_liquidate
Smith, A. (1776/1997). *The wealth of nations* (Books I–III). London: Penguin.
Smythe, D. (1981). *Dependency road: Communications, capitalism, consciousness, and Canada*. New Jersey: Ablex.
The Guardian. (2001, February 12). Court rules against Napster. *The Guardian*. Retrieved from www.theguardian.com/technology/2001/feb/12/copyright.news1
Tschmuck, P. (2012). *Creativity and innovation in the music industry* (2nd ed.). Berlin: Springer.
Veblen, T. (1923). *Absentee ownership and business enterprise in recent times: The case of America*. New York: B. W. Huebsch.
White Jr., L. (1940). Technology and invention in the Middle Ages. *Speculum, 15*(2), 141–159.
Wikström, P. (2013). *The music industry: Music in the cloud* (2nd ed.). London: Polity.

Chapter 2
Michael Smellie, Global Record Executive

Abstract This chapter is an interview with Michael Smellie. Michael is Australia's most successful major label record executive. From his beginnings as an accountant in the publishing business he became Chief Operations Officer for Sony BMG (Global) and led the company through what was to prove an historic merger. His time with Sony coincided with the advent of the CD and the subsequent explosion in revenues for the major record labels. Michael also played a major part in funding and conceptualising one of the most exciting and successful independent record labels in the history of Australian music, Rooart Records, the many achievements of which include the international success of INXS. An accountant by training, Michael brought a new management ethos and radical financial logic to the music business. The interview covers expansive ground, including Rooart; Warner BMG (the merger that almost happened prior to Sony BMG); the relationship between sport and music; and commentary on the nature and quality of management in the major labels sector of the music industry.

It's a curiosity to me as to how you ended up in the music business, Michael. You were an accountant, a non-musician, and ended up as the country's most successful label executive. Tell us a bit about how you came to be in the music industry first of all, and what it is about you that made you so successful.

Well I think, I've got to start off and say, like probably the majority of the population, I really had a passion for music as a kid and went and saw bands and all sorts of things as an 18 year old, a 19 year old whatever, and so you know I always had, I think, a better than average interest in music. How did I get started? More luck than anything else. I happened to know somebody just through a mutual friend, someone who was looking to hire a CFO for a music publishing company. I went along, interviewed for the job, and got it.

Who was that?

The guy?

Yes.

He's long since moved on, but his name was Colin Cornish. He was the managing director of Chappell Music in Australia at the time and, interestingly enough, for a short period of time was the US CEO of Universal Music Publishing. So he was

P. Graham, *Music, Management, Marketing, and Law*, Music Business Research,
https://doi.org/10.1007/978-3-030-02143-6_2

quite successful as well, but has long since left the business. I think it's in some respects being in the right place at the right time. When I think about later things in my career, I suppose it's also that you have to put yourself into the right positions. Whether that's through networking or knowing people, you've got to put yourself in the right position.

How did you know Colin?

Through a mutual friend, but we'd met at social functions and things like that. I'd chatted to him and obviously made enough of an impression that when he was looking for a CFO our mutual friend said "Well, why don't you go talk to Michael? He's an accountant". I was working in the advertising industry I should say, so it wasn't as if I was working in, I don't know, mining or ball bearings. So it was sort of vaguely related in so far as it was another Creative Industry. And that's what happened. Our mutual friend said "You've met him a couple of times, you know what he's like. Why don't you talk to him?", and that's exactly what happened.

That would have made you fairly young to be Chief Financial Officer of an international publisher?

Yeah, I guess I was. And if I look back it was a very successful company. We were the biggest at the time. It was a very old company called Chappell at Bond Street, London, and was founded in 1812. At the time it was owned by Polygram and it had the catalogue of the greatest writers from Tin Pan Alley: the Rogers and Hammersteins, the Irving Berlins, Noel Coward; it had a fabulous catalogue of musicians. It was a bit short on contemporary musicians at the time, but it was a fabulous company. We did really well and I suppose I probably stuck out because I conceived of a deal, which I think at the time nobody else had done. We acquired the catalogue for the Little River Band, who at the time were definitely the most successful Australian band in the world. They'd had a successful career in the United States, with at least three or four top ten albums at that point in time. Maybe even a number one, although maybe that's wrong. Anyway, I conceived a very fancy way of acquiring their catalogue which shot me to prominence. The CEO, the worldwide CEO, got this proposal on his desk and scratched his head and said "Bloody hell, who came up with this idea?"

What was unique about the deal?

It must have been about 1981. We effectively leased the catalogue, just like you can lease a car. We put a bank in the middle. So we said to the bank "You buy it and just let us use them". In simplistic terms, that's what we did. I mean it's been done subsequently on a number of occasions but I think—I might be wrong—but I think it was the first time that it had ever been done in the music publishing industry. Anyway, he got this deal dropped on his desk in London and he must have scratched his head and said "those guys in Australia have been sitting in the sun too long". But at least he was curious enough to get on a plane, fly out to Australia, and sit down with me. He must have walked away and said "hmm, this guy is quite smart", or something. So that got me started.

Coming into this business from advertising must have been a big change. The financial flows in advertising are fairly straightforward, especially at that

time before things got a bit blurry post-Keating. But you would have faced the vague problem of valuing catalogues.

Yeah, a lot. I mean the biggest issue that Chappell had was that we had an enormous catalogue. I don't remember the number but I think over 100,000 songs from memory. And lots of earning—20 cents and 50 cents and a dollar and things like that that needed to be aggregated. So at least one of the things I was confronted with was this enormous processing function that I had to try to come to grips with in order to properly pay the artists. That, to me, was the biggest thing that I found different. In the advertising industry we generally had a few clients with big amounts. Here I had effectively 100,000 clients earning small amounts. And then I remember, for example, we had the Bee Gees at the time. And this was just after *Saturday Night Fever* and *Grease*. So the money flowing through from the Bee Gees catalogue was extraordinary. We had auditors and all sorts of things floating around.

But getting back to the second part of that question, what is it about you that made you so suited to the industry?

I think there are a couple of things from that perspective. If I were to do anything else, a lot of people have asked me, I said I'd probably only ever work in sport. The two things music and sport have in common are people, and possibly unusual people. So I think I enjoy mixing with creative people, with unusual people, with unusual personalities. I think that was a key component. And I was very lucky to get some mentors early on, and in fact I'd probably argue that the CEO who flew out from London took an interest in my career. It was funny because many years later I ended up as his boss. He ended up as the head of BMG Music Publishing worldwide when I was the Chief Operating Officer of BMG. So he ended up working for me. But I think over the years I was very lucky to be in the position where these people want to mentor you. There's a personal interaction or something like that. So I would say those were the main things: I was flexible, I suppose I was above average intelligence, others may have their own views on that, and I had an interest in unusual people. Straight away I was able to deal with artists. Because even though I'd never dealt with artists before, I was interested in them.

And do you think that first strategic move in your acquisition of the Little River Band catalogue characterises the rest of your career? Did you keep innovating in those ways for the people you work for, do you think?

Well I hope so. The further up you go in the management chain, that's the fundamental thing that a leader needs to do. You try and put a structure in place that can deal with the day-to-days, and I think your role as a leader in a business, as a CEO, even if it's a relatively small business of maybe only ten or twelve or a dozen employees, is that you should always be looking forward—what's next and how do I move the organisation? How do I move the product? How do I move the artist? Whatever it is, you need to ask how you move into the next stage.

I think one of the things that I did early on in my career was to put the basics in place, get good people, delegate to them, communicate with them, clearly let them get on with things, and that enabled me, because I was confident that they could get on and do their jobs. That enabled me to spend time thinking about the future "Okay, so what do we do next? How do we move this up a notch? How do we do we as I did when I ran Polygram in Australia? How do we get involved more in Australian repertoire? How do we get involved in RooArt and various other kinds of things?" But constantly think about the next step, and I think that's characterised my career. I think I'm like that still today, trying to think about the next step.

I think making a lease deal out of a musical catalogue actually changes the character of what that catalogue represents and changes its economic category. I think if you went to a bank tomorrow and said "Look, I've got these great songs, would you buy them for me and I'll lease them back from you?" it would be a very hard ask.

By the way, just to complete the picture, we went to the Australian banks at the time and I guess it was Westpac and I don't know, ANZ or somebody, and they just looked at us as if we had three heads. There was a bank operating called, I'll never forget it, the Philadelphia National Bank. It had a little representative office here and somebody suggested I go speak to them. I went and spoke to them and the guy just said "That's a fabulous idea, I've never heard of that! We'll talk to our head office about it!". But you're right. If we were to go to the Commonwealth Bank today they'd say "We cannot".

You once said to me, and I'm quoting roughly here: "The music industry threw itself into decline by turning recorded music into commodities". I think you also said something like "Once new records began to appear on the shelves of Woolworths and petrol stations, the writing was on the wall for the industry". I've thought a lot about that since and I want you to explain those comments and ask you whether you've changed your mind about that given the number of places music is now available.

No, I haven't changed my mind. Let me explain. Up until, I don't know, probably say the early 1980s or at least the mid 1980s, that 95% of music sold in Australia was sold through specialist music stores. The CD probably changed the music business as much as anything, partially because it was very durable. So you could put it in a store in Woolworths and not worry about it as you used to with vinyl records. Because once a bunch of people took a vinyl record out of the cover three times it'd be scratched because they were very fragile. That was 90% of the music stores, and if you were a sales rep working in the music business in those days you went to record stores and basically record stores sold music—that's it!

I think that the advent of CDs, possibly, also with the advent of television advertising which took it to the masses at the same time, music ceased to be special. Up until then it was sold by people, by artists. By artisans, I should say. You would walk into the store and you could chat to the bloke about "Well, what's the newest record this week and what would you recommend?", or, "I bought The Beatles last week and what do you think this week?". You could get that kind of recommendation and dialogue that you can get at a craft store today. That all went away and I think that kind of store virtually doesn't exist today. I'm not sure what the statistics are but I doubt that 5% of the music sold in Australia is sold through specialist music stores. The majority of it is sold through JB HI-FI, K-Mart, Target, etc. etc. You go into one of those stores and ask somebody: "What's the new album this week from Missy Higgins?", they're likely to say "Oh, I work in underwear, I'm sorry I can't help you".

I think commodity in that respect means kind of anonymous—undifferentiated.

It's lost its specialness, and look, I'm not suggesting for one moment that it could be avoided any more than the rest of the changes. But it changed the character of music. It coincided with the CD which proved to be an economic boon to the business. Prior to 1980—I've often said this also—the global music industry was really a cottage industry. It was mostly smallish companies. When I went to Polygram in London as the finance director in around 1982, the worldwide revenue was only about two hundred and something million dollars and their profit was about $7 million. It was nothing. It was a relatively small company. When I left Sony BMG our revenue was five and a half billion and we had a profit of $750 million. So in 20 something years, you can see how it fundamentally changed in scale. It became big. When companies started to list it became a big business. You had shareholders and investors and all sorts of things. It wasn't people like Chris Blackwell and Ahmet Ertegun, people who owned labels that were basically labours of love. Of course Chris Blackwell wanted to make money, but if he made half a million dollars a year he was really pleased with that. He wasn't trying to make millions and millions.

It's an interesting point to ask why CDs were such a boon. I expect that a lot of it again had to do with back catalogue which is what we're seeing again today in some respects—Elvis on CD and such—I guess what was then 30 or 40 years of recorded music history being reissued in a new format.

Well I think it was for two reasons. I can vividly remember my very first demonstration of the CD. I was at a conference in Florida and the then-CEO of Polygram—and Polygram were really the first company to push it because they were owned by Philips—sat in a room like this and someone set up a CD player side by side with a record player and played *2001 A Space Odyssey*. He played it on vinyl and he said "So listen to this" and then he put the CD on and he swapped it and I remember we sat there and went "Oh god yeah it's much better. Yeah, that's great!" Anyway, he then basically picked the vinyl record up and threw it to the back of the room. It bounced on the carpet three or four times and he said to the bloke it landed near "Stamp on it then bring it back to me!". The guy stood on it, brought it back and put it on and said "Have a listen to this now" and it was "sccccrrttch, sccccrrttch, sccccrrttch"—wrecked. So then he did the same with the CD. Threw it up there and said "Stamp on it and bring it back to me". It just played exactly the same as if it was brand new, and I remember at the time thinking "Oh my god, that's amazing!". That to me at the time, to people of my era, that was just amazing! They were so durable, and I think that's what, more than anything else, fundamentally changed music again. It was easily portable, you could put it in your car, and you could do all sorts of things with it. It was durable and it was high quality. It was the first digital music, effectively.

The other thing is I remember vividly is when we just sold CD in Australia, there were so few factories in the world and there was a bit of a demand. But if you were a retailer you had not much choice: you had to buy it in lots of 20 and you could either buy pop or classical, that was it. You just got 20 assorted compact discs, that was it. We were landing them for $9 and the retail price was $20. About 3 years later, we were landing them for a dollar, or $1.50. Nobody expected when we said a price of

$20 that the manufacturing cost would decline so rapidly. We all thought "$9 would be the price and one factory in the world". But in fact within, I think, 5 years there were three factories within Australia.

So you thought you were doing a boutique kind of thing with the CDs originally?

Yeah. I know none of us dreamed it would dominate the business and so fundamentally change the economics of the business. I was working in London, ironically, a year later, alongside the very guy who'd done this demonstration. While I was in the office with him I got to know him pretty well. His name was Jan Timmer. I think without him the CD would never have taken off and the music business arguably would never have achieved the size that it did by ten or so years ago. But I don't think he ever believed it would so fundamentally change the business, but it did.

So how do you look at the vinyl revival?

Vinyl today? Look, I don't really have a view. There'll be always niche markets. There always has been niche markets and there always will be. If you're asking me "do I think vinyl will become the dominant carrier in the future?" well no I don't. But it's a nice niche. When you see Peter Colby, who I think is coming in 2 or 3 weeks, ask him because I think he's building a plant particularly to focus on the niche vinyl market.

Oh great, because they pulled the one out at Homebush down.

Yes, he might have bought that one.

Good.

And he's going to put it in Byron Bay. Where else would you put it?

When you quit Sony, Patrick Riley, I find this amusing, Patrick Riley, VP of SIRIUS now, and former BMG exec said of you in a Variety interview, that you "had no patience for the monkey business that went on in the industry", yet he was thoroughly of that industry. What did he mean by "monkey business"? I guess I could ask you in technical language what kind of reforms you brought, but I'd much rather hear the stories about the monkey business.

Well I think that from my perspective what happened was that the music business had basically boomed from the introduction of the CD. Relatively speaking the profits exploded, and I think the lavish expenses, let me just say the expenses grew commensurately with the revenue and they shouldn't have. When I first went to work in New York with BMG, the company was losing money and I remember very clearly doing a presentation about what we called the "Limo Culture". We used a photograph. We got the senior executives and we said "We're going to have to turn this company around, we're going to have to be focused on things". The picture that we took was a photograph of our building on Times Square at around 5 o'clock and there were about 15 limos, stretch limos, lined up with drivers and all waiting for the record label executives to leave. And this was at a time when the company was losing money. We were laying off people and all sorts of things. And to give you an example, that was one of the changes I made: "This just isn't going to happen". It's simple things like that. It's just not acceptable. We're not going to pay for these guys to sit around here for hours being paid $150 an hour just to wait for you guys. It's just not going to happen. There was a whole series of things like that, and overspending on all sorts of things. I think that whether you liked it or not, and because I'm now talking in the year 2000 or thereabouts, by then it's a big business, there's lots of money involved, there are shareholders and investors who have certain expectations.

My view of the music business at that time was that it was just bloated—the whole business had gotten bloated. It's interesting in my view that the number of jobs shed since then, is more than half, I think it's about 65% of the people who have gone from the business. I think the recorded music business is probably today at the size it should have been in around 2000.

How do you explain that?

Poor management, generally speaking. I've said this before and, as a general rule, and there are exceptions of course, but as a general rule, the quality of managers—and I'm not talking about artist managers here—the quality of managers in the corporations involved in the music business, and I include publishing and rights management and recorded music in that, generally the standard of management has been poor. If you want any evidence just name me one senior executive in a music company that went on to do something else.

I can't.

Yeah, well I rest my case. Nobody went on to work at Disney, run Disney or run Newscorp or run whatever. Pictures theatres, nothing, they couldn't cut it anywhere else.

That's getting to a point we're going to talk about later. During the time you were involved most actively, was it a change from, as you said, a cottage industry, family owned, business approach to these massive multi-national corporations run on strategic management principles and post-Reagan, Thatcher type of ideals. Was it an expansion of that "I'm in this for the love of it" or was it the personal aspect bloated out of all proportion?

I think what happened was that too many people got paid too much money and there was too much of a sense of entitlement. And that's not only corrosive but it's also contagious. I'll give you an example. One of the record executives that I worked with who was most respected in a creative sense is Clive Davis. You've never met him, but Clive has a pedigree as long as my arm, starting from Janis Joplin and Bruce Springsteen, through to Whitney Houston and right up to Alicia Keys, and the relaunch of Santana's career, and all sorts of things like that. He was a very highly paid executive, made tens of millions of dollars, but you could probably argue he's a unique individual, probably worth it because he added hundreds of millions to the corporation. The problem was when people hypothetically said "Well Clive makes ten, so I'm his assistant so I should make eight". And then somebody else says "Well I'm his assistant so I should make six". So you've got this contagion spreading. I think that's what happened during the mid-80s to the mid-90s. And because there's plenty of money floating around it's much easier to pay the bloke, give the bloke another rise than have an argument with him or have him leave. To me it was generally just poor discipline and poor management. And too many people, that's possibly what Patrick was referring to, hid behind the smoke screen and said "Wow! you know, it's creative, you don't understand" and I think that's bullshit, frankly.

And what about the artists? I mean, we hear stories now and of course they were rife at the time about people's riders and huge amounts of drugs and big nights out and everything else. I'm sure you didn't have anything to do with that Michael but ...

This is on the record so I'm going to record that I didn't. But there were enormous excesses and artists fell into two categories—well-managed artists who were in the midst of all the excesses but had smart enough managers to make sure that the money flowed in two directions: one, the half that I want to keep because I know that at some point this is going to end. And, two, the other half that's for having a good time. And there are a good number of artists, as I said generally well-managed. You talk to the Paul McGuinnesses who managed U2 for so many years and they're a very wealthy bunch of people because from day one they were smart about what they did. And there are the other artists who just lived this lifestyle. They had limos everywhere and they stayed in flash hotels and bathed in champagne. But when it actually finished they said "Well now what have I got?" and the manager went "Oh, well, nothing, there's nothing to show for it, we spent it all. But didn't we have a good time?" And there's lots of stories like that and they're not stories, I mean they're not fanciful stories, they're factually true.

How does that happen?

Like I said: I think in part it's poor management. I suppose you can't say that the record companies are entirely free of blame from that, but a lot of it's to do with 18 year old kids who suddenly get millions of dollars floating through their bank account. They're not necessarily the most emotionally mature and capable of making good, strong decisions. And look, let's be honest, most creative people are not across those sorts of things and not interested in those sorts of things. So if they're, for whatever reason, badly managed or badly advised they're often end up in a bad state. As I said, there are plenty of examples I could give you. As I said Bruce Springsteen with John Landau was very well managed from day one. Then there's the really sad stories, like Whitney Houston who really was managed by relatives. She sold, I don't know, probably 100 million albums. More, 100 million or more albums I think. She played shows for the Sultan of Brunei, was paid $10 million for that alone, and basically ended up broke. You just sit there and scratch your head and say "How's that possible?" I recall her making records because she needed advance payment that recording would trigger despite her being in poor health. I just want to say, Whitney was an extraordinary artist. Probably in her prime the greatest voice in the world and you just sit there and think "How?..." You wonder how it's possible, but it is.

That leads me onto the next question. You presided over Sony BMG over one of the most turbulent periods in recent history for the music industry. Do you have specific regrets about the way things went or about how you did them?

I think the answer to that is yes and no. I don't think that merged company turned out the way I had envisaged it. When we began the negotiations, if you'd have asked me then "What do you think the merged company will look like, let's say after 3 years?" and then compared the actual outcome, I think my expectations were severely overstated.

In what respect?

Well I think creatively, firstly. I think we lost of a lot of market share. There was organisational chaos for a long time, not chaos sorry, it's too strong a word: organisational discord, disharmony for a long time after the merger.

Discord between the two merged cultures?

Yeah. Which unfortunately when I left it precipitated a major drama and they fired the CEO and all sorts of things. And that precipitated arguments between the shareholders and so I look back and say "Yes, it didn't achieve what I would have liked to achieve in that respect". But you also have to say, "Well, the music business was contracting at the time". You have to ask whether BMG would have continued to exist on a standalone basis, and would the shareholders have continued to support it given that the size of the worldwide music business between 2000 and today has halved? But it was so. I mean I'm saying I'm now justifying my decision, post-justifying, but it's all speculative as to what might have happened. So that's my balanced scorecard. I think we were in a position where we had to do something. I think again—and the record shows we wanted to do a deal with Warner—and I think if we had been able to do that it would have been better, but that got ...

So you wanted to do a three-way deal?

No no no.

Warner BMG?

Just Warner BMG. And we had negotiations over about 6 months. But for various reasons we were incapable of being able to conclude those. I think the cultural issues and some of the management issues that arose as a result of Sony BMG would not have arisen, or would have been less likely to arise, if we'd have done the Warner deal.

Why? Were the cultures similar?

Yes the cultures were similar. At the time I can say that the guy who was the head of Warner Music was an ex Polygram executive, the modern founder of London Records, Roger Ames. He was the CEO of Warner at the time. He and I both worked for years at Polygram. We had a very good and close understanding. His CFO had worked at Polygram. There were a number of people at BMG who'd worked at Polygram as well. So our cultures were much closer. The essence I think of running a good global company, is in my view, particularly in creative industries and music industry as I've encapsulated it, is in decentralised entrepreneurship. Okay, that's a strange term and a bit wordy. But I think that's how you have to run companies and both Polygram and certainly BMG were run in that way. We delegated a lot to our local management. They made the local decisions and we only measured them on the overall outcomes, not on the individual decisions.

So as an executive at a global level, and a financial executive, what connection did you have with signings and general A&R processes? How close were you to that? Was that one of those delegation things where you just left it and didn't have any interest in that sort of thing?

Well I suppose, like everything in the majority of cases, not a great deal. It was delegated. But in some cases you have to deep dive. I remember when we signed The Foo Fighters I got very personally involved with that, with the management, with the band and involved in bringing them into our company. Was I involved in choosing singles and things? No. Do I hang out in the studios with the bands? No. There were people who did those kind of things. But I didn't sign a deal with, for example, just The Foo Fighters and pay them millions of dollars and then go "Oh it's fine now, don't have to do anything". I check in now and then and say "So, tell me how are things going?". And you don't sit back and just wait for an email. You want to go and talk to the band and ask "How's the process going?". So to that extent, I think, as it is for all big decisions, you remain engaged and, again, sometimes even small decisions, you're called on to help out.

Would you say that the relationship between how closely you were involved in that process was proportionate to the amount of money in the signing?

Yeah, look, in some cases not, but as a general rule yes. The bigger the risk, the more involved. Yes, as a general rule.

And so how did you make those decisions as to whether a particular signing was a good thing or whether it was a bad thing, or greasing the wheels and sort of lining that up too?

Well I think there are two things: one is you have to trust people, I think that's the key thing. There are people you trust. You also trust your judgement. Even if, for example, I was to say I'm a specialist on rock music, I can tell you whether a Foo Fighters single is going to sell or not. Even if I was I'd have a bit of difficulty with Simon Cowell's pop music and I certainly would be screwed on figuring out what the latest classic recordings should be. No-one in a large international company that sells in all sorts of genres, in all sorts of languages across all sorts of countries, can be a specialist in everything. So even if you wanted to be, you can't do it. So you have to rely on people. You don't blindly rely on them. You rely on them within a framework of controlled mechanisms is probably how I would best put it.

I remember the 1980s as a period during which majors started to draw fairly widespread criticism from artists and musicians and the general public as being run by bean counters. It was an era that saw the rise of strategic management principals, as I said before we're in a post-Reagan, Thatcher revolution. Do you think those really broad trends, first of all, warranted criticism, and second, how did it affect the creativity in the industry more generally?

I think that's the really big balancing act and there have been plenty of examples recently. If you look at the modern history of EMI, which let's say in the 1980s was a very successful global company and then they bought Virgin in about 1990 and paid an extraordinary sum of money, I think $1.2 billion or something of that nature, and listed separately. They were part of the Thorn group, and I've forgotten so I may be out by a few years, but suddenly they're a separately listed company and suddenly they've got their share prices quoted every day. That fundamentally changes the nature of everything. They brought in a new CEO who subsequently went on to found North Face. I think he'd come from Boston Consulting or something like that. He was a strategic financial guy but EMI needed that at that point in time. But I think when you look at EMI's trajectory, and as I said, it's a really good example. In the end they got rid of him and I think they then brought in Alain Levy—he was a music guy who'd worked at Polygram—and David Munns. They really set about trying to rebuild the creative process because, going back to the comments I made before, the music industry was bloated with costs. So bringing in some of these guys to drive out some of the costs was easy. Knock off a 100 million dollars a year with the costs. You could do that and you do your multiples, your price to earnings ratios, and so you've just added maybe a billion dollars to the value of the company. But the trick is to keep the creativity going. I think if you look at what's happened at EMI that's the biggest problem: there's been at least three different lots of bankers own it in the last 20 odd years.

Like the latest one.

And they've screwed it! They haven't had a hit record. They haven't broken any new artists since I don't know when. I can't remember the last one and I'm sure there is one or two but, literally, for a company of that size, they haven't had a new record, new artist for a decade or 15 years, and that's what I think we did really successfully at BMG. It's acknowledged by our competitors, in the press, by various people: BMG was to be able to rebuild the creativity. At the time we were able to break Alicia Keys and, as I said, relaunch Santana, and do a whole series of successful things at the same time as reducing costs.

The strategy was effectively to say:

"You guys are the creative people, we're going to put a ring around you, you're a bit protected here but we have expectations of you. You've got to produce records of a certain quality at a certain time. If you do that, you effectively buy a bit of freedom from us looking at your costs too heavily. The rest of you, distribution and sales and administration and royalty accounting and stuff like that, we're going to go through you with a fine-toothed comb."

So that was the trick, to try to be able to increase the creative output at the same time as reducing the costs.

It seems the artist has a strange place amongst all of that. I'm hearing you talk and it seems like there's the company and then the artist and the creative aspect. So you've got this massive system going on at one end that's fairly stable in terms of personnel and so forth, I mean you spent 30 years in the business. At the other end there's a constant churn of artists and probably the A&R department was the fastest churning department of all. Was that the case?

No. It's no different than playing rugby league today. There's a decent proportion of churn, either through injuries or just poor performance. It's the same in music. I don't think A&R churn was particularly higher or lower than anyone else in that respect. There's a definite churn though. It's a difficult place to hide. You can be an average accountant and you can hide. When you're in the music business, they publish your charts every week and they're public. Every week people see how you're doing. Everybody knows it. It's a bit like sport in that respect as well. You can't, if you're coaching a team, as Stephen Kearney knows, the Parramatta coach. He knows you lose five or six matches in a row, or seven or eight, and you're gone. That's it. Everybody knows about it, and I think A&R is a bit the same. You sign five acts in a row that don't work and you're on the endangered species list.

That's for A&R but what about the artists' end? It's like they never become part of the company.

I don't know whether that's correct because a lot of them have long, long careers. They form good relationships at various levels throughout the company. We talked about Whitney Houston. Her entire career, which was, I don't know, 30 years, was with one record label: Arista. So you form strong bonds across a number of parts of the organisation. In fact I would argue that part of the reason that some people in Australia have not been successful overseas is they haven't built long-term relationships. If I look back at the successes that artists and record labels have had, the greatest ones were where they worked closest together, where the management's vision, the artist's vision, and the company's vision are in sync. So they're all working for the same thing. They're all working with the same work ethic, the same expectation, and those are the arrangements that work over the longer term.

Interesting, so, this was to be a later question but it kind of flows on from the last one: The new 360 deals are that are appearing kind of mitigates against that and there's a whole lot more of the artist being bought at the time when they get signed. What do you think the future of that sort of thing is and how would you advise budding professionals?

As a general principal I'm not a great believer in 360 deals. I think you do a deal for what you think you get back in expertise. You go to any of the major recorded music labels today and say "Will you please work with A&R, work with me at an A&R level on my record, will you help me then package and promote it, and will you help market it and distribute it?" I'd say all the majors are pretty good at it. That's what they do pretty well. But if you then say "Well, would you help me promote a show?". Well, it's not in their DNA. It's not what they're necessarily good at. So I wouldn't be rushing out to do a 360 deal today.

But I think the rationale for doing 360 deals is money. Artists and managers all exist on percentages. So you want big advances. If you come to me as a head of a record label and say "I want a 100,000 dollars or 500,000 dollars in advance", it's basically "Well if you want a 100,000 you can give me this much, you want 200 you give me this much, you want 400 you give me this much, and you want 500 you give me your first born child and everything!" That's the only rationale for 360 degree deals. It's not because of an expertise level, it's about an investment level. It's not being driven by record labels wanting to change their business model; it's being driven by artists and managers requiring a certain amount of money and the only banker effectively is the record label, and it's the only way the record label can make sense of the deal, because they've got to look at risk and return. "We'll just keep throwing more rights in there and eventually this'll even itself up", is the equation. That's the driving force.

But it's not a strategic rationale. None of the record labels said "Oh, we must get into this concert promotion business, it's a great business to be in". A lot of people lost a lot of money out of it. So that's my advice to anybody confronted with a 360 deal: look at the deal on its merits. If ultimately you think that the rights that you're giving away are going to be well represented, or I'll take it up a step, excellently represented, then do it. But whether that ends up being 360, 270, 180, 90, or whatever, in my view it should be driven by you being comfortable that they can tick the box and say "that right will be excellently looked after".

You were a key figure in RooArt. What an experiment that was.

Yeah. That was a great time in my life. I've often said that one of the most exciting times in my life was coming back to Australia and running Polygram. I'd come back from London and one of the things that struck me was that there was a big gap in the Australian market. Our rock market, essentially we're a rock market, was very focused on—I'll call it American rock. There was in those days The Angels, The Choir Boys, The Radiators.

But that was all sort of American rock and there was none of the alternative rock. Having been in the UK with the likes of The Cure and other things like that that, I'd been very exposed to the alt rock movement and saw how very successful it was. I thought, "Well, there's nobody doing that here" and I was fortunate enough to have met a guy called Chris Murphy who is well-known because he managed INXS. The truth of the matter is he and I came to Brisbane to watch a State of Origin match in god knows what year it was, must have been 1989 or something like that, maybe 88. And the next morning we had breakfast at the Beaufort Hotel. We went outside and sat by the river and started talking about this idea. He had to say he'd already started, that he was more advanced than I was. He already had Sebastian Chase and Justin van Stom working with him on exactly that.

Maybe our audience needs to know who RooArt is.

Oh, sorry. Well in about 1991, maybe I got the year wrong, we just, we basically funded an independent label. We won virtually every ARIA award for local artists like Wendy Matthews, Ratcat, Screaming Jets, and Crow. We even did an album with someone called Monica Trapica and won the best jazz album. We couldn't believe it, we just won everything, and it just went from this independent label that was nowhere to being the most dominant label in Australia at the time. I was effectively a co-investor as Polygram. It was an extraordinary time and it just blew us away.

What was it? How did it work and who funded it?

Well we funded it. The true story is we, as Polygram, put up all the money. The first year we sold bugger all. We had lots of critical acclaim and sold bugger all records. There were artists like Martha's Vineyard and others that no-one ever heard of but drew lots of critical acclaim. I remember saying to Murphy after the first year, "We're in a big hole here, I'm a million dollars or more in the hole here. We have to do something". He went out and did a record with a band called Absent Friends. It was a song called *I Don't Want To Be With Nobody But You* which Wendy Matthews fronted. It was completely not an alternative rock song which was what we were trying to do. It just became a big hit and it just went from there. I think Ratcat was the second one. That was exactly our sweet spot, that kind of rock, that alternative rock was what we were after and Simon Day was the Australia Robert Smith. Younger, and I remember thinking "That's exactly what we talked about and we've pulled it off". It was fabulous. I think the issue it highlighted was that we had very significant success in Australia and bugger all success outside of Australia. I think we sold a few records of Wendy Matthews in France and Germany and a few Ratcat records in Germany and a few places but we didn't really crack the UK or the US.

What happened was for various reasons, which in part led to me leaving Polygram, was that they canned the deal and that's when Rooart went to Warner. As I said we were the most successful label in Australia. We had about ten number one records in a year, but because we didn't have any success outside of Australia the fundamental economics of it were just sunk. And that's exactly what happened. So they went to Warner. They didn't have as much success in the Warner days as we'd had in the Polygram days. But the answer to that is that if you're in the business long enough you know fundamentally that you have to have some international success if you're going to invest significant amounts of money. That was what we were doing, and we didn't have significant international success.

Why are we so patchy at getting international success in this country?

Do you really want to know the answer?

I do.

I think we accept mediocrity too easily. I think it's interesting to say at the moment whilst the Olympics are on. You want to crack the world market? Look how hard it is! Look at, what's his name, James Magnussen, ask him how hard it is to win that 100 metres or whatever it is today—bloody hard work. To crack the international music market is that hard as well. There are more gold medals handed out in the Olympic games this year than there will be number one albums in America in the next 4 years. And that's just a fact. How difficult it is to get a number one record in America? It's *bloody* difficult, and you've got to be really good and you've got to be that dedicated.

When you say mediocrity it's a catch-all term. What do you mean in concrete terms for people who are aspiring musicians?

We're talking about cracking internationally here. So if you want to be world's best then you need to be able to compete on even terms in the US and in the UK, and that's extremely difficult. You can't do it by living 90% of your life here. If you want to look at the most recent success, a really big success, unfortunately you've got to go back to INXS. They spent 3 years living outside of Australia. They lived in the UK and then they lived in the US. And they toured. What was the album before *Kick*? *Shabooh Shoobah*. They toured it for 2 years in America. They lived in vans and stuff and that's hard. They had family and all sorts of things and they stayed away from them. But again I say it's like the sacrifice that James Magnussen has to make: it's bloody hard work and you have to set extremely high standards.

At every level? Business structure, networks, creative?

Every level, everything. You have to accept that your songs can't be good, they've got to be world's best. Your production can't be good, it's got to be world's best. Your performance can't be good, it's got to be world's best. And then you've got to have the marketing, the support, the management, the sponsorship—all of those things have to be world's best and I think there are very, very few people in Australia that either have that understanding, that vision, and very few people that can actually deliver that.

You're talking there at a really high level, and other conversations going on these days are all about niche markets and the 1000 fan model and such. I mean, that's a very different kind of thinking.

Totally agree. I think that increasingly what exists today is the ability to tap into niche markets, and you see that often, where people can sell the digital equivalent of 50 or 60 or 70,000 albums because the distribution costs have largely gone away. The issue is marketing and promotion and that hasn't gone away. There's a certain amount that you can do through social media and things like that but also there's a certain amount you need to do. You need to be in the market. You need to be seen. You want to sell your music even in your niche in, I don't know, Iowa? Then there's a certain amount you can do through word of mouth and things like that but there's a certain amount you can only do by being in Iowa, by seeing the people, by being able to identify with what's going on in Iowa at the time.

Yeah, this is an issue that keeps coming up and up again is that you need to get out of this country.

You have to. If you're serious about it, I mean Australia is about 2% of the world's music market. Well in theory if you want to be a number one artist in the world you should give it 2% of your attention, but that's just the maths. And you've at least got to start thinking about it that way if you're going to achieve any level of success. And I think you know, as I said, if we're talking about, let's say, swimming, there's a well-established infrastructure and support for that. There's a lot of people who understand and they know it and they know what they've got to do and the expectations start from when you're, I don't know, 12 or however young they take swimmers. They know from that date what the expectations from them are and that doesn't exist in the music business in Australia. I think it did a little bit in the 1980s, maybe in the 1990s, but we seem to have lost that.

It's not as clear either. We know exactly what it takes to be a world-class swimmer: you get in the pool and you flail your arms and legs and get up the other end in a particular time and that's that. There's no mystery.

And I agree with you. I'm not suggesting that the process, per se, is the same. The way you've got to go about it or the standards that you must demand of yourself are the same.

I hear over and over from lots of people and you've said it yourself, Australia needs more high quality music managers and we've kind of heard why but I'd like you to be a little bit more pointed about that. Second, how do we make that happen, because it's a percentage based living and 50% of nothing isn't much at all, so how do we do it?

Well I do think it's true. If I had to identify the one thing that we lack more than anything else in Australia I'd say it's good quality artist managers who have the vision to do what I've just talked about here: to be able to speak to artists, understand them, and have a clear understanding of what their expectations are. If you want to be the biggest artist in Fortitude Valley then that's fine. That's fine, but that comes with certain expectations and outcomes. You can then say "Well I want to be the biggest artist in Brisbane". Well, okay, there's certain ways to do that. I want to be the biggest in Queensland, Australia, whatever, you can work your way up. They all come with different levels of expectations. I think we have almost none—we have very very few artist managers capable of having that discussion at a level at which an artist would say "I want to be a major player in the world's contemporary music market"—pop, urban, rock—doesn't matter whatever the genre is, but "I want to be able to play on that stage" and then have a manager that can figure out how to do that.

I'm not just going to keep going back to swimming, but if you do that there are coaches and because they've got track record they know how to win gold. That's passed onto others because they've got assistant coaches and assistants' assistants and all sorts of things. We don't have that in music and I've heard dozens of people talk about it but nobody's really done much to deliver it. I mean, to be honest, part of why Stuart and I originally conceived this series was a way of starting to try and tap into that. We've got people like Harley Medcalf who's a very experienced manager and John Watson who's a very experienced manager. Hopefully the series continues in other years. We'll continue to tap into these people so that knowledge will be institutionalised, captured in a way that we can build on over time. But you know, it's the single biggest challenge in this country. I think we've got people working at record labels and things who are good and are reasonably experienced in international. They're really the support players. You know, they're like the masseurs or the physiotherapists or I don't know, sports psychologists or whatever they are. They're not the real drivers, the drivers have to be the managers. I mean that's obviously assuming we have the talented artists in the first place. By the way I think we do. I don't think that we lack the talented artists. I think we sometimes lack ambitious talented artists, but I don't think we lack the talented artists.

And would you say that was the number one make or break factor for any artist that you've been involved with—management?

Yep. When you go to America, and I've been down this route dozens of times, dozens and dozens of times. To get an international company to put a significant market behind you involves lots of dollars, firstly, and lots of organisational effort. Even in my own way when I was running Polygram Australia, what was my job? It was to make sure—I had about 200 employees at the time—that the 200 employees went out and sold The Dire Straits or whatever it happened to be that week, the whole 200. My job was to be able to go to Ed Bicknell, their manager, and say "I'm going to put 200 people's efforts and money and things and we're going to make this happen". When you go to America and say "I want you to put all your label resources behind this", then it's has to come with what they're looking for. Of course they're looking for talent. But they're also looking for the backup systems that go with that. The artist will work hard, has the right work ethic. The manager who can be a facilitator as opposed to a pain in the ass. And there are many managers who are that. Many an Australian artist's career has ended because, in my view, 90% of them do end because they've got poor or barely adequate managers and the Americans just say "These guys are clowns. They're just not playing at the same level that we're playing at."

So how do we change it? How do we get a system in place?

Well I think you know. Partially as I said, it's firstly a question of recognising the problem. I think it has to be dealt with in a much more formal method than it has been, and it's about seeing Australia as an integrated part of a global music market. I think at a policy making level I see people doing the opposite. Let's build up barriers, let's protect our industry. It's like the car industry—God, we've been paying Holden money since before I was born. We've been paying it in the sort of hope that eventually Holden will become profitable. Well, I turned 59 yesterday, 2 days ago, and as far as I know we just wrote them out another cheque for another couple of 100 million, didn't we? At a policy making level it's a question of instinct that's existed for almost as long as I've been involved in the industry to protect it. In fact you can't protect. You've got to put them out there in the glare of the spotlight. Facilitate them, don't protect them. You've got to be able to create a situation in which our artists go out and compete. Any protection should only be to get them to a point at which the mother hen then kicks them out of the nest and says "Fly". And if you don't fly you go splat.

A lot of people in our audience today aspire to be involved in the music industry, as artists, as producers, as engineers, some as writers. What's the best way for them to approach the future? Is it worth pursuing a signing or are they better off staying independent?

That's an individual decision. I don't think there's any right or wrong answer to that. But I think that if somebody wants to work with somebody else, it's no different than a signing in some respects. As I said earlier, the best record relationships are long term. As I said, Whitney Houston signed with one label and Bruce Springsteen spent his entire life with Columbia Records. Lots of artists have done that. Tony Bennett, I think, spent his entire life with Columbia Records. There's a lot of people with these long relationships. They're the ones that work the best. You find that it doesn't depend on individuals because, for example, Columbia Records have had ten heads in that time. I don't know how many they've had but dozens of heads. People come and go. But there's an ethic, or a way of working, that gets passed on. And so I'd say to you if you find somebody who's interested in working with you and the deal makes sense then you should do it. Because I think you can never have too many people supporting you. On the other hand—and it's what I said before—if there's niches you are interested in and you believe that the other people don't share your vision then you shouldn't sign. Do it yourself. Find a few people, a few supporters who can help you go out and do it.

I don't think there's one size fits all. But recognise that to succeed you'll need really good support and you'll need really good levels of trust. And I'll tell you this: it's nothing to do with money. The vast majority of acts that I've seen fail, fail because of a focus on money. They say "Ah, he's offering more money I'll take that". Again, that's a failure of the managers. I've seen it time and time again. Because they get a percentage, they want a percentage of the advance up front, so it's in the manager's financial interest to go for the biggest advance. But it's not about the money. It just isn't. And the vast majority of artists that I've seen fail have valued money over relationships and that level of commitment, that intellectual and psychological commitment, which I would urge you if you are in that business, really if you're going to be successful that extra $10,000, I know however desperate it may seem, doesn't mean anything if you want to be successful. Sign up with the people who you really feel comfortable with. And if it's $10,000 less, that's what it is. You're an artist, so tell your manager that. Remember, the manager's ultimately there to guide you but he's not there to make the decisions for you.

I'm going to ask the last question Michael: if you were allowed to give only one piece of advice to aspiring musicians, what would it be?

I think there are two really key things. I take for granted that whatever you do, whatever aspect you're involved in, is your talent. I think there are two things, one is you need to be resilient. You need to expect that you're going to get lots of setbacks. Virtually every artist, even huge, big artists that I've dealt with have had them. You know, the other night I talked to some other people about Alicia Keys. Well she was dropped by Columbia Records before she was picked up by J Records, she had to learn and re-write albums and all sorts of things. So you have to be resilient. It's a tough, tough gig and you have to bounce back. And you have to bounce back stronger, but you have to bounce back. You have to learn. Don't be in denial. Every setback you have to see as a learning experience that makes you get better.

The second thing I would say is when the fun goes out of it, get out of it. Because it's too bloody hard. It's very hard work if you're not enjoying it. Get out. So be resilient and have fun.

Chapter 3
Peter Colby, Production and Logistics

Abstract This chapter is an interview with Peter Colby, our technological and logistics voice in the collection. Peter began his career as a recordist for the ABC, Australia's national broadcaster, and was at the time of the interview Global President of Sony DADC, the company's digital production arm. Peter has been responsible for the development and implementation of numerous new music media and platforms for mass and niche markets and has overseen the building of massive plant and equipment for both the production and distribution stages of commercial recorded music, including the legendary Armstrong Studios in Melbourne, Australia. Peter details the history of production technologies used in both the recording and distribution phases of the record business through his experience as a professional involved in practically every aspect of commercial music and video production, packaging, and distribution.

Welcome Peter. You began your career as a broadcast engineer at the ABC in the late 1960s and became an expert in the running and building of very large AV facilities. Being a music and sound focused talk, the first question I want to ask you is: how, in your opinion has the experience of sound and audio in particular changed for the engineer and for the audience?

I'll answer that one and we'll take a bit of time on it. But first I'll put on the record that I've been in the industry for 40 years and while it doesn't quite get to the 60s, I've actually seen the transition from mono, valve-oriented technology all the way through to some of the latest stuff. When I first got involved in the audio side of the ABC I got involved with the Melbourne Symphony Orchestra and actually doing their recordings. In a lot of cases their high-end stuff was done direct to disc. In a lot of cases it was done just to two-track.

What you find in those days was the discipline was very much about the creative aspects of recording, the people who were actually doing the job, the engineers and their attention to detail. You talked about things before you actually set up the Orchestra. They went around and they virtually made sure that every cable in the whole place was exactly the same length. They made sure that all the phasing was right. It went through all those disciplined processes that maybe you don't necessarily have to do today because of the digital domain. In some instances just to record one track for

P. Graham, *Music, Management, Marketing, and Law*, Music Business Research,
https://doi.org/10.1007/978-3-030-02143-6_3

the Melbourne Symphony Orchestra could take 4 or 5 days. They could be placing the chairs. They could be placing the microphones, checking the phasing, doing those sorts of things, because the luxury of being able to actually shift the time domain of the end product wasn't necessarily there. It was done in more of a mechanical sense. In the early days they had no mechanical reverberation units—which you probably never hear of now—which actually have a steel plate with springs on it. They used to send the signal in and actually dampen it down and then mechanically create reverberation.

I think in those days the art was very much with the engineers and the producers and everybody else that went into the studio. They had to offset any limitations that they had in the technology. I think as we move through time that the discipline's actually changed in all genres in the studios. When they put the first digital tape machine into the Melbourne Symphony Orchestra—it was very early days of digital records—they had this problem because they could hear a squeak but couldn't work out what the squeak was. Turns out it was the old-style cane chairs that they used to have. Every time the lead violinist leant forward to turn the page on the score it squeaked. We had never heard it before, but it was probably in most recordings that were done in that studio for many years.

After nearly 9 years at the ABC I also moved into television post-production and the music studio of Armstrong's audio and video. There was some interesting stages in that because they had five studios in Melbourne. It was probably seen as a very top shelf studio. People like David Bowie recorded there, and a lot of other people too. But the disciplines changed when digital came along. In a lot of cases it highlighted the musical limitations of the groups being recorded. I remember being involved at a management level in the studios and having a huge furore in one of the studios because, with the clarity of digital recording, they found out that the bass player could actually never really play the bass. With the purity of the signal and having 32 tracks, they eventually worked out, after years of playing together in a group, that the bass player couldn't get himself to the stage of professionalism they needed. So that was one side effect of digital technology. That group went back to a more analogue-approach to try and make the transition more palatable.

We also put automated mixers into the studios. If you go back to the ABC, they would set up the studio, they would set up the orchestra, they would set up the microphones, they would set up the mixers, the tape machines, no-one else was allowed to touch it. The setup sat there for the period they wanted it. It might have only been a 5 minute orchestral recording, but nobody touched the setup. Whereas if you go into the commercial studios like AAV (Armstrong) at that stage where you had automation on the desks and you could record the automation, you could set up your own files to come back the next day, reset your mixing desk, and do all those sorts of things. In some respects I think that took away from the art. It allowed people to mix for a day, go away, come back, reset the mixer, and start back into it again with all the delays and limiters and compressors and everything else set the same. They achieved a different sound.

You can see the evolution of it now. We've seen the evolution into the digital world in delivery, whereas in those days we were talking vinyl, which moved into CD, and now we're talking about MP3 and all those other formats. Mastering and all those things really are playing different games now. I think the real core issues at the end of the day could be with the people at the front end. I was talking to Phil earlier about the fact that there is the creativity, the dynamics, the lifestyle, and there's the emotional part which sits at the front-end to create the intellectual property. But then there's a huge supply chain issue at the back end which is really seen as a separate driver altogether, and we'll talk more about that later on. But in general terms I've seen the evolution, and if you go into a studio now and you can see the producer will be looking at a screen. He'll be looking at a screen to see what his track numbers are, to see what the bass response is. He'll be looking to see whether he's got his phasing right, whereas when I started it was effectively done with the ears of probably two people. Therefore the artist I think has to be reinvented in some respects because involvement in the recording process does give people a lot of satisfaction.

Do you think it's better or worse with the digital versus analogue? What's your general view? Let's compare, say, the best digital recordings with the best analogue recordings.

I think that the dynamic range and everything else that comes with the digital world is certainly there. I'm a grumpy bugger. I can look at the analogue side and think of how nice it was and mellow, but ultimately, if you listen to the type of music that's being played, the dynamic range, the ability to actually hit that purity of sound has improved three or four fold in the last few years, just by the improved filtering in digital. I must say that, yeah, I'm comfortable with listening to the digital environment. But I also like to listen to high-end analogue. I'm not a great lover of MP3. I think that we've got another few levels to go, but we'll talk about that a bit later. But in the real world there's this stance that now the digital world is here, improved technology will only make that better. At the same time I think there's still that bit that requires a large level of human interaction and interface to make it work because they're the people who've got the ears. They're the people who feel it and the technology can't do that for them.

Some people say that audiences just can't tell the difference in sound quality. I'm not convinced, but ...

No, I don't know whether they can. It depends what you're used to. If you listen to vinyl, some people say it distorts gracefully and has nice round edges. If it's properly mixed, properly recorded, and if it's properly cut it has a fairly good sound—it's quite acceptable. But at the same time if you look at digital, the early CD players were atrocious. They had shocking filtering systems and in those early stages you could actually hear the transients, and in some instances their second and third harmonics. I don't know if you've ever heard the term digital fatigue. That was an effect of the very early prototype of the CD players. People would listen to a track and think "that's really great, the dynamics are there, the sound's there, the bass is there and everything else but it just sounds a bit loud". So they'd turn it down a bit. That was actually the overshoots on the filters that were subconsciously getting the brain to turn the sound down. But now the filtering and everything else has improved so much that if you've got bandwidth there and you've got the dynamic range there then a digital recording is quite good—it's very good.

There have been occasions on which people have introduced formats, DAT for example, or laser discs were another. They sounded quite good but got left by the wayside. What is it that makes a format work? Even cassettes outsold everything for a year or two there. Why do you think that is?

I think it gets back to the basic core issues of convenience and money. In a lot of ways you can produce the product and you can produce a very good, high quality album. Put it out on vinyl and it goes to somebody's house, they play it. You put it on a cassette, it can go into the car and people put it into a Walkman—people can carry it around. It's easy to transport, not affected too much by the sun, you can leave it in the sun for a long time compared to vinyl records. So it has a certain level of robustness and affordability. Even though the creative aspects of it are exactly the same, it's that convenience thing. You talk about MP3—MP3 is a convenience product and allows people to go jogging with music. It allows people to plug it into their computer. It allows them to do a myriad of things they could never do even with the CD. Therefore you can now see the commercialisation of the product is actually driving the business and it's not necessarily the quality; it's the commercialisation and the ability to sell into a market.

Almost everywhere we look in the history of recorded music, the major players seem to have misunderstood the implications of new formats. Sony and the CD would be the big exception there. The LP was another one. What's your take on that and why were the effects of broadband and digital distribution such a shock? They shouldn't have been.

No. It shouldn't have, at least if you had been reading the technology and seeing where it was going. I'm just harking back to the early days of the internet and the fact that the assumption was that when you go to somebody's place and say "look, I've been watching the kettle boil for the last 12 hours at Oxford University, isn't it fantastic". But it's free. So it developed this whole genre of people who were developing ideas and ways of communicating with one another, sending product backwards and forwards. Ultimately it was only a matter of time before it started to deliver a commercially available product to end-users.

People who were interested, and I think the majority of the music industry, and to a certain extent a lot of industries, missed the implications of something being made available globally and people having easy access to it. I think in general terms why it was such a shock is because they lost control of the supply chain. If you take a CD, you take a DVD, or a Blu-Ray—any of the packaged media products that you see in the market, even in pre-digital days—is that the label controls production, they control the marketing of the product, they control the distribution, the logistics, all aspects of the product and how it was delivered into markets, in whose market it was available, what license rights were available—all of that was just a supply chain to the retailer.

They even had control in some respects of the retail market, what each retailer has available, what retail they could do, and how they could do it. They lost control of that because all of this intellectual property suddenly became available to anybody who had the ability to go onto the internet and download it. They didn't know how to manage that and I think a lot of people are still struggling with it in other industries as well. That's why it came as a shock: all of a sudden you saw the whole supply chain being threatened by the technology.

The industry's full of really bright people, as far as I've seen, and you'd think that say, in 1999 when the Annenberg School in UCLA did the MP3 Napster survey of students and they saw that people who were downloading things were actually twice as likely as people who didn't download things to go out and pay for the product, that the majors would have noticed. Yet they still reacted by suing their customers, or even criminalising their customers in some cases.

Well I suppose that's how you react to it. How do you actually engage and embrace those people who are ultimately your clients in a different format? I think basically the speed of it was one issue: it took off a lot quicker than they expected it to. I think that in a lot of cases they felt the market still would recognise intellectual property values and all those sorts of issues, and I think they didn't actually focus on the fact that technology was ramping up much quicker and it was going to impact on the musicians in as short a timeframe as it did. I don't know whether there was anything more Machiavellian about it other than that. They didn't see the change in technology having such a material impact in such a short time.

We hear whispers about a new vinyl facility in Australia. Do you think that the vinyl resurgence is a fad or it's going to last?

Well, I can give you a couple of stats on that. We've got to think about what base it's growing from. In Australia there was a 23% growth in vinyl records last year. In Europe it was 25%. The plants that are currently running in America are all full with orders. So yeah, you can say it's a fad. But I think it's an interesting position to be in because there are people who like vinyl. There are the audiophiles. But it's also a bit of a novelty value—it has all those sorts of things and people can touch and feel it.

I asked someone the other day at a restaurant, one of the young waiters there, what he thought about vinyl and he said "Well, when you go to a disco it's a lot easier to ask somebody to come out and listen to your vinyl collection than it is to look at your MP3 files". So I think there's maybe there's a bit of that as well. Whether that's a driver or not, there's a market out there. I don't think it's going to reinvent itself and become a leader because it's too cumbersome. It's not designed for mobility, for portability, for anything else other than sitting at home and listening to it and pretending that it sounds fantastic. But there's opportunity for very much the, what I'd call a limited edition product that's probably been remastered, redeveloped because all those tapes still exist in most cases. The original 16 tracks, the original 2 track masters still exist for a lot of that product and I think you can redevelop another market for it. Not for retail. It's not a retail product. It's very much an online product.

Do you think that there might be something to do with the size of the format and the tactile nature of it? When they first started putting out CDs some people put them out in the same sized packaging for retail.

Well, you can fit a poster in a vinyl jacket and it only has four folds in it. If you try and put the same sized poster into a CD ... So it's your marketing material, your promotional stuff and the quality of the actual covers. In some instances people have a thought process that says you should advertise and sell vinyl records which you offer with a free MP3 download of the record, so you can get the scratches and bumps and whatever else on the MP3 player and you don't actually have to take the cellophane off your vinyl. It's a novelty but I think there are genuine audiophiles out there, and particularly the baby boomers of my era who still like to listen to AC/DC on vinyl.

If it's going to get revived as a distribution format, if it's going to keep growing at 25% a year, there are huge implications for mastering. There's probably half a dozen people in the country now who really know how to master for vinyl, and we've now also got the iTunes mastering chain for when you're mastering for the iTunes standard. Vinyl's got all these requirements based on the dynamics of the needle. Do you think mastering might be a future boom area, or is it just going to go the way of everything else in audio with cheap technology and "I'll do my own mastering and here's what I think"?

I think there's two answers to that question. One answer is about everybody in the commercial world having costs. I think that sometimes people totally focus on cost and then at the end of the day sometimes it has a detriment to the long-term value of your product. If you go back and you look at mastering I think it will be an important component and we'll talk about opportunities in a minute. But we'll talk about vinyl more. As you say there's probably about half a dozen guys who are actually used to running modern mastering machines and doing that sort of stuff in the country. They're in my age bracket, they're sort of looking back to the schools, there's no-one to actually pass their knowledge onto as such. They developed a methodology and a discipline that knows how to eliminate the phasing issues with vinyl, how to maintain a nice clean profile and reduce noise, and all those sorts of things. Those skills should be passed on because even though it might not necessarily be a leading-edge technology, it will be there, it will actually be a skill base that people will appreciate. Vinyl will be around for a while yet. If you search the internet and look at the number of companies that are selling amplifiers, turntables, needles, and belts, there's a whole industry, a subculture. So the quality of the product has to be there and that's the sort of base that should be there. I think it will evolve further. There might not be hundreds of people involved in it but certainly it will be a skill that people will need to pass on from these guys that have been doing it. They were pioneers because they had to deal with noise, how much carbon you're actually putting into the vinyl. The more carbon the less noise, but the more carbon the more transitional issues you have, and all sorts of things. So they had a fairly interesting time developing all of that.

You can see it again now with iTunes Plus. They entered the market, they got their market share, they've got their market penetration, they need now to raise the quality to the point where they can continue to market and grow that business. There are mastering techniques that they're expecting now with the sampling rates, with the amount of limiting they put on, and the compression and so on. I think you'll find that mastering will be a key part of any business that actually needs to take intellectual property and turn it into a commercial product.

So that's a future career?

Absolutely, yeah.

Are physical formats in general dead over the long term?

No. They have a life. We see now CD is still in some respects stronger than everybody expected it to be. If you look at the numbers that have been going through Australia in the last year, there hasn't been any real decline in the actual number of units. Three or four years ago you were seeing 5, 7, 10% decline each year. Now it's levelled off. That's driven by a number of factors. One is that the groups are out touring around the country. You see a lot more groups touring Australia and promoting their product—they're pushing it, they're a usable gift: there's no sense giving your grandmother an MP3 download of something. There's no romance; there's nothing in it. It's the same for some of the young kids who are now working out that if they buy themselves a CD it's actually a master: if they do have a crash in their computer or their MP3 player they can reconstitute that without having to go back to iTunes. So I think there's a whole myriad of things that are happening in the market.

The CD will decline, there's no doubt, and I think it will go down once iTunes gets to a much higher quality format. I think that would accelerate the decline because it's not as if there's an intolerable difference between formats. I think that in most cases it will decline over the next few years to have a real life of ten, 15 years at the most because music is more durable and anybody who's involved in the music industry is probably in a better place than somebody who's involved in the packaged media video business because people do listen to CDs more than once, whereas if you buy a DVD or a Blu-Ray disc you watch it maybe once or twice. CDs or MP3s are always being played.

After so long in what I guess you'd call large-scale, physical format production, and you've had a very specific career in that, you must have developed some kind of philosophy about what it is you're doing, is it selling emotion, are you contributing to audio visual culture? How do you see it? I know at one level you're just making money for somebody—being a business you've got to do that—but what is it that makes things successful, or what is it that makes you feel like you're doing something useful.

Well I think if you look at it my background and how I got involved in the post production of the music industry and went off and built the first compact disc factory in Australia in Melbourne, it's interesting because in a lot of cases when we first did that and went to the major music companies in Australia and said we could make CDs in Australia they wouldn't believe us. They thought that initially we were importing them from Japan and putting labels on them. The satisfaction I got out of that was very much the case of bringing the technology to Australia and developing the industry here. I think if you look at the packaged media industry in Australia you would probably have to say that it employs thousands of people across the full supply chain. If you take that we are a service organisation, what we do is we take people's intellectual property—and that could be anything from music tracks to video or whatever it is—and then spend a lot of money and a lot of time and a lot of emotion and a lot of commitment to producing that product. Our job is to commercialise intellectual property, to take it from that particular emotive piece of information and actually turn it into a saleable product, through retail, or the next generation digital format, or whatever it is. So you are part of that full supply chain.

And although you're at that primary part of where the money is made, in a lot of places it is a place that has the responsibility of also protecting people's intellectual property. I get a lot of satisfaction out the fact that we can build those large technology facilities in this country. I was thinking about it on the way here that when we first started to make CDs in Australia. It took us four and a half seconds to mould a CD or injection compression mould a CD. Now we do it in 2.8 seconds and that has brought the product which was probably a wholesale price of about $2.50 for a CD in 1987 to where it's probably 30 cents. The development of expertise in technology for the industry now is probably world class.

Does Sony do small runs?

Yeah, it's moved into that. Most of the industry's now moved into the point of catering for what the industry's going to look like in a few years. You made the comment that there's a lot of warehouses in Australia that have got a lot of product. The average order sizes are actually reducing and in most cases you'll probably find a back catalogue that people are looking for will probably come out of small-run technology where, instead of doing an average run of 4 and a half to 5 thousand units, which is what it used to be a few years ago, we're probably looking at the order of 300 now, and that's a just-in-time approach. So in other words they'll get the orders in from the retailers on that particular product, it'll go into the warehouse before lunchtime, and then you'll look at manufacture for a day and a half and it'll go back in the warehouse. So the whole supply chain will be shortening right down to provide that service. This is all part of the strategy to prolong the life of packaged media into retail.

I saw something that said the number one record album in the UK last week sold about 7000 albums which was the lowest ever since they've been tracking numbers. In the US it was 9000 which was the second lowest number as the number one.

Yeah, I need to qualify that because if you're doing a new release, like an Adele album or something, I think Adele probably sold over half a million units in Australia which still happens once in a while. In general terms a new release may run 6 weeks to 2 months. Then it drops into a back catalogue status and then that's when the average order size drops down.

So you house the masters and then just do runs according to retailer demand?

Yeah. We get daily orders coming through, basically. So what happens in the supply chain is that you'll have someone like a JB HiFi or Woolworths or whatever placing orders into the warehouse. If there's not in stock in the warehouse then they'll place an order at the factory and the factory will manufacture that. It may be that they look at the stock terms and say every month there's an order of 300 come through or whatever, so you do 2 months worth. But in general terms they will put an order into the warehouse, including printed parts. They'll do all the packaging and everything else and it'll be sent out to the warehouse from there. So most cases back catalogue now will be running at 300–500 units per order.

And that's all the way back? I mean, are we talking Bing Crosby here?

Yeah, it depends on the music company of course. And when you think of the amount of product that's probably sitting in some of these warehouses that have been around for 20 odd years, there'll be a lot of Bing Crosbys.

So there will be a lot of changes in the market, and in the way packaged media runs. Just to expand on that: You'll find that there'll be two stages of back catalogue. There'll be people who go out and buy the new release stuff, there'll be people who look for it on CD, but the third stage of that is that people will download it, so it will be available in huge files sitting out there in the ether. If you're looking for Bing Crosby's *White Christmas* you can't buy it on CD, you can actually go online and be able to download it. So it'll be three stages of the transition from the packaged media sale to the download.

Do you ever see the time when a company like Sony Digital does what, say, Red Dog or any of those sort of small manufacturers do: dealing with indie folk—people who are knocking up stuff in their basement, 3–500 or 1000 and putting them on CD or whatever, do you see the day that that happens or is that already here?

I think that's already here in a lot of cases because of the contraction of the market. You take some of the small indies and you also take some of the small video distribution companies—their markets are shrinking too … well, their ability to enter the market is shrinking—but the market is still out there. So rather than selling 500 units into New South Wales they may well sell, if they expanded into Fiji and into New Zealand, 500 units. A company like Sony who actually has a global footprint with its manufacturing and distribution should ultimately be able to provide those services into other areas so people will be able to gain access, either physical media or a download service.

And what's the link at that point between what you call the marketing department of the record company, what you do in the factory, and Sony's global distribution and manufacturing footprint?

The basic core issue is that we are a service. So Sony Music is a separate entity. They tell us what they want us to do with their intellectual property and we deliver it in physical format, or in digital format to ISPs, or direct to consumers. That footprint will be where it's at. But it'll be hybrids. They may say "We want 10,000 CDs. This is a mixture, 300 of this, 500 of that or whatever it is, delivered direct to retail in New Zealand and at the same time we want you to put it on some of the ISP sites in New Zealand so we can actually deliver that as well".

Sony was a clear leader in the introduction of CD as a consumer technology. But in other cases such as cassette tape and MP3 the consumer led the charge. To what extent do you think future strategic choices of the music majors have shaped consumer behaviour and how's that going to change into the future? It used to be the case that the majors would just own the whole chain.

I don't know. I think the world has changed so much. I think you see a clear match between people like Sony, people like Audio Technica, Panasonic. You see lot of the major organisations are involved in media and try to control people's behaviour and they come up with formats to achieve that. If you look at the VHS and Beta format wars, it's a classic example. It was a race to see an end and to a certain degree it was the same with HD-DVD versus Blu-Ray where you had competing technologies and you're trying to penetrate the market. Ultimately the winner of the VHS war was consumer behaviour and the consumer behaviour was that they were used to buying a fridge or a television set so it was that VHS actually entered the market through 13 or 14 different brand names in Australia. Sony hung onto the Beta format for itself, so you see where people are going and they would buy themselves a Rank Arena TV and they'd buy themselves a Rank Arena VHS player. So they controlled the buying behaviour by actually spreading the market, and I think that's what will happen in the future: it'll be the adoption of the consumer, the consumer will say "well I don't see any upside to that technology, I'm happy with what I've got". We're seeing that with 3D TV. We're seeing it in a lot of those other areas where there is certain consumer resistance to it because people become more assertive about what they actually want out of their technology, and so manufacturers have to think harder and smarter about what the adoption will be. Sony is no different to any other major organisation. They have to look at how people want to buy their TV sets, what they want on the TV sets. Do they want to be able to watch YouTube on their TV sets, which is now becoming part of the offering. They've sort of moved away from 3D because, and I think we'll talk about 3D a bit later, because 3D is not what the consumer wanted on their TV set. They wanted to be able to sit there and watch YouTube or reality TV, and so the consumer drove that decision. If major corporations like Samsung and Sony and Panasonic had their way, people would be buying 3D TV sets.

Apple really scooped the vertical integration pool with iTunes software, iPods, iPhones, iThis, iThat, i everything. Can you see any challenges to that model coming in the near future?

No. I think people will want choice and through the natural way that the consumer works. I believe that they will look at opportunities not to have to lock in. iTunes will have to grow its business, it will have to offer better quality and everything else to maintain their client base. There is another product which is coming out which is not directly related to audio but it may do it which is called ultra-violet. It is endorsed by 70-odd of the major studios and manufacturers around the world. It tries to cover off packaged media side as well as the download levels.

What is it? Is it a codec or a format?

No, it's actually an authorisation software system where you go out and you buy a Blu-Ray disc or a DVD or whatever it is, and then log on to a website. You get an authorisation number off the Blu-Ray that you've bought—it's a bit cumbersome—and then it authorises you to have any sort of download. So whether you want a portable download for your phone, whether you want to put it on your computer, it allows you to do all those things. So it expands the format genre that you get by buying the product. I think that was a way they saw of competing against iTunes but it was driven very much by the 75 major studios and manufactures. So it's early days yet to see whether that goes. But in general terms I think you see iTunes will continue to dominate the market. There was a recent court case between Apple and Samsung over the iPad, some of the software, and I think you're going to see a lot more of that over the next few years.

So the ultra-violet part of it, is that actually a technological change? Is there better quality or is just entirely an authorisation.

No, it's authorisation.

Multi-format?

Yeah.

Is there any kind of media format you're seeing as challenging what's around now? FLAC has been talked about as an audio standard going forward because of its quality.

Yeah, I don't know. I think there's a lot of people who are working with a lot of ideas. It's the old story: how much quality and how much bandwidth? The consumption of bandwidth has grown astronomically around the world and you need to be able to transfer products cost-effectively with the minimum amount of bandwidth. But until you can get over the algorithms to make the quality as good as you can get it, I think we'll see changes over the next 5 years with people trying to enter the market differently. iTunes are making a quality standard for themselves because they've got effective people who are going to bring the technology forward.

Getting back to the formats and these ideas about the sensory intensification: things like 3D, "smellavision", adding touch sensitivity to movies ...

We actually tried at one stage to make CDs that when you scratched them made the smell of flowers. It didn't work. It was a bad marketing idea: scratch the CD then smell the flowers while you're listening to it. It didn't work.

Is 3D too intense an experience? 5.1's another one. I just can't see a long term domestic use, even though they're still ticking along and people are actually selling them as features in new homes. You've got to be in exactly the right spot at exactly the right angle to make the most of it. What do you think's the future of all these experiments?

I have a personal view that I think 3D's a very particular experience and people treat it as such. You go to an IMAX theatre to see 3D. You sit there and you watch it. The problem with it in the home, and that's why there's been a certain more move towards YouTube and the internet on TV, is that it's not as antisocial. It's not socially acceptable to sit there with six people and a pair of glasses on in front of the TV and somebody from next door pops in with a bottle of red wine and says "I'll sit down and watch too". "But we've only got six pairs of glasses". What happens? Six, seven drinks of red wine while everybody else is watching. It's very antisocial in that way. Add to that the fact that as a mature age person I get home I like to lie down on the couch. With polarized glasses when you lie down on your side the picture disappears so you can't actually watch the TV while you're lying on the couch. I think it has its limitations as a family device, because you have to sit there and you have to focus and intensively watch it. It was probably great and had some real value if somebody went out and bought a 3D Blu-Ray disc and sat home and watched 3D *Pirates of The Caribbean* as a once-off scenario. But to sit there and watch 3D all day every day, until they actually come up with electronics that actually take away the need to wear glasses and allow you a much broader viewing arrangement, it will have its limitations to much more event-driven programming. I think that's where they all have to move with that technology to make it work.

I've seen three or four attempts at 3D in my lifetime and I can't see them ever working.

No. I think it still sits in the cinema and when you wear the glasses you find also there's a certain real light-loss in them and you have to focus a lot more. When you lose sensitivity in your eyes, as older people do, it becomes harder to sit there and watch these sort of programs. Whereas the kids love it. They get that perception, and I think that until they can get rid of some of those inhibitions it will always not necessarily get high penetration. And it's like you say: in a lot of cases everybody raced off and bought 5.1 surround systems. We've got one but we leave it turned off because you can't sleep when you get 170 dB of dynamic range comes through the system and you're asleep on the couch. It doesn't work for me. I'm quite happy to listen to the news subliminally.

Coming back to the issue of vertical integration, it's been the case for years that tech companies continually seek lock-in. A classic example: if you're running an Avid system you've got to have this hardware, that software and it makes for really inflexible outcomes. It sounds like ultra-violet might be another technological lock-in strategy. Is that where it's going?

Well everybody likes to control the vertical market. It's a bit like buying a car. You buy yourself a BMW and the services are free but they've built it into the costs. But in some instances you go out and you get your 50,000 mile service and it costs you a fortune. In some instances companies survive on selling the initial hardware and then living on the upgrades, living on the software development. I think that there are advantages and disadvantages, and I agree with the point about inflexibility, of being able to run a multitude of different software on the same platform.

The advantage is a bit like if you're running multiple studios and someone visits halfway through a recording session and you only have a 32 track tape machine and someone says "Oh shit the desk's just blown up, it's going to be 5 days before you can get it back up because we need the parts out of Germany". You can take that tape, you can take it to a studio next door that has a 32 track machine and you can actually fire it up and rerun it, so you don't lose that flexibility. It's a bit like running a desk that's got automation and you can actually take the disc out of the desk and take it to another studio. So: a common platform interchange.

Once you get into multiple platforms, and you might be running a computer with three or four different software packages that are interlocked together, that locks you into that computer for the period of time you're mixing. So it does create inflexibility. But on the other side it allows people to experiment. Once you have a common platform you can have different software. It allows your intuitive juices to flow with people bringing in different software and saying "Well I'd like to try this with you because it sounds better than Charlie-Down-The-Road's software, so I'm going to try mine". In a commercial sense, that's why you allow people to actually go out and develop their skills, their intuitive skills, in the craft outside.

But in a place like Sony, it's a "keep it simple" and "this is how it works" approach. That's why you need to develop the craft outside where people get a computer, get different packages of software, work on different ideas, and come up with different sounds and different products. Whereas at Sony we just take people's product and make sure it's 100% perfect. So there's a balance. It's from experimentation that all the ideas come, not the companies. The ABC doesn't generate experimentation. You have to get outside of that to studios and other areas and that's where the new things happen.

Studios are another thing that's changed. Production technologies have been dropping in price and increasing in complexity and quality for close to 30 years now. It's been a really rapid transformation. We were talking about Rhinoceros Studios earlier. Many other big studios in this country that have really vibrant histories have disappeared. Is there going to be a time at which there's a future for those types of facilities?

I'll go back. We're talking sort of 1987, 1988, 1989 and AAV had five studios. It had two studios designed for music production and very much designed around big large desks, 32 track tape machines, a lot of room. They were the sort of places that we were nanna napping in the afternoon halfway through a 24 hour recording session. Then it had these other three studios that were much smaller but designed primarily to develop radio commercials, jingles, and products for television commercials. Eighty per cent of the revenue came from those three studios. The other 20% came from the music studios because it was seen as the market you needed to get into. So there was an oversupply of studios. There was discounting on rates and only a certain number of bands around who had potential to invest in their production and could afford to spend $200,000 on a record in those days.

The technology has significantly changed and I think in a lot of ways labels look at it now and say "Okay, that's an upcoming group, I think that we can actually make a 12 track album for $40,000". So they give them the money and they go off and they either go and negotiate the position with the studio or they actually go out and buy the equipment and do it at home and if it's good enough it gets remixed or whatever it takes to actually produce it to broadcast quality.

So I think in a lot of cases the market has changed. The big studios are still there. Often they're working in a sort of a training capacity. There is a certain aura in a large music studio and they've got a lot of nostalgia attached to them. But the market that the people are driving to at the moment is online and self-sufficient. A lot of the groups now, if they can afford it, will go into a studio and do it. But if they're up and coming groups the company generally gives them the budget to go out and produce it and they hunt around for the best prices and the big studios will always be there, but not many of them in Australia. They still seem to sit overseas in L.A or wherever where people can afford to spend their half a million dollars or a million dollars on a record because of global sales.

The Australian market is generally going to shrink because of Australian sales. It'd be nice I think for some of them to come back but they are expensive to run and they are expensive to equip. We need to have a re-realisation of the music industry before it will pay. With the transition to digital the revenue streams have to come from digital. It's an interesting commercial phenomenon that if you sell a John Farnham album—or it could be a Wolfmother album or whatever it is that's got 17 tracks on it—when they buy the CD it's got 17 tracks. If you go online you say "Oh well I don't like I don't like track 5, I don't like track 7, I don't like those tracks so I'm not going to buy them". So the revenue for that album drops significantly when it's online. Therefore the royalties and everything else going back to the artists, and also the revenue back to the music company, drops, and so it's not the same.

We had a couple of changes, one in about 1992 with the Keating government changing the cultural import laws. Then there's marketing theory that says advertising is 95% visual and so nobody wants music for advertising anymore. I don't think there was any large studio around in the 80s or 90s that wasn't making it's bread and butter doing advertising, TV work, titles, and everything else like that. That work's largely gone as well.

Well even on the video side, when they allowed the import of American commercials into Australia, you could get a Colgate commercial and someone's driving around in a left-hand drive car talking about how white their teeth are. It's culturally different to having somebody who's driving a right-hand side vehicle. I think we suffered immensely in the industry in Australia because we didn't have the advertising agencies to actually push back against the idea that they could use overseas commercial material for their production. Post-production businesses have major investments in sound studios to actually sweeten the commercials and the jingles, the radio jingles and everything else. We've lost that revenue stream and it is lots of overseas commercials that have flattened out those revenues.

We lost a great training ground there.

Yeah, very much.

I know that you've got a combination of audio and video in your background. They're strange bedfellows in a way. I mean at one level they've got a lot in common, but they're economically separate areas of activity with completely different approaches. Film's this massive enterprise that's very hard to do by yourself. Some people make one-camera iPhone movies but I don't think we're ever going to say that's the future of the movie making industry. Audio, and especially music, has come off as a poor cousin to the moving picture in Australia. You see it in funding contracts for film grants, even though we know that if the audio's not up to spec or even if it's a bit dodgy and not really well thought out that the movie's going to look terrible as a result, no matter how well it's filmed. Do you see those attitudes reversing, or do you see any kind of recognition of the role of audio in film and television in this country?

I can say firstly that, yes, I believe there is a change. If you go and you look at some of the classic movies that we've seen in some respects that are Australian-made like *Priscilla Queen of The Desert* or *The Sapphires*, which is probably one of the better movies that's come out, everybody relates to the music. Everybody relates to that, and I made the comment earlier that sound reinforcement in actual films is just so important because that's the dynamic—the major dynamic that drives people. Have you ever tried to watch a James Bond movie without any sound? You'll just go to sleep. There's nothing there. It's basically a lot of action and a lot of movement. But it's the sound, the energy that comes out of the sound, that's so important. You need to make sure it's always continually pushing forward.

People listen to CDs much more often than they watch movies. They listen to them five or six times—I think the average listening was about five times for a CD—whereas you might go to see a movie once. So I think the sound is just so important. And I don't know whether it'll actually reverse, but I know that video people are becoming more conscious of music and sound. You can shoot what we'd consider to be acceptable reality TV with a single camera, HD, and edit it up later. But it doesn't sound any good, there's nothing there, it's dead. We talk about the loudness and we talk about the energy that's being put into the sound to the point where people will actually sit up and listen. If I go to a movie that hasn't grabbed me within the first 20 minutes I go to sleep. The only thing that wakes me is when the sound goes up because I know the action's happening. I know it's not the pictures because I'm not watching the screen, but subconsciously I'm listening to it. All of a sudden the action starts and you sort of wake up. Sound is what imparts emotion and I think we need to put more energy into that as an industry.

So it's a problem of education?

Very much so. I think there's a skill base that is still out there, and there's a lot of young people that need an opportunity to learn those skills. As an industry I think it was let down because there wasn't constructive drive to make sure those skills were passed on in the media industries because everybody just started focusing on games. I got involved with a company called Lake Technology. They developed a time domain filtering for surround sound and sound reinforcing studio. All they worked on was the sound for games because it was so important to the gamers that when they turned their head towards the sound of a flame, that the flame was actually in the right spot, so the sound was the primary driver for games that were being developed.

This is quite out of left field in terms of what we've been talking about, but can you identify changes in legislation or regulation—we talked about broadcast standards and so forth—in Australia that has dramatically affected distribution formats?

I think when legislation came in to say "Okay, we're going to allow importation of CDs into the country", and that was probably 18 years ago, retailers could suddenly bring product in directly and sell it and compete against the local distributors. Everybody thought that was going to be a major downturn in the music industry in Australia but I think it had no material impact because the supply chain for music is sale or return. You go into a retailer and put in 20 copies of a particular product, they keep it on the shelves, if they sell 15 of them and they find they're not going to move the rest then the other five get returned. But if they've ordered them they're basically getting sold. So it was the service elements that developed within the music industry after that which enabled the quickest response times, delivery, the manufacturing, and supply chain processes to actually move product. To import a product into the retailers slowed that down to a trickle because the local service and supply chains were providing an on-time service and they didn't need to necessarily go offshore to procure the product. If you've noticed, the retail price of CDs has held up pretty well over the last few years. It's more in the competitive market now than it was a few years ago, we were selling below $19 for a new release or $21, depending on who you knew. But it's still got value and not a lot of it's directly imported, maybe some small volumes come in, but certainly a lot of it is packaged here.

Standard pricing is the strangest thing. You'd think you'd pay $3000 for a Rolling Stones album and $2.50 for the latest unheard of indie release.

Yeah, I dunno, it's all market-driven. I remember in the early days the blank VHS cassettes that were made in Japan were three times the price they were in Australia, and that was really on the basis of what the market prices were. I don't know the fine art or the black magic of standard pricing but someone worked it out.

Getting back to the value of sound and music, I think in our culture at any rate it seems to have gone through a few audiophile stages. There was one in the 1960s, another one in the 1980s with the emergence of digital, and it seems to be there's been all of a sudden people have realised that MP3s sound rotten. I have a friend who's an audiophile. He's telling me that the recent explosion in audiophile fashion underpins one of the largest consumer areas in sound technology. Do you think we're really in the market for another audio uptick in sound quality consciousness?

I think so. It depends on what you use it for. If you were sitting at home where you'd built yourself a surround-sound studio and a nice room with the right set of speakers or whatever, you're not going to put an MP3 player through it because there's severe data compression and the limited dynamic range and everything else that goes with it. It'll sound okay but it won't give you the presence you really want out of that music. Whereas it's fine when you're walking along the beach or it's fine when you're listening to it in the car where there's a lot of ambient noise around or you're doing other things. People accept lower audio quality in a transportable product and they're happy to listen to it. But with the next stage of technology we'll expect the quality to increase. I see it now in that 2 or 3 years ago people used to have earbuds. Now they're going for the full earpiece because they want better quality. Next thing they'll be saying "Oh, we want better quality out of our digital portable devices". So the next format that comes out whether it's an iTunes Plus or whatever it is will drive that higher quality because people with the technology are now coming to the stage where we expect that. Marketing companies are asking "Well how do we raise that bar to sell a new whatever it's going to be called—MP3 player, new headsets, all that sort of stuff?" We drive the quality because that's the only thing we can drive now. Again, it's consumer driven.

It's an odd thing. If you look at the trends in presenting audio to pop audiences in particular there's a lot of talk about the loudness wars alongside the MP3 quality issue. That's kind of presented a lot of music that smacks you in the face and goes away and you can't remember what it was. Do you see engineers are almost scared to not be the loudest? Even mix engineers seem to be aiming at loudness rather than space or dynamics or anything else.

I think that's an education thing. In early days of television programming, and to a certain degree in commercials on radio, there was a lot of drive to get as much energy into that bandwidth as you could. Therefore loudness became the underpinning driver of commercials. I don't know if most people here would remember that you could be watching a program and it could be a very nice sort of romance movie and it's got reasonable dynamic range on it and suddenly it'll cut to commercials and it'll be commercials about buying furniture at Charlie Joe's Furniture Shop in Lismore or whatever it is and the energy level just goes through the roof. It's designed so that you ask "What's all that about?" rather than going to get a cup of tea. It's actually designed to sort of wake you up to the point of saying "You should watch this commercial". Then the television stations got over it and the radio stations got over it by actually putting limiters into their transmitters to make sure that there wasn't such a dynamic swing from programmed material to commercials. Now we're going into the MP3 player and its limitations, how do you get people's attention? Rather than having dynamic range, how do you get the presence in the ears? You do it with loudness and energy, and once you get back into having good dynamic range and once you get back into having a good soundfloor in the product, it will sound different. What will happen is that people, when they get to a quiet patch, will wind the volume up until they get used to it. Classical music's probably a good example. You could never actually run with modern loudness on it because there is such dynamic range built into the music. It would just destroy the music as such and I think that what will happen is that people's expectations are that if they want the quality they're going to have to wind some of the loudness out of it and they're going to have to wind it out to make sure people appreciate some of the frequency response and dynamic range and the real message in the music and get away from just banging people's ears because it makes them feel better. Does that make sense?

Yeah, certainly. It's just hard to see how the transition will happen.

Again, I think it's education. I think that MP3 and iTunes absolutely blitzed the market with the transition from what people thought was a good audio format which was a super CD or whatever it was, or CDs, to a convenience product. They've got a convenience product now and they can walk around and listen to it and they can plug it into their computer. They can do whatever they like with the MP3 format, but it still has its limitations because of its ability to actually recreate the purity of the original music and I think that's the next stage. I think that next stage will be newer technologies and newer formats which our people are expecting. As I said earlier, the reason being is that you're starting to see people walking around with higher-quality headsets rather than just buds in their ears, so they're looking for that bit of extra purity in the music. It'll come through education and it'll come through people wanting to listen to their music even more.

It's like when they built the Walkman. The reason Sony built the Walkman back in the 70s or whenever was the fact that when the trains were so crowded in Tokyo people didn't have their personal space. They were all standing there looking at one another and they had eaten garlic or whatever, and they were just crammed into the trains. So Sony thought "Oh well", whoever the bright person was who came up with it, "Give people their personal space". How do you give them their personal space? You put a headset on them and you give them music that takes them into their own space where they don't have to worry about anything that's happening around them and that was the philosophy behind it.

My friend, Greh Hearn, calls it a synthetic emotional environment.

Yeah, and that's why the success of the Walkman was to put people into their own space.

You've been involved in some massive initiatives with large scale media format productions. Most people would have never heard anything about it even though it's shaped markets, it's shaped listening habits, it's shaped

viewing habits, it's shaped consumption patterns, it's shaped consumer behaviour. Why do you think you managed to get away with doing all these things for so long without anybody noticing? You're one of the most difficult people to find anything about. So congratulations on one hand, but I'm interested to know why and how.

I don't know. If you look at the market that I've been involved in and you start talking about building compact discs here and building overseas and building facilities here and restructuring businesses and things like that, I don't believe it's generally newsworthy. It's a process of building technology and service organisations; it doesn't need advertising. It's not dealing with front-of-mind consumer based technology. Our client base is clearly defined and quite niche.

In real terms it's our client base in those particular cases. Our music companies, video companies who are forward-facing into the consumer market, so they're the people who really need to have advertising, marketing, promotional stuff. But in most cases like building these compact disc plants and DVD plants and Blu-Ray plants and things like that around the world, that was really a process. That was really just building the plant, going out and getting the client base, building the structures and doing all that sort of stuff. It was very enjoyable, it was a great time, particularly with the leading-edge technologies—building the first one in Australia. The challenges that it brings on and the intuitive demands—I think that's one thing that we really need to get into our businesses even more is that intuitive thinking so that you can actually think outside the square if you need to. At 2 o'clock in the morning when you've already got a delivery to Michael Smellie at Polygram or whatever it is and the machines aren't working, let me tell you, intuitively you work out how it's going to happen and that's what it's all about. That's what really develops the satisfaction is being able to deliver and provide those sorts of technologies. It's been a lot of fun.

I'm assuming you don't have to take a hands-on interest in actual audio engineering any more.

No, I'm over the hill when it comes to that. I even have difficulty reading my Blackberry now, and I have to put on glasses to read a Blackberry. I get more involved in commercialisation now, working through a lot of those businesses and their development to actually get them to the stage where they make money. I now get involved in a couple of areas. One area is in building a strategy for a long-tail soft landing for packaged media so it doesn't fall into any disarray as things move forward. It's designed to provide the services with the continuity of content through the next 10–15 years or however long the format survives. The other part of what I'm involved in is commercialisation of the digital side of the business and how you actually take all these great ideas and make them commercially viable. There's a lot of young kids out there who have these great ideas and they want to develop the software. They do all sorts of new stuff, and then they get someone old and grumpy like me to do get involved and asks "Well okay, how are we going to make money out of it? How are we going to deliver it? How are we going to monetize the back end of it and those sorts of things?". So it's a bit like a saying what we're doing on the digital side is a bit more in the mentoring vein of "Can we make money out of it and what do we need to do to make money out of it?". Sony is an organisation that makes money to fund any future development and research, contrary to belief around the world is that most companies are in business to make money.

I've got one last question before we turn you over to the audience and it's one I've been asking all our guests: if you had one piece of advice to give aspiring professionals, what would it be?

I would say don't inhibit your intuition. I always took the philosophy that if you're not leaning on the edge you're taking up too much space. So as you're moving into some of these areas, and new corporations can be great places, some, if they're intuitive enough, will actually support great ideas and new things going forward. Some will actually try to control it into a pattern. But my personal philosophy is don't be scared to step outside your comfort zone. Don't be scared to actually go forward with what you truly believe in and follow your emotions because ultimately you always rise to the satisfaction of doing what you wanted to do and not saying "I wish I had". I think it's important in life to not to actually say "I wish I had" but to say "I want to do this", so that's my piece of advice.

Questions?

Audience member: Are streaming services like Spotify just another fad?

Yeah, I think they are. I think in a lot of cases people see it as easy. You pay your $10 or $20 a month and have unlimited downloads. I think everybody's looking at ways to actually monetize the business and that's one. I think even Sony is involved in one of those and, yeah, I think it's just another format to access content.

Audience member: For independent musicians like myself who are releasing stuff for the first time, do you think there's an argument for bypassing physical releases entirely? Just releasing on aggregators and that sort of thing?

It depends. There's a double-edged argument to that because if you're an independent musician and you've developed your own content and you think that you can actually market it, the biggest problem with the internet is getting people to find out who you are. If you look at most companies throughout the world they actually say "Okay I've got a product, I want to sell and market it on the internet, I'm going to spend $10 million locally on traditional media to actually promote the fact that I've got it on the internet". As you're probably well aware, once you get on the internet and start to deliver content you need word of mouth. It's a trendy place to go, you need to create a need for people like Google to actually promote articles about your product, so it's really a marketing exercise.

If you go to a major record company then of course they will search around and say "Well, okay, we need to spend $200,000 or half a million dollars on promoting the product but we need to recover that before you get any money back" and those sorts of things. So really it's an issue of how you want to develop your product. Sometimes publicity is good publicity and I don't mean that in a negative sense, but you do create your own image and that's what sells the product. I can't give you any firm answer on that, I'm not an expert on marketing on the internet. All I know is that you need to continually push yourself to the front of the queue all the time and unless you've got the financial backing I think it's always a struggle. Unless you put something on YouTube like Justin Bieber and these sort of people and it becomes a phenomenon overnight for no reason.

Audience member: You were saying before about when an album is released by an artist after the first 2 months there's loss of sales. What about having a strategy where you release one or two songs every couple of months online, would that maintain a constant interest from your fans do you think?

When I was referring about that I was referring very much to the packaged media sale where they do the album and then the tracks and then they release that and generally, there's about 2 months or 3 months when it's released then it's dropped into the back catalogue. If you're doing it online, I don't know. I can't answer that specifically. I would have thought that's to do with how much advertising and promotion around that you can do to maintain that drive because, as I said, sometimes people release an album and there's 17 tracks on the it and it virtually takes up the full 72 minutes of a CD. In general terms, online, they only buy three or four of the tracks. They don't buy them all and then therefore the royalties issued are only on those three or four tracks.

It seems at least on some level there are entirely different rules operating there in terms of the longer you leave it there the more it's going to sell and you can only do so much at a time, you can't sort of do it in small bits rather than big bits because then you get ten things to talk about rather than one.

Yeah, exactly.

Audience member: I've seen on Amazon that when some people release their music digitally and they release it as a product and a copy of CD as well, they allow certain songs to be bought digitally but they hold back one or two, probably the best songs from the album and say "these are only available if you buy the whole CD". What do you think of that as a marketing strategy, and the other part of the question that I was going to ask before, what advice would you give to somebody who wants to start out an indie label?

I'll answer your last question first. I generally believe two things: one is that you should follow your dreams and secondly that God loves a trier. So I don't think you should inhibit yourself and I think that the internet and online is opening up a whole new area for the indies. The small people who want to start their own businesses and sell online are now at the forefront of most people's mind. A lot of people, as you probably know, are going to the retailer and actually scan the product with their iPhones and work out where the cheapest price is or whether it's online and they go and order it online. That's always going to be there. But the marketing aspects of the online world is where you need to develop a maturity. It's not so much whether you've got the quality product or the smartest technology to sell online and build online; it's how you actually get to those people who will buy it. Sometimes you have to develop a publicity machine that continually drives it. The Amazon thing is their way of placating in a lot of ways the packaged media market and the online market. Because they are really a book seller and they've got a huge logistics and distribution centre built in around the world, these places that send books and you name it, and there's a whole area set aside for CDs and DVDs and Blu-Rays, so how do you encourage the distribution centres because everything that's in there has to move at some stage, and there's a feed attached to that so to make money out of that you need to encourage people to buy physical media as well, so you have a bit of a trickster game and so you hold back.

So would that be a good strategy, say, for me as an indie record label if I want to maximise the profit for my artist, maximise the royalty, to follow that strategy and hold back a couple of their best songs and say "well you can only have these if you buy the whole CD"?

How do you determine they're the best songs?

Put videos up on YouTube and see what you get the best response to.

Yep, absolutely. Do your marketing research and then you may say "Yeah, I'm going to release these", or "No. It's not going to work". It's all marketing at the end of the day: who's onto it, who will take to it, and the physical media has got a huge supply chain globally with thousands of people involved in it. There are huge machines with huge investments in them, and people are driving these all the time.

Audience member: I'm not sure how familiar you are with electronic artists, uh, but I know Carl Cox and Avicii released their latest albums on USB flash drive with special contents like ongoing subscription sort of stuff as well. What are your thoughts on USB flash drive as a medium?

Solid state media, I think whether it's an SD card or a USB stick I think, is probably going to be it. There's no reason why you can't, the only thing that inhibited USB drives and also flash cards and SD cards being used for it was the cost of manufacturing. I go back to my comment earlier where you can actually make a CD, a physical media CD, a raw disc, not in the box, not packaged, nothing like that for probably 30 cents out of the factory, for a lot of people in huge volume. But you try to make it an SD card or a USB stick and probably in general terms you probably can't get it under $5. Therefore the cost inhibits. But now that's coming down at a much greater rate, so you'll probably see that there will be a lot more product released on flash drives and such. It's a convenient way of people loading music into their computers, because most computers now don't even have a CD player. Most of it's in firmware or it's actually online. I know that in China a lot of the new laptops don't actually have a CD or a DVD drive in them any more.

Audience member: I've got a follow-up on that. I just bought a new laptop and it's got a CD/DVD drive. I wouldn't be happy without one because you can load your programs on if you've got them on the CD/DVD and you've always got it there as a backup. So I think it'd be counter-productive not to, but some of the CDs that I have, they're like enhanced CDs and they've got a video on them which it's programmed and it only plays on the computer. It doesn't play on a DVD player, it only plays on the DVD drive on your computer. How much extra would it cost to produce a CD like that, that's got that value-added thing of a video of the artist performing on it?

It's actually, it's embedded into the CD?

I think so, yes.

Manufacturing wise it's probably no different. But if you take a step back, when you're doing the disc mastering process for all this it's all done at the pre-mastering stage. Once it goes onto the laser cutters in the manufacturing plant, the laser cutter actually makes the impression from the data that's been delivered to it. So if that's all embedded into it, the manufacturing process should not be any different. In other words it's, it looks at the data and it makes what it needs to make out of that and doesn't differentiate between video and audio.

Audience member: So if I already have a master from an artist and it's just audio, I couldn't add something like that into it? It would have to have been added when the master was made?

No, I think it'd have to be remastered. There's obviously been software that's been used to embed that. There would be two separate files. You'd play the music and then you watch the music video. Or does it sit there? Is it an embedded file?

I think it's an embedded file because you can play the CD normally and just listen to the music but you can only get the video if you put it into your computer and then it comes up and asks you if you want to play the file. I think one of them actually plays through a flash drive or something on the computer.

Well see, that's probably something that sits outside the normal record and goes past the standard for CDs and DVDs, but that's where it's all going anyway. I would imagine there's probably a lot of that stuff starting to evolve now.

Audience member: Why can't you get the information about who played the saxophone solo and all that stuff? I thought I heard someone say the other day that the format doesn't allow that and I was wondering why or why that would be? You were saying it's just data, it's just digital.

Yeah, it's one of the things, it's interesting that you talk about that because in a lot of cases, and you might and someone says "Okay, we're going to put these 12 tracks online" whether it's iTunes or whatever it is it doesn't matter, and it usually takes a couple of hours or 4 or 5 hours to actually download and put all that data on but it sometimes can take up to 2 weeks to get the metadata right, because you go back and you look at things like who was the actually drummer in 1998 on that particular album? Is he dead or alive? Does he have a trust fund? Does his family still have the rights to that? So there was a lot of backroom work that was done on an album before it's actually put online. In the longer term I don't think there's any reason why the metadata can't be included. If you're doing a direct download why it can't actually provide that information if you want to print it out, I don't know. In a lot of cases I think there are sites you're talking about providing you with the ability to actually make your own covers and do all that sort of stuff. But I think most people are just focused on the MP3s and downloads. If you want to make an album it's a different story.

It's gone a long way from the days of 2 inch tape. You opened a 2-inch box and you've got all the information in there. It's all there all the time.

Well that's one of the things that's been happening down in Sydney. The 16 tracks and all the 2 tracks that we've been sitting around for a long time in some of these studios and the metadata that travels with that 16 track tape is some illegible piece of paper that was written inside that basically says that Charlie was the drummer on this for four songs and then Harry came in 2 days later because Charlie had OD'd or whatever it was. It wasn't possible, and so you know actually collecting the metadata on historical stuff is really, really hard and so there's a lot of work going on in

Sydney in the studios that we have in the manufacturing plant. They're spending a lot of time. They actually scan the boxes so they give all the stuff that's written on the outside of the Ampex box from 1975 and on the edges and everything else just to make sure that they've got that data and it's all file stored, along with all the 16 tracks and the 2 tracks, and everything else, so all this stuff's been stored. At the moment I think they've probably got close to 300,000 tracks. Then there's all the physical tapes, and we're not talking about EMI, we're not talking about Warner, we're not talking about Universal, we're starting to move into a lot of those areas but everyone's making a conscious effort to try and protect that property and the metadata and so that they can actually historically capture it.

Well I understand that because I've been very involved in the whole metadata business in the UK. One of the ideas is to have the ISBN number attached to all that information. But I'm thinking more about the added value, the marketing value of the booklet or the sleeve. You can read the back of the sleeve and say, you know, the blurb on some Bob Dylan album that has a Hunter S Thompson style blurb and the whole idea of the sleeve and the cover, I just wondered why it seems such a, to me it seems such an obvious, that's just a straight PDF or a JPG. You can download cover art in iTunes, but you don't get the sleeve, you don't get the book. I don't know why there's not that detail. You get the picture on the front but nothing else.

It's interesting because if you look at, even on the physical media side, the average booklet size in some were actually 16 pages. The average booklet size now is probably 6–8. So a lot of the data and information that you're talking about is actually coming out of the physical media side and that will be stored, but it won't—and I think if I digress across to MP3—they probably looked at it and probably never thought there would actually be a secondary market for downloading that. It may just be naivety, but I think MP3 is very much a case of people storing it on their computer, storing it on their MP3 players, and not being particularly worried about the track listings and they weren't particularly worried about the metadata. But the metadata is important in the longer term to maintain the integrity of the artists and their product.

Chapter 4
John Watson, Music Manager

Abstract This chapter is an interview with John Watson, widely recognised as being one of Australia's most successful and innovative artist managers. He began his management career with Silverchair in 1995, helping to sell six million albums for the band. In 2000 he established Eleven: A Music Company and took up the management of Silverchair once the band had finalised its contract with Sony. In 2012 the company managed a small but influential roster of artists that includes Gotye, Missy Higgins, Cold Chisel, The Presets, and Birds of Tokyo. Eleven was in many ways a pioneer for a new music business model. It combines the functions of a label with the functions of management and has been widely emulated, at throughout the Australian industry and elsewhere.

Welcome, John. I'm going to start with a quote by Shane Simpson. He says in his book *The Music Industry* that "the perfect manager would be an amalgamation of hard working business executive, snake-oil seller, economist, tangier rug trader, kick boxer, parent, stand-in spouse, friend, confessor-psychologist, fall guy, punching bag and standover merchant. He or she would also be on first-name terms with all the big hitters of the industry in three continents, enjoy an independent source of income, love your music and have a bulletproof belief in the future". How close do you think that does describe what you do and who you are?

Well, unusually for a lawyer, I think he's oversimplified things. I'll start by saying there are, in any talks I give, the same couple of themes, so if anybody's seen me say them before I apologize for repeating myself. I'm not going to do it all day, but there are typically three ways that I will explain what a manager does. The first kind of fun way comes from my dear friend John Woodruff who managed many legendary bands—the Angels through to Savage Garden. He had a great line. Every time he started work with a client he'd sit down with the band and say: "Just remember one thing—you're in charge of fascination, I'm in charge of bullshit." I think there's a lot of truth to that line, and that's probably the simplest way to describe what a manager does. A slightly more developed metaphor that I typically would use in sitting down with an artist is that there are a number of different styles of managers.

P. Graham, *Music, Management, Marketing, and Law*, Music Business Research,
https://doi.org/10.1007/978-3-030-02143-6_4

If you think about your career as being like a truck going down the highway, some artists just want to drive the truck and have the manager be a bull bar on the front of the truck: "Don't tell me what to do, don't have any advice, just mow down the stuff that's in the way, I'll work out where we're going." That's fine, providing the artist has got all the answers, they know everything, which a lot of artists think they do but not many artists actually do.

The second type of manager-artist relationship is the artist who just wants to party in the back of the truck; the manager can drive wherever the hell they want as long as the hookers and the blow keep coming back there. And that's a lot of fun for a little while. Typically there's one day the artist wakes up, the truck's gone over a cliff, the manager's run off with the money and they've spent the rest of their life wondering what happened.

The third type of relationship—which is the one I would typically hope describes all of our relationships with artists—is where the manager is essentially a navigator in the passenger seat and the driver is the artist. So the artist is ultimately behind the wheel of their career. The manager's role is to say, "Up here I think you should turn left for this reason and that reason, I think we should be trying to get to this point". But ultimately the artist is the one who decides whether to make the turns or not. The manager's only sort of recourse at the end of the day is, as the truck goes off the cliff, you get to say, "I told you you should have turned left."

The third way that I describe is a more sophisticated way of thinking about it. Most managers exist to do what artists either can't do for themselves, or don't want to do for themselves. As such, every artist-manager relationship is different. The manager, if you like, exists as the mirror image of the artist. So if, for example, you're managing Britney Spears, you're going to need to be finding pop songs, need to be able to find stylists who deals with the perfume ranges, find lawyers to bail her out of jail. But if you're managing Neil Finn then you presumably don't need to do any of that because he has a different set of needs. So the needs of the artist and the capacity of the artist define what the manager is required to do; the manager's skill set has to be the mirror opposite of the artist's. Think about it if you like with the old hippy yin-yang symbol. You draw that differently in every manager-artist relationship, but when it works well, each party's doing the thing they're good at and the other party's handling the rest of it. And that's why there's no such thing as one type of artist-manager. There's no such thing as "a" manager—you get lots of different types of people known as artist-managers. That's because they exist as a function of the artist. Now, if you're managing The Rolling Stones, Mick Jagger's studying at the London School Of Economics so he's already got the business side under control, largely speaking. He needs someone to help give it flair, which is where Andrew Loog Oldham was such an amazing manager with the photos and the press manipulation and producing the records in their early days. If you're managing The Beatles, they've already got all the flair stuff going on, they needed somebody to help try to organise things for them so they're with Epstein—the respectable small business owner. Brian Epstein and Andrew Loog Oldham: you couldn't meet two more different human beings but they made sense as the managers of those bands at that point in their careers.

So the artist-manager relationship works like a yin-yang symbol and to expand that out to see how the whole picture works, you need to think about that yin-yang symbol as being like the hub on a bike wheel: each of the spokes is a different facet of your career. So a publisher, an agent, perhaps a label, an accountant, a publicist—whatever the case may be—they're each a spoke coming out of that manager-artist 'hub'. The manager's job is to put all the spokes in place, work out where the wheel is supposed to get to and then to coordinate, to motivate, and to persuade to get it rolling and keep it rolling in the right direction. They're the three key verbs of artist management, I would say. To coordinate, to motivate, and persuade, all of those spokes have to spin in the right direction to get the artist's career to where the artist wants to go.

So given the variability of the task, say in comparison between Cold Chisel versus someone who you might not know, or even Silverchair for example, how do you adjust your yin to their yang?

It's why the key thing in management is actually getting to know and understand the artist's needs. Not their wants, their needs. And you're right, different artists would have different needs. They'll even have different needs across their career—the needs Silverchair had as 15 year olds compared to their needs as 27 year olds were quite different. Their level of involvement in certain areas that I would have been expected to take care of when they were 15, they were much happier to get involved in when they were 27.

So you're always re-drawing your lines of responsibility, and it begins always with a really open communication process. It's why a lot of times people, artists will say to me, "Who should we get as a manager?" It's like asking who should marry. You need to actually really understand the areas in which this artist is truly strong, and in which areas do they need some help? Some artists are going to look for musical input, others aren't. Some are going to need a lot of help organising things, others aren't. Some are looking to have a really strong visual flair, others aren't. And so on and so forth. So you need to be able to work out quite quickly how to develop a relationship with someone that, (a) allows you to work out what the needs are, and (b) puts you in a position of trust so that they're willing to take some kind of navigational guidance from you in areas that they require help on. It's also then your job to meet those needs and you won't be able to do all those things yourself. So part of the role is to build a management company that *can* offer all those things. For example, I like to think I'm pretty good with ears stuff but I'm definitely not great at visuals. Melissa—our GM—has that skill, though, so she plugs the gap there if our clients require help with photo shoots and videos. Ultimately, the specifics of the tasks vary but the manager's job is always simply this—you have to add more value than you take away by commission. You have to grow the career 'cake' by more than the size of the 'slice' that you take away. That's your role every single day when you get out of bed. And on the day you're not doing that for your client then you should be fired. You're there to deliver a service and to add value. It's not about you, it's about them. If you can't deal with that reality then you shouldn't be a manager.

So it's been an amazing learning journey for you. You started as a bass player. Can you tell us about the early years between your Townsville freelance journalism and your job with Sony international?

Well I like to joke that my career in the music business has been a long, gradual descent. I began working in record stores, which I still think, to the extent that they still exist, is one of the great things to do, and I played in bands when I was at high school. So I think those were probably the two most honourable things that you could possibly do. Then after a few years, looking to pay the bills I got asked by a friend who ran a magazine to do some record reviews. So I became the person that every artist knows is pretty much scum, which is a music journalist, right? So I'm stepping backwards. After being a music journalist for a while I became the person that music journalists think is scum, which is a publicist, a promotional person who's always trying to sell stuff to music people, to music journalists. I then got a job doing A&R at Sony, and you know, as a music journalist you just pick up these records everywhere and ask "What dickhead signed this?". So I became one of the dickheads. Then anybody who's ever worked at a record company knows that the true vermin in the music business are the managers that make your life hell. So after 5 years of working at a record company I descended to being a manager, from which I think the only point further that I could sink would be to become an investment banker. So yeah, my path has been a sad and sorry tale of repeated failures.

We should all fail so well. So this early job in Sony International and A&R seems to be a key turning point in your life.

Yeah, it was really formative. I mean working in a record store was the most formative thing I ever did.

In what respect?

A whole different set of them. I mean, it was from when I was 15 until I was 20 which is pretty formative years to begin with. The guy who ran the record store was really a father figure to me, an entrepreneurial guy in a way that I probably hadn't been exposed to at any other point in my life. A natural promo guy, a natural marketing guy from whom I learned a lot, and he gave a real sense of possibility. No-one in Townsville ever thought of releasing records in those days. He was the guy that said "Why not?" so my band just went out and did it and everything rolled out from there. So that relationship was really important to me. Also working at a record store was incredibly useful in other ways too. Most kids in those days, when there wasn't Triple J and there wasn't the internet, were just exposed to the stuff that was on Countdown. Working at that record store was great because it sold a lot of niche music. It exposed people to a lot of different types of music, and really gave me a much more broader musical vocabulary than any 15–20 year old had any right to expect in that era. And that's stood me in good stead through all sorts of other things. I'm a total music nut, but I wasn't just a music nut about stuff on the charts because I was exposed to all this other stuff. Such useful training.

Anyway to answer your question properly: I moved from Townsville to Sydney with my band at the end of 1986. We toured around for a couple of years and during that time I started doing the freelance music journalism to help pay the bills. That lead to me getting the job at Sony in early 1991 and I was there until the middle of 1995. I started off in A&R. Then I also took on international marketing about halfway through that time. That job was all about getting Australian artists' music released overseas, trying to ensure that it was followed up with promotion, and that was when I got my passion for wanting to take Australian music into overseas markets. That's been the defining ambition of my career. I learned a lot from working for Denis Handlin through those years. He's one of the legendary figures of the Australian recording industry. It was a really formative period and I was really lucky to get to travel around the world in that way. The record companies couldn't afford to do that now.

Did Sony have an actual international group at that point? Did they have someone somewhere in the world coordinating international?

Yes they did, but they only did basic coordination tasks. My job was to kind of work more directly with each affiliate to drum up interest in our artists. Fortunately Midnight Oil was the flagship act at the time. They were already a huge name globally and it was my job to walk around behind them, trying to help them in whatever way I could to help them maximise their sales internationally. That opened the doors for me, so I got to go to the marketing meetings and whatnot. More fundamentally, I got to understand different markets and I got to meet lots of people, which is what business is always about: making human connections, building relationships, and getting knowledge of the subtly different ways in which each market is different. Then Silverchair came along in 1994. John O'Donnell and I signed them to the label and I subsequently left Sony to manage them. But I had this glorious 9 month period where I quietly knew I was going to leave to manage them, but I was still within the record company. So I had every manager's dream position of being able to have a meeting with myself and say, "Should I send this band to Europe to do three shows, make the cost flat, give them a week off to make sure that they're refreshed for the gigs? Yeah, yeah I should!". They ended up selling over five million albums for Sony so it ended up working out pretty well for all concerned.

Looking at your history it seems you've done a fantastic job leveraging the power and interest of the majors into your own aspirations and those of your artists. Has that been an entirely strategic effort or has it just been luck, or has it been a combination? How have you looked at that relationship?

I've been very fortunate to have generally positive experiences in dealing with larger labels. There have been some negative ones over the years as well, but the good ones outweigh the bad. I'm not one who subscribes to the black hat white hat view of the music business; that indie equals good, major equals bad. There's plenty of indies out there that wear black hats and there's plenty of majors that wear white hats.

I think each situation is different. I mean, major record companies have changed and the business has changed, particularly in the last 5–10 years, so the nature of my relationships with labels is very different now from what it would have been back in the mid-90s. It's a more complicated thing we could delve into for ages if you wanted to. But generally speaking, it's been a positive thing. Generally speaking I've found that there are ways to navigate through that system that can still allow the artist to get what they need, which is the key thing from a manager's perspective. You begin by saying, "What is it the artist needs out of this situation? How do I. . ."—I'm trying to find a nicer verb than manipulate but I can't—"manipulate the situation to get the thing that the artist needs?"

Hopefully the best way to manipulate it is by working out what the record company needs and aligning those two interests. One of the good things about my background in business was that I had a little taste of doing everybody's job before I became a manager. I had a bit of retail background, a bit of background as an artist, a bit of background in media, a bit of background in promotion, I studied a bit of law. I'm not really good at any of those things, but I've done enough of them to have some ability to walk around and sit in the other guy's or girl's shoes, and that's really useful when you're trying to work out how to get them to see that my objective is also their objective. So the question becomes: how do align those objectives?

So there's a great deal of empathy built into your approach?

Well I suppose there has to be at some level. If you don't understand what the other party needs out of the situation, how on earth are you supposed to negotiate with them? Any negotiation begins by trying to have a really good understanding of what the other party is trying to get out of a deal and then finding a way that they can get that out of the situation without it costing you more than you're willing to pay.

We hear all the time that Australia doesn't have enough good artist managers. Do you think that's true and if so what can we do about it?

Yes I think it's true, and I think it's always been true. I think it's fundamentally due to the scale of the market. You know, at any given time in Australia, there's probably between five and ten artists who are really making seriously good money, and then you very quickly drop to artists who are still not quite household names. That second rung is probably making, at the most, average weekly earnings. I'm not going to name individual artists, but you know, there a plenty of local artists in the Triple J Hottest 100, sometimes the top ten, who are probably making less than they would be making if they worked at Woolworths. So if you're a manager, you're making 20% of what the artist's making and you're running a business out of that 20% so your actual earnings on that artist might be less than 10% of average weekly earnings. It's pure maths. So what you end up with at any given time is, three, four, five managers who between them will look after most of those ten popular artists. They're the ones that are then actually able to build a proper business. It's not necessarily that they're the best managers either, by the way, just that they're lucky enough, skilful enough, or whatever, to get one of those five to ten big names. There are lots of other good managers who just never got that kind of break. And so that next level of managers have to manage six, seven, eight artists without a proper infrastructure in order to pay the bills and they therefore can't do a great job because they're spread too thin and they often burn out due to the workload. Alternatively, they have to take on day gigs where they're working in some other role as their main bread and butter and managing an artist or two part time, which is fine. But again: there's no way to give the same level of service which means they're compromised in a different way. So is there an issue? Yes, but I think it's actually structural. Therefore in most cases for artists, I think, particularly in the early days, the answer is to take more control for yourself and to look close to home for your management options. Except if I'm trying to sign you, in which case I'm the answer!

The truth of it is that most successful managers become successful with the first artist they look after, you know, when Paul Pitticco started managing Powderfinger he wasn't what he is now. Same for me. Prior to managing Silverchair virtually the only band I'd managed was my own, which I'd literally managed into the ground with a smoldering van, our gear all burned to a cinder by the side of a highway, and a $20,000 debt which we all had to go out and get day jobs to pay off. That was my performance with my band. That was basically my CV when I became Silverchair's manager. So at the time you take on your first band you're not necessarily the name choice that'll make the artist's mum and dad feel comfortable, if you know what I mean. Even so, the 'name' managers typically have too much on their plates so it makes sense initially at least, to look closer to home for the sort of person who can coordinate, motivate, and persuade. Look for the kind of person that learns fast and doesn't repeat mistakes. Look for the kind of person that's passionate about what you do. If you can find a person with those qualities and you're an artist who's willing to actually turn up for work, then that combination is much more likely to lead to success than sitting around hoping you can find a perfect way to configure your demo CD to get one of those five 'name' managers to step on board. As I say, we've probably we've all got full plates already so sometimes the rank amateur with the right skills and passion is the best choice. If the band really blows up then that person can quickly become one of the handful of successful managers for the next generation.

So do you hire other managers to delegate things to?

We have a larger company but we don't do it that way typically. We divide our staff up according to function rather than delegate according to clients in the American way. The typical American way of doing it is that you typically have the fat, grey old guy who has been doing it for 30 years and knows everybody. Then under him you have the hungry, 30-something year old who's worked their way up from assistant to now being the day manager of 2 or 3 breaking acts. She or he spends every waking hour scheming ways to stab the fat old guy in the back and walk out with the artists on which they're actually doing most of the work for a fraction of the commission. That's typically the American management model. That 30-something year old has three acts and there's ten people like that in the company so the old guy therefore notionally manages 30 artists which makes him appear very powerful. I'm simplifying a bit here but, broadly speaking, it's true. That model kind of works because it's 30 artists that make financial sense in America. I refer to my previous point—there aren't 30 artists that make serious money in Australia to start with. So that model just wouldn't work here. There simply wouldn't be enough gross income to cover an overhead of that size. Instead of that model we divide our company up according to tasks. We have somebody that looks after promotion, someone that looks after touring, someone that looks after marketing, a finance person, and so forth. They oversee those areas for every client on our roster, Melissa and I cover various other elements and we also do most of the artist interfacing. That's really the core of the role because, as I said at the start, the key is to have a relationship where the communication is open and strong so you can be clear about what needs to be done. It's a very personal thing. You can get pretty deeply into stuff. You see a lot of these people at their most vulnerable. It's a very intense, personal relationship and I don't particularly see that aspect of the management role as being particularly delegable.

And how emotionally taxing does that become? If it's like that, I mean I haven't really thought about it, and of course it's like that, but I haven't really thought of the implications of the emotional effort it takes to manage.

It's an interesting question and it's been one of the real learning things for me over the course of my career. I think at the start of my career, certainly the first 4 years when I was working with Silverchair, the first three albums, I was very much strapped to the roller coaster ride with them, with Daniel in particular, and his roller coaster ride's a matter of public record. Even though we had some fantastic times and have wonderful memories, I don't know that I was the most effective manager precisely because of times I was a little too close, a little too emotionally involved. One of the interesting things that's happened over time with other clients who've come along later is that we're still close but I've managed to maintain a more professional kind of slight remove. I think that makes it easier for me to be objective, or at least more objective than perhaps I could have been when I was reading the reviews and being every bit as outraged by them as Daniel was.

Now I would have thought it was really odd if you'd said to me back then that what I actually needed to do was manage a few more artists precisely so that I could be more considered in my viewpoint. At the time I thought it was all about getting deeper into the tragedies and having total empathy. Don't get me wrong I still care deeply about my clients, but I'm not strapped to the same emotional roller coaster as them these days. I try hard to maintain a more balanced perspective as that's usually what they need in times of stress. Where the artist's on the roller coaster I see my role as trying to level it out a bit for them. You're never as good as they say you are and you're never as bad as they say you are so part of my role is to help them keep things in perspective rather than utterly sharing their world view at all times.

So there's a management of expectations in there?

Everything in life is at least partly about the management of expectations. Happiness is a function of expectations and results.

Well your focus on promoting Australian acts overseas resonates with the next question which is that I'm often struck with a sense of parochialism in the way new and emerging artists approach their aspirations. They're more worried about being popular in the Valley than being popular in New York, for example. In this day and age when the world's literally on our doorsteps, is there any point in new and emerging acts spending years of time and money and effort in making it in the Australian market?

Yes would be my answer to that. I wouldn't say to be exclusionary to anywhere else, but here would be my kind of in a nutshell advice to an artist that's starting out today: don't orientate yourself towards the industry, orientate yourself towards the audience. Spend 95% of your energy on writing better songs and forming connections with fans rather than sitting around and thinking about how to get a record deal, how to get a big manager, how to get stories in the paper, or songs on the radio. Now more than ever you have the ability to receive immediate feedback from consumers. It used to be, when I was a boy, that you had to get yourself onto *Countdown* or *Hey*

Hey It's Saturday or onto 4IP in order to get heard by the public. Only then would you find out if you had what it took. So you needed to convince those guys—and they were always guys—in the middle to take a punt on you, so it was quite right in those days. You would focus on the gatekeepers like managers and record companies and media types because the public was on the other side of the gate.

Now it works in the opposite way. Now the first step is that you're showing a room full of people at your show, a whole heap of Facebook likes, a lot of YouTube views, heaps of people searching your song on Shazam, whatever the case may be. Now the first step is *reactivity* with the general public. If you don't have reactivity you'll find it virtually impossible to get anyone to step in and help you grow your audience. But if you are showing reactivity, then the industry people come to you so fast you won't believe it. And when they do you have the advantage of being able to say "Hey, creatively what I'm doing already's working, don't try and mess with it. Don't tell me to get a perm and put a disco beat behind it, it's already working". And you also probably have a couple of them chasing you because that's typically how it happens. So you now have the ability to do a better deal for yourself. "Build it and they will come" has always been my advice but it's truer now than it's ever been, because if you're a gatekeeper why on earth would you sit down and listen to a hundred CDs and try and work out which one's working when you can look at what's charting on Shazam and see right there what's working with real people?

If you're a manager or an A&R person or a booking agent or whatever then you don't have to just blindly trust your own taste anymore—you can trust the wisdom of crowds to help you filter what you hear. It's right there. You're doing your duty paying some attention to it. You're obviously still going to trust your own ears as well; you've got to see the person and work out whether it's going to work. So if you're an artist the best way to get industry people excited is to virtually ignore them and build a real fanbase because then they'll all come running. Now if what the artist is doing is not resonating with an audience then it's possible that it's due to the audience being stupid or perhaps you're exposing yourself to the wrong type of audience. However, it's much more likely to be due to the fact that what you're doing's just not that special and you've got to be remarkable to attract attention from real people who are bombarded all day by entertainment options. The good news about all this stuff about audience accessibility is that the barriers are down. The bad news is that the barriers are down, so you're going to have to be willing to cop the "That sucks!" comments on your videos.

In short there's much more onus on the artist now to get themselves to first base without anybody else. The music business is entirely about perception of momentum. I think most businesses are. Everybody wants to jump on board the train that they perceive to be leaving the station. If a band looks like they're happening, if everyone feels like this band's happening, then that's the band that Rocking Horse wants to put in their shop window, that's the band that *Time Off* wants to put on the cover. That's the band that Triple J wants to playlist. That's the band that festivals want to give one of the new slots to, and so on. That's the band that iTunes will give a little title to on the front page, the one that they think's going to work. So the entire business is about constantly exceeding expectations and the manager's job is constantly to kind of heighten that, to present anything you do in a way that makes it look like a win, make it look like you're the artist that's got momentum: "Have a look at our YouTube views, don't mention our Facebook likes". Do things that generate more Facebook likes so it looks like you're happening. If you build it they will come, but you actually have to look like it works, like it's already working, and then everyone wants to get involved. It's a real paradox—it has to look like it's already working, then it will work. If it doesn't look like it's working, no-one wants to take a punt on it.

Inertia is a very powerful force and it works in both directions; if you're totally still you tend to stay that way. If you're rolling you tend to stay that way as well. So your job in the early days is to do whatever you can make it look like this roll is happening. Don't play too many shows so that they're not selling out, do only the ones that sell out, then it looks like you can sell out more shows. Make sure you aggregate your Youtube views if you shift your content—do whatever you can to strike a chord with the public and to make it *look* like you're striking a chord with the public. The whole game is about that, about generating a perception of momentum.

We've heard this quite a bit. We did a series of think tanks through Australia with various people to discuss what digital meant across all areas of the industry. We heard this a lot from publishers and labels, in particular that they were interested in evidence online and I just wondered how that's changing the structure of relationships between persons like yourself, various others and the majors, and other people who can help along the way later on?

Well we're in an odd relationship as far as that's concerned. Now we're half-owned by Universal, but in doing that we actually gained more independence for ourselves because they only do our sales and finance functions. We outsource promo/PR and we do everything else ourselves. So we have a very unusual structure. We don't have to convince anybody if we want to take a punt. We just take the punt. Then we have to convince different gatekeepers. We have to convince the radio programmer or whatever in due course. So we have the same game, but we're not selling each song to a major as part of that process, if that makes sense. Again it's changed the business to a point where someone once told me—I don't know if it's true or not, it could be complete bullshit, it is, after all, my job to bullshit, band's job to fascinate—but someone once told me that Michael Gudinski used to have this line that A&R was really simple: you walk into a pub, you look to the left, you look to the right, if you can't see the walls on either side of the people then you sign the band. And you know, conceptually that's pretty much still what we're talking about.

That was the 70s, but conceptually it's the same thing, except that you're walking into a chat room as it were and looking for those signs of connectivity. That's really what it's about; it's about having stuff that strikes a chord, which sort of leads to a whole other thing, which is the thing that's really changed. My opinion is that it used to be enough to just make something that didn't offend anybody, because then you could find your way through. Radio wants to playlist the song that doesn't make anybody turn off. If you give a radio programmer a choice between two songs, one that 90% of people absolutely adore and 10% hate, and one that 100% of people don't dislike, they'll program the second over the first every time because the first one's going to make 10% of the listeners change stations.

In a world where it was about getting radio airplay—that plus a bit of TV and press was the whole game—people shopped from that small menu. In those days a lot of lowest-common-denominator type music became commercially successful because while it may not have been great it didn't alienate listeners and thus fitted harmlessly in between radio advertisements. However, in a world where discovery requires friends to tell you about it one way or another, on Twitter or Facebook, the stuff that gets noticed is the stuff that's unusual—not so much the lowest common denominator stuff.

There's this American marketing guy, Seth Godin, who talks about how in a fragmented media environment, the stuff that works has to be "remarkable". He doesn't just mean shit-hot, he means people literally want to *remark* upon it. It has to be *Gangnam Style*, or it has to be the *Somebody That I Used To Know* video, or it has to have some quality to it that makes you want to say to your friends "Hey, check this out!", which is something that would not have happened for . . . I don't know, I could pick some radio band from years ago, but it doesn't really matter. Some bland radio rock thing. Once upon a time that was sort of good because it didn't offend anybody and fitted through. Now you actually need to be out to the edges in some way to cause people to talk about you. Parkway Drive's going to make a lot more sense these days, The Hilltop Hoods in their own way make a lot more sense than they would have when artists lived or died by mass media exposure. Even if you're going to be pop these days, you have to be Lady Gaga. Just be bigger, be more exciting. Now you're competing with Halo, you're competing with *The Dark Knight*, you're competing with, I don't know, with everything. You're competing with people snapchatting you photos of their genitals. It's like you've got to have something really compelling to get noticed these days. That pleasant enough song about your relationship breakup might not cut it anymore as much as radio might prefer something "safe" like that. These days the middle of the road is where you're most likely to get run over.

Radio seems to have lost the plot, at least in Australia, what's your take on where all that's headed? Is it still going to be a major. . .

So this could pop up online later on? My take on radio is the answer is to play more artists on the Eleven Label, then all of radio's problems will be solved.

It doesn't necessarily have to go public.

The thing about Australia is this: we have a very unusual climate when it comes to radio specifically. Triple J is a game changer for this market; the Australian music market only makes sense when you understand Triple J. If you're coming from overseas, you'll just think: "What? Why? How?" And then if someone spends time to understand Triple J, "Oh, hmm, interesting," you know? Of course it's an exasperating thing and everybody likes to bag them out and we all wish they did more of this and less of that and that person's an idiot and this should be different, but let me tell you—no Triple J? We're all dead, you know? It's, is it perfect? Hell no. Is it better than anything else going on in the world? Hell yeah.

But why has commercial radio lost the plot? How did they-

I think that commercial radio is in a particular kind of game. It's a very odd time for commercial radio when it comes to local artists because pop music is so in the ascendency right now. One of the advantages of getting old is you see music trends come and go. Now Australia has traditionally done rock music really well, singer-songwriters really well, pop music and urban music pretty poorly. There are some exceptions, you have your Air Supplys. You have your Kylies. You have your Savage Gardens. But they're exceptions rather than rules. The dominant musical forms here have tended to be organic forms of music that exist mainly to be performed live, which is not true in most other markets.

It's an unusual quality and a large amount of it stems from Triple J, at least in the last 20 years. But pop music's kind of a dominant form globally at the moment. It's just in fashion for pop and urban music to be largely what people listen to, so Australian music is struggling a bit at the moment because there's just not that much good local pop stuff out there, apart from the occasional thing like Guy Sebastian or whatever the case may be. If you look at the top 50 singles I think we're at just about an all time low for the amount of songs that are actually cracking through on commercial radio. My prayer is that it's to do with fashion cycles rather than to do with something fundamental. There could be broader impacts behind it which is about the types of music that major labels will support, the fragmented media environment, the ability of certain things to cut through. It's a more complicated picture. But I think part of the reason for the current disconnect between commercial radio playlists and the local music scene is to do with the current dominance of musical forms which are traditionally our weak suit in this country.

It's as if there's been a lot of work done by CRA to basically wash their hands of Australian content in many ways, and I just wonder why that is.

One of the arguments would be that pop music—I mean pure pop music that can go toe-to-toe with Pink or Katy Perry or Will.i.am, those sorts of records—is typically a very producer-driven genre. You usually need your Dr Luke or someone like that to drive that kind of sound. With the occasional Charles Fischer-type exceptions, Australia hasn't traditionally has not had producers who compete on a world stage in that genre. Our producers who've competed best on a world stage have tended to be more on the singer-songwriter end, or on the rock end. Perhaps it's to do with ethnicity but it shouldn't be to do with ethnicity because we're such a multicultural society. Back in the day you could have said it's to do with being a particularly Anglo culture, but that doesn't add up. Canada's much more Anglo than us and they've got a more diverse production culture. I don't know what it is, but there's definitely an element to that at the moment.

And it seems also to be, there are rumours rife about the disconnect between the majors locally and our commercial radio stations. There was a kind of fairly smooth system going on over what you'd call the Countdown years I suppose, but that seems to have broken down and that system seems also to have suffered under new media.

Look, the media landscape has changed utterly and the music business has had to change with it, and record companies have been stuck in the middle of that. If you think of—it's all about metaphors today—but if you think about an Excel spreadsheet where the rows across are artists and the columns coming down are different forms of media. If you go back 20–30 years you would have had your FM radio, your daily newspaper, maybe some street press, a couple of monthly music magazines, and one or two TV shows. That would have been pretty much all the columns. The record company's job was to have a priority list and the artists on the top five lines would get all their boxes ticked. They're on the radio, they're in the newspaper, they're on TV. For boxes they couldn't expose the artist in, they'd buy an ad because they'd have the marketing funds to do it. As you moved down the rows some holes would typically open up for those artists who weren't priorities but the ones up the top could generally expect the record company to expose them through all the available channels.

That was the old model, and in that model the manager's job was to use relationships, motivation, and persuasion to get the artist high on the record company priority list. Once that was in place then the manager had to be like a cattle dog nipping at the label's heels strategically to make sure that the boxes were ticked in the right order, and that all the boxes were ticked. Make sure that the label got the review in that magazine and make sure the label bought some ads on that radio station and that they got the artist onto that TV show etc. Then once you were exposed to the public it was "Please God don't let it just be a turntable hit, please God let it react". That was the old model. Now, keep that same spread sheet in your mind, but just keep adding column after column after column. You've still got all the old ones, you've still got the Rolling Stone, you've still got The Courier Mail, you've still got 4MMM, but now you've also got Vodafone and you've got Channel V and you've got Facebook and Twitter and Faster Louder and Mess and Noise and an endless proliferation of channels. You're not reaching more people, it's just that the people who used to be reachable across a few columns, are now spread across dozens of columns. You've got three times as many boxes to tick to reach the same number of people now. So if you take the record company's position, over that same period, for various reasons their revenues have probably halved. Their staff has halved, so you've got half as many people trying to do three times as much work.

For half as much money.

And they don't have the money to buy the stuff to fill the gaps. So if no one's gotten around to booking an interview with *Rolling Stone* for you, they're not just going to jump in and buy a full page ad. They don't have the money for it. So even your ability to fill the gaps with money has gone as well. Now what does that mean other than we should all go out and get real jobs? It means that anybody that sits back and expects the record company to tick all those boxes is just an idiot. The reason they're not ticking all the boxes isn't because they're lazy or they're stupid. The vast majority of people who are still left at major record companies work their asses off and are really smart. The reason they're not ticking all the boxes for even their high priority acts is because there aren't enough of them to cover this fragmented media picture. Plus they don't have enough resources, so your role as a manager or an artist has now changed. Your role is to get in there as well, roll up your sleeves, and tick as many of these boxes as you can yourself particularly by going directly to the audience.

If you go directly to the audience and you can really strike a chord then that will eventually drag a lot of these media organisations along with you. If you're already top 20 on iTunes, the programmer of B105's going to notice that and they're probably going to start playing you. If you're trending on Twitter then iTunes might give you a tile on the front page of their store. And a hundred other versions of the same thing. So the entire game has changed because of that fragmentation of media and, to a lesser extent, retail, which has massively added to the to-do list at a time where the number of doers has shrunk.

Two questions that have been asked over and over by students and young musicians are: when do I need a manager, and how do I go about getting one? What do you tell them?

I would tell them not to focus on getting a manager but to focus on getting a thousand true fans. I'm sure at some point we've covered that hoary old article which is now 3 or 4 years old and which is possibly geriatric in our terms. There's a lot of good in the idea of chasing a thousand true fans. Do that. Not only will it make you do better work because you'll see when you're striking a chord and when you're not striking a chord, it will also allow you not to get discouraged. If your goal is to get a thousand true fans or a thousand people following you on Twitter, if you wake up in the morning with 42 and you go to bed with 48, you're six people closer to your goal. What did you do today? Well I didn't fail objectively, I made a little bit of progress. If your goal is of getting out of bed in the morning, and get Paul Pitticco to manage you then you're going to go to bed that night, and unless Paul's called, you failed. So it's a very demotivating process as well.

Paul will probably call if you've got enough of all this other stuff going on, because the thing that people vastly underestimate is how much people in Paul's position are actually really keen to discover the next big thing. By the way, I'm just singling him out is because we're in Brisbane, it's his town and he owns the place. The thing people don't understand is that it's a bit like when you go to the high school dance and you're afraid to ask a girl on the other side of the room to dance. You don't know that she's over there hoping against all hope that someone's going to come and ask her to dance. I wish someone had told me that when I was young. So that's the truth of the music business as well, that the people who are running A&R and the people in management, they're desperate to find someone that's going to work, *desperate*. The reason they're not committing isn't because they're not interested. The reason they're not committing is because they're looking for the signs that the artist is going to be The One. So there's no point saying "The reason you should sign me is because I'm really good," because everybody wants the one they can't have—just ignore the industry people and go out and get it happening. Be just that little bit unavailable—a little bit, but not stupidly so—just that little bit unavailable and you'll find that's where you start to attract interest. Every woman in the audience knows what I'm talking about and every guy doesn't. Just don't be the guy across the bar that's just looking desperate. Be the girl that plays it just right. And there really is a lot of that kind of wooing process going on here.

So: when's the right time to get a manager? As I said before, I think there's no right or wrong, there's no rules in this business, but doing it yourself for a period of time's really good and looking close to home, if you can find somebody that's got the qualities I'm talking about, is usually a better answer. If you're going to get a manager, I would suggest to don't sign anything until you've seen a good industry lawyer and have a trial period of 3 months or something like that, just so you can figure out if they've got a crack habit before you get too deeply embroiled in something that can end up costing you a lot of money or a lot of time and net worth.

Eleven's an interesting phenomenon. It's been with two different majors now, it's closely associated with the management team, it seems a hybrid of sorts, a hybrid kind of company, a very new, historically new, kind of company. Even as far as it wraps around your artists in a number of different ways. I had the recent pleasure of talking to Troy Barrett and both his company and Eleven have a lot in common in many ways, I think. Can you tell us how you think about the company and the way it relates to the artists, the labels, international development, publishing, and so forth? How do you finesse all of that as a manager?

Eleven's had two different incarnations. There's almost been a mark one and a mark two at Eleven. Mark one was our period with EMI. Mark two has been our period with Universal. Eleven mark one was actually started for a reason. It wasn't that we got it one day and said "We want to have a record company". It was my belief after many years of working at Sony and then working with Sony in trying to make overseas affiliates pay attention to Silverchair, it was my belief that worldwide signings to major labels in Australia rarely lead to global success. If you look at the history of the music business in Australia, the vast majority of local artists that have gone on to have success around the world, AC/DC, Little River Band, INXS, Jet, The Vines, Natalie Imbruglia, Kylie Minogue, they all had someone behind a desk in London, New York or LA, preferably all of the above, who would get a promotion if they had a hit and they would potentially get fired if they didn't. They had skin in the game. They were directly responsible for signing. However at the same time, 80 or 90% of Australian artists have signed worldwide deals with major labels in Australia, which means when their music goes overseas, the person over there is not as invested in it, financially or emotionally, so you're always the foster child with that sort of deal structure in my opinion.

There are exceptions, Silverchair was one of them but I've told you the circumstances behind that. Men at Work, Midnight Oil were others. Some extenuating circumstances surrounded those cases too. Anyway, my point is that worldwide major label record deals out of Australia were something I wanted to avoid. We had Paul Mac who we were wanting to get signed. A lot of labels were interested and Tim Presscott from BMG said, "Look, we can't sign Australian and New Zealand deals, we're not allowed, if you were a label we could do it, but . . .". I didn't even let him finish the sentence, I said "Stop, we're a label!" And that was literally where we had the idea to do a label. It was a device to allow us to split our deals. So Missy Higgins was signed with our label in Australia and she was signed with Warner Brothers in America. They put the money out to help develop her and all of the money she made in Australia came straight to her. It was what you called "uncrossed". So separate recoupment accounts. The money that's invested over from the US isn't recovered from the revenue here, so she's making money from record one in Australia and all the losses are quarantined over in America. That was a really good situation for her. So the reason we started a label in the first instance was largely for that purpose. It then had the additional upside that my background's in A&R and Melissa, who's the general manager of our company who I've worked with forever, her background is in marketing. So it also allows us to take control of the creative side on behalf of our artists. Under their direction we would make the records, the artwork, the videos, the photo-shoots, all the tools of the project. Then, in mark one of Eleven, we would march into EMI, lay them all out, and there would then be this wonderful to and fro that we would have. They would kind of go back to first principles, question everything and we would tweak the plans according to their input which was always helpful. They'd then pick up those tools and implement them, so we had a product manager there, the promotion, the publicity and sales all happened at EMI. So it was an unusual hybrid in those days, we were neither all in nor all out. We were sort of half in.

What happened in 2007—it's a long answer but it was a complicated question—there was a particular moment when we were following up Missy Higgins' first album and there's a lot of times you have a big first record but the second record stiffs. So we were going out with that song "Steer". It was the lead single off the second record. If it works then she establishes herself as a career artist as we believed she should be. But if it doesn't succeed then she'd become another one of those one hit wonders. And with that as the backdrop, EMI came to us and said: "Look, in a couple of weeks time we're going to have to lay off half our promo staff and they're nearly all the ones that work Missy". So that meant that we'd have to launch the key Missy Higgins track arguably of her career, other than the first one, with a team of promotion people literally who had never worked one of her records and it's happening in 2 weeks time. So I cancelled all of my stuff because I'm taking the record to radio myself now with all these new promo people, "Hi, pleased to meet you, let's go sell Missy Higgins, I'll do most of the talking". So all of the stuff that was going to be my work during those weeks suddenly became Melissa's job. All the stuff that was going to be Melissa's job over that period was passed to someone else, and before you know it, literally by Friday afternoon, I'm realising we don't have enough staff, so we have to run out and hire somebody else. This was all in the space of a week, and I looked at them and said, "Wow! EMI's headcount reduction just became our headcount increase!". There she is sitting behind the desk over there. And that was the moment where I realised that it had actually gone "crack" and the old way of working was no longer tenable. The folks at EMI were fantastic, some of our best friends. They loved Missy, would have done anything for her. It totally wasn't their fault. They were being told from overseas they had to fire the staff. What are you going to do? There wasn't enough money flying down the recorded revenue streams to justify the level of promotional support we required. Fact. So what do you do about that? Then we moved onto Eleven mark two, where in 2008 we sold half the label to Universal, taking some of the money they gave us to bring the product manager function in house. So we now do all of our own implementation of marketing ourselves. Then we employ promotion and publicity on a project-by-project basis. With the cost of those things being paid for not just out of the records, but also out of the tours, we have additional resources. So instead of having the record company buying an ad for the record and the artist or the promoter buying an ad for the tour, we're just buying an ad then splitting the costs and that's our way I guess of cutting a 360 deal, but it's a 360 deal from the artist's perspective in that the marketing and promotion services are applied across all facets of their career at all times.

Oddly enough, what we did with Universal effectively took the control back in-house. We now do the whole thing instead of being half in and half out like we were at EMI. The only thing that we're relying on Universal for is finance and sales. The marketing and promotion and publicity we were able to bring in on a project-by-project basis so we didn't create an overhead for ourselves. Which, as soon as you create the overhead it's "Meet the new boss, same as the old boss". You've got a beast to feed, a machine, you know? "The album's coming out for Christmas". So that's been our approach to Eleven, and ultimately it's allowed us to view ourselves primarily as a management company with our label being a device for our management company. As a management company our job is to serve our artists' needs. So our view is that we exist to add value and help the artist realise their creative vision, which all seems very highfalutin' but it's actually sound practice. The artists have full creative control, their masters revert to them. As a consequence we've never lost a client.

You know, it's interesting that you say it's a 360 degree deal from the artist's perspective because I was looking at it and thinking, "Is this just a different way to do a 360 deal?" We've had a lot of discussion about those contracts in this series because it's become a new way of approaching things. What's your thoughts on the Sony 360 deal?

Everybody's coming at the problem in different ways, because that spread sheet, that to-do list, is now too big to be funded just by selling the bits of plastic and the little downloads of single tracks on iTunes. So how are you going to fund all of that marketing and promo activity? That's the key question. Everybody talks about the decline of the music business and sales, they always look at it as a revenue story: "How much less money are you making?". That's part of it, but the truth is most artists outside of the pure pop genre never made that much money out of record sales anyway. The problem from an artist and management perspective is the decline in promotion and marketing. You no longer have somebody to tick all those boxes. How are we going to tick the boxes? How are we going to let people know this thing is out there? How are we going to cover all the bases? We're going to have to find some money and some resources from somewhere else because there's not enough coming in from these bits of plastic any more to fund the whole thing. And there's so much more to do now! So that's really the fundamental conundrum.

Now in answer to your question about 360 deals: I have no problem with a 360 deal if it's a description of the services being offered. I have no problem if someone is saying to me, "I'm going to give you a best practice merch company, a best practice booking agent, a best practice publisher and a best practice record company and we're all going to add value to your career and we're going to prove it to you". It sounds like I'm being facetious but I'm actually not. I'll give you an example: Warner Brothers in LA. Missy was signed there and Tom Whalley was running it and set up a merch company. They found two people who had a background in merch from outside the company, brought them in, set them up in a separate bit of their building and gave them a genuine budget. It was really cleverly done. You walked into the reception area, there was this whole block of offices there, that was their merch company off to one side. They made a point of going out and signing some artists that weren't on Warner Brothers so it was a real merch company within a record company. Those guys had better designs at cheaper prices on quicker turnaround times than the merch company I was already working with. Why on earth wouldn't I do a deal for Missy? It was better for her. As it happens it's also better because then the merch person sitting in the marketing meeting every week is an extra voice. Warners are making a bit of money out of the t-shirts and they're going to reinvest that possibly in paying to do a few more promo things on TV or whatever the case may be. I have no problem with that.

What I have a problem with is when you're acquiring rights that you then have no ability to exploit. So, "we now own your merch rights—how do you sell a t-shirt to kids?". That's the approach I have a problem with. I have no problem with the idea of participation in additional revenue schemes if you're truly helping to grow the streams. The whole business is going to revert to something we were talking about before we came on air as it were. The business used to be that you had artists and you had fans, and in the middle you had a bunch of other companies that unfortunately or fortunately were gatekeepers. The fans couldn't hear about you until you were on TV and radio so that meant you had to curry favour with all those programmers. Then they couldn't buy your LP or CD until some big company was magically able to manufacture it and get it out to 500 shops around Australia all on the same day, which sounds easy, but was really quite hard. So these companies that were sort of strategically situated in between the producer and consumer, anybody who's studying economics will sort of have a sense for what I'm talking about here, they were able to extract "super profits" by virtue of their position in the supply chain.

In a world where the artist can go direct to the fan, the only businesses that will exist are those that add value to both the artist and the fan all the way through—particularly to the fan, because they're the ones who are coughing up the money. So if you're going to exist as record company or a merch company or a retailer or a manager that sits in the middle, that mediates that relationship, you have to add value on the way through. You can't just punch the ticket, let alone punch the ticket for an inflated price as was probably happening under the old model. This is all, for anybody who hasn't studied economics, a simplified version of the theory of disintermediation.

There's a lot of different views afoot about the future of the music industry. Some people think it's a wonderful time, some people think the end is nigh, and so forth. Things are in transition certainly, maybe even chaos, but as far as aspiring musicians in Australia go, do you think the future is more or less hopeful in terms of the prospects and opportunities compared to when you began in the business?

I think it's more hopeful. But it depends on what you define as success. Why you're doing it. If you're doing it because you want to make music, you want to express yourself, you want to make sound recordings, you want to connect with an audience, you should be hopeful. If you're doing it because you want to get your face in the cover of *Rolling Stone* and want to get laid a lot then it's less rosy. If you're doing it for the right reasons though, it's probably better than it's ever been. The two aren't mutually exclusive, so I'm told, but the truth is now that it's easier to make a record, because the costs of recording are lower. It's easier to distribute your recording than it's ever been. It's easier to make a video for it and to put it out in front of people than it used to be in the days of huge budget film clips and Video Hits. So all of those elements have lowered the barriers to entry. Compare all that to the efforts that I had to make back in the mid-80s with my band. We had to find a recording studio in North Queensland, there wasn't one so we made it in a garage in Kuranda and it was the only thing that was ever recorded there. There was no one to print the covers in QLD or press the 7″ singles. My uncle worked at the printing factory so he had to print it. We never thought to measure what the bags should be, so the bags were all a centimetre and a half too big fit any of the record racks. We couldn't access any video cameras so had no music video and so forth. All of those barriers to entry are largely gone nowadays. It's easier to sell a thousand records now than it's ever been.

The downside is it's harder than it's ever been to sell a hundred thousand records, or a million records; to scale that up, to reach critical mass, because everything's just splintered apart. We see it in venues as well. There's fewer and fewer new artists coming along and selling out arenas, but more and more artists coming along and selling out The Zoo or whatever. That's not necessarily a bad thing. It's probably quite a good thing for the quality of music, I would guess, as far as there's more of it around, there's more people making it, and that you don't have to depend on some middle-aged guy selecting you in order to be allowed to make a record and get it heard any more. If what you're doing's interesting it'll probably find its way to an audience somehow. So I think there's lots of positives. The downside is if you kind of thought it was going to be rock and roll and partying every day, then no, it's not about that any more. The artist, he owns his back more and more and the artist and manager do a lot more, they can't rely on a marketing, promotional muscle, or oblige corporations to do their thing for them. So in the new world, you know, it's a good news story if you were always that way inclined. It's a bad news story if you were kind of hoping you'd just coast through and have some wizard pop out of the sky and tap you on the head and say, "I want to make you a rock star."

What about making it overseas? Do you think it's a bit kind of easier to take an act from Australia and promote them elsewhere, regardless of where? China and US, or?

Well if you go back to my spread sheet, along the bottom there are tabs. So I just talked about the Australian tab, there's an American tab, it goes for miles! There's an English tab, there's a German tab, a French tab, there's so many bloody tabs! There's Indian tabs, there's tabs in places that don't even release records. So the to-do list is unfathomably massive and the amount of work that it takes to actually go out and do the promotion that Pink does, just to pick an example as I go past the poster on the way in, is—I don't want to sound presumptuous—but it is truly incomprehensible to anybody who hasn't done it. You cannot to begin to imagine how much work it takes to break America. It's like eating an elephant. It's a fantastic challenge and a wonderful kick when you find yourself actually getting there. The internet will help you, certainly with the Gotye video and all the views that had opened a truckload of doors for us that wasn't there when we were starting out, or the first Wolfmother record when we were breaking them, which is not that long ago. So you know, there's lots of advantages to it, but it's a massive, massive task.

The thing about it is this, though, from an Australian artist's perspective—again, I've talked a lot today about the history of the Australian music business—I guess it's because when you've been looking for a while you tend to see things with that longer view in mind. If you look at the history of the Australian music business, if you put all the artists who tried to break international markets into one pile and the ones who didn't into another pile, you'll find that this pile, the ones who tried to break overseas, tended to make better music for longer than the other pile. There are some exceptions, but generally speaking the artists who are engaged in trying to crack overseas markets do better than the ones that run into a ceiling in Australia, figure they'll have a nice life, get complacent. They tend to break up, they get frustrated, whatever the case may be. The artist in the first pile, if you think about the bands when I was a kid, back in those days, you had Cold Chisel, Midnight Oil, Split Enz, INXS, you know—INXS: you could put them any category that you care to name, Split Enz had a better image, the Oils had a better image, Chisel had a better image, INXS didn't have the best image, they didn't have the best songwriters at that point—in the early 80s I'm talking about—they weren't number one in any category across those artists.

What they were number one in was the desire to make it work. When everybody else found producers they liked and kind of settled in or let their internal conflicts destroy them in different ways, INXS pushed on, had Chris Thomas who pushed them as a producer, they raised the bar with the videos they were making, they kept challenging themselves, and that's why INXS became INXS. And it's why the other artists didn't, and still you go back and listen to those records, INXS were an amazing band but I would argue with anybody about Cold Chisel's ability or Split Enz's ability or Midnight Oil's ability to go toe-to-toe with them. Why did they become so much bigger? Because they had bigger ambition and they worked harder.

At a certain point, your success will be defined by your work ethic. Your talent will get you so far, I think that's true, by the way, behind the scenes as well as on stage. It's a really boring, family values thing to say which I would have thought just was so un-rock and roll when I was 19 or 20, but I swear to you it's true. The people who are hungriest for it over time will tend to be the ones that have the success, particularly those that are actually engaged in it for the right reasons. They love music, they're passionate about their music, and they really want to connect with their audience. The business can be really unfair over any given one or two year period: good things happen to bad people, bad things happen to good people. But over a ten-year period, people who don't take the shortcuts, who work hard and who cultivate genuine relationships and do things for good reasons, they tend to rise over the people who are cutting all their corners, burning all their bridges, they might make a quick pay-day here or there but they tend to sink. So taking that longer term view I think is critically important if you're looking to turn this into a vocation.

Let's say you decide as a new or emerging artist that your music really is going to take off in London or Austin, Texas or somewhere else. Would you stay

in Australia and wait until you got a certain amount of cash to get over there or would you just talk with your colleagues about pulling up your stumps and going to stay in wherever it is your music fits—which is it?

The fantastic thing about the music business is that there are no rules. Every time you get to a point where you say "It always works like this," it's about 5 minutes after that someone else comes along and does the exact opposite and proves it wrong. So there is no right time. The reason that seems a bit blurry is because it is blurry. The Birthday Party pulled up-stumps and moved to London, Nick Cave became Nick Cave, the cult of The Birthday Party and the cult of Nick would never have been what it was had they stayed in Melbourne. That's sort of a textbook example of that. The Saints out of Brisbane, different but similar. On the other hand, INXS, those first couple of records if you know them, there were some cool songs on there but really it's not until their third record, and arguably their fourth and fifth records, in fact their fifth and sixth records, that they were truly ready for the world stage. So it's an artist-by-artist thing. What's the need of the artist?

The great advantage that you have now is that you don't actually have to sit and wonder how you're going to go in Srebrenica. You just check out where you're getting the emails from on your website, trawl out your Google trends and look at where people are searching for your name—that's going to give you some kind of insight. There are websites like Reverbnation and Songkick where people can sign up to have you come to their town and so you can work out which markets to go to rather than guessing.

So now you can actually look market by market and say "we're out on this tour". Back in the day you'd have to call up your radio spins and your sound scan sales and try and work out which markets to go to. You can still do that, but it's a pretty blunt instrument compared to the finesse that is now possible. So, you know, I think it's more a good news story than a bad news story as far as that's concerned. And in terms of when to do it, if you can find a government grant to help you do it or anything else, then that's better than sort of parlaying a kidney to get yourself over there. The one thing I would caution against—which we sort of touched on before but I'll say it again—I just really always caution against the, "You know what? I've been trying to crack it in Brisbane for 2 years, no one's paid any attention to me, it's because they're all absolute cloth-eared dicks. Really, Austin Texas will get me. My genius is too great for Queensland." Maybe. But probably not.

Mistakes are always interesting to hear about, they often teach far more than success. Can you tell us, without necessarily naming names, about one or two mistakes you've made as a manager and the lessons you've learned?

The good one, which again sounds very family values but it's true, is, is the natural order of a person in their 20s and into their 30s. I hope to be obsessed with building careers, to be obsessed with it. It's also the natural order that, if that continues, it can ultimately be quite a destructive thing if you let it—destructive to health, destructive to family. So finding a point in your life at which you are consciously willing and able to inject some balance into existence, that definitely came to me later than it should have come to me. I'm glad that it did because I look around at some people who it didn't come to and the price they paid for that. They ended up quite unhappy later in life as a consequence. So allowing all of the good stuff about life to actually turn out to be a negative thing for your life is definitely something to avoid. There's definitely some times when I got way out of balance, when it came to work versus self and family, and that's an inevitability I suppose, of all businesses to some extent. But two really important things: just be watchful. Divorce is very, very expensive. Kids are very precious and it's tragic to miss out on seeing them grow up. Fortunately I haven't had to pay that price, but I could have. So that would be one.

I guess the other one is a hard one to talk about. It is—I always talk about these things and again forgive me to anyone I've already said it to—I've always had these eight things that it takes to be successful for an artist when they're starting out. Number one, most importantly, is songs. Always the most important thing. Number two is instrumental prowess, typically the most overrated by musicians. Sometimes a factor—Keith Moon, Eddie Van Halen. Generally speaking, vastly overrated, you can probably get by instead of spending that extra 3 weeks perfecting your guitar tone, you probably should have gone and written three more songs. But it's sometimes a factor. Third thing is the voice, there is something about certain voices that have a certain connection with an audience that it almost doesn't matter what they sing, they just have that ability. Having the voice is a key thing. The fourth is image. Typically that means sex appeal, but doesn't always. It's not sex appeal with Iggy Pop or Meatloaf, but largely it's sex appeal, something to look at, something that is remarkable. The fifth thing is a narrative, a story that will allow people to kind of connect all of these things, and you're really in a sweet spot when your narrative comes through. You've got the image that looks like a story, the songs about that theme. Typically these things get heightened by managers and record company people. So the delivery boy from Memphis who's a mother's boy turns out to actually be Elvis the Pelvis only shot from the waist up on national television. Because he had certain sex appeal if you looked at him the right way. James Blunt became the sensitive singer-songwriter that was actually a fighter in Croatia. And so forth, so you have this sort of connection between narrative story and music. Pete Murray, the rugged sportsman that's still got the sense of heart and ability to write, you have this sort of narrative—I'm exaggerating for effect of course. The narrative and its ability to weave through everything else is an important part of striking a chord. You also have luck and time and these are the two variables that are not within your control out of the eight, but they are both important and at least you can be mindful of them. If you know you're having a particularly good moment of luck and this is your time, put your foot to the floor and go! Don't go on holidays. If you know your time just sucks a bit at the moment, you've just had a bit of bad luck, be mindful that will help you to not get discouraged. So at least be mindful that you can't control them, they're worth having in your head. And the eighth thing is hard work which I've talked about enough, the work ethic. Now these eight factors, to my mind are a little bit like lotto numbers—it's really easy to find an answer to three or four of them. Very hard to find an answer to five or six. Virtually impossible to get seven or eight. But when you get seven or eight, that's the holy grail.

It's taken me about 10 minutes to answer the question, so what's the mistake? The mistake is going to into a project where you know, from the start, that some of those variables are missing. And you know that they're not gettable. I'm not talking about luck and timing. The work ethic's not there. They just really don't have the voice. Those sorts of things. The image is just not right for this artist and they're never going to really have it. With the singer it's just not going to work. Those sorts of things are essential and, really, convincing yourself that you might not love their songs or love their voice, but then letting yourself be swayed to ignore the fatal flaws is a big mistake for a manager to make.

How often does that happen to you?

Not much anymore.

We've had a number of views on streaming services during the series. What's your take on Spotify and that sort of thing? The criticism is that they return nothing to the artist, it's basically leveraging the loss of the majors though whatever partnerships are going on there, and then the deal is kind of separated, so there's a revenue issue there. On the other hand, people say "Well, it's the new TV, it's the new radio."

The history of the music business is a history of exposure versus return. At any time, there is no manager alive who doesn't get at least once each day somebody trying to send them something on the basis of, quote: "It'll be great exposure." Sometimes it is and there are certainly examples where streaming services can be that. My particularly quirky take on it is that there's still a missing piece to the streaming service model. It's starting to happen and it's been promised for some time but it's still not there in the way it should be. If the artist was being truly compensated by way of exposure more broadly in streaming, then the fees would be less of a problem. So if when you stream *Last Dinosaurs* a thing popped up that said, "Hey, did you know that they're coming around the corner? Did you know that there's a new merch range just available? Did you know you can get a free plastic dinosaur by clicking here?" Sign up to their fan page, their mailing list. At that point, it's a pretty strategic moment where the consumer is experiencing the music possibly for the very first time. That's their point of connection with the artist. At this point, can we please engage them more deeply? Can we sell them a concert ticket or a t-shirt or just get their e-mail address? It wouldn't really cost the streaming service anything other than development costs. I'd think from a consumer perspective, providing you're not shoving it down their throat, providing it's just popping up, if you've just discovered this artist you love, and this streaming service is actually going to do you the service of telling you they're playing around the corner at the moment, and that clicking here will get you a ticket, you don't have to click it. It's just this nice additional benefit to the streaming service. So I would be much happier with the deal if there was that deeper engagement rather than it just being song-by-song exposure.

One of the real problems with the business at the moment is that suppliers expanded massively, demand has expanded too. But going back to basic economics, if price is an indicator of value, demand goes up a little, supply goes up a lot, price comes down, perceived value comes down. So everybody has this reduced perception of the value of the artist and the value of the song. How do we more deeply invest people beyond the song and into the artist? So if it can be a gateway to that, come sit next to me. Without that, you know, the other part can go. If it's an opportunity to inject some more marketing and promotional aspect into the business, if, as seems likely, streaming services are not actually capitalising sales but rehabilitating file sharers, there's a lot of data to support that at least in the UK, not the US so far but in the UK, then there's possibly some small upside in that as well. I can still see a justification for it.

There's also a data option too, I mean if you get returns from some of those things and you see what x-hundred people played this song on this day, or it got x-hundred spins on this day through Spotify or Rdio or whatever kind of platform, there's absolutely no way you can find out how that happened if it's a blip in interest on those platforms you've got no access to any indication about why that happened.

Yeah, all of that. I mean of course there's all sorts of privacy issues and all that stuff. But none the less, it's true on iTunes as well. We'd all love to have the iTunes database. But I don't know. At this point, if the music business has learned anything from the last decade or so, it should be about letting the customer consume music in the way they want to consume the music: step one. Step two, try and find a way to monetize that. But that should be the order. We lost a generation of people by trying to do it the other way around.

Your career straddled the end of vinyl, you would have come in just about when cassettes had its year in the sun, through CD, and into digital distribution, and then of course it's a thorny and ugly issue with lots of casualties along the way. In some areas of industries there's been little or no adverse consequences. Harley Medcalfe said "it just helps and makes my job easier and I've had a great time thank you very much". In others it's been revolutionary in IP law, physical sales, and so forth, which has damaged people or made a monster for copyright lawyers and the lot—how has it affected your area of business over the years? How do you see it?

There's positives and negatives to it. The change has been substantial. Substantial change will always produce some winners and some losers, some good things about it and some bad things about it. On balance I'd say the good marginally outweighs the bad. The downside from a manager's perspective is all this stuff that used to be other people's job is now mine, and last time I checked no artist is offering to pay me 25%. But that's the new deal. The good news is that you have more responsibility now. You have more control. The bad news is you have more responsibility and control. So people who are capable of exercising responsibility and control will be okay. People who are really good at being party rock stars and bullying managers and your old-school theatrical kind of table-thumping rock impressario manager types. They're going to find it real bloody hard, because they're actually used to doing all the talking and someone else did all the work. Now you've actually got to do all the work. That doesn't particularly concern me. In fact it was interesting. I did a workshop for John Butler. He has this charity, JBC. We do it every year and we all come and Bill Cullen—I trust he wouldn't mind me sharing this because he did it in a public forum—was talking about the difference between working, he's got a Sarah

Blasko and Paul Kelly record coming out like, right now, a week apart from each other. One last week, one next week or something. One through a proper label, Dew Process, and one that they're doing themselves, Paul's record. Bill was making the point that it's sort of interesting because you'd expect that Paul's would be a lot more work, and in some respects it is. But equally when you're doing it yourself you don't have to keep double-checking that something's been done, there aren't as many cooks in the kitchen, and so it all sort of tends to even out a little bit. So even though one is notionally a lot more work, he said "For the per-hours basis I think it ended up being about even". So there's a lot more responsibility falling on artists and managers now. If the music business, I'm just killing the metaphors today, but if the music business is a big eco-system and the record companies were the dominant species in the eco-system, they haven't died but they have shrunk a little. And so the other species either need to be symbiotic and shrink with them, or expand to fill the space that's been left, take on those extra tasks to tick those boxes. And so that's, what technology has meant: we have more control but we have more responsibility.

So given that the Bill Cullen story about those two records, which kind of work would you prefer to be doing?

See we prefer the Paul work all day, every day. Because my background's in A&R and I was in marketing, the truth is we just don't like being second-guessed on that stuff. We would rather engage in a dialogue with the artist and say "This is the kind of record we want to make". We'll have the back and forth there, we'll arrive at a decision. But ultimately it's the artist's call, they're driving, I'm just the navigator. Same with everything else—we know what's been done and we know why it's late. We're not running around recording, we don't go, "You know, you said you were going to do that photo agreement, I'll just double check, do we have that yet? I'll get back to you." Perhaps it's because we're control freaks as well. We quite like it, but it works for us. Our thing works well for us. I'm not saying it's everybody's answer, but our little thing works well for us.

Coming back to your momentum talk, which I've seen you talk about in a number of forums, it seems like you're saying your perception of success can actually substitute for actual success. Is that right?

Momentarily. You can find gravity for a bit, you know? Wile-E-Coyote runs off the cliff and it takes a while for gravity to catch up. That particular bit is another that I've ripped off from John Woodruff. I've borrowed a lot of stuff from him over the years. Years ago I did one of these seminar things, and for those of you who've never seen John speak at anything, he's very larger than life: comic, funny as a hatful kind of guy. Anyway, we're on this panel. There's, like, eight people, and they begin by saying, "We'd like everybody to say their title and what they do for a living." The guy at the extreme right goes, "I'm the senior vice-president of corporate communications and development for the blah blah corporation for Hong Kong, with responsibility for..." Yeah, it goes on for ages, and each person somehow feels compelled to say as much as he did. So by the time it gets down to John Woodruff who's at the other end of the line, it's like 25 minutes later and we haven't even started the panel, we're just giving our business card, basically. And Woody leans into the microphone and says: "My name's John Woodruff, I'm a really good bullshit artist. I bullshit for a living." And he then went on to say that, basically, if the artist's reality is at a certain level—and I am answering your question with this, believe it or not—if the reality of what the artist is capable of is at one level, it's John's job to make it look just that much higher. And the gap between the two levels is the "bullshit quotient". That's stuff like "The lines were around the door at 6 o'clock", when really, we were 50 short of sell out but don't tell anybody. We just held some people back so it looked like a sellout. We wallpapered the venue with our friends. Whatever it was, the venue was sold out at 6 o'clock. If you keep doing it over time you're going to get found out. But for a period of time, the reality will follow up with it if you're plausible enough. You don't have to be telling a lie, but you can be framing a conversation in a way to give it its most positive face. You can talk endlessly about the amazing story that the band's got going on in that market and not mention that they aren't selling tickets anywhere else but in this or that market. You're not lying, you're just focusing on the positives and creating the perception of momentum. So it's all about how you spin something to keep the good news rolling along. You just want to spread it around everywhere. The bad news you want to bury deep in a lead vault and put it way underground, never to be seen again.

Eventually though, in this day and age it will be found out, you can't really hide from it as much anymore. So the ability to hype a record in the charts, a lot of the stuff that used to go on, it's all sort of fun and games and what not, but the ability to really heighten stuff in the ways that used to happen are long gone. But there are people out there every day who are goosing their YouTube views, who are goosing their number of Facebook likes. There's all sorts of ways that you can create the perception of success.

We're just about out of time, I've got one more question to ask before we turn over to the audience. The question that I ask of all our guests—if you have one piece of advice to offer aspiting artists or managers in our audience, what would it be?

We'll go two. The first is that ultimately, the success or failure of business is based upon your reputation. Every decision you make every day has a consequence for that reputation. It sounds like something your mum or dad would tell you, it's so dull. But it's really true and I don't think I was really conscious of it all the way. You just kind of walk around bumping into things and you deal with people in the way you deal with them so when you get 10 years down the track, you realise, "Hang on a sec, I've just painted myself as a particular person here.". Just as well as I've painted myself as someone I'm comfortable with. If I'd been a different type of person then that could have really caught up with me. So avoid shortcuts and be aware that every decision you're making is affecting your reputation and ultimately your reputation is what you're selling. If you're going into any business and saying, "Sign with me," they're going to ask around and at that point that really clever thing you did to make an extra 50 bucks could just come around and cost you a million dollars. Plus you've got to sleep at night too.

The second thing I would say is a lot of times in this business, and again this is the guy from the record store I worked at as a kid gave me a fantastic piece of advice, one that I always find is useful for people, it's not my line, it's his. There was an artist, a very famous artist, who came to me for management, but they'd made a record that just wasn't going to be successful but they were convinced that it was. So whoever managed them was basically in for an absolute flogging from the artist. Because when it failed it was going to be the manager's fault. That's always how it goes. Success is the artist's, failure's the manager's job. But I was really torn, because I loved the idea of being able to work with this artist. I could see myself how great it would be, getting to go to shows every night. I called this mate of mine and said, "I just can't figure out whether to do it or not," he said, "It's really simple—*ask yourself, is it a temptation or is it an opportunity*?". I found that advice early in my career to be like a knife through butter. If you ask yourself when you're not sure whether something's the right or wrong thing to do, ask yourself if it's a temptation or an opportunity. Nine times out of ten the answer will be stark, you know? So yeah, that would be my advice.

Fantastic. Thanks John. Questions?

(Audience member): I was just wondering on more the A&R side, what suggestions would you make to be able to work your way into a record label company, or what sort of position as an intern or a publicist or A&R or anything like that?

It's an interesting question. A&R's an odd job because there's no well trodden pathway to it. People come from all sorts of odd backgrounds to end up there. Typically, people who end up in A&R have had experience in various facets of the business and have established a reputation as being good with artists and having good ear and a good nose for the next big thing. So, typically, my advice to anybody would be to get a job somewhere down the track, start local, start small. Do as many things as you can possibly do that relate to music to help pay the bills. Go volunteer for a show on 4ZZZ. Do the door at The Zoo. Do reviews for *Time Off*, and a hundred other things like it. Manage your friend's band just to see what happens. Because the things you learn will stand you in good stead. But the people you meet will end up opening up, providing you treat them with respect and have an eye for reputation. That will be your calling card. I wasn't doing it for those reasons when I was doing it. I was doing it because I really didn't want to get a real job. So I cobbled together a whole bunch of part time jobs in the music business through which I met a whole bunch of different people which turned out to be what now would be called networking.

I really don't think I'd have known what the word meant, they were just other people that liked the same music I liked. The guy who booked my band, which was a $200 band, used to book its $50 support bands off, who wrote for a fanzine, and who I would always go to as the guy I knew who got the copy of *Nevermind* 2 months before it came out. Everybody loved it, we were all taping his cassette of that album, literally. He now promotes *Homebake*. I didn't become friends with him because I thought, "One day this guy's going to promote a big festival and if I share this cassette with him that's going to stand me in good stead down the track." He had a cassette of the Nirvana record! So follow those sorts of instincts and if you're doing it for the right reasons you'll do well. There's a great line in a Hunters and Collectors song that if "success is on your mind, the true direction is missing", and I think there's a lot to be said for that. So follow those passions, follow those instincts, do as much as you can possibly do, treat people with respect and one door will tend to open another door.

(Audience member): Hi John, I really appreciate all the advice you've given us, it's been fantastic. I just wanted to ask a little bit further about the case of the role of Triple J in the Australian music industry and if you have any advice for up and coming artists on how to get played and get involved with Triple J?

Look, Triple J's fantastic at helping people get to first base, you know? Their role is not to take you beyond that. So what tends to happen is that artists have an inflated expectation of what Triple J support means. It's a fantastic first step. It's unreasonable to expect them to be the ones that also take you on your second, third, fourth, and fifth steps. That's not what they're there for. They're there to get it rolling. And what are you going to do with that? In terms of how you attract their attention, well obviously Unearthed has become the be all and end all of existence right now. Your ability is another thing. I haven't mentioned it, but of all the reactivity measures that I've referred to it's probably the one I should have mentioned first. You know, I think they're really smart about sifting out the bullshit *Unearthed* reactions from the real ones. I don't know quite how they do it, but my perception, which could be wrong, is that they're very good at filtering. There are plenty of things on *Unearthed* that just smell of being hyped, and they never play them. Maybe it's just because they've got pretty good taste so they filter out the bad stuff. I don't know. But again, if you're already filling some venues, getting put onto the right festivals, I'm assuming you're a band not an electronic act, DJ-based thing. If you're a DJ, if you're already showing well on Beatport and you're already getting asked to DJ at the right clubs. That sort of story is going to mean a lot more to Richard and Nick than, "Oh great, they put a rose on the front of the CD and then put five songs, clever!"

It's amazing. I will guarantee that there are people sitting in this room right now whose real question is, "How do I get someone to listen to my demo tape?" That is not the question to ask. Be audience oriented. Don't worry about the industry. They'll come to you.

(Audience member): With your eight things, when you are starting to develop an audience base and trying to promote your own stuff, you know that you're really, really crap with number five or number six, I assume that you just try and network and work with people who are good at it. Do you have anything else to say?

I should have said that it's not like I sit down and coldly dissect that before I start signing artists. That came out of being asked to give a speech about why do you sign certain artists, and I tried to take what was essentially an unconscious process and deconstruct it. I realised that what I was actually doing was looking for a reason *not* to do it. If I couldn't find a reason not to do it, then I did it. So I made a list of the reasons why I've said no to things. That's how I ended up with that particular checklist. You can totally develop some of those things. The narrative for example, all of them really in different ways, they all require work. I think the only reason that it might be useful to be conscious of them is for exactly the reason you say: it's like, "We seem to really have the songs but the voice isn't connecting, maybe we don't have the right singer in our band. Maybe actually I need to be Pete Townsend, we need to find Roger Daltrey. You know, maybe there's something missing in our narrative here, I need someone to help me,". Because the narrative part of it's a really interesting one. It's the one aspect where management in my opinion can make the most difference. Because most people have a story, but they're actually not great at working out what it is. It's the ex-journo in me that makes me think it's usually there. The media will always make a two-dimensional version of your three-dimensional self. You might as well pick the two dimensions for yourself. Pete Murray's a lot more than a football player that happens to write sensitive songs. He's a dad, he's a surfer, he's all sorts of things. But those are the things that all, in the first instance, got people intrigued. So what you do is take your Elvis thing for examples about that. I made a comment about Elvis the Pelvis, right?

I always tell a story about Elvis when he was first starting out was in a County Fair singing and people were sort of not paying that much attention. He swivelled his hips a bit, a few girls down the front reacted, so he swivelled them a bit more and the whole front row reacted. So he started doing it like crazy and the whole crowd went nuts. Now swivelling his hips, to some extent, was a natural thing for Elvis. The show biz comes in with the hyping of it, the magnifying of what's special. You're not going, "You know what would be great? If you swivelled your hips, that would really work," that shit never works. When it's imposed from that side, never going to get there. But when it's already there and it's just magnified, it's drawn out and made bigger. That's when the magic happens. And that's where listening to your audience is important because you'll start to see certain things: "I love the way the guitarist does that windmill thing!", or whatever. So I'm not saying you should pander to your audience either, it's not like you get out of bed every day and go "I'll make myself into whatever it takes to win their acclaim". But stuff you're already doing that's working, why would you not do more of that? What's the harm in that, if they're already liking it.

We have time for one more.

You talked a lot about a lot of interesting things to check out like the theory of disintermediation? I'm really interested in learning more about marketing and how to market my band better and I just wanted to know a bit more about those websites you were talking about that show Google Trends and show which town and stuff receives more of your music and stuff like that.

There's a lot of those sorts of things out there. Google Trends, if you just Google Google Trends, you'll see it come up. Type in Gotye and muck around with it, you'll see what I'm talking about, that's more a country by country thing. If you look at *TopSpin*'s website they do a whole bunch of metrics. Metrics isn't the right word. Tools that can be used for measurement purposes with all of this. As far as marketing itself is concerned, be very careful of courses in marketing. I did one some, not that long ago, about 7 or 8 years ago. I got to the point where I just felt like my brain was rotting and so I started actually doing some study, really just to stop my brain rotting. I did a marketing course that was so funny, because you go into this classic marketing theory says firstly, you begin by going out and identifying the need in the customer. "Customers are looking for a toothpaste that whitens as well as cleans", Ah … So we go back and design a product that whitens as well as cleans, we work out who those customers are, they are people, women between the age of this and that, those women come of this and that, and we design the perfect toothpaste, get the packaging right for it, we work out that those people read this magazine and we get an ad campaign that's right and we're hitting that target. And they do this thing in our course. It's a room like this and they go around, it's all, it's post-graduate so they're going around and the woman from the baby food company goes, "Yep, that's how we do it, we've got nine different forms of baby formula, they're all basically the same thing but we package this one for people that are particularly colic-y babies and this one for older babies and this one for younger babies. They're all basically the same thing just different branding, different market segmentation, right?" And they go around the whole room and they get to me and go, "What do you do?" and I go "Well, our artist has a breakup, pours their guts out in a song, brings it to us and we go, "Hmm, how can we possibly expose this in order to sell something?"" It's completely backwards, it's not like the artist goes out and says "Excuse me, are you in the market for any songs about breakups?" So marketing theory, and the reason for this—and I have a serious point at the bottom of it—which is that what we sell, thankfully, is one of the few products, and I hate that word, that exists for multiple purposes other than just being for sale. So you know, the toothpaste only exists to be sold, the song exits partly, in fact, largely or even totally in the case of some of my clients, as a means of self-expression, as a means of catharsis. It is a product only incidentally or partially, so the usual rules of marketing, while they can sometimes be helpful, don't necessarily apply. So be cautious in getting into marketing theory because you have to remember that what you're selling is fundamentally different from toothpaste, at least if it's any good that is.

Chapter 5
Michael Taylor, A&R Manager

Abstract This chapter is an interview with Michael Taylor who is today joint managing director of Universal Music Group, Australia. At the time of the interview he was Australian VP of A&R for Universal and head of Island Records, a Universal imprint. Michael's career began at Clark University where he booked nationally and internationally significant acts as President of the Student Entertainment Committee. His first music business job was at the William Morris Agency in New York. He then became an A&R scout for Columbia Records and went on to be A&R Manager at Madonna's label, Maverick, and Senior A&R Director at Epic Records. In the mid-90s Michael founded the Go Big label, a project that fused music licensing with lifestyle sports, which he ran out of his kitchen in New York. In 2001 Michael moved to Australia to head up A&R at Sony Music. In 2008 he established Island Records Australia as General Manager. Michael was promoted to Executive VP of A&R Universal Music Australia in 2013 and in 2014 became co-Managing Director of the company. Michael's interview shows how the A&R function extends well beyond the mere discovery of talent.

Welcome Michael. Our audience may only have a passing notion of what and A&R Manager does, so could you paint us a bit of a picture of where you've come from and what you do today?

A&R is the aspect of the record company that works directly with the artists. So we're finding the artists, we're helping the artists make their record, and then we're working with that record through the record company, helping the artist through their career. That's the core of it.

A&R stands for Artist and Repertoire, which at one time, I guess like in the 40s or 50s, there were singers and they needed songs and so you were the guy who put artists with repertoire. So, for example, Frank Sinatra didn't write any of his material, just like Elvis didn't write his material. He had an A&R guy that found those songs and said "Hey Frank, here's this new song by Sammy Cahn called *Three Coins in the Fountain*, what do you think?" and Frank said "great" and recorded it. So that was the role in the beginning.

Over the years it's evolved into a whole different thing now where most artists are self-contained writers. Or if they're pop artists looking for songs then the A&R

P. Graham, *Music, Management, Marketing, and Law*, Music Business Research,
https://doi.org/10.1007/978-3-030-02143-6_5

person might take that old school traditional role. If not, you're helping the band that might be writing their own songs to do their best, to find a producer, work with them on their recording budget, assisting their imaging, it's really all aspects now. At one time it was very specialised but it's grown, it's quite broad now.

Why do you think that is?

The music business, like any other business, is cyclical. So you go through periods of up and down. Right now we're at kind of a plateau but the music business as a whole, starting about 10 years ago, really took a dive—internet piracy, all those things, and 30% of the business eroded. So with that staff got cut, fewer people, and the people that were there took on more responsibility, did more things. So partly just due to the changed economics of the business, A&R started becoming a broader role.

Is it different here in Australia? In America you've still got dedicated songwriters and dedicated performers who, probably, in about half the cases in some genres, never meet.

It's different in every genre. In the country genre, a lot of those artists are looking for songs, outside cuts. So in country there is the more traditional roles—here's the artist, here's the song writer, here's the producer. Australia has really just two genres in terms of domestic or Australian-created product, you've either got your indie or your alternative—let's call it alternative because indie gets way too confusing and it's a bunch of bullshit what indie is anyway—but you've got your alternative music and you've got your pop and with alternative most of those artists are writing their own music, sometimes producing it themselves so you're coming more from that background.

And so you've got pop artists looking for songs in this country?

Yeah, and then you have your share of pop artists and some of them consider themselves song writers so you help them co-write. If not, you go out and look for outside songs for them. It's really genre-dependent and skill-set dependent.

You started out in music as a drummer. How did you move from being a musician to doing what you do now? Do you still consider what you do primarily about music or is it mostly about business? How does it all work?

I specifically focused on getting into A&R because I knew it was a job I could do creative work in, focused on music, as well as having some control over my destiny. As a drummer—if there's any musicians that are in the audience who are drummers—you just don't have that much say over how well the band does at the end of the day. You can be a quarter-member song writer or something, but a lot of it depends on your front-person and all that. I was playing in a band, we were on tour in America, we were opening for Faith No More at the time, they weren't big, it sounds impressive but they were really small at the time, and we had a gig and the guitarist just had a freak out and decided he'd quit and walked off sound check and said "I don't feel like playing tonight". I said "I can't do this for a living, I have to find something else to do". So that's when I said "Okay, I'll continue to play drums and make music for fun but I'm going to try to get more into the business side". I was booking my band at the time, the band that I played in. I was kind of the *de facto* manager so I enjoyed that aspect of it too. So it was kind of a natural progression.

So, there's been a fair bit of historical criticism about A&R throughout the years: "they're just doing what was done last year" or at the other end there's so much control over the artist's material that it loses its integrity. And I guess it's positioned almost on the horns of a dilemma, caught between the demands of business and the demands of artistic temperament or instinct or whatever you'd like to call it.

Art and commerce, shall they ever meet? I don't know, that's kind of my job is to ride the fence somewhere between art and commerce, you know? I know I'm supposed to make money for my company but ideally I want to do it making the best possible music at the same time.

Is that a common attitude do you think, amongst A&R folk?

I don't know, there are different A&R types out there. I got into it because I love music and that's my goal: to help my artist make the best records possible and make money at it. But it's hard, and sometimes you have to make smart decisions rather than just go with what you feel is right for your audience at that time. And it's a process as an artist, but I find that if you let your artist do what they do, I mean if you're going to sign an artist in the first place as an A&R person you should ideally love what they're doing, right? And be extremely passionate about it. I remember an old saying: "If you're not ready to get fired over the band don't sign the band". Because at times you have to stand on a desk and yell at people to get things done for your act. So yeah, I think you have to really be willing to go down that path for your bands.

How do you negotiate those tensions between art and commerce on a day-to-day basis, are you a more hands-on person, where would your creative influence stop for a band?

Well I give as much advice as I think they can take on. I'm not ever going to hold back. I usually have a meeting with my artist and say "Listen, I'm going to tell you what I honestly feel all the time. It's your job now to determine how much of that advice you're going to take and I'm hoping that you're going to take some of it and it will lead to success". But, you know, do I sit and say "Oh that high-hat is too loud and if it doesn't come down 2dB I'm not going to release your record"? No. Are there A&R guys that have done that? I'm sure there are.

So you have that much control about what gets out? Do you have to sign off on everything?

It's different with every artist. I worked with the Hilltop Hoods and my relationship with them is they call me and they say "Mike, we finished our record. We want it to come out next Tuesday" and I haven't heard it yet, and my relationship is "okay cool, I'll work on it" because I know they're probably going to produce something amazing and the deal was I'm going to stay out of your music and I'm going to help you business-wise. I have other artists that really want a lot of input from me and need a lot of assistance for song writing and production and engineering thoughts, so I get more hands-on. So it depends. I have about 17 artists on the roster, 18 artists, and every one of them is a different level of involvement.

And is that kind of involvement negotiated at the deals stage, or is it something that evolves, how does it all work?

Some artists want to have security and they'll say "I need a creative control clause in my contract". Okay. Sure, I'm not signing you to tell you I want to change who you are. That would be a bad signing and I guess past experience and stories lead artists to think "I have to have this protection". But the artist really does have control, I can't release anything until the artist approves it, so I can't just put out any photo or any video, bio or song. They have approval of every step along the way. And you know, almost all my relationships with artists are really good where I'm helping them and I might call and say "Oh god, I hate that picture!" and they'll say "No we love it!" and I'll say "Okay cool, go with it" but I did my job in terms of giving you advice, and I guess for A&R my job is to kind of amplify the artist's vision. So if I don't have a desire to change their vision, I have a desire to make their vision bigger. Wider to an audience.

How far into the future do you look in terms of longevity? It seems to me that a lot of the revenue now for the majors is coming from back catalogue, so how far into the future can you bet on an artist?

Well I mean, back catalogue sales aren't a huge percentage, they are definitely a percentage but the driving percentage of revenue is almost always new releases as far as I see. Maybe when CD first came out or when digital first took off, people then go and buy Dark Side of The Moon again in a different format.

I'm thinking of Spotify not being able to go ahead without Beatles and Stones and all the major bits and pieces and people signing up to those sorts of things, there's a ton of revenue associated with that stuff and it seems like in some respects the past is the future of the business.

Well you've got to create that new catalogue though. It's only going to come from new artists.

Well that's what I mean, and do you look at it over "oh this'll make us a buck in the next year" or in 10 years' time this is going to make us a fortune sort of thing?

Well, I think with some artists that you sign you truly believe they're going to be a career artist and you want to help them along their entire career. I work with Boy and Bear and I think *Moonfire* could be an album people care about in 10 years. They might go back and say "Oh I love Moonfire, I want to go check that out again". I have a couple artists that are much more in a current trend in, say, pop music, where their production is going to sound ridiculously dated in 10 years. It sounds amazingly awesome right now but radio softens everything after repetition. So if you think about The Presets, *My People*, first time you heard *My People* you thought "Shit! That sounds amazing and aggro and heavy and how is that ever going to get on the radio"? You could probably hear it on Mix FM now. So certain things—and I'm not dating The Presets, I think they will be around for years, don't get me wrong—are very much of the moment and might not have that longevity but that's the artist's vision of how they want to make their music.

My daughter was watching TV at one point and she said, I think it was an Elton John concert or something and she said "oh it's really sad", she was 13, 14 or something and I said "what is?" and she said "there's going to be no-one like this in years to come, they're all going to be small" and I thought that was a

reasonable and insightful thought. What do you think? Are there going to continue to be these mega, long-term career artists?

I mean, I certainly hope so. You would hate to think that Elton John is one of the last of those artists. Every once in a while somebody will come along that blows off all expectations and they just lift the bar higher, and ultimately it's about great artists. If great artists exist, people will come to them and hopefully there'll be another one of those great piano singer songwriters that gives us those songs for the next decade. Is it harder now? Could be. There's always those conversations. Could The Beatles or The Stones exist in today's environment? I don't know, I mean I can't name you a One Direction song, but they're huge, right? Will it matter in 10 years to them? Probably not, but there certainly are still massive artists on a massive scale. I don't think that's going away. People want to feel a sense of community and a sense of community through music and so everybody kind of coming around one artist does that.

But still people talk about niche, niche, niche, you know?

Yeah, it's cool to like the newest, hippest most coolest Brooklyn band in the world that nobody else knows about. But then, you know, 3 years later everybody knows about them so do you give up? No, I still love Grizzly Bear. I saw them in a shitty little club in Parkslope 6 years ago and still love them now. But they are definitely a niche band. There are people that grip onto that niche stuff.

Why are we suddenly seeing producers being put in the role of A&R and I'm thinking here of Rick Ruben and Scott Horsecroft in Australia.

Scott would love his name being mentioned along with Rick Ruben. I think there's always been producers in A&R roles. Jerry Wexler produced Aretha Franklin records, he was an A&R guy for Atlantic in the 60s. Herb Alpert fancied himself a producer and had A&M records. Jimmy Iovine, engineered Born to Run by Springsteen, now he runs Interscope records and he's on American Idol. So I think there's always been those people in roles. Some are good and some are not. I personally think it's a really hard thing to do the two because the roles are really different. If you're a producer, what you love, what your passion is, what you're best at, is sitting behind a console working with a band and closing the rest of the world off. You can't do that in A&R because if you're in A&R you've got to deal with the shipment for your sale coming up on Saturday, your schedule with your promo people, and there's just tons of calls and emails. You can't do both. So a couple of people try to do both and some succeed and some don't.

So, at the level of conducting business, what would make a producer a good call on all of that, I mean, why would you do it?

Well some of them do succeed, you've got Jimmy Iovine who's a producer and an amazing record executive.

At the same time?

Yeah, so there are plenty that can do it and can do it very well, but it's not the norm. I think it's a rare thing.

So when we spoke at Song Summit you said that YouTube revenues were now in the top 5 revenues for Universal after iTunes, JB Hi-Fi-

Sanity, Leading Edge, probably yeah.

Do you think it's going to continue like that and do you do A&R on that basis? How do you factor those new platforms into what you do for a job and how do you think about them into the future?

With YouTube, it's not something that I think about in terms of the song. I don't try to create a song that's going to get more attention from some novelty video or anything like that, but a very good video or a video that's going to excite people or be viral can do huge business for you, and so it's a factor to that extent where videos are that much more important now because people are watching so much content on YouTube and it's creating a lot of revenue. So whether people switch in 6 months time and everybody is on Spotify and nobody's listening to music on YouTube, I don't know, I can't predict that.

Does it factor into the decisions you make about who you sign or how the artists get developed?

No, I'm sure some people do. I don't particularly do that but you know that Korean artist Psy, Gangnam Style? I think it's like 125 million views when I saw it 3 weeks ago it was at 60 so it's just a phenomenal amount of people are watching that. He's just recently gotten signed by Universal Republic in the US, Justin Bieber's label. The guy that runs Scooter Braun picked it up. That's going to create a heap of revenue and perhaps that drove some of the thinking along with "Hey, that's a funny video, let's go for that". So perhaps some people do it that way. I just kind of feel like I'm a little bit old-school in that respect. I still feel like it's got to be about the music and the marketing comes later. If the music's great then the marketing stuff that happens around it will just fall into place.

And is that formulaic? Is your approach to marketing a formulaic approach, you do X, Y and Z or is it about building an audience around it?

It's different in every respect. You don't want to make it formulaic because then everything you put out is a cookie cutter replica of the other and that doesn't work, so you've got to really tailor your marketing plan to your specific artist. I have an artist named Gin Wigmore who's just got a sync with Heineken, and Heineken decided to put it into the new James Bond commercial which is coming out in a couple of weeks. Then they decided to shoot a commercial with Daniel Craig who plays James Bond with Gin Wigmore performing in the background. This is now a huge opportunity for us because it's a $45 million campaign that's global and based around the new Bond movie. So off of that I got a whole new marketing plan in place.

I take issue with what I guess what you'd call "marketing 101 theory" when it comes to music. You know, "product price place promotion" sort of thing. It's a very cookie cutter approach and it seems to me that a lot of entertainment companies right across the board have fallen for it rather than thinking about "how do I, through what do I, develop an audience for this act or this artist or this show or whatever else". Why do you think it's gone like that, or has it?

I think what happens is there's a lot of volume that happens and people have to get things done and off their desks to move onto the next thing, so you get the "tick the boxes and move on" mentality with some people. As an A&R guy who's personally invested in all these artists—and I spend time with my artists—I know them and I've probably met their mum. I really don't want to see by-the-numbers marketing; I want to see something unique that speaks to the music and speaks to the people who are going to want that music. So one of the first things we do when we're signing an artist is ask "who are the fans? Do we know who these fans are for this artist? And then how do we reach them? How do we get them to hear the music?" And if you're not doing those things, even if that is step 1, 2 and 3 then all the rest doesn't matter to me because you're not really doing the right job.

You've done A&R across multiple areas including TV, recorded and live music, you've even spent time in a talent agency, and you've also worked across multiple geographic markets. In terms of being in A&R development, how different is the Australian industry from elsewhere?

Well it's small in Australia, and the size of the market dictates budgets and so in that respect it's different. You know, when I forecast for a record, when I'm saying "okay, what can I spend to make this album", if I think it's going to do 20 or 25 thousand, which is a good result in this current market, I know I probably should be making an album that doesn't cost more than $60,000 because then you also have your advance to the artist and your videos and photos and art, and without spending much time you can be $150–200,000 into a project. So you've got to just really step through it and make sure that you're plotting for the right release.

So how do you decide what a thing's going to do in terms of numbers? How do you make that call?

To some extent it's a bit of guesswork. To an extent you base it off either past sales or what the buzz is on the artist in the marketplace and, perhaps, off past singles. Although with pop you can't really do it that way because in pop music the audience loves the single and they don't care about the album. Ideally, if your last record went platinum a conservative estimate then would be "okay, let's say this one's going to do 50,000" and then you base your budget on that.

Is it in your interests as an Australian A&R guy to encourage your artists overseas?

Yes. A big part of my job is getting a US or a UK label excited about my artists—if I have worldwide rights—and hopefully getting those artists released. One of the things I do twice a year is just get on a plane and go to New York or LA or London and I just say hi to everybody and play music and talk about what I'm doing and hope there's some reaction. You can't force a release into another country. I mean people do it, but the result is you just spend a lot of money and spin your wheels and don't get a result. Because for an international company to put out a record that was made in Australia they're going to have to feel some passion for it, that they want to break it. Because it's not their baby, it's my baby, you know? To do that you have to get some buy-in, so part of that is just getting the stuff out there.

But is that a relationship with you and the A&R departments in the other places or is it more about their tastes, the state of what they're doing, whether they have a good day, you know what I mean?

Well I tailor what I play to certain people. I know most of the A&R team in Universal in the US and when I'm in New York I'll go see certain people if it's rock and certain people if it's alternative, and certain people if it's pop. My roster is kind of all over the shop. The guy who's doing the LMFAO record isn't probably doing the Feist record, although that's the one example where he is, so skip that one. But anyway, you know what I'm saying, if you're doing hip-hop in the states you're not doing pop, rock, you just don't cross over in that way.

How different is Universal from Sony or Warner or EMI or any other company in that respect? Is there a system in place where successful stuff from one geographical region sort of gets pushed through the system on a worldwide basis?

So for Universal their international division is out of London. There's an international team, and when one of the affiliates, one of the smaller countries (not the US or the UK) is having a hit then the international team gets behind it and gets it going around the world. So I have an artist, Havana Brown, a pop artist, has a song called *We Run The Night*. It came out probably 2 years ago here, is just coming out in UK and Europe next month, spent a year on the US charts and went platinum. We needed that US platinum hit for the UK to decide to go, but all of that was kind of shepherded through the system with the international team. Sony's very similar, although the international team's out of New York.

You've worked for Sony?

Yeah. I've worked at Warner too. Warner's international team was out of New York as well.

And how different are they to work for, those companies?

Well the difference between Sony and Universal is vast in terms of corporate culture. But I'm sure it's like that in any business. The culture behind Sony comes from the fact that it's owned and run by a Japanese mega company and has a much different culture. Universal traditionally was an American company purchased by a French entity, so they have a different culture as well. Warner's always been a US company, so very different as well. And it's a weird thing, company culture, what is it? But it's so obvious. You just walk into the Sony building in New York and it's this monolith with heavy marble and security guards and it's just not friendly; it's mean. Some people want that, you want a mean guy in your corner kicking goals for you. You go into EMI and it's really warm and friendly and huggy and some people want that, they want that teddybear in the corner. It's what you want.

We were talking about musician earnings at the APRA panel earlier this year when we discussed the plight of musicians' earnings in Australia. We almost always hear comparisons between music and sport, and I know you've had a bit to do with sport at one point and you've had a go at integrating the two with Go Big Records. It'd be good to hear a little bit about that too but can you tell us where the crossovers are and how you're thinking with Go Big and what happened with it?

Well there isn't a lot, I don't find a lot of similarity between music and sport because music is so subjective and sport is so finite. You won by one point. But I had a record label that I ran out of my kitchen with my roommate in New York called Go Big Records and he was a total motocross nut. He would take me to these motocross events, and they're this weird phenomenon where there's 60,000 people in a stadium and just some guys riding around in a dirt bike trail and I don't really get it. But the scene was awesome and I loved the scene behind it, and the music, don't judge me, we're going back to 1994, 95, but the music was like Limp Bizkit and Kid Rock and Korn and all these nu-metal bands which were kind of cool at the time—not cool but kind of cool—so what we did was we started to build soundtracks for motocross and supercross racing. Then we built soundtracks for the extreme sports world and got involved with ESPN and their extreme sports games and became music supervisors in that world. It was a great outlet, just like music and surf or music and skate were connected, so were those extreme sports. But it was definitely a mid-90s thing with metalheads and those kind of artists and bands that worked around that. So we enjoyed that and did it for a couple of years. We actually sold the company and made a little bit of money from it, but it was an idea that we ran with and we really just did it because we liked the party aspects of these events which is why so many in the music business get involved, because they like the circus that goes with it.

In 2009 we did a round of interviews canvassing multiple parts of the industry, up and down the east coast. One of the recurring comments we heard was that publishers and record labels were turning to online as a gauge, as opposed to turning up at gigs at the Manzil Room or whatever it was in the 80s, early 90s. How much of a role does online play in decisions about the acts you sign or at least think about signing? Do you have people trawling the internet and Facebook?

It's changed the business completely. Nothing's changed the music business as much as the internet. The last time a change that big occurred was when somebody figuring out how to record music. That's probably the two big changes. You know, as an A&R person, if you hear something about a band you instantly can look it up, learn their entire history, see all their songs, learn everything you want to know about them within seconds. You can just sit there and do it. That was not the case at all prior to the internet. When I started in A&R scouting, if you heard about a band you would get on a plane and go see them. So when I first started doing A&R I was working at Maverick Records which was a small but quite well-off label from Warner Brothers owned by Madonna. We had The Deftones and Prodigy, Alanis Morissette. But yeah, you would just get on a plane to go see the band. So I spent a lot of time doing that, which is where the joke "A&R stands for Airplanes and Restaurants" comes from. But you don't have to do that now, I mean you can see the band instantly. Then if you like them you get on a plane and go see them. You take out a little bit of that guesswork. Is that a great thing? I don't know. Because suddenly the artist is more reliant on creating really great tools online rather than getting a huge buzz off of a live show. But that's just the current environment we're in.

Stats can obviously be gamed online. Do you often get fooled by online fluffery, if you know what I mean, by people buying likes and so on?

For a while the industry loves whatever is hippest and newest and that's just the nature of the music business. When MySpace came along everyone was like "this artist has 200,000 plays on MySpace so they must be awesome!" But we soon found out when an artist really fabricates how many plays they had had with a bot, or in the case of one artist that I signed, you know, I did really truly love her material but I think I would have been much more slow in moving forward with her if it wasn't for the fact that I saw her MySpace at the time and I was like "Wow, she has millions of hits". She actually had several sisters who would just do that all day long. So yeah, it happens. You know, I think you just live and learn with that stuff.

At what point do you sort of draw the line between, as you say, you loved her music anyway and she had millions of hits, where does the balance lie?

If I just loved her music but she didn't have millions of hits, then she is a brand new artist who you're going to have to go and establish and develop. I probably would have just done some demos with her, maybe done an EP, built it over a year and a half, I still would develop the artist but in that case I got fooled into thinking there was a base already for her so all I had to do was put out a record and if 10% of her base bought that record we're doing great, but 10% of her base didn't... (laughs)

So when you look at an artist signing, what do you look at more closely, their ability to sustain a career over a long period, their ability to succeed in sync or alternative revenue streams, their ability to sell records from day 1, their ability to succeed internationally, or is it a combination or is it something else entirely?

Well, songs. If they have great songs. I mean that is the hardest thing to get. You can have someone who looks like a star, they play amazingly, they sing great, they could have all those elements but if they don't have songs you're still starting from square one. So if I come across a band that just has amazing songs that's the hardest part of it. It's a huge excitement factor for me. That's with my creative A&R hat on. So if they have the songs and then they have the x-factor and they have the skills and the live performance ability then that's a whole package and then you get *really* excited. Then there's this other thing that I've learned, really only over the last couple of years and it's intangible, but they actually have to be 'smart' and they actually have to make smart decisions because it's amazing how often you're like "I wonder what happened to that artist, they were so good". The truth is that they probably made some really bad decisions over the course of their career and that's why you don't know where they are now. It's a really hard thing to know when to say yes and when to say no to certain things. Also the team that you build around you as an artist is paramount to success. If you don't have the right team around you, you just can't do it.

Just about everyone we've spoken to has emphasised management as being critical to all those sorts of things, would you agree with that that it's 95% the management they've got that determines their career success, after talent and songs and so forth?

If they had everything else and a horrible manager it could still work, but the likelihood's a lot lower. Great management is invaluable. I know of artists who've gotten signed by certain A&R people not because the A&R person loved their music or the artist, but they knew the manager was going to do a great job. It's not really a great business model but, yeah, it happens. There's very few great managers out there in Australia and I'm not the only one who says that, and that's because it's economies of scale. It's just very hard to make money as a manager. With a brand new artist you aren't seeing money for about 2 years down the road until money starts to flow in if you have success, and how do you sustain yourself for 2 years? It's quite difficult so you have to have do other work as a manager then, and if you're having other work as a manager at that time you're not able to focus fully on your band or your artist. It's a real challenge. It's one of the hardest jobs out there in music by far, too, because you're doing everything as a manager. You are babysitting and you are taking meetings at high levels and everything.

It really points towards the online thing, the 2 year development stage for management, the expectation that people have a fanbase at the point of signing, it's a huge benefit to them when being considered. All that leads to the suggestion that an artist that gets to that stage almost doesn't need a record deal, almost doesn't need the help of the company. What does that mean for the future of the majors?

That's why at major labels we have to develop artists. We can't just jump on the back of things that are successful and try to make them bigger. You have to invest in A&R to be relevant in 10 years time if you're going to be a label because, yes, bands can get from 0 to 50 on their own but to get from 50 to 110 is a lot harder because that's when you need money, because you just can't go into commercial radio and say "play my song" because commercial radio isn't about music whatsoever; they're about commercials and music is the annoying stuff between their commercials. How're you going to get them to play your music? You're probably going to have to show that you're truly investing in the artist and you're going to run some campaigns with them, you're going to do some advertising. We're not saying "payola" because obviously that's not what it is. They want to see some commitment on the label's part if they're going to add the artist.

I've heard anecdotes about de-linking. Historically, in the 50s, 60s and 70s, the majors and the radio, commercial radio, both here and everywhere else, were kind of linked. Their fortunes were very, very linked and there was a lot of to-ing and fro-ing between those arenas. People have started telling me that there's a big de-linking now, and that's why we're not hearing, for example, a lot more local artists being played on Australian commercial radio. I don't know what's happened there but it's a strange, it's interesting to hear you say that there's a kind of co-operative arrangement going on there.

Well I could go on a rant about radio in Australia.

Go ahead.

No, I'll just get in trouble.

No you won't, we won't tell anyone.

I mean, Triple J is just a disaster at the end of the day. I find it very challenging to listen to because their playlist is all over the shop. But if you go back my biggest issue, and there's several I have, but if you go back to Triple J 10 years ago, when they decided they were going to support an artist they would *really* support that artist. So you might hear that artist 30, 40 times a week so you get 30, 40 spins a week. That's significant, that creates impressions. Now I think the highest spins you'll get is 16 spins a week, so high rotation on Triple J is 16 spins a week, so what is that? Two times a day, maybe three on Sunday, and 3 am and 3 pm probably and it's just not breaking new artists. So you go back to the time 10 years ago when you were looking at some of the artists that break off of Triple J—Jebediah, Killing

Heidi, Something For Kate—they were big bands, multi-platinum bands. You're not seeing that right now and that's a direct link to the fact that they're not spinning songs at the rotation that breaks bands, and so what are they doing? In my thinking they're hurting the ability for Australian bands and artists to truly succeed.

And why do you think that has happened to Triple J?

Well I mean, they're such a unique beast I can't really point to why they do what they do, but you know, one of the things is right now—I'm going to get shot for this—but they really only play stuff that *they* discover, right? And we could really just pick out some great examples, but if it doesn't come through the Unearthed program, they didn't discover it. If they didn't discover it it's not theirs and they really don't want ownership of it. So either you have to sign a band that is already on *Unearthed*, or pretend they didn't get signed and then put them into *Unearthed*, which I've done and they've then picked up and added the band and I've said "That's awesome, I signed the band because I heard them on *Triple J Unearthed*". If I have to play that game I will, because Triple J are that challenging.

And then you have a completely different scenario where they're adding six or seven things a week and they're all unknown, one spin a week from *Unearthed* stuff. Well that's sucking up a lot of playtime from other stuff they could be building bigger. It's their station, they can play whatever they want. But if their directive is to reach the youth market through Australian artists and help build Australian artists, I don't think they're reaching their directive.

Are they really youth market radio anymore?

Well that's a whole other conversation isn't it, when the hottest 100 of all time pulls up, what was it, Nirvana? I mean it is a 20 year old record, so-

Radio's changed like that. It seems to me that because Triple J is a national public broadcaster it's bound to have quirks and so forth. But you'd think that among commercial radio stations, there'd be at least one youth channel. Youth used to just feed off the popular music radio channels, whereas now you've got the TripleM station that has their audience from 1985 and seems to have just held onto them, and the same goes for most of the others as well. It seems like there's this passing parade of what-used-to-be-youth through a radio station then they get old and listen to the ABC. It's kind of become like capturing a new age demographic every 5–10 years and sticking with them until they're dead. It's a strange thing.

I can't really speak to it because I don't know what they think over there, but it's frustrating. I mean, they're really concerned about their brand and branding their station and that's all fine and good. If a record label is investing in an artist financially over time, helping develop that artist, you know, if there isn't radio for them, if you're playing alternative music, you're just not going to have a live base in Australia, Triple J has a live base. It's rare if you're doing alternative rock where you can have a live base without Triple J. So they're becoming integral to the financial success of artists. Can we break records without radio? Yeah, I think we're doing that more and more now and radio's a bit less of a gatekeeper than they were before. But you still need it to feel that real impact. You still need it to get beyond your platinum record.

I mean, they seem quite hostile in some respects towards Australian music,

You mean commercial radio?

Commercial radio, CRA I'm thinking of. You know the type of comments: they'll say "that's not our business, we're not here to break Australian music, we give the audience what they want" which is like the opposite of trend setting.

The big issue with their internet radio where Australian internet radio felt that they didn't have to have Australian music quotas, they're digital and they go global, but that was really just a ploy because we know that all digital radio's going to cross over to terrestrial soon and it's all going to be digital stations. They're going to have that precedent that they're not going to have to play Australian music. Why don't they want to? I don't really know. I think there's perhaps the feeling that their audience doesn't want it.

Well that's the constant story, that the audience doesn't want it.

But you look at the chart and I run the numbers every year and the Australian music business, just domestic artists, account for about 30–33% of the top 100 chart share every year, so the numbers disprove that theory.

During this series—this was on the nature of contracts and I'm still kind of unsure how much the A&R rep has to do with the signing of the contract and the negotiating of the contract—but we had a bit of discussion around the trend towards 360 degree contracts. Would you used or recommend them? Have you signed anyone to a 360 degree?

Yes, we're getting non-recording activities rights across almost all our deals now for local artists. The feeling is, and the reasoning is, that the record income has just shrunk but artist management still wants us to invest at the same level that we always have. The only way to keep that investment is to see other revenue streams.

So everything?

It's not so blanket as that. It's much more specific to certain things. So let's say I was looking at signing a band who had a fantastic live business. They built up that live business all on their own and I think they have a good case for me not to have any revenue off that live business. But their brand business might be zero and I'm going to help them create that brand business and I'm going to have staff working on that, So I'm going to have some revenue share if that makes sense. So yeah we're getting it, it's a new hot topic, it depends on who you ask.

So is the major label in this day and age capable of building an artist's business outside recordings?

Well yeah. We don't call ourselves a record company anymore; we call ourselves a music company and the thinking is "Well, we're doing all aspects of that. We have a merchandise division, and a brand rights division, Universal has ties with Helter Skelter, a booking agency, ties with promoters". So yeah, we're doing more of that and building an infrastructure for it, because ultimately we will all move to the streaming model.

So you don't need your full sales department any more, do you? And you don't need your physical manufacturing plants anymore, so you know, what is the team then? Well it's going to be more about helping the artist as a whole rather than historically over the past 40 or 50 years helping with just one aspect of the artist.

And do you have publishing as well? Does that come into it, or?

Well if it's the 360 model then we would share in all revenue streams, but it's not like a rights grab. Rather, we are saying that there's things we can bring to the table and hopefully help you get bigger and in return we'd like some revenue share from that. But we're investing to get to that point, so it's more symbiotic relationship than just "Hey, give us some of your publishing money".

It's an interesting trend.

You know, managers have the 360 model all the time, I mean that's what managers do, yet a manager doesn't invest financially, rarely ever invests financially, so you have to say to yourself "well if they're not investing financially but the label is, does that make no sense not to have some of the same rights that the manager might have?"

So relationships between publishers and record companies have, when platforms change there always seems to be some kind of jostling about, how do you see those relationships as having changed around sync issues, and how does that change what you do as an A&R person?

I try to work more closely with the publishers and just keep them across what I'm doing. If we're going to push a certain single, I'm reaching out to that publisher who might have the rights to say "Hey listen, this is our big push right now, can you help us focus in on this?". So it's more communication with the publishers.

Does it still make sense to have them as separate entities? I mean, in some cases you can look at publishers and think "well they're going to go more like record companies into the future and vice versa with the"

Well they're still very different businesses, you know? The publishing business is like bonds and the record business is more like stocks. It's nickel and dime in publishing but lots of them and just ticking very slowly. I've always said publishing would be a great place to go and retire. Working at a label has a different pace, it's a lot more frenzied, if you will.

I'm thinking about sync issues in particular here, and the new opportunities around sync. It seems as if someone wants to do an advertisement with something off the Checkers catalogue and they've got to go to music sales for example and say EMI or Sony and balance up, those rights seem to be costing more and more and taking more of the people's time, music placement people and such, are you finding any effects from that? Are you feeling any of that yourself?

Well, you know, we often engage independent song pluggers, not song pluggers in the publishing sense but sync pluggers, and cut them in on a percentage of stuff just to create more activity. But you know, for the most part I find the publishers pretty helpful. If we want a sync that's not going to pay very well and they don't really want to drop their rates but I think after stating "Hey listen, it's more of a promo thing for us this time", most of them will play ball.

You've had a lot to do with independent labels in your career and Island, would you consider that indie? It's pretty big.

Island UK which is the original, that's 50 years old and Island Australia which is 5 years old. Island Australia is just three people, so is it indie in that respect? Yes.

However I do have the whole Universal arm to then dip into and I have the Universal promo team, marketing team, sales, all that aspect. Could I make a case to call myself indie? I probably could but don't.

What's the role of the indie label now? I'm thinking especially of your role and of how sales are declining for number 1s. I mean is that the niche end of Universal Records or, how do they fit in? Are they still development arms or identifying new and emerging trends and stuff?

The indies are able to sometimes take something and give it 4 or 5 years to see a return on it, so they are repertoire sources for the majors, and I think a lot of the indies want the majors to help upstream their product when it comes time, because it just gets really hard and expensive to take things wider, especially when you're small indie like I was with Go Big working out of my kitchen. It was just two people.

And so at what point do you stop being an indie?

I don't know. What's the definition of major right now? Indie is such a weird term because people use it for their art and it comes with this badge of "I did it myself". I don't really think that's a valid hand wave, because if you're an artist, why do you want to spend your time doing business shit? I mean, doesn't that take away from your art? I get if you're an artist and you have to get your art to a certain audience to the next level. I think there's a myth of indie that it's some "true art", you know? So if you're an indie label you're more authentic than a major. But I think indies make more decisions due to money than the majors because they have so little of it they have to be really cautious. Whereas the majors are usually more willing to give "Hey sure, let's try this idea, it's a whacky idea but we'll try it" because they have the bigger releases to back it up.

So in signing with the major, it seems to keep coming back to this giant machine for getting stuff out to a market. Is that the one remaining advantage, or what else do you see?

Well, like we spoke about earlier, I don't think the majors will continue being powerhouses in the music business if they don't continue to develop artists and invest in A&R and the creative side of the business because it's really easy to put stuff up globally on iTunes. I think it cost like $20 to put your song up through Tunecore and you can check every box and your stuff's up globally by every digital platform in the world and you pay them $20 a year and they're very transparent in their accounting and it's a great system if you want to be independent and put your music up yourself. Where the majors can remain relevant is (1) if they're developing new artists and investing in A&R, and (2) their marketing dollars.

So what advice would you give to emerging artists who want to attract the interest of an A&R professional like yourself?

That's always a tough one, isn't it. I would say really making great music, I don't mean to sound glib, but if you're focusing on your music and you're truly making great songs and great art people will find you. If A&R people are good they'll find you subsequently. So rather than focusing on sending your stuff to A&R people or trying to get a deal, I think that's misguided. I think it's more about focusing on your art, your craft, your music. That's going to be your best calling card.

One final question from me before handing over to the audience, everyone gets this question—if you had just one piece of advice to give to our audience, what would it be?

I saw a great quote from the film director Jim Jarmusch. He's done wacky films to documentaries. He has this great quote that is "steal from everything", and I think that's a brilliant idea for artists. It just means you should really be taking from everything. From architecture to fashion to all forms of art, movies, music, and paintings and pull it all in and then create something yourself. Nothing can truly be original any more can it? Everything's been done, you know, the colour yellow's been used. So: how are you going to be original? It's by taking something that's already out there and creating it in your own way.

Thank you. Questions?

(Audience member) I just wanted to ask: with management we were basically doing everything ourselves which I thought was a hindrance to the creative side of things. We tried having a friend manage us which I don't think really worked. As a band it's sort of developed to the stage where we know the next thing we need is a proper manager to do the things we don't know how to do. How do you recommend attracting the attention of that sort of person in a city as small as Brisbane where people don't just happen to come to a show to check you out?

Sure, well you know there's, if there's somebody eager and passionate to work with your band that's probably the first requirement of manager, isn't it? It's somebody who's passionate about your music. If they're smart it's not an impossible thing to learn, it's just making contacts and learning the business. There are some great club bookers up here who probably would have great contacts with agents and labels and promoters who could become good managers if they were passionate. There's a good indie PR scene up here and some of those indie PR people could be really good managers, so maybe it's not just reaching out to a top-tier manager, but reaching out to somebody who might possibly have the passion and connections and growing with them. A lot of tour managers become managers in time because they grew with the artist and they got to know the artist, so perhaps it's searching not with the usual people in mind.

At some of the Creative Industries master classes there was discussion on the value of having an artist package that includes having a fanbase and a back catalogue of music before you approach a major record label like Universal. Would you necessarily need the same thing before you approach an A&R person?

Well, you know, I think the first thing is when you play your music, are people responding to it? Are your friends loving it and playing it on their own, are you building fans just in that really small circle? If you are then that's probably a good testament that your stuff's reacting. I mean, other than a great song and maybe a picture that's all I look for. Great song first and maybe if I love the song I'll reach out and say "Hey, you know, you got anything you could send me? A video of you guys playing in a basement, a picture?". But start with the music. If the music's great the other stuff falls in pretty quickly.

And is it sort of like an artist development thing that usually happens? I saw some reviews online and stuff, artist development doesn't happen much anymore, does it?

Well that's something a lot of managers are complaining about right now. No, for me, I have a lot of unknown baby artists on my roster who have only released an EP or building an EP. I mean it depends what your music is and what genre it's falling into. But I would think a lot of the labels do artist development because you have to, because you can't just pluck something that's awesome and already selling tons of CDs and get it for a good price and bring it into the label. You have to sometimes take the risk and then grow with that artist. There's artist development deals that labels will do, they'll say "Okay, I'll sign you to just an EP and not commit to anything further". It all depends on where you guys are at in your career.

(Audience member): I imagine it's a combination of both in most cases but if you have an artist that you're really passionate about but the contemporary market doesn't really have a niche or a following, I guess major record labels have more power to create a market behind an artist, yeah? But also I imagine major record labels would be looking for artists to fit in existing markets—what's more common in your world?

Well we certainly can't force demand. If we did then everything that we put out would be successful. I love stuff that's left of centre, that doesn't fit the mainstream. I like stuff that cuts its own path and hopefully can be the leader of a genre. Those are really hard to come by but if you do that's fantastic. Am I looking for something that sounds just like this? No, that would be really boring and I think radio would say "oh that sounds just like this, we don't want to play it", fans would say "that sounds just like this" so I look for something that feels original or different in its own original way.

(Audience member): You were talking before about the difficulties between art and commerce and how sometimes it'll be really good but it may not sell. What do you think is the major differences between something that's in your mind really good but not what would sell?

Well sometimes I'm wrong, so I might think something's amazing and nobody else does. I have an artist named Andy Bull. I think he's absolutely amazing. He's yet to really sell a lot of records and saying the name I don't see a lot of recognition in the room. So we have a long way to go obviously with Andy. He's just somebody who I totally believe in so I'm going to back and continue on a long path. But I thought he probably would have reacted and connected quicker.

So is it about trending styles and genres or image or what?

What did Ray Charles say? "Ain't no man alive who could pick a hit"? It's calculated risk, it's finding something that you truly believe in, that's the first stop. And then my job, if I truly believe in it, is convincing others in my team. I just don't make a record and then tell my team to put it out and they just go do it. I actually have to convince them. I have to sell them on the idea that this is going to work for them, so my radio person actually feels that it should be the top of her list.

(Audience member): If you have a band and you feel that you're particularly niche, say you're playing a certain genre that's particularly unpopular but you

feel that there could be an audience out there for you somewhere but perhaps you think that might be a bit difficult to get much of one in Brisbane for example, what would you recommend to someone who's in such a position?

So are you like polka death metal or something?

Oh, me? I do like, a sort of eclectic folky, gypsy, sort of thing.

Well you can reach people on the internet now globally. You're not tied to just dealing with the Australian media with your music. So find where your fans are, like we talked about earlier. if you want to make money out of your music you've got to know who your fans are and who's going to buy your music. You don't always have to make money out of your music; you might just do it because you love it and your mum likes it and that's it. I'm sure there's an audience for folky eclectic gypsy music out there, and how do you tap into that? I mean is it like, Los Lobos, Latin? You don't have to answer, I'm just saying there are a lot of artists who live in very niche markets who have careers and can be self-sufficient. I love a genre that doesn't really exist in Australia, it's called I guess alt-country, Americana, but it's country rock really basically but in the states there's a radio format for it called triple-a. I love triple-a radio and there is no triple-a radio in Australia. But now I just tune onto my favourite podcast or stream of my favourite radio station that plays that stuff or I build a playlist in last.fm and find new music that way.

(Audience member) You were speaking earlier about revenue from YouTube—are you able to elaborate on the numbers with that, like how many hits equals how many dollars?

I can tell you the scenario Universal has is through a company called Vevo. So when we upload music to YouTube we go through Vevo. It's ISRC coded and all the ads that surround, those annoying things that you have to click off of, that's creating revenue for that song and for those songwriters and for the master rights holders.

Obviously you've got a busy schedule and you've got people who come to you with music, how much time do you, do you ever go looking for music? Is there, you know, do you get much time to actually do that or is it thrown at you?

When you're making a record you start to live in demo world where you listen to 60 songs and that just takes time and when you're making a record you can't just listen to verse and chorus, you really have to dive into it. So if I'm in a record making process I'm probably listening to less new music. But you know, I probably once a week go onto *We Are Hunted* which is my favourite Spotify app, and they do the top 100 things that they think are cool and then I go to Pitchfork and they do a similar thing so I'm getting a lot of new music that way through just hitting play and then I don't have to think about it the rest of the day because it's just going. And it's actually a really interesting thing when you're listening to music while you're working and you hear a great song and you suddenly stop and you go "Wow, that was good", and it's a good indicator of what stands out.

(Audience member): What's your relationship with A&R for creative control and that process where your sub labels are concerned?

Universal is set up so those labels internally compete. So I will often go head-to-head with the Dew Process guys for an artist. Sometimes they win, sometimes I win. Same with Mercury, Modular—I'll battle with them internally, so it's interesting.

Not only do I have to fight Sony and Warner and indies on stuff, but I've got to do it internally too. But that's the culture that Universal has created globally. They want that internal competition.

PG: We've got time for one more, I think. Karl?

You spoke earlier about your responsibilities to the financial director. Do they have an effect on your job? Is there anyone else that affects your position with the band?

Yeah, I report in to the President of Australiasia for Universal. I have to submit budgets before I start albums and I have to submit budgets before I start videos, so you know, it's monitored. We spend a lot of money in local A&R so they want to know what's coming out and hopefully what's coming in. So, yeah, they're across it all. There's that aspect of it. It's not the most fun part of the job but it's the reality of it.

Chapter 6
Stuart Rubin, Global Marketing Manager

Abstract This chapter is an interview with **Stuart Rubin**. At the height of his career, he was Senior VP of Worldwide Marketing for Sony BMG. Stuart's career in music started in New Zealand in 1976 with PolyGram. He "crossed the ditch" to Australia and held a number of senior marketing roles in PolyGram and BMG before moving to Hong Kong in the 1990s where he became BMG's VP of International Marketing for the Asia-Pacific region. In 2001 he moved to New York, becoming Senior VP International for BMG. Following the merger with Sony 3 years later, Stuart was made Senior VP International of Commercial Marketing. Stuart's interview reveals a person fascinated with people, whether they are artists or music lovers. His long experience in selling music to a global market, and as an A&R professional, gives him a unique perspective on the industry. One of Stuart's unique contributions to this series is his analysis of the "prefab" phenomenon that has been a topic of discussion where the majors are concerned for years.

Welcome Stuart. Can you begin by telling us how you first came to the music industry.

I got into the music business purely by applying for a job vacancy in the New Zealand Herald. I know that sounds a bit strange, but in the 70s, certainly in New Zealand, the music industry to me was going to a record store and buying my albums. No-one understood what the music industry was all about. You just saw your artists, read magazines, saw television, and I worked for Unilever, so I used to sell soap and toothpaste and shampoo and deodorant. So I had a good background in marketing discipline in that sense, and they were looking for a national sales manager at Polygram, so I applied for the job and I walked into the Polygram offices which were surrounded by gold records.

I walked in and I went in a three piece suit because, here's good old conservative New Zealand so you're taught to go for an interview in a suit and tie, and the managing director was wearing a polo neck and his marketing manager had a safari jacket on with a double pockets and here I am in my three piece suit. So I thought I'd interview well and thought I'd love this job. This great product—I thought it would be great. Well I had three interviews and in the end I rang them and said "Look, I've had three interviews, it's been five weeks, what's going on? I mean, is it yes or no?".

P. Graham, *Music, Management, Marketing, and Law*, Music Business Research,
https://doi.org/10.1007/978-3-030-02143-6_6

They said "Well, you know there's another candidate and you know him". I said "Oh really?" and they said "Well he works for you". I asked "Well why would you employ him if he works for me? Surely if I'm his boss I'm a better candidate", and they said "Well we think you're a bit conservative because you always turn up in a suit".

So I got over that and that's how I actually got into Polygram. I was applying for a job because the government in New Zealand in 1975 had just doubled its sales tax on recorded music from 10 to 20%. So they were looking for someone who could rearrange territories, work with disciplines, and train people to sell rather than just wander in, click your fingers, and have a joint out the back when Pink Floyd's new album arrived in town. And that was a timing issue. But when I walked into Polygram's office I thought "I fit in here, this is what I really want" and I was in it from 1975 onwards.

On one of the criticisms that we've heard of the music business: Michael Smellie said during an MCA think tank event that he thought the downfall of the music business, or at least the beginning of its decline, was when music started being treated like a commodity, in other words once it became available everywhere. What do you think of that?

Look, I think it's easy in hindsight to say that. But when you're working in a consumer-driven business, which the music business is, and sales go down, everyone looks somehow to increase the sales. Now one thing's for sure, having the chain sell the top music was not a bad thing for the industry, but it's a bit like the digital business today. Do I think Woolworths ever broke an album for anybody, broke an artist? Absolutely not. But in terms of the way music was marketed on commercial TV, we spent an enormous amount of money all around the world. You needed point of purchase for that to get some return, so it's a bit of a catch-22. But Woolworths were really never interested. Same with Coles and all the chains. They were never really interested in breaking the latest Gotye, for example. That's not what we used them for, so I think you've got to look at it on balance. To be fair to Michael, who was my boss and a very good friend of mine as you know, Polygram would have never become as big as they had and U2 would never have become as big as they had if they hadn't been marketed at the middle of their career on television and had people being able to buy it when they wanted.

What I do believe, though, is that discounting music doesn't help sell more music. Good marketing does, but people will buy the album they want if it's at the price they're prepared to pay for it. Now, whether or not music is overpriced is another question and, look, I still buy a lot of music, I actually do buy it, whether it's on iTunes or whatever. I bought the new Mumford and Sons the other day so I might be old but I'm up with the play. But I think music is still overpriced. I went to JB Hi-Fi and bought a couple of jazz albums, mainstream jazz, and they were $26.99 Australian. That doesn't make any sense to me in this day and age. I just think it's way overpriced. But if people are prepared to pay for it I guess it's like anything else.

I don't know what they're buying frontline at any more but I think we've got away for a long time in the music business because it was protected here by import laws. So there were a number of factors that helped keep the price high. But retailers are going to go out of business because even iTunes, which I think is overpriced here, put Mumford and Sons at $16.99 for the full album. And yet iTunes' pricing, and I think Kate Miller-Heidke said it, is rubbish because iTunes when they started said "we're going to have a price of US$0.99" which at the time was about $1.69 Australian, and of course they haven't reduced it. So I think music is overpriced but I don't think that Woolworths ruined the business. I think certain changes have happened that don't make it available any more. And it's the digital change which, in America, is about 53% of their business and I think globally it's probably about 50%.

To me standardised pricing has always seemed anathema. I just don't understand why a Stones album isn't $200, for example, and the new emerging act's album isn't 5 bucks. But you say that discounting music doesn't make any difference.

Well I have to tell you it doesn't.

Well what is it about music that allows a standard pricing thing where all artists are the same price, basically?

Well they're not all the same price. Let's go back before digital, let's have a look at the history. We had a rather large domestic roster of people from the Goo Goo Dolls through to Farnham that was huge, obviously, and that's mainstream, to Southern Sons to Beatfish which was a combination of James Freud and Martin Plaza which we put together as a dance act. Now, if we'd reduced the price on that it would send a message to radio that we didn't have any faith in it. I was saving this for the end but you've brought me into it.

I think it's all about the music. At the end of the day it's all about the music. It's about half price Tuesday at the movies—if people want to go and see the latest film and are prepared to pay $17 or whatever it is for a ticket, it doesn't matter about half price Tuesday. They're not going to go and see a film they don't want to see. I think it's overpriced now and when I used to go to America on business I'd buy a stack of albums because they were, I don't know, $11 or something. And I think that's probably about right. We've gotten away with high pricing but I think catalogue can be sold at a different price if it's older and it's been around a long time. I think that's where iTunes haven't quite got it right. We used to have catalogue in our business, anything that was 18 months or older. Well that might not be quite right but it worked for us. It might be anything over 5 years and you can buy the tracks at, let's say half the price, and then if it's an absolute collection, if you go to buy Lester Young's Verve classic box set of the Verve recording sessions, even on iTunes that box set's about $269 Australian.

Now for a collector that probably makes sense, not digital though because you're not getting anything. If you're buying a box, you know, you've got something. When I worked for Sony in New York during the merger, we put out a coffee table book of Johnny Cash that is the most beautiful book of pictures and 8 CDs and I remember the Australian arm said "Oh, it's too expensive for Australia" and I said "Well how do you know until you've tried? I'm going to try to sell it through Visa or somewhere". So I think everything has a price. It depends on the packaging and the marketing and where you put it. But the general price of music with iTunes today I think is a bit too high.

You've worked at senior levels across almost every part of the major record label scene, manager director, artist development, international and marketing. You've also had extensive stints in film and video. But it seems you were naturally drawn to the marketing end. Is that what you like to do most or were there other factors at work? Why marketing?

Well, I'm not a finance guy, I guess. I'm not a numbers person. I had a short stint working for Kerry Packer to set up a video business in the days when I think one home in two in Australia had a VHS video recorder. It took off very quickly here and the reason I got out and went back to music is because I loved the music business. The video business is like planned obsolescence because it's already been released at the cinema. If it was a hit it worked. If it wasn't, then no-one would rent the movie. I went through an era when we could pack in B and C-grade movies because MGM would send you a package of 20 films. So you'd have Dr. Zhivago, Ben Hur, and all the classic MGM films, maybe some of the James Bond through Columbia or Universal or something from the MGM studios.

But once you got down to the other end of the package, no matter what you did, you couldn't sell it. You could put a great package out but if people didn't want to rent it you just couldn't do anything about it. Also, no film company wants to promote a video (or a DVD I should say now) because they've already paid for the promotion on the film. That's why music to me is always about trying to find and market something from the ground up. Always. Working with people in the music business, with the artists, and putting it all together for marketing, sales, promotion, in all its spheres, is fascinating. There's never any one straight answer to it. It's working with the people that really made me want to do it. And it's a passion too, it's a major hobby of mine. I can't play anything musical, by the way, nothing.

So can you talk about the different kinds of talent and intelligence and so forth that you need for being a salesperson in music versus being someone who identifies and develops talent, because you've done both those things.

I have. Look, as I said, I got into the music business at a time when it was certainly changing in New Zealand and I think was changing globally because, and I don't mean this in an unkind way to anybody that clicks their fingers and loves music, sales guys in the record business knew nothing about selling. They knew a lot about music and they'd hang out with their favourite retailers, but when the tough times came they couldn't sell anything. So I think the music business relies on a combination of disciplines, the same as any business.

But one thing it does rely on is people having a gut feel for product, which is an open envelope with music. It's not a piece of soap and it's very hard to research it, but we can talk about digital and how that's being handed now. I think it's a lot easier today because of social networks. But when I got into the business we didn't do any market research because it was very expensive and someone had to make a call on how we were going to market the new Santana album, for example, or the new Roxy Music album. It came out of a catalogue of very trendy, hip albums and suddenly we were handed this amazing album called Flesh and Blood, and the minute you put it on you thought "Hang on, this is going to go". It's an instinct. So I think you need disciplines and to find people that have disciplines but who are also passionate and have an instinct about what it is they're trying to do.

A lot of the time we hear, particularly from MD types or even production types, that you can't actually push an album; that, music is somehow impervious to the "K-Tel" style of promotion where you get free steak knives and so forth with every order.

It is. But the industry's seen a lot of changes. I think we were very fortunate to have the old school way of marketing because we controlled how the music was marketed. We'd get a single. We wouldn't even hear the album. In the 70s we'd market a single with only two or three tracks. The album would come 3 months later and you'd hold it. You wouldn't let it go to radio and radio would have no other way to get this product because nobody sent it to them. Some of the radio stations had accounts with America but we were the provider of the product to radio. So we ended up setting up the singles for the album.

We controlled the calendar. We pretty much controlled how everything happened, which is a whole lot different to today with the digital world because once it's out there, it's out there. You can't control it. It's almost like day and night. But I do think you can market it. When U2 first came out it was a very indie band. Only the people that really liked indie rock bought *Boy* and *War*. Then *Joshua Tree* came out and expanded that act into something bigger than Chris Blackwell at Island perhaps imagined. I think Chris Blackwell actually had that vision, but I think to the general public they were an indie band. But it was set up well and everyone would import it. I remember Festival Records had Island. They'd import a few, they'd put a few more in the shops, ultimately U2 became one of the big TV-marketed bands. But it was done after so many singles and video clips, and stage by stage, so I think that was a good part of our business. I'm not talking about steak knives, but it was only the hits that we created that made people like K-Tel actually, because K-Tel marketed established hits, they never broke an artist. They took compilations and mainstreamed them out of original hits.

But you take my point that there's an idea that for years pop was a manufactured thing and that people only bought what the record companies told them to.

You know I think it's interesting. I think there's a certain audience that will buy what's marketed to them. Take boy bands: they appeal to a mainstream pop audience but there's nothing wrong with that because there's always been boy bands.

The Beatles were a boy band.

Well yes, they were. But what I'm saying is that manufactured boy bands of today have been working since Bros. It's nothing new, I mean I've been involved with Take That, Westlife, of which we've sold in Asia Pacific probably three or four million copies, Take That is a phenomenon and they're quite packaged. I don't think there's anything wrong with that at all. If you think about the 50s, the songwriters Jerry Leiber and Mike Stoller, or Doc Pomus and Mort Shuman, out of the Brill Building, they almost had a formula for pop records and then they'd find singers to sing them. So it was a bit of a factory, no different to Max Martin today. So I don't think that there's anything wrong with that, but I think without the majors, and in this current day and age people slag off majors somewhat, but without the majors financing some of those independents, some of the artists we know as global superstars would never have happened.

Oh yeah, I'm not suggesting that there's anything wrong with the process, although there might be, who knows, but it's not my question. I'm asking whether it's a fallacy to say that you can set up an act and be sure of selling it in any market or is it entirely unpredictable?

I don't think it's entirely unpredictable because genres of music have a base. You can see what's gone before you in certain genres of music. Then the question becomes setup, timing, good luck, and good management all of which come into play. Now, for every boy band, for every One Direction, there's quite a few that don't make it in certain markets. We used to choose our markets quite carefully. There was a methodology at one point that said "we want to have global superstars and you will do everything we tell you to do in every market". That doesn't work, by the way.

That's the question that I'm really asking.

I got to be the head of international at Sony. Sony has a way of saying "If you don't make this happen in your market you'll be out of a job". So Sony did it very top down. Bertelsmann, being German, had this think global, act local thing. While we wanted to create global superstars we understood that some acts wouldn't work in every country, so we had to grow the markets that really believed in that act and support the act by investing money ourselves and putting our priority system in that worked or tried to make it work to help the country. So it's no good saying to Japan in a market that's 80% Japanese and 20% English, a big 20%, if you get a share of that 20% in Japan I think you've done very well. Bodyguard sold 3.5 million copies, TLC sold 2.5–3 million copies. So if you get a share of the 20 and do it right you're doing well.

But they can't handle every act that you've invested in and the one thing I loved about BMG was they had this attitude of trying to help the countries promote the artist that they felt best for their market. I think that's really important. There is always a "hit and miss" part of the music business and I think there always will be. Because if you take that out of it, and take the passion away from it, there's no music business. So no, it's not an exact science.

I also think just putting something on television and thinking it's going to work, in the days when we used to spend a fortune on TV, didn't necessarily work. We had some huge disasters. You've got to sell a lot of pieces of plastic to make money when you're putting 150 grand into television advertising. Some of them didn't work. It was a wing and a prayer on some of them. But I think it comes down to good judgement and it's a bit like the movie business. Hollywood's track record is about 2 out of 10, if I'm correct, and music over the years will be less because you have to sell less of certain genres to make it.

If you go to America there are so many new jazz and Adult Contemporary artists that we never even get here because it has a big enough touring market, it has a big enough digital market, big enough bricks and mortar support through Barnes and Noble and people like that. That's enough to support all these people that are writing some of their own music and singing some of the old jazz standards. I do a radio show so I tend to look at what the stations are playing. A lot of it doesn't even come here so you go looking for it, but every market can't sustain that. There's only so much populations can handle.

Over the years you've worked successfully with both breaking new talent to the world and selling the most established talent there is, namely Elvis who's sold somewhere between 600 million and 2.5 billion records worldwide over the years—what's the difference in the types of approaches that you have to take in those things?

Well let's go back to the Presley example. With an artist like Presley or The Beatles or even The Rolling Stones, or any of the acts that have got a track record, one thing you know is you know what the sales are and you know where they've come from so you're dealing with known numbers. Now with Presley, the reason that we worked with Presley—by the way, we bastardised Presley as a company, I'm not saying I did, but the company. It's an interesting story. When Presley died, Tom Parker sold the catalogue to RCA for a lump sum and the estate never received another cent in royalties, ever. Now I don't know how much it was for but in those—the early 70s—it wouldn't have been that much. So every time we didn't have anything to sell, RCA would put out another compilation of Elvis Presley. So there'd be the deluxe box sets or Elvis at the Movies or 20 Great Love Songs, 20 More Great Love Songs, and on and on. So when I sat down in New York and worked this out 1 year, we had 1550 different iterations of the Presley catalogue available in the world. Now The Beatles didn't do that because The Beatles controlled their catalogue. They also didn't make as many recordings, but they controlled it better. You couldn't compile a Beatles record until the 1 album came out. It was the first compilation of number ones from their various albums that came on one album.

One year I thought "We really need something big". so I went to Michael Smellie and Rolf Schmidt-Holtz who was the chairman, and I said "We don't have The Beatles but we've sold all this Presley, but the reason we're not selling a lot more is because there's too much of it around. So if you're prepared to delete most of the Presley catalogue from the world for a year and take the business hit, I think we can sell the number ones". Now Presley had more number ones on both sides of the Atlantic than The Beatles by two. Schmidt-Holtz said "Yep, I agree". So we just deleted. We went down to 50 different titles around the world but we also did market research from the UK into Presley. We knew what his earnings were in merchandise year on year. We knew what the sales were. We knew what his chart positions were because we had all that history. So we could target our marketing and ended up doing that.

I think The Beatles *1* sold about 30 something million, and to a younger audience of course, slightly younger because they'd been around less, but I think that album now of Presley has sold about 11 million. 9 to 11 million, and I have an email in my file from the boss of RCA Records in America that said "This will never work". They sold nearly four million copies of that Presley album but we also went to an outside agency and said "Look, we need a buy-line for this because we're all too close to it". I think it cost a quarter of a million US dollars to work with that agency and they came up with that line that before anyone did anything. Elvis did everything. And, by the way, the campaign worked. The commercial was the same in every country. Except for the language, everything was identical: the packaging, the date we released it, we backed every country to do a television campaign, it did them some insurance against royalty payments to put more money into TV so we gave them all a corporate royalty break and it was one of the most successful campaigns I've ever worked with. It just showed what a company can do when it's got the information.

It's very hard to do that with something new because what you need with a new artist is everyone to buy into it. You can't hammer them across the head to do something that's creative with intellectual properties that they don't believe in because that's a complete recipe for disaster. You'll have retailers full of music that no-one believes in. So you take a different approach. That's all setup, getting people to buy them, getting one or two countries to have a hit with it, and sometimes some countries even did better than the country of origin with different artists which happens quite often. For example, the biggest market for Pink the world is Australia.

ABBA was kind of the same as well initially.

ABBA, yes. Dire Straits is my best example. Dire Straits had been available to the world for years and I believe that Holland, Australia, and New Zealand had a hit with Sultans of Swing on almost the identical month. Not in the UK. America didn't quite get it because they were with Polygram and Polygram in America was a complete disaster in terms of a company up against the American labels. I remember Dire Straits played to about 28,000 people outdoors in New Zealand which was the biggest concert they'd ever done. They were doing pubs and clubs in England and then they came here. Then they broke America because I think they went to Warner—either Warner or Atlantic—in America. So they went to one of the American labels. But in this country I think they held the record at the entertainment centre in Sydney for numbers of people in a row at the time. So it doesn't necessarily follow that where you sign them is always going to be the most successful first.

You started with Polygram in 1975 and it was a completely different world. But rather than talking about the million and one things that have changed, can you tell us what the important things are to you that haven't changed in the record selling business?

Well I think it comes back down to what I said before. I absolutely believe that it's all about the music and I don't think that will ever change. But I think technology today has made it possible for anyone with a computer to make a bit of music. So I think what's happened is you've got a huge proliferation of music available through the digital world that is almost limitless. If you look back there was pop music, there was jazz, there was classics, there was country, not contemporary country, it was boots and hats country, there was no world music because people in English-speaking countries said "We're not going to play that, we're not going to play African music". All that's changed. So I think the freedom of choice has allowed this huge change in the availability of different types of music that suit different people's taste. I think the availability of music has changed an enormous since I began in the 70s.

I have a daughter who's in the movie business and I used to ask her what was playing on Triple J to give me a bit of feedback when I was in New York about what was going on. But I think even people today find it very hard to keep up with this proliferation of music. The digital age is obviously the biggest change from physical distribution and is the most significant thing that's happened in the last 5 years. Mumford and Sons last week is the highest scanning number this year of any new product released and it went to just under 600,000 in the US, which is a phenomenal amount of scans because you've been able to get a number one in America for under 10,000, which is scary. But that's because I think charts have changed because people have got this freedom of choice and also what's changed is the ability for people not to have to buy an album. We used to sell singles but we also sold albums. The last Santana album sold 28 million copies around the world and when you're part of a business that sells 28 million things it's really exciting. It's so good. It's also really good for a baby band that you suddenly have a number one single with, by the way, that maybe hasn't sold a lot but radio are playing it. Having a number one radio hit is very exciting. But I think the overwhelming choice has made a big difference in what people do and it's going to get scarier for the majors because the buyout of EMI has now been approved by Europe, so Universal, between Universal and Sony are going to own about 80% I think, roughly, 75–80% of the music assets in the recorded music world, which I think is sort of a scary thing to be looking at. Whereas there was a lot of competition when I was involved in it.

It seems to me that if I were a major I'd almost not make a new record for a little while. Given what they're managing to do with catalogue now, the amount of juice they're squeezing out of a catalogue with licensing to hundreds of digital services around the world, the massive amounts that the labels make when they re-release compilations of famous acts like Elvis and The Beatles and everything, why would you go and work hard to sign and develop a new act?

Because I think the lifeblood of a record company, whether it's an indie or a major is its new artists. Without its new artists it doesn't have a future. That's what I believe. But I think the way they do it will change. They'll probably start to work more with independents and fund independents more than the way they used to own the artist because they wouldn't want anyone else to have them. And whatever book you read, whether it's the *Hitman* or *Stiffed* about MCA, or you read the Warner Brothers story, the story of Universal, these guys were like the guys that ran countries. They had to sign and re-sign artists. They had to have Dylan. They had to keep Whitney. Sony had to keep Mariah Carey. And they paid stupid amounts of money. But on the catalogue side—what worries me about the assets is the people that are involved in the company. I'm not saying we should put in a whole lot of old people, but the people that know what's in the catalogue now are few and far between. so I'm not quite sure how they're going to manage those assets. The young people that are coming into the business, the jobs are fewer in the majors. Well, in the music business, the music business last year I think went down by about 3–4%, it's down from the mid 2000s where it was about 32, 33 billion, it's down to about 16.7 billion.

3–4 percent's not too bad.

That's only in a year.

Yeah, but the years before that it was 9% year upon year since 2002.

Yeah, but Price Waterhouse did some research in the early 2000s and said it's going to come down and by 2011 and would be at about 23 billion. Actually it's come down even further than that because what's happening is the people aren't selling the numbers of full-price albums, whether it's digital or physical. So if you're not selling a unit at, let's say the wholesale price for argument's sake is $15—and instead you're only selling a huge number of tracks at $1.69, it's very hard. Even though digital's gone up to 52%, physical's down to 48%, and the numbers of pieces are becoming less and less. Now I'm not sure how you arrest that because the future, to me, seems to be streaming. Everyone's really very excited about Spotify at the moment. I've got a lot of friends who aren't computer-savvy but they've all said to me "We really want to be part of Spotify", and you know, if I didn't want to buy music Spotify's a pretty good option to stream. But I'm very old-fashioned; I like owning my music.

I think that's common, I think the research is showing that ownership is a trump.

But if the streaming happens for a fee, ownership will change. The way streaming services relate to the sales picture is going to happen in a different model. It must because to monetize your assets under a streaming model is very different to monetizing them under a full purchase for a wholesale price. Having not worked in a major company at the moment I'm not sure how to deal with that and there's another company just opened up here called Deezer which is the French equivalent of Spotify. So I mean the question is if there's a proliferation of streaming services and you can stream on a whole lot of other services it's going to become quite interesting to see how they monetize the assets.

But the lifeblood of our music business is new artists. I mean I just think it has to be. You can't make a whole lot of movies with Dustin Hoffman any more. The business needs new film stars. And while the model changes, the lifeblood of their business is to bring on new people. I think the music business, whether it's majors and a combination of majors and indies, is very important. I think what I saw in New York in 2001 with mobile phones and computer companies is they only wanted music in principle to sell their product. I was always very aware of not giving Motorola our key acts to be loaded onto their phones unless they'd take four or five new artists with it. But they didn't want to do that. So I'm very conscious of the fact that breaking acts is still an indie or an independent or an individual or a major's role to break new artists because the hardware companies and the service providers are only going to use it to sell their services. I think we've got to be very careful about where we put our artists, and that's not anything to do with synchronising your music, which I think is great. But I think just getting a phone loaded with music, if it doesn't include some new artists, then the new artists have to struggle even harder. Just listen to someone whose life is built around their next album. They need that support from both sides and I think that's very important and I think the role of the majors will change somewhat.

I've sometimes wondered if the marketing 101 mindset by which I mean straight out "product, price, place, promotion" hasn't hurt the music business, mainly because the research basis is retrospective. In other words it's like the

difference between a new artist and the Elvis thing you were talking about before when you said you know the numbers. The actual research model is retrospective of what kind of music do you like? where do you go to listen to music? how do you pick it up? All consumer behaviour type questions. But it also assumes that there's a pre-existing market for a given product when in fact the market for a new act develops firstly through new audiences. I'm not sure audiences and markets are the same thing. They've got different names for very good reasons. And radio and TV seem also to have fallen into this same trap where they think the actual audience is their market rather than their product—for radio the audience is the commodity they sell to their advertisers who pay their bills.

It's really interesting. It's interesting because one thing I would love to be doing is running a music company, a multi-national in the digital age, because one thing you have is the social networks and you have people that know about artists before you do. We never had the benefit of that, and that's what you're saying. The old model was very simple—radio would say "a retailer's stocking that music, if they're not we won't play it. If you're not making a video clip it's obviously not very important". We had indie acts that we couldn't afford to make videos for so we had to grind out time on radio. I don't think radio is ever any different. I think they've always had minimal acceptance of new music. You always had to convince the program manager and the music director anyway. They always thought they knew better than their audience. And we used to have different ploys: we'd do competitions at retail to get people to ring up radio, just to try and move these immovable guys that were only interested in their advertisers.

None of that has changed, but the digital age is forcing a change and the other difference is on radio. If you go on the net or you tune in radio on your iPhone you can get any radio station anywhere in the world for nothing. So there is a bigger outlet for music today in that sense. This is what I thought was really interesting about Mumford and Sons: they don't dance, they don't wear designer clothing, they don't do beer commercials, they underplay and undercharge.

But they underplay to any audience and undercharge to any audience. They work and they've come from the UK to America so the market's sort of against them because UK acts have always found it quite difficult to break into America because America's got so many of its own. To do that—and that's what they're doing—and then go and sell on its first week on debut 600,000 up against Green Day's debut which was 135,000—what Mumford and Sons believe in is their audience and they're forcing it through the other way. So I think that's important. But that comes down to the other three things in the music business outside marketing 101 which are: people, partners, and processes, because the processes are working with digital, working with television, or working with advertisers to sync your music, going live, doing everything else before you've actually put that single or the four track EP up on iTunes, whichever service provider you're going to do it, or physical, it's turned around. I mean the live business today is very much more part of the business than it was. The old model was once you'd sold a lot of records your promoter would say "We've got to have so and so and we're going to pay that amount of money".

When we remarketed and licensed Geffen, MCA Geffen, when we were at BMG for a lot of money and part of the catalogue was the Neil Diamond catalogue with Hot August Night, one of the biggest selling live vinyl double-albums ever. And I said to my marketing guys "For Christmas it's about time we did an anniversary version because the people who bought it on vinyl and cassette probably haven't bought it on CD yet, so let's package it special anniversary edition, nothing extra but a slip case". It went to number one in Australia and I remember Paul Dainty ringing me up and saying "is this true or is it fixed?" and I said "Paul, we've sold 100,000 copies". Suddenly his career was reborn, but that's how promoters always do that.

Today the bands are doing their own work through social networks, so I think it's forcing a change. It needs the company to support it because these kids don't have a lot of money so they do need the support to do it. But I think that's where the people issues come in, and that's something that just fast-moving consumer goods, you know, they are what they are, you can research them, you advertise them, you get your return on investment and either the perfume's right or the packaging or it doesn't fit into your hand. That's what I learned at Unilever. And some of those disciplines apply, but it's about the people which means it's about the artists, the managers, the guys on the road, the people at the television station, the people in the press, the people at iTunes, your staff, your promotion people, to the person that answers the phone—they are all part of it and that isn't part of marketing 101 in any normal sense. And the processes through which the partners get involved make it all work.

The live scene today . . . I always used to feel that if you can't deliver your song live and you want to be a band and you've got no presence, then we shouldn't sign them unless we're a music publisher that just wanted to sign people that are great songwriters. That, by the way, is a very good vocation. To be a great songwriter and sell your songs to people and to write music for movies or for television, that's a fabulous living. I mean that's a very respectable part of our business. But I think the bands today and, as I said, the reason I go to Mumford and Sons is because I was a bit concerned they wouldn't do it twice because they were the darlings on their first, but it looks like they're going to be a really big band which I think's fabulous because I really love them, I think they're great.

You've worked through four massive phases of commodity music licensing—vinyl, cassette, CD, and into the digital era. When you look back at the transitions from one to another what strikes you as being most significant in terms of the way the industry responded to the changes?

Well I'll tell you what I saw from where I was sitting. As a marketing manager going from vinyl to cassette, that seemed to be quite an easy transition because what it did was it made music a bit more portable in a sense. You had portable radios but suddenly with Walkman and cassettes you could make your own cassette and mix tape. But I think the industry was always a little bit selfish. When CDs came, well there's a lovely story about CDs in the *Hitmen* book—if you want to read a very good book, by the way, it's a book called *The Hitmen* and it's about the industry and the giants of the industry and it's all quite true—but when the CD was invented and someone told Clive Davis who was running Arista at the time, he said "I knew they'd name a music carrier after me", and that's true story.

But when CDs came out we were scared because we thought no-one will pay the price for this new manufacture just because, at the time, it was a sterile process, it was brand new, and Philips invented it. They had to have glass masters and it was a very different process. I think the business has always been a bit scared to change. To be fair about our business, we always wanted to protect the levels of income and the margins. They were always resistant to change, and I think the Americans were always very resistant. If you read any book about the business of the presidents of the big companies, they were always quite resistant because they were looking at how it was going to affect them.

I got to New York in 2001 when the Napster crisis erupted and I'm not a technocrat so I didn't understand it. I knew how to use a computer but I don't think anyone in the industry realised how quickly the digital download business and digital transmission and the internet were going to affect things. I also think again they were a bit greedy because it became a legal battle about who gets what, how do you copy-protect it. They understood that copying was going to be very easy. With Napster they understood the file sharing issues but it became an inside argument between the industries so I think my answer there is I think they've always been a bit resistant to change and to new carriers from what I've seen having worked in the business for 35 years.

And it seems to have been the deal the whole way through.

It seems to be their paradigm and history's going to show that had they reacted in 2001 quicker, and I'm not saying I'm smart, but had the industry reacted to Napster in a better way, iTunes today may not have 95% of the retail digital download market. One thing we know is Kieran Fanning understood that people wanted to share music. Now admittedly he wasn't paying royalties. But that can be fixed. Instead of suing him, if they'd adopted that software and brought him on side, there might be two or three global digital stores with some competition. But it's going to be very hard to peg back iTunes from its 95% on purchased digital. I'm not talking about streaming, and I know the chairman of Bertelsmann at the time bought the software off Napster because he said "we can use this software" but I don't actually think it's ever been used because Thomas Middelhoff left the company and I'm not sure what happened to it then.

It's out again now as a legal service.

Yeah, but the lawyers had really made a meal of file sharing. We went through copy protection that we put on all our discs and they stuck it in CD players and somebody said "Look, if it screws up a car stereo or a computer there's going to be a public liability suit against the company". So they dropped copy protection because no-one had come up with a foolproof way to do it. Also, I'm not a lawyer, but there's also the argument that says that if I buy a CD and I want to make a copy to play in the bedroom I don't think that's an issue in the business. Look, I used to make—arrest me—I used to make copies of my albums for my friends that didn't buy albums on cassette. Did that stop us from selling hundreds of thousands of copies? No. I think the piracy issue's a different issue to that and I think the American lawyers suddenly worked that out because if you make the copy on your computer on iTunes, you get a little window that comes up saying "you're allowed to make five".

I think that's fair and reasonable. But to actually say you can't make just one copy for another room of something you purchased, it's yours, and I'm a great believer in protecting people's talent and intellectual copyright but the pirates forget that someone's made hardware, someone's copied it. I remember the blank tape business was enormous for Phillips. The retailers would give away a blank tape with a cassette album with a so you could make a copy for a friend. It wasn't legal. That's sort of entertaining piracy, that's how blank tapes, the Japanese and Koreans made a fortune out of blank cassette tapes, but then CD of course changed that because it was initially very hard to copy a CD.

Viewed in one way the internet should have made things really easy for the majors, if you take the book club model or some such. How did you guys not see the opportunity?

Well the book club model's interesting because when I worked for Polygram we had a record club. We were constantly arguing with our retailers because they wanted protection against the mail in the sense that they'd thought it was taking their business away from them. Now the contracts, we had to get permission from the artist, I think it was a 3 month window minimum so you couldn't put any product in a direct mail club until 3 months past the retail date anyway. Now we used to extend it by six. In my experience sales through record clubs never affected retail sales at all. When I was in New York BMG owned www.getmusic.com. We owned it. We weren't selling CDs on the internet in 2002 because nobody anywhere in the world wanted to upset the retailers. No-one spoke to the retailers about setting up a business and sharing it with them. We didn't use it. We sold it to Universal. So Universal, who now have 50% of the global music business, have the best URL, getmusic.com, that anyone could ever have. But we didn't use it.

We were very slow. We let Barnes and Nobel and Amazon and all these people get into it and I remember at the time going to lawyers and talking to Sony, Epic, and our own label saying "why don't we just do a trial?" I mean I understood that we had this thing that we could sell, if someone went to Phil Graham's site, you're our artist, got all the information, why couldn't they press a button and buy your CD? Why? There was no logic in it except we were scared of the bricks and mortar retailers. But as I said, no-one tried to build a hybrid with them and in the end it's happened anyway, and it's just happened a lot quicker and I think it's happened the wrong way because it's destroyed the specialist retailers whose businesses we could have helped build, actually. They could have been our sub-agents because we didn't want to process the money but we could have directed it to them. But they all said they didn't want it because they wanted to keep their own size. I really think no-one understood in 2001 to 2004 how quickly this whole digital business was going to change the world we're in. I don't think anyone really realised it, to be honest.

You work with lots of really high profile, global acts, and I'd just be really fascinated to know how the process goes with the campaign for someone like Pink. How much does the act get involved, what kind of say do they have in

terms of how things are presented, and where they're going? How does this all happen?

I'm not being flippant, but any artist should have and does have a major say on how they're promoted. Now, the record companies may not always agree to start with, but if you don't have an artist that's going to buy into the way you're going to treat that artist with your blessing you have a problem. Without a doubt a happy artist, happy manager, and they're always going to want something, but it's any business partner and you're dealing with people again, and creative issues, so it's vital. There's no way around not having them on side. No sense taking them to Japan to do a promotional tour if they don't want to do it because they're going to piss the Japanese off and then everyone's unhappy.

Walk us through the process, you've got something new for Pink happening, what happens?

That started based on the fact that once we got past the video clip business and what started to happen was promotional tours, because in the 80s you had a lot of people who could perform with backing tracks. So if you just think through it: in the heyday of The Beatles or The Stones, you'd never get Jagger in Australia or New Zealand doing a full performance, right, unless they had the whole band in the studio and it was rehearsed and everything. Then in the 80s, technology changed and a lot of these people would sing to track, as we've heard, because people went to concerts and they actually thought they were doing a terrible job so the promotional tour was born and we thought "okay, we could bring Take That", or a band which were not very big here, Westlife. "Bring them out, we can take them out to Australia's Wonderland, we can bring all the fans from radio, from the magazines that have won competitions, they can perform four songs to track without any instruments, that's what we do". So the promotional tour was born and that's why I think you've seen more artists coming out more regularly to do pre-promotion of their new material.

Now I don't know if Pink performed on this particular tour but that is an inherent part of setting it up because the people here want to see her, the media want to see her, they want to have their own pictures, and it's become very established because this is her market. On the other hand it's also quite difficult to do promotional tours for a lot of these artists because the promotional tours before you've sold anything cost an enormous amount of money. So you've got to be sure you're going to get the right TV shows, the right magazines, the right press, and that the artist is up for doing it. But it's a very important part of the marketing campaign. Also you do teleconferencing today, and because of the whole satellite thing it's a whole lot easier to do it from a studio into different countries. But promotional tours became part and parcel of our priorities system—if the artist wasn't available to do pre-promotion in certain key markets that wanted them we wouldn't make it a priority in those countries.

So how does the artist get involved, I mean at what point do you have to discuss it with management to say "they want to do this"?

You do it when you know the album is going to be released, theoretically, which is a moving date mostly. You'd sit down and say "Well, okay, that's the rough date, these are the countries we're going to need you to go to so in your plan for live performances we need you to think about these are the countries we're going to need you in and these are the dates". So the planning process starts probably a year out, at least.

And how about imagery and setup and style, look, campaign?

Well it's not an exact business. If you look at the Japanese, their lead times were the longest in the world and sometimes we wouldn't have an image that was suitable for Japan until a month out. Part of the business, part of the excitement of the business, is working with great deadlines. Digital today makes it a lot easier because you can send a digital image and it can be released to everyone with the press of a button, so it's changed it a bit, but it's not exact. Normally with a major artist you'd be talking about a year out, at least. When the new Foo Fighters album comes out they'll know exactly where they're going, how many interviews they're going to do, probably 6–9 months before that album or the single's even released.

What's a typical relationship between marketing and A&R in a label?

I know why you ask that question. We've got an A&R man sitting up there. I know, Mike's listening carefully to this. You know, artists and repertoire, obviously it's one of the key parts of the company because they talent scout. Can we call them talent scouts? But again that's an instinct, that's not something you can learn. Now I worked for two Dutch-German companies. Polygram was Dutch-German and German companies. I went to a key management course once and they had a guy that came from Munich who said "We can solve the whole thing for the next financial year, we'll set up a university for A&R people!" No, you can't do that. It's an instinct. A person who plays a guitar is born to play a guitar. You can learn to play a guitar but Clapton was born to play. That's in him. Jagger's performance was always Jagger, he didn't learn to do it. He may have perfected it, but it's something that's in him. Same with a good A&R person. It's about instinct.

What they need to do is not just have the instinct, they also have to understand artists, the trends, where the world's going, and that's the key, in my opinion. I always thought Chris Blackwell who brought reggae to the world went out on a limb when he signed Bob Marleyand Marley became a worldwide superstar. U2: Chris Blackwell signed them as well. The guys at Chrysalis, Terry Ellis and—I can't remember his partner—but Chrysalis was a boutique label. I always thought Herb Alpert and Jerry Moss who started A&M on the back of a garage band that played mariachi brass understood what the public were going to do and what was going to work.

But does the A&R person talk to marketing when they say "we want to sign these guys, what do you think?"?

Yes, of course they do. And that's where there's always a conflict. Because the A&R guys will always think they're right. Marketing will always think they're right. But the guy who always thinks they're right is the salesman because salespeople rely on fixed results and bonuses and so they never want to be wrong. They will always take the line of least resistance. What I found in my companies was that I'd sit the A&R guy down, they'd do a full presentation and give us samples and let everyone live with it, then come up with how they thought they should be packaged. We'd go and see the band, or if it wasn't a working band, go and meet the guys, talk to them so I'd encourage that to happen and then we'd sit down. Again it's about belief and passion because someone has to drive it through. But you can't have any one person just saying no.

When I joined BMG, the reason I got into BMG in Australia, is because RCA had just been bought by Bertelsmann and it was an old man's company. It relied mostly on Lionel Richie and they had Motown at the time and they didn't break any artists here at all. I got this job and the boss at the time said "It's not really what you want to do but we'll bring you in as the product development manager". Then I found out that the Germans had told him to do that. Not me specifically, but find someone, and it's about managing people and ideas and passion. If you're paying an A&R guy, they're only as good as the last act that works, but you have to rely on their judgement, that's why they're in that job and if marketing have some issues to polish off some corners or say "We don't think the cover's right, talk to the artist". Now some artists are impossible to talk to, by the way. They're only one person and they would only talk to the A&R guy so you'd have to send smoke messages around.

I always had a policy of making sure that any artist we signed I knew, and I'd make sure I'd had dinner with them, they'd been to my house, I'd sat and talked to them so we had an understanding of our cultures and where we wanted to go and I'd always say "Well what's your vision? Where do you want to go? Is it something I can deliver for you, do I agree? Do I not agree? What do you think about this?" You have to do that. But at the end of the day there will always be some conflict in a creative business and I think that's good for the company.

But someone had to make a decision and that's your A&R guy. Take Rick Reuben who started Def Jam with Russell Simmons. Now Rick Reuben's a great A&R guy, partly myth, partly real. Rick Reuben's first signing was a rock act. In the last couple of years Sony signed him to be the boss of one of the labels—a disaster. He's not a marketing manager or a company manager; he works with artists. He rebuilt Diamond's career and Johnny Cash's career. The American recordings are some of the finest tracks Johnny Cash ever made. They're beautiful albums. But I think you've got to find the balance and to my mind that's what good A&R guys are there to do: they're there to sit with artists 24/7 and nurture them to a point where you can take them and market them and sell them. But you've all got to be a part of that culture. You can't do it in isolation because that's a recipe for disaster.

Who are the best, meaning easiest, and the worst, meaning most difficult, artists you've had to deal with in terms of your job?

Look, every artist is a human being and some of them are made worse by their managers because they have people that run after them and make life difficult for everybody to justify them being there. I think probably the most difficult that I worked with was Whitney in terms of being on a pedestal and being part of a cocoon. She was such a diva that you couldn't talk to her. Very difficult to get her to do any promotion, talk to any of the companies, just difficult. Talented but difficult.

I found most of them at the end of the day really, really easy. If you take care of business you'll get on with your artist. They want to sell records and be famous. And people like Elton John were very easy, eccentric but really easy. If you were selling records and had their albums in the charts while they're on tour and looked after their business, no problem. I mean they'd take you out to dinner. I've had some funny times. Touring with KISS for seven days was pretty bizarre because they only wear makeup when they're on stage so you're sort of in a cocoon for seven days because no-one knows who they are except them. But I can't tell stories out of school.

But you treat an artist as you'd want to be treated yourself and deal with their eccentricities, and remember it's a business. At the end of the day it's a business and they're the stars. They want to be successful and you've got to do your very best. If it's the best you can do and it doesn't work and you're honest with them, that's usually okay too. I remember Barry Manilow being in Hong Kong selling out two concerts, 20,000 people, Chinese audience but the new albums that he did didn't sell and he asked me "Well why didn't they sell?" and I said "Because it's not what the people want. They want to hear you sing Mandy and Copacabana because that's what they buy". He said "No-one's ever been honest with me, they come up with all these stories about why my new albums aren't selling but you're telling me it's about the music?". I said "Yeah, it's about the music Barry, it's purely about the music. You've got a core audience that love what you do live but they're not really interested in your new music because they've gone away from whatever you've done". I've still, to this day, got a good relationship with Barry and his manager. In fact we're trying to find a way to bring them here because they've just done these huge concerts in the UK and we're trying to find a way to resurrect some of the packaging and do it. But of course I have to say that Sony's not really interested because they just don't think all that stuff works any more, so we're not quite sure how we do it.

Coming back from the top end of town, we've got a lot of hopeful young artists here, if you're starting out a musician today how would you go about selling yourself? Building an audience, making a living?

I had a young guy come to me and we sat down for about an hour and a half and he said "Can you help me market my music?" and I said "Well, I'll have a listen to it". I mean I'm not an A&R guy, but I said "Well let's put the music aside just there for a minute. How often do you perform? Have you seen any publishers? How big's your social network? Have you got a website? Who have you talked to? Have you talked to any press? Have you talked to any TV? do you need some names?" My advice is you need to talk to everyone that's anyone and everyone that's involved in the business you want to be in to get a sense of whatever it is you need to bring together first. You need a lot of courage because everyone's going to get knockbacks in the music business. I think what you need to be as a new artist is very strong. You've got to have real strength of character and you need to draw today from all the elements because there are more elements today than you can draw from. It's not just live, you can draw from the internet, you can social network, you can build a little community, and before you put your music out there you need to at least make a judgement of all the elements and understand what it is you want to achieve and who you're going to sell to.

But first and for most is ask a whole lot of questions of people in the industry. People will talk to you. Media will talk to you, radio will talk to you, internet radio will talk to you, community radio's good value. FBI and their equivalent in Queensland, you've been to seminars where you have access to the right people but most people in our industry are very happy, generally, to try to give you positive feedback and I think that's where you need to start. Just to walk in to someone and say "Look, here's my music" unless you're a child prodigy is really difficult. And again, I come back to the fact you have to pay your dues in the business. Not because I've done it in terms of being a musician, but if it doesn't happen, or if something's a one hit wonder—I've got cupboards of great albums that never sold—there's nothing wrong with the music but there might be some other element missing. So if I was a young musician I would certainly talk to my peers. Other musicians can give really good feedback I've found. They're not always easy to get to but you can get to them and certainly people in the industry are very important before you make that first step. But you've got to be of a very strong character as an artist because you've got to fine tune it and fine tune it and fine tune it whether it's a manager or a song or whatever.

You need to find a good manager ultimately, not initially. I've always thought there's no point in paying out a lot of money to someone until you're ready and you don't have the time to manage yourself. So you need to lay a very strong platform by finding out. Talk to managers by all means, say "Look, this is what I want to do, what would you suggest? But look, it's a very tough business. It's like actors. Everyone's an actor today. It's a tough business. It's really really difficult, and I think strength of character and asking questions of all people before you jump off is important. I certainly wouldn't put my music free up on any website. I just wouldn't do that, because if you put it up free and it doesn't work, what do you do next? There is a temptation to put stuff up on a site. But until you're really ready and you've got the packaging and your little community and some feedback and some gigs lined up or press lined up and radio and or, I would hold my treasured possession which is my intellectual copyrights, until I'm really ready and I've fine-tuned it. You might listen to everyone's opinions and say "I don't agree, I'm going to give it a shot". I think that's also great, but you've got to at least get that feedback first and I think it's an industry where you can get it and it doesn't necessarily cost you money because people love to see success in our business.

If you were running the worldwide marketing for Sony BMG today and I know it's only been a few years and things have changed radically since what, 2007 was about when you stopped so about 5 years. If you were doing it today how would you approach the issue of streaming? It seems to me that there's almost no opportunity to intervene in the way those platforms work because the deal between the major and the streaming platform is separate to the deal between the streaming and the audience.

When I got that question I started to shake because I'm not very technical, but I understand streaming. To me, and I might be wrong and people in the audience might have another opinion, streaming is almost like a wholesaler. If you look at it in the new way of distribution you either buy something or have it on loan, are we talking the same thing?

Well I just think the streaming listener has every kind of music, every catalogue available to them in theory and they press go and they might so

"oh, today I might just let it run and see what it throws up to me" whereas the tradition in the old school model was, as you said before, you had control over what people could get access to, it was very piecemeal in terms of what was let out.

Well it wasn't piecemeal, it was an organised release schedule based on the music, if you like, or the artist we had available. But today a lot of the streaming is not just artists that are signed. There's a lot of streaming of unsigned artists so I don't think if I was a major I would try and organise my artists. It's all about how much, whatever the contract is, but at least if it's being streamed legally somebody's getting something back for it, right?

But if you want to promote something in that environment, how would you do it?

I've just got onto Spotify myself and I just figure it's quite good in the sense that you can get a radio station of your own from the artist you like and you can share people to say "Look, I've just added this to my Spotify list" which I think is all that's helping. But I don't know that because of the change in distribution you have a choice—you have to be in it. I mean, what are Universal going to do? Not allow all that stuff to be streamed? And I think, someone can help me here, I think there's AC/DC still aren't available on iTunes. I think Led Zeppelin have finally allowed their catalogue to go on iTunes.

That was recent, yep.

I think AC/DC still don't which is quite interesting because to me in this age, I know they want to sell albums, but in this age when anyone can hack into anything, I just think that doesn't make any sense any more, to me. It doesn't make intellectual sense to me because they've sold millions. Surely they're better off to get something and people buy their favourite tracks than get nothing and run the risk of people just pirating files. So I think the streaming thing to me, my understanding is they're the same as movies, people are going to start streaming movies in every month for a package fee because you don't need to pay Foxtel and they can watch them over a month whenever they want and they don't want to buy them any more. There'll always be some people that will buy them, but if it was my company I'd make sure I was on the best streaming deals I could get for my artists. I see it as part of a very important distribution mix to a forever-hungry audience that's out there. As long as it's a legitimate, well-organised service, which I think Spotify has proven that they are. Well, up to a point it's very professional, I mean it's a good site, it's quite easy to manoeuvre through. I think iTunes is quite difficult sometimes, by the way. I can tell you they don't get their genres of music right, they absolutely don't. Someone just says "what's this? It's gospel" No! But anyway, that's another discussion.

One of the old advertising sayings is "we know that only half our advertising works but we don't know which half", it's an old adage, how true's that for recorded music when you're promoting it?

You know, it's a good question and I think it's true still to a degree, even with all the sophisticated market research of general advertising today. One thing we used to do, and I've noticed there are a few albums still on television, but the ability for us to do a marketing campaign, say, with three single grabs off an album that we'd normally feature in that TV commercial. We knew that people had already bought the singles so we were just highlighting to people that hadn't bought them that these singles featured on the album, so I think that was good. I always remember arguing with people saying "Well we're going to buy this spot on Channel 9" and me saying "But those people aren't going to buy Santana, they're not going to buy The Foo Fighters". "But this is a highly rating spot". I said "I know but my gut tells me that they're not". So I still think with advertising that there will always be an element of some of it being wasted, but I think less of it's wasted today because their research is far better, their numbers they get on programs. But it comes down to if you want to market a new range of high-class perfume or clothing or whatever it is, you can do your research but then the person that's created it, that has a feel for that range, knows their audience maybe better than some of the research numbers. But that's the human element and that's what I loved about music. There's always a little bit of a challenge. You could get to some of them but how you finally finished off that campaign and saw stuff get out of the shops there was always a gut feeling, in my opinion. Always.

We're down to our last question Stuart. If you were allowed just one piece of advice for aspiring artists in our audience, what would it be?

I've talked about character, which I think's really important, but my underlying success and my belief is my passion. Now I know that sounds very airy fairy, but it's true. You have your disciplines, but if you're not passionate about something you won't drive the disciplines over and above the hurdles that you come to. It's about having a sense of character in a business that's not exact. Now you talk about leadership, you can talk about reality, I think reality's important. But to be involved in the creative process, you need to be totally passionate about it. Because if you're the only person that knows because you created that piece of music, you've got to convince the people that are backing you that you really believe in it. If they knock you back they're really saying: "Well he just doesn't really believe in it". So my advice about the music business, the entertainment business, is to be passionate, absolutely madly passionate about everything you do. Now you can be a bit wrong, but people can deal with passion and anyone in the music business that can't deal with that passion doesn't actually survive in the end. And all the artists, they're eccentric but they're passionate. If you write a piece of music and you've got to convince someone, the only way you're going to do it is because you're absolutely passionate about it.

It's an odd thing that it seems to me that a lot of the success that people had that I saw when we were dealing with younger artists in Sydney had to do with their belief in themselves way over and above their talent if you know what I mean.

But you know I think, I'm a frustrated air guitarist, right, I wish that my parents had made me play an instrument, I really do. But I think the passion goes without saying. At the end of the day there's got to be a touch of reality. But as I said before you've got to have character because you're going to get knocked back. Now we all hear stories about these arrogant people that, regardless of what anyone ever says, don't change anything. At the end of the day very few of them actually get through.

But I think all performers have a touch of arrogance, it might manifest itself in a different way, and in people that are young—I had this instance the other day being on the board of a community radio station, young guy, we put him on nights. He's got a great voice but he started saying too many four letter words on a community radio station and he happens to be an Eastern Suburbs Jewish kid so he's a bit cocky and a bit arrogant, so I had to sit him down and he said "Yeah but I want to". I said "Look, you just have to tone it down a bit. Don't lose your passion but just tone it down". I always hear people say "You've done this and you've done that and I want you to talk about it". I'm always scared that it comes across as being a bit arrogant but there's a lot of it in our business and I think you can tinge arrogance with a little bit of softness sometimes to be honest. Elton John, can he be arrogant? Of course, but he's also eccentric. So I think it comes and goes but it's about being real, it's about having a bit of reality to it.

Okay, thanks Stuart. I'm going to turn over to questions from the audience now.

Audience member: If musicians have the opportunity to do marketing courses do you recommend us taking that opportunity because it would give us an understanding of how to market our product?

Absolutely, I think that absolutely yes, I teach an undergrad course at the Australian Institute of Music in Sydney and the class this semester is 20. I do International Business with Marketing to help them with different cultures, how to do contracts, just general global marketing management, and half of them are performance students. So I would say if you get the opportunity absolutely yes. It will help you immeasurably.

Audience member: You were talking about the priority sort of system you were using in Germany, I was just wondering what that system was and how did you work with it?

That's a very good question. With the company we had so many different artists, new artists, brand new albums no-one had ever heard of. For example when Pink was new or Avril Lavigne, no-one had heard of them, so we had to work out how do we break this artist. Then you have artists who are onto their second or third albums. Then you have The Eurhythmics or Elvis Presley and they have decades of history. We had to work out where to go, rather than every company in every market, because not every market's as big in America. In America you have a label system. So within BMG and Sony you had Epic Records, Columbia Records, you had a classical label, you had Nashville, you had Alistair Records, you had J Records, you had RCA so all these people exist in America as individual businesses putting into the world four or five albums every month. If you multiply that into Australia you've got to handle 60 records, 60 products. So what we came up with was the priority system, which wasn't fool proof. What it meant was that a release had to at least have been successful in one or two major markets in the world, a new artist had to be available to do promotion in a market that wanted to bring them in, the artist and the label had to be prepared to invest airfares to get them to a country, to physically get them there to pre-promote, and the country also had to be prepared to back it and put some money in. Now, that was on a new act—an existing act was a little more easy because if it's been successful more people will buy into it and then the catalogue side you've already got some information so that becomes almost like a top-down project on maybe on a year. It wasn't foolproof but it was one way of managing our resources a little better than having everyone do something different all at a different time without planning when we were going to have Pink, when we were going to have the Foos come in and do some promotion, or when we were going to have whoever it may have been at the time, Alicia Keys or whoever.

Uh, you were saying before Stuart that you couldn't learn A&R at a university it's more of a talent or an instinct. If that's the case how would you get involved in A&R? What would employers be looking for?

Well, you know, most artist and repertoire people—and look, I don't know the history of A&R, but let's go back to the 30s and 40s, Ira and George Gershwin were song writers, Cole Porter was a song writer, Jerry Leiber and Mike Stoller were song writers. They used to write songs because they just wrote songs and they'd sell them to an artist. So if you like they were A&R people and they'd find the right artist and then they'd produce it. That morphed into people being talent scouts and hanging out with the artist at night, exercising their instinct. They might have been musicians, most A&R guys I've met were musicians, not of necessarily of note, but they knew their way around clubs and they had an instinct for what people liked. If you look at the very successful people in the hip hop era like Puffy, Russel Simmons, or you look at Chris Blackwell at Island, or you look at Clive Davis or Ahmed Ertegun, if you can get hold of a DVD called *The House That Ahmed Built*, which is the Atlatic Records story, he's a guy whose father was Kemal Atatürk's ambassador to the United Nations in the USA. A very privileged guy that decided to skip school in New York and go and hang out in clubs in Harlem. For a white guy to do that and go visit black record stores in the 50s was unheard of. He was the first person to sign a black artist to a record label, which was Atlantic Records, Atlantic Jazz. He didn't have a background in music at all. He was a very privileged guy but he had an instinct and he knew what the people he thought would want and it proved to be correct. The artists adored him because he gave the artists space so I think that something was in him. That was him and it manifested itself through the company as the company got bigger.

I don't think you could learn to have that sort of instinct at a university. You might fine tune your skills in managing people, but either you've got a lot of feeling for music or you don't. What did the great movie makers have, the guys that set up Warner Brothers, that made MGM Studios? If you read the books about those guys, they were refugees from Eastern Europe who used to make fur coats. But they understood that if they could make something move on this Edison moving picture thing when Edison created the movie projector they built these massive studios. Sam Goldwin, Jack Warner and his brothers, Louis B. Mayer, they'd built these massive star systems based on the fact that they had a gut feeling for what people would go and see. Now it's changed a lot. They still have studios but it's more independent. But, if you like, they were the A&R guys of the film business and I think that's something that's inherent in a person. If you give me something, I think I can market it with my skills and my feel for it but I don't know if I'm the right guy to find the trend in the next lot of music. I think it needs people in this audience to do that. A

65 year old's not going to tell you what the next trend in music's going to be. I just don't think we can do that.

Audience member: In terms of proving, if you weren't already working for a record label, how could you prove your worth as an A&R person? Would you network, try to connect with a label?

I absolutely would. These people are always looking for the next big act, you've got to remember that. That's what they want, that's where the money is. At the end of the day one big act will help grow a lot of small acts, so it helps the balance. So connecting, and if that's what you think your skills are you should make yourself known. And by the way, it may take one or two artists to prove it, but that's how it is. Clive Davis sitting at the top of the record company doesn't go to every nightclub across 50 states of America. He has people feeding into him and the ones that step up step up and say "Clive, what do you think?", that's how he finds them. It's impossible to go and research all the artists. But I think today with social networks it's a lot easier to find a thread of new artists, whether it's through YouTube or Spotify or whatever. Lots of things happen through YouTube that may make someone at a record company, whether it's an indie or a major, go and look at it. If you can be the catalyst you can be the next artist and repertoire person. But I think that's an instinct. A university won't teach you how to tell what the next trend is. It will help your disciplines to grow your business but creative people have an instinct—authors have instincts, musicians have instincts, film stars: "I want to do it this way". Directors have instincts, but's that my opinion, by the way, only my opinion.

I was wondering if you were able to give any hints on how to create or grow a trend or a market for culturally different music?

I think marketing people will look at someone that brings that, particularly in the music business. Like hip-hop, and I can use this as an example. Clive Davis introduced, and I don't know what his name is these days but last time I looked it was Puffy, but he introduced Sean Coombs to us as the hot shot hip-hop producer with Bad Boy Records. We couldn't get arrested around the world with hip-hop and American hardcore hip-hop is very hard to sell outside of its culture. But as things have turned out that trend has grown as more and more people have become involved and there's a bigger audience and so other countries have got onto it. But then they've made their own form of it. Has anyone seen Gangnam Style from the Koreans?

Who hasn't?

Now we had a very successful company in Korea. In the day, we couldn't get arrested in America with any Korean music at all, even pop because K-pop hadn't quite happened. J-pop was very big. But the Japanese being Japanese didn't want any of their music sold in America because they were scared it was going to be made cheaper and the discs flow back into Japan. Very Japanese: we want you to sell it but we won't give you the license. Whereas the Koreans did it the other way around, so K-pop's success has come out of the distribution, because it's visual and it's quite quirky and unique. How long it's going to go for I don't know, but I think any trend from any marketer depends on the time in which you get onto it, whether it's fashion business. There was a time when we had these big caterpillar boots that had sort of a yellow suede. Reeboks, everyone wanted white running shoes that these South Africans made that were white with the union jack on them. Reebok suddenly started this huge trend in people wearing athletic shoes with suits, so I think a good marketer—someone creates it. The creative business creates it but a good marketer knows where and when to get onto it, and if you're lucky and have good timing, you'll do it the right way. Some trends had been missed, of course, but I think it depends on the whole system coming together to do it.

Chapter 7
Shane Simpson, Music Lawyer

Abstract This chapter is an interview with Shane Simpson (AM), Australia's best-known copyright lawyer. He set up his practice in 1986 and has since acted from many of the leading artists in Australia and elsewhere. He began his career in more conventional areas of the law, coming to the bar in New Zealand in 1973, in New South Wales in 1978, and stepping down in 1986 to pursue his work in the arts. While he is perhaps best known for his work in the music business, Shane's experience and influence extends far beyond. His first work in copyright, and an enduring area of personal interest, was in visual arts. He has extended that work into areas such as museum law, media law, information technology law, and of course music. His contributions to the Arts in general include the establishment of Australia's first Arts Law Centre, a free service for artists who could not otherwise afford legal advice. The most striking aspect of Shane's interview is the historical depth and detail of his legal and business knowledge.

Welcome Shane. You've clearly got a passion for the arts and the establishment of the Arts Law Centre attests to that, it's a wonderful institution. Can you give our audience some background about your personal and professional journey into copyright law?

Yes, I'm an immigrant and I always tell people that because clearly it's a large political issue in our community. I came here when I was 23 as a piano player from New Zealand, and then there was a series of serendipitous, happenstance things. I ended up teaching law at the University of New South Wales from when I was 23 to 30. Then I decided I'd go to the bar, and I think it's an interesting lesson to hear people say, at this stage of my career, that one of the bravest things I did in my career was to leave the bar: I found that I was very good at being a barrister, I was making stacks of money—and I was deeply unhappy. So I decided to stop legal practice. I sold my chambers and I packed all my things up. I went back to New Zealand without a clue as to what I was going to do. For 6 months I sat on my arse and got quite depressed. One thing I would say to people who don't know what they want to do is, "Panic not, but be prepared for the loneliness of not knowing".

It was only because I took that time out, went through that process, that I had lunch with my parents who had invited an artist friend along. He'd just been stiffed

P. Graham, *Music, Management, Marketing, and Law*, Music Business Research,
https://doi.org/10.1007/978-3-030-02143-6_7

by his gallery and I went into barrister mode and told him what he should do to fix the situation. Eventually he looked at me and said, "That's just a load of crap. You don't know anything about what I do and you don't know anything about my gallery". So after I'd picked my ego off the floor, I thought about it afterwards and I realised that I didn't—he was right. It was very pretentious of me as a lawyer to think that I could be telling somebody what to do without understanding their business. So that was an important lesson for me. But then because I'd really spent the last 8 or 9 years of my life as an academic I thought, "Well, the only way I can really find out anything is to write a book on it". If you don't know anything write a book.

So I applied to the Queen Elizabeth Arts Council in New Zealand for a grant to write a book on visual artists and the law. They thought the idea was great but they didn't have any money. So I thought there's nothing to lose. I'll send the same letter off to the Australia Council, and lo and behold they came back and said, "We've been waiting for somebody for years to write this book, we'd love to support it".

I spent time in New York and London and Paris where lawyers actually worked with visual artists, which is where my focus was. But during that time what became clear to me that there was no point in raising the awareness and level of education of the artists, which was my focus, if you didn't have other things which also support that. For example, if the lawyers didn't understand the art business, you also had to teach lawyers. Then you had to be able to provide a link between the artists and the lawyers at a price that they could afford, which was essentially nothing, and that was where the idea for the Arts Law Centre came from: it started as a concept in visual arts but became arts across the board.

I came back to Australia, sold my apartment and lived off the money I made out of the apartment, while I lobbied and, in 2 years, got the Arts Law Centre up. I did that for 3 years and when that was firmly established and happening then I set up my own practise—with no clients.

And can you tell us a little bit about your first forays into the record industry?

Well, the first clients that came in with a record deal I will never forget because it was a deal being offered by CBS. I rang up the managing director and I said "I'm Shane Simpson, I'm representing so and so, and I'd like to come in and discuss the record deal". He said "who are you?". "I'm Shane Simpson". He said, "I don't talk to fucking lawyers, I only talk to artists, piss off!" and hung up. I was sitting there thinking, "Well, this could be the end of a very short career, because if I can't deal with the Majors as a lawyer, how is this going to work as a business?". Eventually I got the deal done and all was resolved but it was very difficult in those early days because lawyers weren't really a part of the music industry landscape. Standard deals were what people signed.

It's interesting. Look at an example: I've done quite a lot of work over the years for the Bee Gees and when we acquired the first album they did, which was owned in Australia, it was very interesting seeing that first record deal. It was two and a quarter pages, and yet those two and a quarter pages represented millions of dollars over the years!

It's not necessarily a good thing having the lawyers involved, but lawyers are agents of change. Part of the downside is that the deals became heavier, more sophisticated, and more complex.

So the first one you saw was a 1960s contract?

Correct. But the upside of the legal involvement is that nowadays you've got terms in there that are fairer than they certainly were in those early days of the record business. So there's pluses and minuses in that.

At one level you've been an artist-side lawyer for many, many years but you've also dealt on behalf of Warner-Chappell and for the Majors as well. How did that transition occur and did it temper your view of what you did as an artist-side lawyer?

Well it's an interesting question because in fact I've never acted on behalf of major record companies. I've acted for most of the major publishing companies and in fact in, a corporate sense, my client base was really heavy in publishers, not in records. I've acted for independents but that's a different conversation: independent record companies, but not the majors.

I suppose it's because what gets me out of bed in the morning is the music and the makers of the music are very important to me. The composers, it seems to me, are the very apex of a triangle upon which the whole industry sits and I think composition is—it's certainly a talent that I don't have—is one that we all need to cherish. So my practise developed through, yes, the artists and the composers, and through doing deals on the behalf of composers. That's how you get to deal for the company, because they figured it was going to be better to have me on their side than on the other side. But that's another story also.

I want to have a talk about some recent legal decisions. There are a couple of notable ones. The first one I want to talk about seems to have highlighted the odd position of musical talent in relation to the music industry and broadcast media. It's as if the music and the musicians have the same relationship to those industries as does coal to the power industry, I mean they're necessary ...

Music as a utility?

I guess as a natural resource, to be mined, harvested, and what comes out at the other end is a completely different, far more complex thing than it starts out as. The case in point is the recent challenge by PPCA to the 1% cap. You might have to explain that to the audience in the answer. The high court ruling's a fascinating read. It cites the Statute of Anne in describing the public good basis of plate makers' rights, which is a seemingly archaic law to be drawing on since it's 300 year old. Also, given that digital technologies do away with plate making, which in the record company's place would be-.

Which you're saying, makes the Statute of Anne seem pretty irrelevant to quote in the High Court?

Yes. that and the fact that the law's 300 years old and that its current use guarantees, basically, this very influential group of people, an instant absolution from any rights infringement, regardless of how that might happen.

Can I take your question slightly differently?

Yes, by all means.

I think it's interesting that the Statute of Anne is taken as sort of the birth of copyright—1710. It's a very common feeling this thing that you express—"My god, it's very old". I think it's very important to understand this as a music practitioner: if you want to understand what's happening now and have some insight into what's likely to happen then I'm a great believer in the importance of knowing where we've come from and that whole cliché about how, otherwise, you keep making the mistakes of the past.

The story doesn't start in 1710, it starts in 1403. 1710 is actually not that interesting. 1403s really interesting because in London they set up the Guild of Stationers. The members of the Guild of Stationers was made up of the people who made books and the book sellers. (Now when I tell this story, think about record companies in another period). The purpose of setting up the Guild was to control the manufacture and sale and distribution of books. So in 1403 we were already seeing a group of business people trying to establish a monopoly and a monopoly of rights.

Then you have in 1440 the invention of the printing press, think, if you like, digital. In 1447—and forgive me, this history lesson won't go on all night ...

No, go right ahead.

In 1447 the Guild gets the government sanction and actually incorporates, becomes The Company of Stationers. In 7 years between 1440 and 1447, already the technology had moved so much that printers are starting to become part of the Guild of Stationers so when they incorporated they were an important power base in the Guild. It's estimated that in that 60 years from 1440 to 1500 over 20 million volumes were published. So it was a complete revolution of business, of the knowledge that was books. By the way, they got exclusivity in return for a censorship role so that they would not publish, and also have search and seizure powers over, books which were not approved by the church or the state. So again they were selling off author rights in order to get a personal power.

1710 comes along which is where people think the story starts, and the only reason that the printers and booksellers and so forth suggested that the authors get any copyright was because they knew that their monopoly was not going to be renewed. So a deal was done, even back then, in order to keep the monopoly intact for a bit longer: the Guild got the first 14 years of exclusivity and then authors got certain rights after that. So it's not just a three, four hundred year story of trying to keep your rights, it actually goes back to the Middle Ages.

But you can understand I guess at that stage and earlier, of course, if you're printing 20 million volumes you've got some serious capital outlay, in logistics, in printing presses, in transport, the lot. Accounting, as well really. So on the basis of that view you can see that if the plate makers couldn't make a profit then public knowledge gets damaged and you can see the basis of that argument. But today we've got 97 million songs in Gracenote, we've got an hour of material being uploaded to YouTube every minute. When everybody is a "plate maker". In essence, is the law still relevant?

I thought you were going to come out with the wonderful cliché that copyright is dead.

No, absolutely not! I just want your views on this basis for talking about it further.

I think you've actually put your finger on it. I think that the corporate investment in copyright is so enormous that I don't see any threat to copyright itself as an economic construct. Almost every major corporation on the planet has on its books a huge investment in IP, intellectual property. So I don't think copyright's going to go away any time soon. But of course how money is made out of copyright, what those copyrights protect, who owns those copyrights, those are continually changing. They've been changing since Gutenberg and the printing press.

The camera, movies, certainly the recording industry. I'm old enough to remember when cassette tapes came out and it was going to be the end of the music business. Of course it wasn't; it was just another channel by which people could make money from copyright. And that really is the message of history: yes, technology drives copyright change. It always has. It must. But it doesn't kill it. It alters it. And, yes, the development of copyright law is often behind the technology, and that's the way it should be, frankly. You don't want lawyers leading technological and cultural evolution. It's nice if they're a little bit behind.

On the matter of revenues, there's been some recent and fascinating developments around streaming services such as Spotify, Rdio, Pandora and so on. On the one hand we see artists complaining about the really low returns offered by most of these things; on the other, we hear the services claiming they're paying Majors the bulk of their income in what's called an advance, which seems to me to be a strange transaction. So there's a deal between Spotify and the consumer and a different deal between Spotify and the Majors and a different deal between the Majors and their artists as well. It suggests that the Majors are passing very little of this on.

The returns are very limited but, panic not, because it's the nature of the way the business evolves. There's a couple of things, I think. One is, and let's look at the financial returns for second, if we look at what you mentioned about the record companies getting large advances and not paying them on, record companies in the last 5–10 years have been in deep shtuk wondering what their future is. Frankly, I think the taking of the large advances from Spotify is using an old record company practice to shore up their books in the short term. Similarly, if you look at when a Major buys another label and it's paying out a lot of money, the purchased label doesn't share that.

They don't get the money, exactly, and it's that part of the deal I'm in interested in.

It's a very similar kind of transaction that's happening. It's not as though it's new and surprising. Whether it's fair or not is a different question, of course. And certainly if you're looking from the artist's perspective, given that if you have a large—we won't call it an advance because advance suggestions that it's recouped in some way or paid out in some way as a royalty of some species—but it's a fee ...

For catalogue use...

Then that's just the nature of the beast. I see it as a temporary holding position. I don't approve of it but I'm not surprised by it. In terms of what the deals are, nobody actually knows what the deals are with Spotify. Well I certainly don't anyway, at least in any detail.

And they're not telling.

No, and why should they? It's commercial in confidence. But in terms of the return to artists, I would still say, I'd be still allowing my stuff to be streamed. And yes, the money now may be less, but it will grow. It's already grown on Spotify, they've already increased the royalty rates. It's miniscule, but it happens. These things are always incremental and that's why I think it's kind of cool when you look at these things to actually see where you are in history. That's why I enjoyed you starting where you did with a little historical perspective, because we're talking about just a tiny blip at the moment.

Let me give you an example. In 1995, so early days of the Internet, I gave a paper to the OECD on how the Internet was going to affect the value and use of government information. And when I say this paper was one of the most contentious papers that they'd ever received I mean—it created a furore! You'll be really surprised to know that all I was saying in it was that the Internet was going to be really important, because governments at that stage still didn't really appreciate that.

What I was saying was that, at the time, all governments thought that their information, call it corporate information, (the analogies are easy to make), must be held to their bosom. They thought that this information was the value of their government or business. All I was saying was that the Internet was going to make them re-think the value of that information and that they would make some of that information available for free, some of it they could make people pay for, and some of it they wouldn't release. The government representatives were horrified. That simple idea was really contentious, only in the mid-90s. Now it's so banal. It's so vanilla that it's embarrassing.

That's only in 17 years ago, so I'm not too worried about the royalty rate that Spotify is paying over 6 months. I think you need to look at really important transitions, and streaming is a really important technological transition, a distribution evolution, so I'm not too worried that we haven't yet got the balances right in terms of who pays who for what for how much for how long. I think that'll happen.

Have you been following the Al Yankovich case on this? He's arguing against, I think, Sony that what's being done with streaming is a licensing deal and should therefore fall under that part of the agreement which is 50% of revenues rather than the 20 or 30 they might receive if it's called sales revenue rather than licensing.

Well the logic is inescapable. Clearly it's a licensing deal, not an album sale. Not having seen his contract, one assumes that this sort of income stream is treated as though it were the sale of an album. But, again, the historical perspective: when I started we were still black vinyl. CDs were introduced. All of the record contracts for artists in those days, and the royalty provisions, said, "CDs will be accounted as though it is black vinyl". And there was a deduction, often a very large one, 25% for new technologies—which was the CD. So it's not new. Then of course CD becomes the primary sound carrier and they're still treated as a 'new technology'. It took some years to get record companies to change the contract so the new technology deduction was dropped. DVDs: same thing. All of these are just ways of lowering the royalty rate. Another one which was a classic, was the packaging deduction on records—a 25% packaging deduction. No there is no packaging deduction on a digitally transmitted product!

Can you explain the packaging deduction?

I don't think anybody can really do that, but record companies had this fabulous thing which said that they'll take a negotiable figure, which was generally 25%, but if you acted for somebody who was really quite powerful you might get it down to 15%, which was only out of the artist's royalties and went to supposedly the paying of the actual packaging in which the product was sold. There was no real justification for it. No record label guy could really say that there was a particular reason. But it's a business so it wants to keep as much money for the corporate accounts and pay out as little as possible—which is a completely traditional economic approach.

Now that we have digital distribution there are still lots of deals around—not as many as there were—where packaging deductions are charged and there are still deals around—before decent lawyers negotiate them—in which streaming is in fact treated as an album sale not as a licensing. Some of the smaller companies, certainly are treating streaming as licensing, but some of the big acts are very unhappy because they are in very long-term deals which were negotiated hard at the time but it was really before things like streaming became important issues. So they remain stuck under the terms of their original contract.

So it's a trap for young players, always assume the technology's going to change.

Well, you must always assume the technology's going to change.

We've had a couple of different views on the 360 deal. One speaker was quite reluctant to endorse them as a strategy for artists based on the fact that the majors are great at promoting distributing recorded music but not very good at the other things that are required of a label in a 360 degree deal.

It's not their business.

What are your thoughts on this trend?

I think that again it's a part of record companies fighting for survival. They're looking for their place in the economic firmament and clearly record sales are not what they were. Recordings can no longer be the focus of everything so they're trying to diversify the sources from which they're earning income—completely understandable.

If, on the other hand you're an artist, I think that the 360 deal is a terrible idea. Let me enumerate the ways. I can't think of any Major that has been successful in truly exploiting all the rights. Take Universal for example: There was a period a few years ago where every record contract that came from Universal said that it gave an option to Universal over the film rights of the artist being signed. The logic of it was that "Hey, we've got these huge Universal studios, we can make you into a star. If you're going to be going to films we want you to go with us". I understand the logic. But it never happened. So all it was, was a roadblock to doing a good record deal—which is what they were good at. So you spend a lot of time negotiating out, or down and around a clause which is almost irrelevant but you've got to try to get rid of it.

There's very little history of Majors providing good management and, I think, one of the really important roles of managers—and I think most record people will agree—is in fact to have the manager chewing at the ankles of the record company, keeping them up on the mark. They're often really unpopular in one sense because they're a pain in the neck. But that agitation is important for both sides, and I think that when management gets too close to the record company it certainly is to the disadvantage of the artist.

In terms of merchandising, I can't see any advantage in artists having their merch signed to record companies, just none. In cases where the Major acquires a merchandising company and then says, "You must sign", it hinders something I like: the freedom of having lots of independent companies that all have an interest in that artist's success rather than a whole lot of interrelated ones that actually have just the one pretty simple, glandular, interest.

I've always been impressed by the country artists. In Australia, country artists as recording artists, is quite a modern phenomenon. Yet there has long been a strong country tradition in Australia and they've succeeded by doing everything themselves—they tour, make their records, and sell them.

You and I were talking a bit before we started about surf movies and how those genres are different. Surf movie-makers are so different from the general movie making world, just as the early country scene was very different from the Major music scene. But even now I think country artists, even if they're backed by a Major, still have a strong sense of carefully looking after each of the elements of their own business.

I learned a great lesson from Garth Brooks. He only did one tour in Australia and, it was really funny. I just got a call at work from the States from a fellow who said "Hello Shane, my name is Rusty. I'm the attorney for Garth Brooks". That year Garth was the biggest selling record artist in the world, so he was a seriously important player signed to EMI. He was doing an Australian tour of all of the entertainment centres. Merchandising is a very important part of his money stream and he wanted us to devise a system to protect the copyright in his merch from all the pirates. I don't know if you know, but all of the major acts, whether Madonna or any of these people, fly around in their enormous planes with their enormous amounts of gear—but the pirates follow as well. So all of the artist managements know all the names of all the pirates because they see them at the airport unloading all the merch and so-forth. It's a huge industry, so protecting the merchandising rights of a major artist is terribly important because what the pirates do is set up in all of the alleys leading to the entertainment centres. So everybody passes by them and by the time they get into the entertainment centre to the official merch, they've already got the t-shirt, they've got the this and the that.

Is it that organised?

It's that organised. I'm talking about the big acts, not you and me going and doing a gig at a pub. Anyway, we needed to go to the Federal Court to get the necessary powers, then organise teams of pros to do the enforcement. There was a moment during one of the early conversations with Rusty, who turned out to be a delightful fellow, when he said, "Shane, you're not talking to me" and I said "Rusty, I'm trying to think what it's likely to cost, because under my professional rules I have to actually give you an estimate of what this is likely to cost and frankly I haven't got a clue, I'll have to do some work and come back to you". He said: "Shane, you just don't understand. Garth doesn't care about how much, Garth only cares about perfect". It was a great line. And when Garth came on the tour he bought all his own merch which was really high-quality. He also bought all his own sales people to set up and sell it. Highly professional. He wasn't leaving it to, you know, some t-shirt distributor to have rights over the tour. He took control of it—and he broke the merch record for every single entertainment centre he played. It was a great lesson: "He didn't care about how much" (clearly unless we're in that stratosphere we all care about 'how much'). But he cared very much about 'perfect', and everybody in that team, and it was a very large team, was imbued with the ethic that it had to be done the best that they could do it. At the end of the day, it was Garth who was in control. And I think that one of the great lessons for people starting out, is this keeping of control over your own career.

Of course there are always things in your career that you have to give away. I'm not saying you can stay in bed all day and you'll be safe. No. There are risks you have to take. But it's about being a tall person. It's about being an adult and not a child. If you look at artist management relations, for example, the successful ones are the ones where the act appreciates that the manager is a professional and the manager appreciates that their act is a professional and they deal with one another adult to adult. The most dysfunctional ones are where the artist still treats the manager as their mother and expects them to do all the crap that they don't want to do: they didn't want to pick up their clothes from the bedroom floor because mum will do that, well now they've got a manager. That doesn't work for me. So that's what I mean when I say you have to be a tall person. You take responsibility for what you do. You look very carefully at who you're going to retain as a manager and why, and all of their characteristics. We might talk about those sorts of things later. But the main thing is that you take responsibility and you keep involved in the business aspects of your career. If you don't, then either people aren't going to be working terribly hard for you because they don't need to. Or maybe you'll be swindled and you won't even know it until it's too late. All of those stories we know too well.

You say in *The Music Business* that the perfect manager is "an amalgamation of hard-headed business executive, snake oil seller, economist, tangier rug trader, kick boxer, parent, stand-in spouse, friend, confessor psychologist, fall guy, punching bag, and stand-over merchant. He or she would also be on first name terms with all the big hitters of the business in three continents, enjoy an independent source of income, love your music, and have a bullet-proof belief in your future."

So I'd had a glass of red wine!

We've heard time and again that the key aspect of sustained success in this seminar series—everyone says good management is essential, critical to success. We've also heard just as many times that Australia lacks enough good skilled and experienced music managers to get our industry ticking to the level that it needs to. Why do you think that is and what do you think could be done to help our talent management pool?

Well I think it's a lot better than it was. Twenty-five years ago it was really hard to find good managers. There were two or three of them that had had a degree of success and we all know those bands that they represented. One of the things that has improved over the last period has been the quality of management. We now have managers who have accounting degrees. It used to be when an act wanted to break its management agreement the first thing I'd do was just call for the books and do an audit, because managers could never keep good books. It was just an easy out of the contract. If they were in some country town at 11 o'clock at night and wanted pizzas, the manager paid and he'd rarely keep the receipts. The receipt-keeping and accounting was very approximate. That just doesn't happen these days, everybody knows how to use MYOB or Excel spread sheets. Nowadays, the figures are there and you should be checking them—and being a tall person.

The days of having managers who are just enthusiasts for the music are over. I guess there'll always be a role for that kind of person but they're almost the worst manager to have because, in a sense, and I say this only in a very limited way, it almost doesn't matter if the manager loves the music or not (although they have to because they spend so much time and so much of their life with the act). But really, the manager's focus is not to be a sycophant, they're not there because they love what you do; it's because they want to do deals with the talent and their product. That's where the good managers really shine, because they can actually love the music but say, "Well, this is my focus". They're not generally getting involved with artistic decisions. I know there are some exceptions that are quite successful but they're pretty rare. Their focus is the business.

Now, things like the courses run at QUT are a classic route to management because people may well start out wanting to be a performing artist but they may, through that process, find that they have a real ability and skill and love of the commercial side of the business. In a sense I'm an example of that, not as a manager, but of that sort of mobility. I started out as a piano player. I'm a much better lawyer than I was a piano player. In fact it was a fantastic career move, many would say. I would say that too because how many piano players are there in the world who make a decent career? Not many. Somebody told me the other day there are 6000 classical pianists living in London at the moment.

I thought there would be more.

Six thousand professionals. I mean it's an inconceivable number really, when really only the top 25 are probably making a living. So it's not just the rock musicians that are having difficulties. But moving from being the artist to being a manager is fine so long as you've got the skill base and motivation. I think that's important.

This issue about artist incomes I think is strange. We see various reports stating that globally people are spending more money on more music than ever before—that's a combination of live, merch, everything.

This year was the first year that the sale of games outsold the sale of music.

Is it? That's surprising, I thought that would have happened ages ago.

No.

The copyright industry in Australia's worth more than the utilities and communications sectors combined and that opportunities for musicians are on the up and up. Meanwhile we've seen a steady erosion of actual income. Last year we saw two surveys pegging the average level of musician income between $12 and $15 thousand a year, well below the poverty line, less than half. Simultaneously royalty collection agencies, their revenues are going through

the roof in one way or another, and there's never been a time in my memory in which copyright consciousness has been so loudly propagated. What's going on? What's happening to music that the artist gets the least share?

Why are you surprised? What's new?

I'm not surprised, I just wondered why it's gotten so bad. Why do you think?

I don't think it's 'gotten so bad'. I think it always has been bad. I don't think that that's in fact changed.

But there's a lot more, when I was a young man there were a lot more opportunities to make a living than there are now, so it seems anyway.

Well I think so, too. Australia of course was an unusual community in that we had a really important live circuit in the pubs and certainly that's diminished. But figures about incomes are again a little distorted in that what it doesn't take into account is the distinction between full time and part time. So somebody could be a professor at a music school and having a gigging career as well and might be making 6 or 8 grand a year out of live music.

Sure, but I mean that's part of what's happening also, is the semi-professionalization of the trade or the craft or the profession or whatever you want to call it.

Well perhaps that's a criticism of the role of universities because universities have become an industry where they churn out students that cannot have an expectation of a full time job in the area that they are trained for, and that's really the same whether you're talking about music or painting or lawyering.

You think we're overproducing musicians?

Absolutely, and that's why, for me, the emphasis must be on flexibility of career. I see nothing wrong with training somebody for 3 years in a music school if they go off and then do something else, because that's been an incredibly important keel that's built into their life which will give them enrichment for the rest of their life. But we have to get away from the fact that expectations of full time employment are really valid. A few people will make it through to that. The cream will rise to the top, but it will only be the cream.

I'm loathe to accept it.

Of course, because you're in the business of producing students.

No, it's because I had a wonderful life as a musician and I don't see why that shouldn't remain as a career option. I mean, it was tough going, there's no question about it, but we've seen the erosion of session work, we've seen the erosion of studio work, we've seen the erosion of gigs at pubs, I think it's more or less the cultural diminishment of music as a valuable thing as compared, say, football.

Well you talk of music as being a utility and as soon as you start using that sort of terminology . . .

Oh, I'm not endorsing that.

No, I understand that. But that sort of conversation does lead to that diminishment of cultural property. So one part of me is always resistant to it. The other part of me admits that as a means of distribution, particularly for music as opposed to other cultural property, the 'music as a utility' analogy fits. But it our career expectations are very important. I think it's very important if people are doing courses such as these, that they be flexible in what they expect to get out of them. Things change: when I started there weren't music lawyers. Now everybody wants to be a music lawyer. Last time we advertised we got 157 applicants.

Wow, that's like 6000 piano players in London.

Exactly. Now how many of those were actually qualified suitable to work in our firm? Not many. Because you have to look at their experience, their level of their commitment to the cultural sector. You interview somebody and they say, "I've always loved music". I'll say, "Well tell me what you've read. Have you read my book?" If they say no, of course that's the end of the interview. Assuming that they say yes, I'll say, "Well tell me what other books you've read". In other words, how interested are you? How committed are you? Because it is about commitment. That's the same whether you want to be a lawyer in a speciality area or you want to be a musician. It's that desire to be the best you possibly can. So what are the elements that show me as an employer that you have that fire in the belly? It won't be just because you 'love music'.

Well I can ask the question in a different way—what I think what I was getting at is that there's all this money being spent on music, musicians are getting less of a share of it, there's less to actually pay for the musician to live. Can you explain that in any legal way?

The only insight I have is that I think there are more people involved in the food chain now.

Which is counter-intuitive isn't it, because you should be able to cut out the middle men with digital distribution.

Of course you can, and I suspect that that's the way that it's going. I really do believe that. But because we've all heard we can all be publishers; we can all be distributors of our own music; the web does that. Terrific. Then we can earn 100% of everything we put out. Great. And there are some examples where that's worked in a miraculous way for less than a handful of people. So on the whole you're still going to need people who market the product, who account for the product, who audit sources, who get you to use my product. So there are many people are in that food chain, all of whom need to make money, send their kids to school, have a mortgage, and all those things—and it all takes out of the income stream.

The classic example is the film business—now we in the music business are a bit shocked this is happening. In the film business it's the absolute standard way it works. The producers make the least amount of money of anybody in the economic triangle. The exhibitors get the biggest slice and then the exhibitors send what's left down to the distributor, and then the distributor takes their slice and sends the balance down to the sales agent, and on it goes down through the chain, and then what's left goes to the producer which is split with the investors and other rights owners. And they wonder why investors don't make money in the film business! Well, it's because of the structure.

Now, one of the great hopes of digital distribution—and I don't think anyone's cracked it—but it's still there as a potential—is in fact you reduce the size of the food chain so creatives get more. To use the Spotify example, (I'm not talking about that specifically), where you've got a distributor that actually has a business in expanding distribution and getting people to listen, which is what most of us sitting at home with our music don't have, we need a corporation that does that. That may be quite a small food chain and as that relationship develops commercially over the next 10 years we'll see changes. We'll soon find that a "neo-Spotify" will come out and they'll offer a different deal, so there'll be competition and negotiation of royalty rates.

Then of course we get to the wonderful thing that the Internet gives us that we never had when we were dealing with atom-based distribution, and that is for something to go viral, and suddenly you get a million purchases. Yes, you can do it with discs but not like the web—and we're almost used to that concept now.

I had a client who was the first person I know of in Australia to make $1,000,000 out of one track. One track, and it was quite early days in downloads and you wouldn't even know the name. Well you might know her name, but she's not a star, she's a music writer, music producer, and this thing just went off, internationally, and it's probably the only thing of hers that ever has, but that's pretty significant.

I thought we'd move on to some issues facing musicians in the future, and maybe quite immediately—many bands struggle over ways to split royalties. It's an age-old problem, the Kookaburra case for example focused not on what song-writers Hay and Stryckert wrote but on an improvised solo in the thing to break it down.

Pity it wasn't improvised.

It was definitely improvised. It was a jazz improvisation of a standard that he used to tag the composition.

Sorry, I take improvisation as something which is not an existing work. I should at this point declare that we act for the owner of Kookaburra.

Music Sales? So in some ways that ruling was a confirmation by the court that every part of an arrangement contributes to the copyright value of the recording, which wasn't always the case as standard practise.

I don't know that it does go that far.

You don't think so?

No. Because it's not about an arrangement, and that was much litigated, believe me. *Kookaburra* is in fact a really straightforward case when you cut away all of the extraneous argument. That recording in fact reproduced two songs, two original works, one which was written by the Men at Work guys and the other which was written by the author of *Kookaburra*. The *Kookaburra* song is very short. It was designed as a girl scout round. It's actually all there. It's not just a sample of it; it's actually the whole work. A short work, but it's the whole work because it's a round. So it always has puzzled me why the case happened at all. I've got some ideas but I'm not sure that I'll share them. But it should have settled with the first letter. It should never have gone to litigation and yet it has been fought by EMI every step of the way. It's gone to the High Court, now it's back in the Federal Court again, still not finished. All of the legal aspects are really finished. Now it's about damages. But it's still going, so that's why I'm being somewhat cautious but it really was pretty easy legally at one level.

Once you get into litigation nothing's easy. You take every point and that's what's happened. But it could have been a straight licence deal which Music Sales would have given—just like that. So it's no different, really, from sampling in the record business. When sampling started everybody thought it was going to be the end of copyright and everybody dealt with it. It was every sample. The first year or so was tumultuous. But after that we all worked out that we could have a penny rate or we could do a small percentage. Mostly it was just done, 50 bucks, 150 bucks, whatever it was or, "No, you can't use it". Which is fair enough. You know where you are: you can go and sample something else. So in a sense a lot of the criticism of the role of copyright in creativity is this sort of post-modern appropriation of bricolage. Fine, use other people's work, but do them the politeness of actually asking. If it's in copyright pay them their due.

Just stepping back from that to get more general: when you're in a band and there's a clear songwriter involved, how do you suggest the band shares proceeds.

That's a really important one because of course you've got two elements within the band—one is the artistic element and the other is the purely human relations element. The longevity of the band depends on getting both of those things right, not just the creativity bit. So there are no set rules. I think that the biggest potential divider, though, is when you have one or two song-writers in a band and the rest aren't contributing to the song writing. That's because the songwriters, it's an old joke, they drive the Rolls Royce and the others drive the VW because they're only getting the mechanical royalty for the reproduction of the song within the recording that the band is selling and promoting and so forth. Now, publishing is a stream the record company can't recoup from. So the songwriters are getting, if you like, solid, stable money coming through whereas the rest of the band is waiting on recoupment depending on sales and touring and everything else. So if you end up with one or two really rich people in the band and two or three who are struggling to send their kids to school then it's not necessarily the artistic part that suffers, it's the human bit. It creates jealousy and tensions and so a lot of the successful acts that I'm aware of have internal deals recognising that the non-writers still play a role in the success of the publishing income of the writers, because they get out there and they work their ass off trying to sell the records.

And they have a distinctive sound and arrangement?

All of that, and there are various ways that royalties can be split but I never think that the non-composer should have a share of copyright. I don't believe in that for a moment. I do believe it makes sense to give them a share of the income stream that flows from the copyright because it's very important for composers to, as much as possible, keep their copyrights intact, keep a catalogue, because that's their superannuation. Looking at ways of earning money when you're too old to go on the road, it's your catalogue that does that.

If you want to recognise the role that the band is playing in promotion of the music then I know of composers that give non-composer artists a share while they're in the band and then once they leave the band the deal's off. In other cases some will give a lesser figure but so long as they recorded it and stayed within the band for a certain period then they keep getting it. So there's various ways of cutting that cake, but it's all about keeping longevity within the act. It's very important. You know, you can make a quick buck out of a one hit wonder, but the real money is in longevity. People want to come to your concerts which is a very direct source of income, and you can do that for a very long time, (as sadly we observe).

Sync deals are always another point of interest for composers. The nature and content of sync deals have been changing for years, I think, even previous to the potential for digital distribution. All I can really say in general is that the deals seem to have tended towards being for less and less up front money and more and more, I guess a higher and higher degree of rights assignment . . .

I think it depends on what area of sync you're talking about. The money in sync for TV ads, for example, has gone through the roof. It's not less and less money. I've done lots of deals in the millions of dollars. Lots of deals in the hundreds and hundreds of thousands mark. You just think of what QANTAS is paying for I Still Call Australia Home. There are a lot of songs out there that make hundreds of thousands from good deals, so I don't agree that it's dropped. I think that in film world, the composer frankly has always had the rough end of the stick because the composer gets commissioned or starts work and starts getting paid at the end of the movie when the rough cut stage is there. They're the last people, really, almost last people, certainly the last major creatives off the rank. So if there's a budget blow-out it's the composer that's always going to suffer, either by saying "No I won't do it for that" or having to reduce a fee. I don't think there is any change, though in terms of ownership. Film studios have always wanted the copyright in the soundtrack.

But they seem to get it now. They didn't always get it but now they almost always get it.

I'd actually say it's the other way round.

Really?

They always used to get it. I'm not talking about low budget Australian movies, I'm talking about generally, you know, a more international perspective.

Top end of town stuff?

Yeah, well if you're talking about a 'John Williams type deal' he can negotiate deals that I can't negotiate in Australia, so I'm not talking about top end of town. Similarly, I don't think it's helpful to talk about the sort of one and a half million-dollar budget movie that's never going to make any dough anyway. A lot of those deals are because the producer knows the composer and they're very much friend-based transactions. I'm talking about where a lot of Australian movies are now, around the sort of $8–15 million mark, where music is a serious component of that property. In those sorts of 'serious investment films' there are so many musical elements within the film that I'm trying not to generalise—for the licensing into films of existing product, there's no problem and I don't agree that money's getting less. I think licensing fees for sync are okay. The part that's the endangered species is the writer who's really doing the soundtrack, the, what's the word I'm looking for? The score.

That's kind of what I was thinking of at one end but also there's this huge move to library music . . .

But again that's in the cheaper films, not where there's a real music budget. I just don't see that that really is an issue. In terms of the demanding all rights: for years I represented a writer called Christopher Gordon who's done some fabulous stuff. He did Moby Dick and Bounty and all sorts of large, American-based mini-series, and he and I developed a really interesting approach. He has his screen music career but he's also a symphonic, classical writer for orchestra, and he wanted to be able to use some of the themes that he developed in his screen work for orchestral development in a different environment. Over the years we've negotiated with many of the major studios and networks in the States about this and of course their initial position was always "No, we want everything" and "No you can't do anything", but in almost all circumstances, we've, at the end of the day, been able to carve out this area which essentially they don't care about. They just want to acquire all the assets, but because of his reputation he can negotiate a little carve out. It's a mini version of the John Williams deal that we were alluding to. That's why it's so good acting for stars instead of start-up artists because you can actually do something with deals.

Digital distribution of all types of copyrights have given rise to new kinds of rights schemes. I'm talking about Creative Commons and AE sharenet and things like that. What's your view of those things? Creative Commons is a good one to start with.

It's not very popular to say this but I think it's quite banal. All it is a form of licensing. That's all it is. It's just copyright licensing and it's kind of primitive copyright licensing in that once you've licensed it, it's gone. With a more sophisticated licence you can do it for a term. You can do it in various ways. I know there are levers on Commons that you can pull, but in essence, once it's out there it's out there, whereas one of the advantages of traditional licensing is that you can do it for a term and then renegotiate your position, so in fact you're keeping the value of your asset. Now, that said, I think there are lots of situations in which CC makes a whole lot of sense. Academia is one, where the general reason that you want to put an article out there is because you want it distributed and read, reproduced, and discussed. It's an educational drive, not an economic drive.

That's also the basis of the academic star system, having it read and cited.

The more the better. So the Commons concept has got a lot of promotion from academics and I can completely understand why. But as a model for someone who lives in the commercial world rather than the educational world I'm not sure that it works. That said, of course, the question is how do you have a system of licensing in an online world that doesn't require negotiations and formalities and so forth and still allows distribution and content protection. I think that CC's a transition in the online world, but I don't think it's the answer.

It seems to me that there was a lot of hope around the commercial returns to individuals from the open access world. One example was that Don Tapscott story. He tells of a gold company, I forget its name, it was a Canadian gold company. Anyway, they had held their data close to their chest—all their geological data that they'd gathered. They were in trouble with stocks falling through the floor and their last gasp was to put the data out, open up all their geological data for a competition in some form amongst geological analysts to tell them where to go and mine. Anyway, that was quite the success and some South Australian guys won it. It was those kinds of stories that were feeding the

idea that if you just put it out there under the right kinds of licensing terms it'd pay off.

It can, but is that a business structure? No, that's a lottery structure. And I'm not against people taking a scratch-it ticket but that really is the scratch-it mentality. You can't build a business on that. Part of your business may be to put stuff out there for nothing. That's clearly a validated part of an online business structure. But there is always going to be a need for some control of the asset and how it's going to be adopted and commercialised.

One of the interesting things about trying to look into the future, which is what we're doing with digital, is that we live in it but we know it's not going to stay like this. In the 90s I actually gave up my law practise for 3 years and I set up a centre within a university looking at the interrelationship of new technologies, law, and management. I did it because I was really sick to death of people developing new technologies and the entertainment business, of course, develops a lot of interesting new technologies. As a lawyer, that was my entry point—only when there was a finished product. I wanted to say, for example, "Look Phil, if you'd come to me 2 years ago when you were working on this we could have got accounting expertise on this and we could have got some regulatory stuff done and we could have actually engineered it in such and such a way". But as a lawyer you were typically the last person on the bus and were given a finished product to protect. And so I spent some of this time as a kind of quasi-futurist, I suppose. That's when I was doing that OECD paper on the role of government information, things like that, and one of the things I did learn is that you can be pretty good at estimating *what's* likely to happen, but I think there's no way in the world you can estimate, realistically, *when* a particular thing is likely to happen. I think that the time aspect of it is just unsolvable.

When I wrote the first edition of *The Music Business*, which was about that time, '94, I remember saying in the technology chapter that by 2004 or 2005 the CD would be dead and it would only be used for blokes going out on fishing holidays because I really thought by then we would have an online distribution system. Frankly, I thought Telstra would do it with *Hello Telstra.* What a waste of a business opportunity—you've got wire into every home in the country, or at least you did then, and you had a billing backbone. So all they really had to do was in fact do the licence deals with the Majors, distribution, pay-per-play, everything gets distributed through the billing network, comes out at the end of the month with your telephone bill. A perfect solution, really, for everybody. So simple. Wrong again. But here I was saying that in 10 years time the CD would be gone because of this. Clearly the CD is in pain but it isn't dead, and it'll be quite a long time before it is dead. So the timelines in which you imagine things are going to happen are almost always wrong.

There are also things that I was guessing would happen at that time and frankly they happened in about a week and then they were dead; they weren't significant. I can't even remember the name of some of them: the Minidisc. DATs. Most of us can't even remember the names any more. But when they first came out they were the new big thing. It was the first time we could get digital quality on a tape. It was going to change the business, pirating was going to go crazy, it was going to wreck the record business. But that just came and went. It was used in recording studios over a longer period but even then, not for that long.

So some of these things come and go in just blips and other things actually have quite long timelines. One of them is online distribution of legally distributed music. We start talking about Spotify, but that's part of that evolution. I know I drive you crazy keeping on talking about this historical perspective but I think it's very important. Otherwise we think that what's happening today is truly significant. No, it's an indicator. If I were a musician I think this is one of the things I would find really heartening because we're at a time in which actually nobody knows the answer. Anybody who says they do? Don't trust them, they're just snake oil salesmen. Copyright is dead? Bullshit. It's changing. The technology is changing, just as in fact music content is changing. Genres change, some things are huge sellers at some times.

But the wonderful thing is that the online world and online communities have done wonders for individual artists and groups of artists in terms of self-empowerment. I think that there are very few reasons these days for artists to seek a Major record deal. There are certain genres which I think are best sold by Major record companies. Pure pop, for example, is certainly one of those things. But we've got lots and lots of examples now of artists who take their own career by the short and curlies and are really creative not just in their music but in the way they develop their career. It comes back to what I was talking about, being a tall person, being responsible for yourself. There will always be a role for Major record companies although it won't be the role they've traditionally had. But remember that major record companies have basically been marketing companies, I think, which is why they are so different from publishing companies.

Depends who you talk to, Michael Taylor would say that they've been historically talent development companies and they keep doing that. Marketing's kind of accidental or opportunistic in his view.

And I'm being cheap when I say they're essentially marketing companies because there is always a talent development side to what they do. But, frankly, A&R guys come and go. It's the marketing guys who tend to go towards the top of the company.

Chapter 8
Shaun James, Music TV

Abstract This chapter is an interview with Shaun James who was in 2012 head of XYZ Music and centrally involved in the direction of Foxtel's music channels, V, V Hits, Max, and CMC. He has since moved on to front Presto, Foxtel's streaming video on demand (VOD) service. Shaun's industry history includes being CEO of Warner Music (Australia and New Zealand) during a time of massive market growth for that label, Chief Marketing Officer of the national TEN television network, and Vice Chairman of ARIA. Shaun's experience across television, digital, and major music labels gives him yet another distinct and unusual perspective on the past and future of the music business. Shaun's is the mind of a technology business strategist. He sees the technology, the rules, the signal flows, the money flows, and the way value gets created across multiple platforms and the connections among them. This interview reveals a sophisticated sense of value ecologies for music that is both futuristic and paradoxical in its implications.

Welcome Shaun. Can you start by telling us how you got into the industry?

The fact of the matter was that I was a music nut growing up as a kid and I loved music. I was into all sorts of music and that's where all my spare change and money went and everything else. The honest to god story is I fell into the music business, and I think it's a common thing for a lot of people in music. There's not defined pathways and there's not clear ways in like you might have if you want to be a lawyer or an accountant, or something like that.

I grew up in Melbourne, and I was studying a Bachelor of Business at Monash Uni, doing a marketing degree, and playing very average level of park cricket with a local club. Park cricket was an excuse to spend a couple of hours out on Saturday afternoon before we could open the fridge and get into the beers, and it just happened to be that the state manager of Festival Records was one of the guys on the team. After about six months he offered me a job as a sales rep. That's really how it started. I chucked the uni degree—I had five subjects to go—and started my career as a rep at Festival Records.

I got a ten year old XF Falcon and was sent off to the wilds of Victoria to go and sell to Brash's stores and everything else. We were selling vinyl and cassette, and all those wonderful things that don't exist any more, and I had a ball. I did that for about

P. Graham, *Music, Management, Marketing, and Law*, Music Business Research,
https://doi.org/10.1007/978-3-030-02143-6_8

18 months, actually resigned, went back, finished my degree. Festival were kind enough to keep the job open for the four months it took me to go back and finish off the last few subjects. I was a very lucky guy. But the honest answer is that I fell into it.

Your time at Warners was very successful. If we look back a decade or so, we see Warner increasing market share of its Australian offerings, of its Australian signings from 3% to 17% of the local market, which was a huge jump. It was also generally a very positive period for Australian acts overseas. What do you think it was about that period at Warners that made such a success of our acts in Australia?

I think there was a number of things. When I first came in, the brief was to get in the game. We weren't in the game with regards to local artists or domestic repertoire. We'd been left behind by other labels and the Sony guys had started the Murmur imprint, Roadshow, which was a film and video, and theme parks, the distributor and theme park operator, and started a label and were starting to play. There was sort of this bubble away, and you'd always had businesses like Mushroom, Gudinski, and Festival and those sort of businesses that were overtly invested in the local business. So the view at that stage was, from senior levels within Warners, that Australia's this really interesting place.

In the words of the Americans, it's a really good test market. It speaks English. There's a lot of things that are similar: it's derivative of a lot of North American culture, a lot of English culture, things that work here can have a tendency to work overseas. Australians travel the world, there's a whole bunch of things going on, but the headline was that we were underweight in domestic artists and we hadn't invested enough. That was one reason why we got into it, and you mentioned that Australian artists at that point in time were doing well overseas, and majors at that point in time—we're talking mid to late 90s—had this terrible habit of "Boy bands are working, so let's go and sign five boy bands," and "Metallica's put a record out that's sold ten million, so let's go and sign heavy metal bands." And the same thing was happening with talent: "Oh, we've just had a hit with this guy out of England, so England must be hot in terms of local talent," or "We've just had a hit out of Australia, so Australia's got to be hot and there's all these local bands down there."

So they were the things going on in the background of doing it, and the other thing that was happening was that, for a long period of time, what was Warners before Warners became Warners in Australia was a company called WEA—Warner Brothers, Electra, and Atlantic, and we were distributers of that wonderful, 70s, 80s catalogues of, you name it: Rod Stewart, The Eagles, The Doors, it just kept coming out of North America. The local arm was a very, very clever and nimble marketing, manufacturing, and distribution operation, but it wasn't really a record company. And that fuelled obviously enormous fiscal success for the business, and there was the odd local signing. I mean, well before my time, but Chisel came out of what was WEA.

Charles Fischer had quite the relationship with WEA.

He did, and there was a band called Radio Birdman that came through that was part of the company's heritage, and they had a hit with another little band called

INXS. So it was the odd thing that they'd spotted, but early in the 90s we weren't really in the game. So that was the brief, and I've always said that for a local record company at that stage, an outpost of a major label, the real litmus test of how healthy the company was how healthy the local roster was. Because that's the bit that, you can become a really good marketer, you can become a really good salesman, you can become a really good manufacture and distribution operation, but someone else had put the time and effort into the Rod Stewart record or that Prince record or that REM record, or, you know?

But not much at the creative end.

You were dealing with finished products, so there was a responsibility there in terms of what you had to do. But to paraphrase it, you had saturation radio airplay. If you had good retail coverage and you were a smart marketer, you could sell records in Australia. So the health check for me, of any business, was the local roster where you've actually got to put your hand in the shareholder's pockets and say, "I'm going to invest in band x, and I'm going to help that band develop and build it from nothing into something," and that's where we started at the end of the 90s when I took over at Warners.

And is the difference, just sheer investment, do you think?

No, because you can throw money at anything and that doesn't work. I think, it's one of those things. People talk about A&R as being a dark art. It's not, it's a bit of a guess at times, it's a bit of a roll of the dice, but I think by doing that any time you're taking a risk, whether it's music or anything else, you're looking at circumstances and factors that mitigate that risk. And it may be that, if the band's got a fabulous live following, they've put a couple of EPs out, that you know the guy that's produced it, but there's all these different things that are going to come through that eventually make a decision. One of the key things for me, too, was also sitting down with artists and finding out what made them tick. It sounds incredibly rude to say about another human being, but you don't go and buy a house without doing an inspection on it. You wouldn't just buy it off the internet and hope that it's not going to fall over in six months. Therefore if we were going to invest and spend money on a particular artist, then we really wanted to know that they were prepared to get out and do the promotion work, that they were okay with getting up at six in the morning and doing breakfast radio.

All these types of things that you're going to ask someone to do, and for a lot of artists, that's a really difficult thing to do because they don't want to get out there and sell themselves. It's not in their physical makeup. I don't mean that as a criticism, and it's not always the case. But it was really important to know that, that if you had someone that you thought musically and artistically was just phenomenal but wasn't prepared to get out there and flog it, then all that was was just something on the sheet of paper when you were making the decision about, "Do we get into bed together or not?". That was just a contributing factor. It wasn't the be all and end all. We were very successful with a band by the name of Regurgitator. Those guys were not going to go and do the B105 rooftop gig. That wasn't in their nature. But by understanding what made them tick, and one of the reasons that Michael Parisi was the A&R guy that found and nurtured and worked with the Regurgitator team, was that we really gave them a pretty loose deal in terms of creative control. We knew sitting down on those very early days that if we tried to pigeonhole or box or sausage factory a band like Regurgitator, we were going to come off second best because they were very, very firm and strong in how they saw themselves and what they wanted to achieve.

If you said to the guys, “Define success,” for Regurgitator it was being able to continue for as long as they could as musicians. It wasn’t about how many gold or platinum awards or how many shows they sold out or how many records they sold. They wanted to be working, creatively free musos, and find a partner who could help them do that. And so I think when we found a happy marriage in that respect, then we understood what each other’s key points were, it made life a hell of a lot easier, and was in the end, successful.

They’re still at it.

Yeah.

So one of the views around the place for a long time was that Australia was basically, for the majors at least, a dumping ground for overseas content. So it’s been interesting to hear people who were around at the time speak in those terms, and what seems to be at play is the role of independents hanging off the majors.

Yeah, we had RooArt which was in there at that point in time. And you know, there was some terrifically successful acts that came through.

An amazing experiment.

It was, and anyone that’s ever spent time with Chris Murphy, he’s a force of nature. You might not always agree with him, but Chris goes hard, and RooArt was his baby which Warners financed and some things went incredibly pear-shaped, and some things went really, really well out of it. But I think that was also driven, too. I talked before about an educated guess and an educated gamble. RooArt was half a punt, you know? “We’re going to put some money into this, but we think you guys are the creative guys and you guys are the ones that can make this happen and work with the local acts and find the right bands,” so it was still, in some respects, half a bet. Rather than actually saying, “We’ll take this on, we’ll do it.” And over time, it’s worked either way.

I mentioned Murmur before, well Silverchair wasn’t signed to Sony. Silverchair came through Murmur and was out through Sony, then globally it took off and it was phenomenally successful. But it came from the imprint rather than the main label, and there’s always been that model. I think what you find in the smaller independents, I’ll use another context, is that every three or four years a new strand of dance music will take off, and then you’ll find that the people signing and creating these dance records that are doing really well are two kids operating out of their mum’s garage, with a really cheap kit who are making these really great records.

So the major comes along and says, “Great, we’ll buy you out because we’re really weak in dance at the moment,” and then they ask these kids to wear a shirt with a collar and turn up to the office at 9 o’clock every morning, and the kids go, “I don’t like doing that, because I’m out all night. I don’t get out of bed ‘til 11, I don’t start recording and creating until 6 pm” and that’s just not the way to do it. So they’ve trousered the cash for selling the label, they wait for the non-compete to finish in two years time and then they fly off and start it under a different banner and do the same thing. And that's where majors are really stupid, and that's where big ad agencies are really stupid, and that's where a lot of big business is stupid. They see someone who's highly creative and highly successful and has come up with a different way of doing something or a new innovation, they go and throw a bucket load of cash at them and then they say, "Now we want you to be like us," and expect them to still be successful. So I think, in a longwinded answer to your question on the independents, there's absolutely a role and there's absolutely a development role, and they're, I think, becoming an even more important part of the local scene because of the way the business has changed.

But if a major wanted to play, or a key investor wanted to play there, the best thing you can do is support them and that may be from providing financial backing. It may be that you've got a bigger distribution network. It may be that you've got some really slick promotion and legal abilities, and all those type of things, and get the hell out of Dodge and let them do what they do. Give them better tools to play with; don't go in and try to run the game for them.

So sort of an ecological approach where you're just basically setting up an ecology around the mother ship?

Yeah, there's some of them doing it well and we were chatting before. We've managed to convince Tim Freedman not to be an independent any more and sign to a major. He was well established, very successful. The Whitlams were three or four records in when they started with us, and it was like, "Well why would I do that?" I won't break confidences, but it wasn't fiscal things. He was really keen to explore some opportunities internationally and we had a network we could bring to the table there. He felt that he never had a fair go outside of the Triple Js and whatever, and he felt that we could bring some weight to the table with commercial radio.

So there were certain things in that relationship and we were playing to each other's strengths. But again, the entity that is The Whitlams and Tim is run very much as an independent, highly successful business that doesn't need any further help. It doesn't need any remedial work with people coming in. It's doing just fine. Don't try and fix it.

What was it like at Warners in terms of international?

Australian repertoire going the other way?

Yeah.

Really, really difficult. Really difficult, and it's really difficult because the record business and record labels, like anything, is a function of human nature, and we had phenomenal relationships. We got hearings on everything in terms of music we wanted to play and bands we were excited about. With success stories from Australia, you're starting to roll the whole thing uphill again. That's really difficult. Getting a shot just through the door in a big market like America or the UK is really, really difficult. And you could have a really solid level of success in your home market, Australia, but it's hard for people to unlearn and go back and start everything over again because that's what happens. I think that the time from then to now in the short space of ten to twelve years, that certainly the digital side of things and the ease that content can move around and the ease for people accessing content is breaking that down and changing it a bit. But, and then you'll get one, a Savage Garden that goes from being a couple of mates in Brisbane to completely blowing up the world two and a half, three years later—it still happens. But the long story is it's hard work. It's hard work even if you've got people in your corner who are madly as passionate as you about what you're trying to achieve on a bigger stage.

During this series, we've had discussion about what streaming services mean and their role. What's your take on them and how do the implications of streaming differ from one medium or entertainment sector to another?

You can do a quick chronological run through it. The first thing, really, was Napster, if you want to talk about a game changer. Napster was not only a game changer, but what it was was actually the music business, the record labels, had actually forgotten one of the key things about what was going on, which was keep your customer happy in terms of the way they want to consume content. And so, I say we, because it was we, missed it. We missed the fact that we'd gone from 8-track cartridges to vinyl to cassette to CD, and then the next one was digital delivery over the net. We missed it. There were a couple of really smart people running around in labels, saying, "Let's stop taking Napster to court, let's buy them, because that's the solution." It didn't happen, so along comes Apple and iPods and we know the story there.

It hasn't completely stopped the illegal market, but it's made a big dent in it and it's also giving the consumer a way where they're saying, "I don't want a pile of CDs at home any more, I'm happy to have everything on my phone, on my PC, on my laptop." So you can adapt that model to any content business, because the only thing that's limiting you is file size and the pipe. So I'm now sitting in there as a TV broadcaster in a big subscription television network, and the next thing on the hill for us is the government's rolling out an NBN which just means big files are going to go around a lot quicker. And, as you're seeing already, there's so much talk in the newspapers about TV networks denuding and we've been very successful in bringing a lot of our first-run content in express from the US. I'll give you a classic example: *Sons of Anarchy*, for anyone that may watch it, out of the US, we have it on air about an hour and a half after it screens in North America, each episode. Which happens to be 3 pm in the afternoon on a Wednesday.

The amount of viewership we get from people who've IQ'd it and they just series link it, and they go, "It's great, I'm not going to go to the torrent site, I'm not going to go to anyone else because at least these clowns have actually got it in the right time. I don't have to wait a week or two weeks." That's been incredibly successful for us, and you think, "How the hell are those guys doing reasonable ratings numbers on Sons of Anarchy at 3 pm in the afternoon?" We're not asking people to watch it at 3 pm. We're saying "It's there, grab it, record it and watch it that night when you get home, or watch it the next morning. But we'll give it to you, as you want it, as quickly as you want it", and that's going to become more and more an issue on our business, the free to air television networks' business, and all those things that the music community's been through. So to me, it's a really simple proposition: how do people want to consume? Find out and give it to them. I was showing you before, we've got our new iPad app coming out, Foxtel for subscribers.

So for anyone that saw the Olympics coverage where we had eight high-def channels, sports subscribers could download an app that allowed them to stream those channels to their iPad. We had 167 thousand downloads, 2.3 million videos streamed, and over the course of the Olympics, we published about 1200 hours of catch-up content. So the example there was, if you missed the opening ceremony, the next morning everyone said, "Oh, it was fantastic. James Bond went to Buckingham Palace, and the Queen was in it, and, oh, it was a great laugh." You go and find that on your Foxtel app on your iPad, at no charge, because you're a Foxtel subscriber. They're the things we have to do to combat people wanting to look elsewhere.

I was in the studio last night thinking about, well, obviously what was going on in the studio, but also about tonight, and I was watching one of the students watching TV from YouTube, catching up. She was catching up on her missed episodes of whatever it was, in between waiting around to do her take. She must have gone through half a dozen TV shows.

Wouldn't surprise me. And we certainly don't think we've got the absolute Panacea and the massive Band-Aid that's going to stop people sourcing and finding their own content, sharing content amongst friends, wanting to get that leg up. Because when I was a kid, the way I used to do it was I'd go and buy an album on vinyl, I'd get a 90 minute cassette, I'd sit there, I'd record it in real time, and then I'd swap them with my mates. So now everyone's sitting around here with their laptops and just spitting files at each other. The concept's the same. You've got stuff that you want to share with your friends, and maybe it's not legal the way you're doing it.

If, as content providers and broadcasters, we can jump on top of that, and I think the YouTube example's an interesting one. YouTube was up and running well before TV networks, content providers, sat down and said, "Hang on, how are we going to play in this space?" So they've carved out a bit of a niche, still got a preview. I mean we've got YouTube channels for all our music brands, and we deliberately put content up there, because we know people are out there that are either Foxtel subscribers or they're not. But YouTube's one of their primary sources for content, so we go and fish where the fish are, which is really important. And not put our head in the sand and say, "Oh, people shouldn't be doing that and they shouldn't be sharing content, and they shouldn't be putting it up." And the interesting thing was, when Google bought YouTube, they did a complete about face as a business. They were behaving like high sea pirates with regards to copyright before Google bought them. When Google bought them, YouTube came across the road to all the content providers and said, "Hey, we want to play. We can all make a buck out of this, we can do pre-roll ads, we can do all of this. We can even help you find our content on our site that you didn't even know was there." And they've developed this fantastic matching algorithm.

I'll give you an example. Let's pick something really boring: the final of the Australian Open tennis this year. Channel Seven can give YouTube the tape, they can run it at a hundred times speed and match it with anything. So if someone's actually uploaded the tennis onto YouTube because they've recorded it off the telly Seven can then claim it and drop it in under Seven and grab the ad revenue from it. YouTube's actively promoting that to content owners and providers. So there's this sort of symbiotic relationship. And it's been a massive change since Google's come in. The head space has flipped 180 degrees, which I think is a good thing.

Michael Taylor was talking about the role of YouTube in Universal and Island's revenue streams. I was shocked to learn it was number five after JB Hi-Fi, iTunes, various other retailers and so forth. Number five source of revenue was YouTube and they expect it to go to number one. Can you see the same thing happening with your business?

There's every chance it could, and I mean Universal in particular's been a particularly aggressive and forward thinking, you look at the VEVO product which they've been behind.

I think that's how they've done it.

Yeah, with the on-demand video player going through and YouTube pointing them to that. And I mean, they've been particularly aggressive in the space and it's a smart move. It's one of those things. I think that's actually a really good example of what I was saying before, of recognising that this is how people now want to consume content. So do we license providers to do so, or do we do it ourselves? They've done both and actually in both cases have been pretty successful. The YouTube model is working for them well, and yes, I can see that. Does it become a threat to us? Yeah. But there's a whole variety of reasons why people buy subscription television, and what we offer. I think it only becomes a threat if we have a false premise in what we're providing. Well before my time, a channel like V used to be, "You'll see it first on V." We don't make that claim any more, you might see it second or third or even fourth on V, right? But we ain't going to be first, and the reason for that is VEVO and YouTube. We have a different offering and we've got a different thing under the brand, and therefore we can still survive in that regard. But the one thing we can't be any longer is first.

We've had a long history of music television in this country, beginning, apparently, with *TV Disc Jockey* in the mid-1950s. At one point, and I'm thinking of the *Countdown* years here, it could have been said that TV was the primary medium for breaking new pop acts in Australia, becoming even more influential than radio for a time. What's the role of television in the music business now, and why do you think the commercial, free-to-air stations have practically given up on curated music offerings in particular?

Curated they've given up on, because the void's been filled by others who do it better, I think is one reason. And in terms of their business model, they can't make the scale of money out of it that they want. I think that *Countdown* was completely dominant: if you didn't have your band or your video on *Countdown* you were toast. But that was when there was only four signals in the market, and Molly was unique, still is unique, and carved out this niche and became judge, jury and executioner for new music for whatever reason. There was a time there where it was heavily important.

The free-to-airs have an interesting dynamic, and this is one of the reasons: music as a TV broadcast entity is niche. There's no two ways about it, it's niche. Music will pull an audience of X and the NRL grand final will pull an audience of 100 times

X. It's just what it is. We'll get the odd big thing that comes along where we'll draw a massive audience, and we'll get the odd thing where there's four men and a dog watching. There's a ceiling for music television, and that's whether it's free to air or whether it's subscription telly. So that's one of the reasons why they've got out of it, because as the market splintered from those *Countdown* times, free to air audiences declined massively. I don't know if you've noticed in the paper 6 months ago, 900 thousand is now a hit TV show.

I walked out of Channel Ten four and a half years ago, and 1.4 million was a hit. So all of a sudden, half a million viewers less on a Sunday night but it's still a hit. Why's that? Because the rules have changed and the free to air guys make the rules, so they can bend and break the rules. The audience has gone elsewhere, the audience is sitting on iPads, the audience is watching Foxtel, the audience is on their laptop, their audience is on YouTube, so you have this fragmented audience. And free to air doesn't have any other revenue stream other than the ads they sell, so they can't run pre-rolls, they can't charge a monthly subscription like we do or Spotify does, or whatever.

So they have to try and hang onto that audience, and they've actually splintered themselves a bit by being forced by the government to launch GOs and Gems and 11 s (Digital Channels Ed). So music doesn't tick that box. What they have gone into is reality music and god help us if we had another format. But we have The Voice, X-Factor. Idol's back next year, you would have read that, and not only is Idol back, American Idol's going on in the first half of the year on Ten, which used to sit on Foxtel, it's gone there. So they're going for what they would term as a big, shiny floorshow that can attract enormous numbers. I think the problem with that is that you get over supply, because, I guarantee, I had a look at the upfronts for the free to airs and there's about another four or five new cooking shows next year.

Because Masterchef's a big hit, so let's go and find another half a dozen of them, you know? And I don't think anyone's seen it, but this is the one that made me laugh. I think Channel Seven's got it, I kid you not, it's called Celebrity Splash. They teach a bunch of celebrities to jump off the three, five and ten metre diving platforms. This format's coming next year: Diving with the Stars. Anyway, so, god. Their job is to hang onto a big, big audience, and that's getting really tough to do. Advertisers want mass. The other question you asked about, "Why has it become our way?" I mean, we're able to do that better.

Subscription television is the antithesis of free to air, where we want to offer our customers choice. You want to watch music? Let's have great music. You want to watch sport? Let's have great sport. You want to watch cooking shows? We have great cooking shows, and that's across a hundred different choices. So the numbers are important, because the numbers are an indication that people are interested. So if you're getting zero viewers seven days in a row, you can probably say we've got the wrong offering here, but in combination, what we want is our customers who are paying us money every month to say, "You know what? There's always something there for me." And that's the difference. So if we're smart about the margins we operate on and what we spend on that content, we can offer a broader portfolio and as a result, we're not dependent as much, we only have free to air television in prime time which runs about 13 minutes of ads in an hour. You'll struggle to find any channel on Foxtel that runs more than 6 and a half to 7 minutes of commercial content an hour. So our ad revenue is less important to us in terms of the overall dollars we're seeking because we have people paying a subscription every month.

I think I remember reading a figure, it was 2004 and I forget the name of the survey, but it was the first time in history that the customer had paid more for content than advertisers in an overall sense across all media. So in other words, the model shifted at that point globally between media developing an audience for sale to advertisers versus media providing high quality, wide ranging content.

And you're also seeing that now, which again is an issue for mass broadcasters, because I've had a bit of a whack at free to air. But let's not forget print media's going through the same thing. The rivers of gold that were the classifieds are now all going online. That's making it hard for your bigger mastheads. Circulation's declining because people are moving online to digest news content, and we were saying before, if you put up a pay wall on *The Courier Mail* or *The Sydney Morning Herald*, well guess what? Go to the ABC iView! It's free and it's got the same news, but they're trying to adapt and adjust to that model, which is really difficult. Print was a phenomenal cash flow business for its owners. So yeah, all those things in combination: you're seeing a difference in how people want to consume content and what they're prepared to pay for it, whether that's a subscription, whether that's, "I'll put up with a hybrid model when I'm getting three ads every five songs," and all of that.

Everyone's still playing with the Rubik's Cube to try and come up with what is the next thing. And there's still going to be, just in free to air television this year, there'll still be around 2.9 to 3 billion dollars traded across three networks, so it's not dead yet. But it's coming under attack from a number of quarters. We're seeing it as well. And you've also got a situation now where from, if you just talk the ad model, I know I'm getting off brief a bit, the supply of available slots to put ads, so digital TV and everything, far outstrips the demand. So therefore it's about having a really premium offering, and that's one of the things we plan to with subscription television. If you want the best cooking channel, we'll have it. If you want the best "how to renovate your home" channel, we'll have it. As opposed to "We had 1.2 million people last night watch Kyle Sandilands dive off a five metre springboard", because you don't know how many of that 1.2 want to buy a new car. But if they're watching Speed, or they're on the YouTube channel that says, "This is the YouTube channel for new Holden cars," you can probably guess they're interested in buying a new car. So it becomes a premium value audience.

Just in terms of the music industry, you've worked in commercial, free to air, in the music industry, and you now run music for the largest pay TV network in the country. How do they differ in terms of what you actually do in relation to music, and in terms of their general relationships with the music industry, the majors and so forth?

I think you hit the nail on the head before. When I was in free to air television, we'd moved away from a relationship with the music business. We had pockets.

When I was there, Idol was a very, very hot format. So that was all about getting through to the final and maximising whichever kid came out at the end.

Were there backdoor deals with that?

No, no, not at all. The Idol franchise, actually, is a really interesting one in terms of how it's developed, because there's actually a template between the broadcaster, the producer, which was Freemantle Media, the label which was Sony BMG and how it works, the contract that's offered to the winner, the runner up or whatever.

Everything's actually enshrined before you even go into production, so in terms of the ability to exploit the young kid coming through or whatever, it's been through a really good filter. I don't like the formats as a rule, but I think that one, and all of them actually, are, that hold up to scrutiny, come off better than the Lance Armstrong test. So the free-to-airs didn't really have that relationship. What we have is a 360 relationship in terms of where we sit because we are a smaller offering. Foxtel is in a third of the homes around the country, and part of what we need is access. We need access to Pink when she's touring, or whatever, because that makes our channel stand out from the pack, and we look for exclusive things.

As I was mentioning to you, we had a secret gig in Sydney last night at a pub in Annandale. We had 350 winners get to see The Black Keys. That's the type of thing we can pull off and activate. You wouldn't see Seven, Nine or Ten doing that, or *The Courier Mail*, it's really just not their *schtick*. The flip side of that is because we're running four channels, seven days a week for 24 hours, we can play a bit more in the development phase. And that's an area where, it's a tough one with the labels because the labels are our partner, and we need to support them, we need the access to their content, and that's whether they're indies or majors or in between.

But we also have to remind them that we are not a charity organisation, that we are a business, and we will make content decisions that they may not like, i.e. "We're not playing your video." So there's always going to be a friction point. That friction point has existed forever, whether it's radio, whether it's a journo giving an album a shitty review. Those things will happen, but if you've got a solid enough relationship and a broad enough canvas, then I think you're going to get through those little arm wrestles. And so we very much see, in our world, not only labels, we want direct relationships with managers, with artists, with agents, with promoters, with festival organisers. We support a couple of the schools' programs. So there's a couple of things there we do. We have a very, very broad pallette, because we're trying to be reflective of what our audience is interested in, and our audience has very broad tastes. So it's not just the labels, that's a starting point, but that broader music community is very important to us as well.

I'm a big fan of the Foxtel radio channels. I came across them by sitting there flipping through the millions of channels to look for something decent to watch, and you get taken by the music that accompanies the guide channel. It's the Chillout Lounge, and I eventually made my way to the radio. There's some fantastic stuff there. What I'm interested in here is, how does programming work for your organisation, and for example, how might our students get their music played, for example?

We love the audio channels because it's ad-free. It's 40 channels, it's easy, it's background. So we, Foxtel, about 18 months, two years ago, revised the offering, and we now work with company called DMD, Digital Music Distribution, for anyone that's wanting to access to get their content played. DMD is a joint venture between Sony Music and Universal Music in Australia, so we have a contract where they provide content for those channels.

How tied down is it to those two majors?

Look, they have other companies' content in there, this is just the business that they've set up. So it's, Sony and Universal fund it, and they've said, "Okay Shaun, you're the general manager of this business. Go out and build a business". It's not only us, they supply to pubs and clubs and shopping centres and anywhere you've got background music, any music you like. So it's not just exclusive to labels, although their content's featured. So we have a long term relationship with DMD to supply that content. We provide them with a brief every month on what we expect across it, so we have final say on programming, channel names, content, genres, all the technical execution at our end. So, if you like, they're a great, big programming resource we've got that accesses all this wonderful audio out there and compiles it for us. That's how it works. If anyone wants to try and access that, or introduce music into it, DMD's the first port of call.

And that's for the inline audio only channels?

Correct.

And what about for your V Max and Video Hits channels and so forth?

For us it's direct. We have programming teams across the four channels, which is all up on the industry directories and bits and pieces, so we deal directly with all the labels, a number of the indies now have freelance publicists and promoters that will come in and talk to us about new releases and things that are coming up, and what they want to do.

A tip for those in the room that it affects: there's nothing more frustrating from our end than when someone comes in and sells us on a particular video along the lines of, "We've just made our new video and we're finishing the album next week, and we're really excited about it. We need it on Channel V, and the reason we need it on Channel V is because when we get that, we're going to go to Triple J and tell them that Channel V's playing it, so that means Triple J will play it, and then when we get Triple J and Channel V's doing it, then we're going to go to Austereo and get them to play it, so we really need you to get on this because we need Austereo airplay." That goes down like a ton of bricks with the programming team.

What really works is, "We've just made our video and we think it would work really well with Channel V, because you're playing X, Y and Z that are very similar to what we're doing, and we toured with those guys last year, and how about if we gave it to you before everyone else, and maybe you could pre-promote it on your website and do an exclusive at midnight, and we'll go to our Facebook fan page where we've got 20,000 kids on it, point them over there so they can see the Australian premiere. Would that work? Because if we make enough noise, we'll go to Triple J and then we'll go to Nova." It's coming in with a plan, and like anything, we've all been sold, someone rings up and says, "Do you want to buy an insurance policy?" and you say, "Well, no, I don't," and they come at you. So I think, sort of overemphasising it, it's really important, whether it's us or whether it's anywhere else, is you look at it and say, "I'm madly passionate about this video I've made or this band I'm in or this band I'm managing or promoting or whatever, when I take this video in or this single into radio or a reviewer or mob like ours, why the hell would they want to play it?" And that's very, very difficult to do because we've all got egos and when we've finished creating something, whether it's a TV show we make or an artist has just finished making a video or just walked out of the studio and made their album, that is, they are unbelievably proud of it. The first time someone else says, "I don't like it," or "It needs strings," or whatever, it's going to break their heart. So that's maybe where your manager's got to come in, that's maybe where your publicist's got to come in, that's maybe where you look at engaging someone if as a performing artist you struggle to wrap your head around that, but by being unemotional about it and saying, "Right, well what do these guys want and how do I turn it around the other way?"

You'd be surprised by how few people do that, and it drives me nuts. It's a thing I learned from Channel Ten because I was guilty of it when I was at Warners. Wander into Austereo, I'll tell them why they had to play this record: because it was good for me. They went, "Well we couldn't care less! You know, we want to do stuff on air that's good for us, that works for...". Channel Ten was really different, because advertisers didn't need us, they had choice. They could have gone elsewhere, so when a Coca-Cola came through the door and said, "We want to talk to 18 year old kids who are excited at summer and going to be at the beach, and they've been drinking Pepsi for two years and we've got to get them back to Coke, so how are you going to help us do that?" We actually had to come up with a plan that said, "Well this is why Channel Ten will be good for that, this is why you should be spending money, this is why you should be sponsoring Video Hits or doing stuff in late night news, or "We'll send Bailey down there to do the weather and he can drink a can of Coke," or whatever the case may be. You had to put an intelligent argument forward, not just, "Well we've got a youth audience and kids drink Coke, so you should spend all your money with us". You had to drill down into it. And that's the point I'm trying to make: if people can do that in any endeavour and run around the other side of the desk and say, "Right, I want this person to do this for me, why, and what are they looking for?" you'll be miles ahead, miles ahead.

How do you think Foxtel sees its music networks in terms of overall strategies, and is it important? Or do you think we could see a pay TV, massive pay TV enterprise like that without music channels?

Could you do it without it? Yes. How does Foxtel see it? We're right in the middle of that conversation at the moment, and the fact is they see it pretty favourably, in that it is relatively lower cost to run than some other areas of the business. It's a funny thing. No one rings Foxtel and says, "Can I subscribe to Foxtel please, because I'd like four music channels and 49 audio channels?" They'll ring up because they want sport. They'll ring up because they want movies. They'll ring up because they've got kids. They'll ring up because they think it's a wonderful education experience with Nat Geo and Discovery and the other brands that we've got there. Then when the guy comes around and installs the box and makes a hole in your wall, hopefully he's not too late, all those type of things, and you flick it on. If the music experience is bad, it's a double negative because the expectation is the music experience should be absolutely bloody wonderful. "I didn't buy it for that, but it better be good". And it's really interesting when we do customer research, these things come out. Thankfully, and I'll break a slight internal confidence, but we recently did a survey of about 1800 customers, and we said to them, we gave them all the genres and we said, "As a subscriber, here's these genres: news, music, movies, sport, weather, whatever else. Is it better or worse than free to air telly? You tell us." And I'll speak for music: music came up five and a half times better than free to air telly.

Not surprising.

Top of the class. Tick. Does that drive new subscribers, everything else? Going back to my earlier comment, no. There were some other genres where we've got some work to do and it's a perception issue, and that's from the people who are giving us money every month. And on the other side of the fence we went and found 1800 people who didn't have Foxtel, and said, "Tell us about these genres." Music was still number one, the perceived enhancement on free to air telly was lower than a subscriber, but the headspace still was, "Yeah, if I had Foxtel, my music offering would be better." Then we went down through the other genres and looked at that. So there's a recognition there, and that's something that we've got to live up to, and it's something that we're constantly diving into because, as opposed to any other business I've ever worked in, I'm now in a business where people pay us every month to be entertained. And not only entertained, to experience a level of customer service if their product or their box falls over, to have a call centre that's responsive if they ring up with a problem or want to get a second room done or refer a friend. So there's a number of different things in this business, and we've been very fortunate with management.

Kim Williams is the CEO now, with Richard Freudenstein who came in in December last year, these guys are maniacs in terms of, "What's that mean for the customer?" You can sit around and pontificate about whatever you want to do with a channel or a program or whatever, and they are very, very skilful at bringing it back to, "What's that mean for the customer?" And that's a really interesting business to be in, because hopefully we will manage to avoid pitfalls and push ourselves further down the right path of anticipating shifts in content delivery of how people want to consume content, of how they want to bundle up their subscription or why they're home, and all those type of things, and not find ourselves in a situation where we wake up one morning and some kid's invented a website and you don't need subscription telly any more.

It's a really hard thing to do, because technology's moving so quick and I'm nowhere near arrogant enough to sit here and say we've got all the answers. But we've got some pretty good ideas and we're testing stuff, and we think that we might be on the right path with a couple of things. If you and I had a blank sheet of paper on the board here and said, "Let's start this company and we'll have a hundred channels of content and we're going to get people to pay for it every month," we certainly wouldn't be talking about cable or satellite delivery in 2012. We'd be sitting here working out how we can pump it down the net, the pipe. And so without giving the forward strategy away, there's a lot of that going on in terms of, "All right, as this NBN rolls out, what's our product look like and how do we potentially offer more content?" I mean you want to have a look at a music offering, go to Sky in the UK, there's 32 different music channels. Linear video music channels, but the danger there is when you dig down a bit the viewing experience is really bad because they've split the market so thin in terms of the audience that there's nothing in it for advertisers. So you get those really cheap.

You've got to change channels to find another song.

Pro-activ acne cream and things you can put your feet in when you get home and give you a massage, and all that kind of great commercial content. So it's a really horrible viewing experience, and some of those channels in there have actually just paid for a slot. So we look at that and we say, "We don't know if we like that too much, it's interesting because a lot of the Sky stuff filters down into Foxtel in terms of learning and understanding, they're about three years ahead of us in terms of market development in subscription telly." And that's one we're just looking at saying from a music perspective, we really don't think that what initially, on the surface, appears great, "I've got 32 channels, I've got everything from R&B to pop to rock to dance to classics, to whatever," you've sliced the apple too thin.

You end up with an hour of content repeating every hour for 24 hours, yeah?

And it's a terrible viewing experience.

Like every other major media business, Foxtel's been involved in a number of copyright actions, sometimes as litigant, others as respondent, which I think speaks to the odd nature of where the pay TV thing sits in the media landscape. But what do you see as the most pressing legal issues for the company going forward, and how do you see those issues playing out?

Piracy's the issue that everyone's going to keep talking about, whether that's piracy of the guy selling smart cards in the pub for $50.

Really?

It happens, there's been a number of people busted who hacked and broke into Austar or Foxtel boxes and all of a sudden you've got subscription television and you might not get a full suite and whatever, but that goes on. So that's an issue where people are knocking off proprietary technology that's had hundreds of millions of dollars invested in it, which is probably a little unfair. The piracy with regards to content, I think everyone gets, but that's a less clear-cut argument, because as much as I can say, "Listen, I've paid for the license for show X," but if I sit here and say, "Just because I've got the Australian rights, I'm not going to play it for 6 months because that's my wont," I'm going to get smashed by consumers. And you're seeing that not just with the content, you're seeing it with the likes of Alan Jones the other week, and the tribe spoke. Now whether that's right or wrong, and I won't dive off down a discussion about trolls under the bridge and whether they should have Facebook or not, but people now have the ability to absolutely get front and centre, and not get shut down by the kid that's sitting at the front desk manning the phones at reception and the person in the mail room who won't deliver that. They can get into anyone's inbox and anyone's face, and that's a really different dynamic, I think, in how this works. You can have your voice heard and you can stir the pot.

So all those type of things means that the consumer, in many respects, in a very short period of time, has got the big stick in a lot of regards. Now that shouldn't necessarily drive a business's behaviour 100%, because part of it, especially in our business of entertainment, is about breaking the mould and doing something different. But you'd better listen, and you'd better have your eyes and ears out there, and you'd better be aware of what's going on. You'd better have a sense of who the tastemakers are and who the people are out there throwing rocks in the pond and making the ripple effect go out. So we've been on both sides of the fence, it's not my area of expertise. I think there's a real recognition from a senior level at Foxtel that content and content creators need to be recompensed for what they create.

Which is unusual for pay TV.

Yep, it is. But we're sitting very comfortably, we pay for our content on the music channels. So we should.

And there's a royalty structure?

All of that, and we've got blanket agreements in place, and we've got all those type of things, and we've got really good, open discussions with the collection societies and the labels and everyone else, and there's a framework in place. Not only those guys, but the artists who get played, you're going to get something for it. So that's a good place to be. Because you can't sit there by the same token and say, "We'll lift The Simpsons off a satellite and bang that to air, but we won't bother paying anyone." So there's that recognition.

There's the recognition that we need to keep an eye on piracy from both levels, and Foxtel has been particularly aggressive in a number of areas, and we're currently, Foxtel as a business, is off in the copyright tribunal with the Phonographic Performance Company. It doesn't mean that we don't think we shouldn't pay for certain rights, it means we think they want to charge us too much, so we'll go and let the umpire decide. So that's going to happen, and we will be probably fairly active in determining what we think is the right amount. Sometimes that will get into a nasty arm wrestle. But the headspace isn't we're trying to duck out of an obligation; the headspace is it's a commercial negotiation.

I first had pay TV in Canada, the Rogers network, and ever since then it's had me flummoxed why companies like Blockbuster hadn't gotten onto all that really early on. Because pay TV, you look at it globally, has had a big head start on everyone else. It's been around a long time. I don't know why companies like that would sit around with their bricks and mortar stores and wait for the inevitable end to come. And the same could be said for just about any area of friction-free goods, in other words cultural goods. Will there come a time when paid television formats are all tapped and are also retail formats where content's concerned?

Possibly, I think the Blockbuster example is an interesting one and the simple answer is they didn't have the rights. So Blockbuster couldn't come in and offer Foxtel the ability to screen Top Gun or whatever the movie is.

No, but to rent them through, for example, as you do through Foxtel On Demand.

They could, but then it gets back to a sort of wrestle that's going on at the moment. Let's say you're the international guy sitting at Warner Brothers in Burbank in Warner Brothers Television, so you're running reruns of Friends in a 120 countries all around the world and you've got god knows what else coming out. And your company in Australia does this deal, we sell DVDs through Blockbuster, so that model used to work where they would pay over the odds, so if the wholesale price on a DVD was ten bucks and it retailed at $9.95 take it home, that probably cost them $70 and then they could rent it as many times as they liked. So that bloke's sitting there doing his maths, saying, "Well, if I cut Blockbuster out and I just go straight to Foxtel, and I'm not paying marketing co-op and I'm not paying any sales rebate, I'm not paying anything else.

What's that worth? And what if I don't even need to get a Foxtel, what if I just told them to dial in warnerbrothers.com just drop the AU off it, and I'll just stream it straight from Burbank? Then I don't have to worry about Foxtel or Blockbuster or anywhere else, it's my content and I'm going to make a lot of money here in North America." So that sounds really, really good, until he sits down and looks at the cheque he got from Blockbuster last year for the hard copies, and the cheque he got from Foxtel for the ability to run programs, and then he looks at where the digital market's at and says, "Well it's not quite there yet, but if I make this plan and say I'm going to go direct to consumer, then it's going to cost me a bucket load of money over the next five years and I don't know if I'm ever going to get back to where I was," and that's the wrestle.

And there's almost a halfway house now, where that guy sitting at Warner Brothers in Burbank goes, "You know what? They're pretty smart boys down at Foxtel, Channel Nine or whoever I'm dealing with and they send their cheques every quarter, and the shows tend to work down there and be successful. I might just leave that one alone because I've got other things going on in my own market." And there's almost that hybrid recognition now that you and I've touched on this before as content curators, that the world of choice is a wonderful thing. So you go into Spotify and you say, "Great, there's 23 million tracks." For a lot of people it's like, "Where the hell do I start?" But if you go into Spotify and there's Molly Meldrum sitting there saying, "Listen, I'll show you the hits of the 80s and here's my channel," maybe that's attractive to people. But all of a sudden you've narrowed that 23 million tracks down to a hundred, and because you think Molly's a good guy and you like what he stood for when he had *Countdown* and everything else, you'll go to that playlist. So you just whack down, so a lot of the broadcasters are becoming filters and curators, and I think that's the next role for those things, that there will continue to be so much choice, whether it's torrent sites or it's apps or whatever, in the end you're going to go, this is a lot of what we're about, is, "I've got the Foxtel box in my house and it gives me everything I need. I don't need anything else, so I'm happy. My favourite TV and my favourite music and there's a nice app for the iPad and I can remote record off my phone anywhere if I forget something, I can zap it and tell the IQ box to do it. Great, I don't need to go and look anywhere else even though there's other options," and I think that's what a lot of people are moving towards as broadcasters as a real old term, but as content deliverers, curators. And I think you're going to see more and more and more of that in a very short space of time.

It's interesting, isn't it? Because it reminds me of that movie where the fellow gets voted in as president and gives everyone the choice on everything, and every decision has to go to a vote, and eventually the people just get exhausted and say, "No, you decide everything, we've had enough of this."

It's too hard, it's too hard! And part of what's happened with this sort of explosion of you can grab content anywhere, any time and you can sit in here and pick up a Wi-Fi single and download an album while we're having this conversation, boom boom boom boom boom. People are getting even more time-poor, so I generally believe in a lot of cases the ability to actually go and explore and to use an old-fashioned thing, to go down to the local record store and shift through the racks and see what's come in, and go to the listening station and put stuff on and hang around down there for an hour and a half, two hours. No one's got time to do it! But if you send me an email and say, "Listen, I know you're a huge Tom Petty fan, I stumbled onto this last night, you're going to love it," bang, that just is a multiple of a hundred versus me thumbing through 23 million tracks on Spotify and going, "God, I hope I stumble across something I like."

And we see that now in social media, you look at something like Facebook, who I think, if they haven't already, they're in danger of browning off a lot of people, so the stuff they've done in the last few weeks, the power of friends recommending, "Hey, you will like this, I've just found this, you will think this is funny, check this out, let's share it." The whole premise of what that thing's built on is having that extended community so you can keep an eye on what people are up to, and, "Great, I didn't forget Fred's birthday because it's just told me it's his birthday, so I'll give him a bell or send him an email or whatever." That's the usefulness there, of keeping that connection as everything started to go like this and get really loose, because it was getting too busy. That makes sense.

How about education? It seems to me that pay TV's, we've got this thing going on now that every university in Australia's going to be hearing the term "MOOCs", which is Massive Online Open Courseware. And places like Berklee and so forth are doing it, they're servicing hundreds of thousands of people, or tens of thousands at least, with this courseware that's kind of like you get a badge and stick that on, and it's good for the university. No business model around it, but it strikes me that the data push potential is so much more robust on a paid TV platform than it is on the internet, and probably far more sophisticated than anything the digital diploma mills are ever going to pump out. So can you see a future in which Foxtel's involved in such affairs?

To be brutally honest, I've never thought of it, I don't know. Does it work where people, they pay and they come in and there's a channel or there's a service? Possibly, I don't know. Would that be a conjunction with institution, would that be--

Well there'd be open university-type courses, or other accreditations, all sorts of arrangements.

The answer is that anything's possible, and as you ask the question I'm sitting here thinking, "God, how am I going to answer this?" Because I actually, I don't have any opinion, I don't know, I haven't thought through it. My gut always says to me that if you're going to have education offered outside of a room like this, then the web is the way to go. And maybe it's a combination of both, maybe there is stuff that sits within the Foxtel environment. And our world is changing too, where you think of Foxtel as coming down a cable or a satellite and into a box, we're rapidly moving as I've mentioned into tablets, into phones, into everything else. So under that banner you can access our offering that way. It may well be, I mean that's probably one that I'm going to give you a really ordinary answer on, because I hadn't thought it through. I don't know, I'm not aware of anything that's been developed in that area. We have a lot of different areas we look at, so let's chase that rabbit down that hole and see where it leads. It's not there yet, but it's an interesting concept.

The ABC used to do it during the daytime, you'd get all the French lessons on there. It still may be the case, they did it at the Armidale University, and they had all kinds of science programs and stuff that was associated with, say, I forget what they, School of the Air or some such, and they were actually parts of curriculum that the ABC serviced.

I remember in primary school flicking on at various times to those various programs.

Exactly, yeah, and that went on, I don't know because I don't get a lot of time to watch daytime TV these days, but certainly it was the case for many years that that was a way of doing it. It was quite creative, and very well funded.

I think the opportunity will become easier as we play more and more and more with delivery over IPTV methods, because the prohibitive thing at the moment would be, and Austar had a good program in the regional areas of Austar for schools, which wasn't education based; it was more community based. The cost of transmitting a signal into a school where would be more like what we do with our commercial installations, so if you've ever stayed in a hotel overnight and Foxtel, but there's a limited choice of eight or nine or ten channels, we bundle it down. There's still an install cost there, and one of the biggest costs we have is install. So if you said, "Yeah, we can do this," from a content creation point of view and working with institutions and education boards would be relatively simple, it's the delivery.

They had the Clearwater thing experiment in the US, with the school that, that pay TV channel doing in-school lessons. I don't know how well that went. It outraged a lot of people. I wasn't thinking of in-school, I was just sort of thinking, but I'll leave that. The whole media landscape's cluttered from one end to the other as you've said, and many of our speakers in the series have talked about the kinds of fragmentation that go along with the explosion in media. There's 97 million tunes on Gracenote, 550 years of continuous listening right here. People are uploading video to YouTube at the rate of 35 hours per minute.

And growing.

And growing, yep. Some people tell us that this will continue at an ever-increasing rate, but I wonder how long it will be until the bulk of people want a curated experience.

Yeah, look, we've touched on it a couple of times and there's also the argument that says there's 35 hours of content going up on YouTube every minute.

Every minute.

That just means there's another 34 hours and 45 minutes of rubbish on YouTube, and there's 15 minutes of good stuff, or 15 seconds of good stuff. So the ability of people to record and publish at a greater rate than ever before doesn't mean that the quality's gone up proportionately. That then supports what you're saying. You're bringing back that curator argument, which is ... the recommendation algorithm in all search engines at the moment: "If you like this, send it to your friends, share with your friends." Share buttons and like buttons and everything everywhere, so I think that explosion in available content plays right into curated experiences: "This is too hard and I'm time poor, and I can't be bothered sifting through this to find the nuggets of gold. So when someone does it for me, that I trust the brand, the curator, the person pulling the strings". The Wizard of Oz behind the curtain, I'll run with that one, and that could be find me, I'm after a pair of shoes, I'm after, whatever it is, because it's all available there and I think the minute those things start to work, and we've seen examples of a lot of them work already at the moment. I mean, real estate is divided into two in Australia: it's real estate dot com or it's domain online. You go in and whack your suburb in and the number of bedrooms, bang, bang, bang, there it is. People will have a choice as to the best, but it's completely flogged classified advertising for real estate. Not necessarily suburban glossies, but that market's gone. Car advertising, Cars Guide, bang.

Carsales.com.

All of that, yeah. So you start to get those type of things, and you look at it now where, I saw an interesting thing on the weekend: we're getting into sub-curation. I saw an ad for Shannon's Insurance for vintage cars, and so Shannon's have basically started their own, what's the best way to describe it? It's Shannon's version of Facebook. So not only do you insure with Shannon's, they've got this website where you can go in and throw up your pride and joy if you're a car nut, which is great, and find other car nuts who are also insured with Shannon who want to talk about, I'm going to get this wrong, '78 Chevies or whatever you're into. And I thought, "Isn't that interesting". They are sub-curating, and they are trying to create a community under an insurance brand, and god help me if I ever thought people would want to get around because they're all with the same insurer.

Are they using it?

I went and had a look, and there's people punching... now whether it's Shannon's punching cars up under aliases, I don't know. There is people in there using this thing. Now, does that become a sustainable business model, or is it a hundred rev-heads who have found something to talk about and they probably knew each other anyway? I don't know, but I just, I found it really, really interesting that you're starting to see businesses now come up with different ways of engaging with this. We know about curation and we know that that can work for music, and it can work for a whole bunch of things. What was the other ad I saw? Super Cheap Auto, so you join Super Cheap Auto's key customer club, and that costs you $10 or something, and we guarantee that anything you buy in the store, if we put it on sale in the next, I think it's four weeks, we'll credit your account the difference. So why they're doing that? To stop people shopping online, price shopping: "We'll guarantee you low prices but if we do go out and you've gone in and spent $100 on a tool kit and we put it on sale for $50, we'll give you $50 back. We'll put it in a credit next time you come in the store". So there's this next layer of people trying to work out, they've got a group and they've got a proposition from a curation point of view, how do you really hang onto them and incentivise them to continue to engage?

Stay engaged, sort of . . .

Yeah, and that comes back to the music thing with these streaming services. Alright, I've bought into Spotify, but I think I've mentioned to you before, my understanding of Spotify is just literally parked at a hundred thousand people using the service in Australia. Took off like a jack rabbit, and it's stopped at a hundred thousand. It'll be really interesting to see if that drops off, because how many of the hundred thousand have sat there and curated their own lists, and gone in and set it all up? How many have sort of signed up, had a play, run it through and said, "Yeah, this is okay, but it's really not iTunes" or, "it's not all it's cracked up to be." That'll be an interesting thing for those streaming services over the next few years. I think that they will end up with a couple, but I think it'll flame out a lot quicker. Because everything seems to, the next gold rush and whatever it is, blows up and there's five or six providers and this is the new beginning and streaming's the way to go, and everyone's going to pay $9.95 a month. Then it all just seems to crash quicker as well. And I've still made the point that I've got three kids and a wife who all love music in a family that, if I find anyone pirating anything, I'll basically excommunicate them. So we probably spend $60 to $70 a month at the iTunes store for tracks, and bits and pieces. And my worry is this with the streaming services, is that if all of a sudden if I go, "You beauty, I can spend $9.95 a month and get all the music I want! I don't have to go to iTunes any more," the music business—labels, publishers, artists, everyone else—has just lost $60 out of my pocket which may never come back.

And the artist isn't getting anything, I'll tell you that much.

I've got a good friend who had a track up on a streaming service in the UK, had a thousand plays in a month and he got a royalty cheque for 20 pence.

That'd be right.

Now you sell a thousand singles on iTunes, between you and the label or you and your distributor you'll probably earn 70 cents out of that dollar per track, so there's $700 to split versus 20 pence.

Yeah, I don't think it's working for anybody.

And so there's that, there's the reduction in my investment into music, and then, I've spoken a lot of these streaming services because they're all very active—and they're all very exciting and they all want to partner and promote and do stuff—is that they've got this view that they're going to, all of a sudden, they're going to find all these new customers who've been downloading illegally. And I struggle, and I can't wrap my head around the fact that if you get a 17 year old who, for the last five years has never, ever paid for music, that just because Spotify's run a couple of ads in

Rolling Stone, they're now going to pay $10 a month for their music. I can't see that happening.

They might take the free version and cop the ads, with an ad-blocker.

Correct. They may do that and use it, which is great and there's a bit of ad revenue. So I just think the model plays out, but the copyright owners and custodians didn't have a choice with this.

No, true.

If the labels had said, "We're not going to play, we'll see you in court," then what if this pops and I'm totally wrong and I don't know what I'm talking about, and here comes the next great funding vehicle for artists and the business, and they didn't have a stake and they haven't licensed stuff? So everyone had an arm tied behind their back that this thing was emerging and we had to get into it. We know that from the Scandinavian countries.

The rise of Spotify, which was one of the first markets in which it really took off, substantially damaged iTunes sales, which supports the point I've made. It went like that. And you know, we've done a lot of focus groups and research with younger consumers—I'm talking 16 to 24 year olds with the music channels—and I was horrified three or four years ago. There was this one guy in there and he was really one of those blokes that comes in and dominates the session when you've got twelve people around a table. And I wanted to jump through the two-way glass and throttle him, because he just wouldn't listen, and he said, "You know what?" he said, "I don't pay for music, because music, when you pay for music, it just goes to the record labels. The record labels screw the artists the whole time." Okay, got that, that's good. He said, "But I'll pay for my concert ticket, because all that money goes straight to the artists."

All right, so you've never met a promoter, but anyway . . . there's this entrenched attitude with a lot of them which is really hard to shake. Case in point: that guy's not going to spend $10 a month on Spotify or whatever. However misguided he is, where he thinks he's supporting his favourite artist by buying a t-shirt or going to a concert, that's fine, but that die has been cast. So it's going to be interesting to see how it plays out.

Probably none of our audience would have thought, "Oh, I might end up with a career in pay television." What kinds of music or music-related careers are there in pay TV? How many people are you employing to do what you do?

In the music channels we have, full time, just over 45, and so there's a variety. We've got people on staff who are programmers, some of those have a radio background, some have come straight in off the street, we've taken a couple of interns in from Macquarie Uni who've become full time employees, which has been great, who've joined the programming team. We have another team who are fantastic photographers and shooters and editors, which is our promo team, making all the 30 and 60-second promo spots, so we do that in-house with a graphic design team as well. So there's seven, eight in that team.

There's a small digital department who runs our websites, our social media, our Twitter accounts, all that type of thing. There's one guy in there who's come from a label background, there's another three that have come from various telcos, web start up design firms, whatever, and found their way into what we do. We have a small sales force, we have a production team which we use to shoot: we shoot, produce, edit and publish content daily, on air and online. So my biggest team is the production team. And we have a small marketing and promotion and publicity team. There's four in that one as well. So there's a variety of areas that fit within telly, and a lot of different on-ramps into that, so it's not just, "You have to be a programmer," or, "You have to understand how to cut and produce." People have come from a variety of backgrounds, and then beyond that, when we gear up and go and shoot something like a Future Music Festival or a Big Day Out festival, we obviously use a whole bunch of freelancers, and that tends to be sound guys, camera guys, riggers, hiring OB trucks, all that type of thing.

So there's a lot of really different, varied careers within there. The other one I haven't mentioned is obviously our on-air talent. Some are ex-radio, some have come up through the channels, some have just turned up because we did a presenter search and they were absolutely fantastic and managed to win out of 6100 entries in the last presenter search, and Marty got through and became our newest on-air talent, which was fabulous.

So to what extent are you a content creator? To what extent do you see yourself as a content creator?

In terms of content we create, we would probably create about 20% of what we put to air on a full schedule, that's Channel V. V's the majority of the content creation.

So who's doing the packaging of, like, the 50 greatest riffs, the 50 greatest Love songs . . .

All of that's us, we do it all in house. So all the graphic treatments, all the programming, everything else. All the clips are delivered from the labels, either physically or now most days electronically. They're in the library and then everything else we create from the ground up, so all the deco-plates and everything you see with number ten, and artist, song and title, we create it all in-house. So I've got a really, I'm really fortunate, I've got a really creative team who get a lot done with not many arms and legs to do it.

Like everyone. I've noticed some of your comments around the place on the nature of the visual aspect of music, and I'd be happy to hear you speak about that. It's become steadily more visual over the years, music, and what do you see as the reasons for that transition, and what's it mean for emerging artists?

I think it's a combination of a lot of things. Costs have come down substantially in terms of being able to film and produce really good looking content. You still see the mega-budget clips on superstar artists, but let's put those to one side. The ability for a new and developing artist to create an interesting clip or piece of content is there, and can be done at a reasonable rate, and I think that's a really, really positive thing. Also driven by, we've touched on the YouTubes of the world, just the available outlets for video content, and people's willingness to consume it. So I think all those things are driving it. And like a lot of things in life, you see some really good, creative clips that have been done on a shoestring budget because the idea was great. That's what we love with all our stuff, we'll play a lot of stuff that doesn't end up on commercial radio or whatever, because we sit there and say, "We're a visual medium, and that's an entertaining clip. It's a good song, but the clip's a cracker because it was a great idea."

And so I think people have the ability to do that at a relatively efficient economic rate, that's why we're getting more of it, and that's a good thing. And I think that will continue as the hardware and the software becomes more effective and even cheaper, it's just going to stimulate more of that. I'll give you the best example I can on that: it was two and a half years between the presenter search audition where Billy Russel became a presenter on Channel V and the one that Marty just won back in June. In that short period of time, the quality of entries coming in that people have self-produced or animate, film and edit or whatever was, I couldn't believe it. I couldn't believe it, I watched this stuff going, "This is all broadcast quality."

Some of the stuff was fun, and you could see that this guy or girl had something going on and they were really interesting talent, and "hey, we want to get them and learn more about them", and there were these other things that were just fabulous. And that is people's ability and mucking around and learning, and then the technology side as well where you could get really good kit at an effective price. So they're good things.

The Max Sessions are a very successful part of what you do. They look great, they sound great, and they're well put together. You've also got the V Guerrilla Sessions working for you, and strong connections with a number of festivals. What's the link between you and live music? Which way is it flowing, and why is it such a central part of what you do?

If you take the link with the festivals and the bigger tours and everything else, it's that we can give the promoters who are trying to sell tickets, that's what we're trying to do: get greater coverage and greater marketing voice than a free to air can. Because a free to air might say, "Listen, we're really interested in being your partner on the next U2 tour, but we haven't got much space because we've got the car races on Sunday, and we've got the news at 6 o'clock and everything else, but we can run some spots on Monday afternoon or whatever." We'll take it for 6 weeks, and we can run a U2 special, and if you've got the interview footage we can do that, we can satellite that in on a Saturday afternoon, why don't we play the last concert that was filmed in Wembley 4 years ago? We'll create U2 month, and they'll go, "That's really good." And all the while we're telling people to go and buy tickets when they tour.

So I think we bring a more holistic package to that, plus our digital and social audiences. The trade-off for us is that we get access and we can offer our customers and our consumers the ability to make sure they get tickets to the concert, so that's a nice *quid pro quo* relationship. We see the festivals as really important, because not only is a third of the homes that we go into do we have audience there, the bigger festivals, we also have potential subscribers there as well and festivals over the last ten years have become a massive part of the Summer music calendar in Australia. So if we're going to be the leading brand in music, which is what we want Channel V to be, then we need to be right there at every key festival. You're judged by the company you keep, and we want to stand next to the right people. And we offer the same thing for Future, Homebake, Stereosonic, Soundwave or whatever festival.

The only one we're not involved with next year is the Big Day Out, and that was a shame. After 19 years that was one of the things where we had to agree to disagree on some commercial terms and everything else, and they've got some new owners coming in from the US, and there's some really firm ideas about what they wanted to do. So we'll see how that goes. But other than that, we're tied up with everyone.

You mentioned the Sessions and the Guerrilla Gigs. That's us putting a stamp on content because we can't spend our lives just holding a mirror up to someone else's content, be that a festival or be that a tour or be that a whatever. So that's our way of doing things, and both of them are allowing our audience to experience something in a small, intimate fashion. The Guerrilla Gigs in a V style, and the Sessions in a Max style, it's sort of the older and the younger audiences. The other thing is that the Guerrilla Gigs have been phenomenal for our social footprint. We announce them on Facebook.

Like the Black Keys, for example.

Black Keys was one. Black Keys was a little different, that was a sort of one-off event, but the whole thing was driven we started with social media, and yes you can win tickets and we partnered with Triple M. The best example of the Guerrilla Gigs was Good Charlotte. We had just under 2000 people come to Rundle Mall in Adelaide for them. We only told Adelaide three hours beforehand that it was Good Charlotte at Rundle Mall.

That's the power of social media, so we've got this really engaged audience linking in. Now, we'd leak some clues and, city of churches, and a few people have woken up and whatever, so it wasn't just one announcement. But that's really powerful, when you've got people that engaged with your brand, so aware of what's going on that the minute you tell them what's going on, they're there. And we like that, and there's one running at the moment, we're doing one with, almost gave away where it is! We're doing a Guerrilla Gig with Delta Goodrem this weekend, and the banter within social media between fans about where it may be, "And I've got a mate who knows a mate whose cousin works at Channel V, who's told me it's here," and that's wonderful to have people interacting with your brand like that. And then give them a reward at the end of it, where we actually are, she is playing and we have got it, we are filming it, and if you miss it you can see it on telly in a few days' time, so we like those things.

Will you ever become a label?

No. It's not because there's not a buck in it, not because we're not... it's just, it's one of those things, we are, first and foremost, a subscription television broadcaster, and we are a group of channels within that. So there's certain other things we'll get involved in. We got involved in merchandise, we sold ten thousand pieces of Channel V festival clothes last summer. We're doing a deal with Skullcandy for headphones because we figure that that's a nice fit. So we'll play in those areas and do different things. What's a TV broadcaster doing selling t-shirts? Well, we can, and we did, and it was successful. But it worked in terms of where the brand was. One of the favourite merch items for the Country Music Channel is a stubby holder. We sell lots of those at Gympie and Tamworth and whatever, but it works. And it's complementary to what the brand's trying to do, so it's that thing about, "Be adventurous, expand your horizons, but don't be reckless in terms of what are we actually here to do in the first place."

We're just about at the end of our time, Shaun. I ask one question of all our guests, and it's this: if you were only allowed to offer our audience one piece of advice as future professionals, what would it be?

Be absolutely passionate about what you're doing, that's really important because it's important for a couple of reasons. It makes the day go quick. And people can see through a fake. If you're not passionate about it or you're doing something for the wrong reasons or whatever that would be detrimental to yourself. And I've been very lucky over a long period of time. Someone said to me a long time ago: "Be honest." Just be honest. If you really believe in something, make your point. If you muck something up, be honest about it, that's okay.

But people don't mind honesty, and honesty is not backing off on something. Honesty can be brutally frank as well. You've got to be honest about it. If you Just don't think you're up to something then it's time to move on. That's being honest, rather than pfaffing around, it's a really good thing and the same person that told me about being honest also said, "You can't remember the lies you've told." And you can't! If you lie about something, you go, "Hang on, where was I Sunday night when I couldn't make the barbeque? What did I tell them?" You know, be honest. "I don't want to come to your barbeque because I'm buggered and I want to go to bed." That, at all levels in business, I think. It just really cuts through. So passion and honesty.

Thanks. We've only got a few minutes for questions.

(Audience Member) I noticed in Pizza Hut and Hungry Jack's Channel V plays a lot, have you got a partnership with them?

No, that's through our commercial arm. So within Foxtel, there's the residential subscribers that we deal with, and then we also have another sales team that deals specifically with pubs, clubs, restaurants, McDonald's, whatever. So we're conscious of that, we get a brief from the commercial team that, "Hey, we are making a play for McDonald's and they want to know what they can play at 6 o'clock when they've got families with young kids in," and we'd probably say, "Don't play V, put V Hits on, that's the safer one." But yeah, that's an arm of the business, and it's the same as I was mentioning before with hotels. They'll approach Hilton or Best Western or whatever, and there'll be a brief in terms of the suite of channels they want. The shame with those type of deals is they don't show up in your ratings numbers, and we know that the music channels do really well in pubs and clubs and McDonald's and Pizza Hut, and goodness knows what else. And we'd probably be able to thump our chest a bit more about the ratings, so that's how that bit of the business works.

Chapter 9
Toby Cresswell, Music Journalist

Abstract This chapter is an interview with Toby Cresswell, one of Australia's most influential music journalists. He edited *Rolling Stone* (Australia) and was founding editor of *Juice* magazine. He has written numerous books, articles for multiple publications both national and international, and has also worked extensively in television and publishing. The worst appraisal from Toby is one of mediocrity, of being part of the "sludge". A song needs a story to be worth listening to or worth writing about and so needs to be a unique contribution to culture. The new media have challenged the role of the music critic as fundamentally as it has the role of the musician and composer. But there is no sense of nostalgia for a lost profession here. Rather Toby has a sense of opportunity and optimism about the future of music criticism.

Toby, in every respect we can look back at the last century and understand the music industry as a subset of the communication industry, or at least being almost entirely dependent on it for its success and shape. Given what's happened with journalism more generally, what do you think the current communication environment means for music journalism and the success of the music business?

Well, the current media environment I suppose is the internet really, I mean it's kind of the only game in town and everything else—print, television, radio, even live performance to some extent—is all subsumed into the internet. I think the internet is the best and the worst thing that could happen to culture. It allows everybody access to culture and allows everyone distribution, which, on the one hand, is a great thing, but it's also actually a really terrible thing. I think what we'll see in culture is the second law of thermodynamics. What we're seeing is good, but once you have a closed system, the amount of energy becomes flat with no highs and no lows—just a grey kind of sludge. Entropy is the state that we're looking at until something sparks it off again.

That's the worst thing about it, you think? The blandness of it all?

I think one of the great things about cultural activity, particularly in something like music, is the number of different people that were involved in the making of a record and the number of different people that were involved in the making of a

P. Graham, *Music, Management, Marketing, and Law*, Music Business Research,
https://doi.org/10.1007/978-3-030-02143-6_9

career. Now everybody can do it and you don't need all of these other things to get out there.

In 1980 for instance, when I was in a group making records, you'd have to get a whole bunch of money, you'd have to find a studio, you'd have to find a producer who was going to help you craft your music and you'd have to find somebody to distribute it. Through all of those stages people were giving input and the quality of that input influenced the quality of the record that came out at the end. I think that once you take all of those things out of it, once you take the record company out of it, once you take the record producer out of it, once you take the engineers in the studios out, then you end up with something that is not as good as it should be just because it's not a collaboration.

So a lack of specialisation?

Well, I'll give you an example. The Rolling Stones made the greatest records of all time and they had a producer called Jimmy Miller. Nobody really knows what Jimmy Miller did, but once they stopped using Jimmy Miller, they stopped making good records. Once they had complete artistic control the records got less good. The Beatles, who were the greatest rock and roll group of all time and created a good deal of the world's most popular music. But left to their own devices, all made really bad records. It was only when they had George Martin there and all those other inputs that they made the great records. Once you take those things out the quality becomes less and less. It becomes less and less interesting. What we're seeing at the moment is that things are very homogenous; you're not really seeing the highs and the new exciting things so much as you used to because it's harder to.

It's a confounding aspect of the whole thing to me. Marshall McLuhan predicted a global echo chamber, and it seems to me that's exactly what's come about. Instead of having a really diverse news-scape, for example, if you look on any news website across the world they'll have the same seven stories, maybe one or two differences. It's the same thing with pop. There'll be a Gaga record and that'll be it for a week or two weeks. There's not a sustained focus on any particular thing. So I just wonder what do you think can cut through all that. You'd think more people would be collaborating and more experts would be attracted towards each other, and towards the kinds of collaborations you're talking about.

Well I think there was a kind of infrastructure that was involved in the creation of popular music. There was an infrastructure that was involved in the creation of those records that isn't there any more, and part of that infrastructure was also people being told things that they didn't necessarily want to hear. So you have to make compromises and you have to try other things and be moulded in a certain way before you could come into your own thing later on. I think it's also a question of developing that infrastructure that allows things to grow, and the great record companies were record companies that took a long-term view of an artist's development. A classic example in Australia is Cold Chisel who made three records and it was only on the third record they did that they actually sold any copies. The first one did nothing, the second one did nothing, and then the third one was where they brought it all home and they went off and did a whole bunch of other stuff. In the age of the LP the third record benefited from the first two and the act had a chance to build. Now everything has to happen on the first record. You don't get three records any more. Even if you're any good you probably don't get three records. So, how you develop? How do you know what you're doing? In anything you do it's going to take you 2 years to work out what the fuck you're doing in the first place. Unless you've got the long term opportunities to listen to that commitment, to go the long term, you're never going to get that sort of sophistication.

I wonder whether you would have thought the same thing in your post-punk incarnation, in regards to record companies and the ecology of popular music in the, say 1980s when you were in Surfside 6.

Oh, I think so. I mean, we grew up with the the mythology of Island records with Chris Blackwell and Atlantic with Jerry Wexler, the other great independents—these were all record companies that were put together by people who weren't necessarily musicians but had great taste and could identify what could be done to take something from nothing to somewhere else. I mean Chris Blackwell with Bob Marley and the Wailers just took 30 hours of stoned jamming from Jamaica, brought in two American session players, and turned it into a record that changed the course of music and gave us reggae. But without Blackwell having that insight into where this thing could go, it would have just stayed being a regional music in Jamaica. No one would have heard of Bob Marley. No one would have heard of Peter Tosh and King Tubby and all the rest of the stuff that came out of that. So understand that those kinds of people were very crucial to the way that music developed. You don't have The Beatles without Brian Epstein; you don't have The Rolling Stones without Andrew Oldham. You've got to have that kind of connection, I think, and I've always liked that. I mean obviously there are areas of music where people just spread and go out and do their own thing and post-punk music was like that. But it's not really very listenable. It's interesting for people of our generation to go and have a look back on our youth. It's not really what has sort of happened in the mainstream. It's not going to rival Tom Petty or Lady Gaga, and it's not supposed to. It's not supposed to appeal to a lot of people.

We had for decades as part of the popular music ecology a curatorial system in TV, print, and radio too, from *GTK*, *Sounds Unlimited*, *Countdown*. Now we're left with, in television for example, one late night show, *Rage*, which is anonymously curated in many cases. Commercial radio has given up on promoting Australian music, quite explicitly. They say it's not popular and doesn't pull the crowds. The street press is also starting to fall. It's kind of like a last bastion. How do you account for the trend in the lack of curatorial interest in popular music?

In Australia or in general?

I'm talking Australia here but I'm happy to talk more generally if you'd like.

I think there are two things. I think Australia is particularly bad at that sort of thing. Australia doesn't really understand how to own its own culture. We pay almost no attention to the history of popular culture in this country. I don't think anybody here's probably heard The *Missing Links* album which was up there with The Velvet Underground but nobody in this country's ever heard of it. So we don't really honour these people. We have an ARIA Hall of Fame that none of the record companies or publishing companies can actually be bothered building. They don't give a fuck about it. All they care about is that they have a party once a year and invite a few people and get drunk and that's kind of how much remembrance they give to their own catalogue. It's absolutely a national disgrace.

So that's why it was very easy for the curatorial aspect of the culture to just evaporate, which I think it has. I mean Meldrum is kind a kind of unique character, as much as he is really stupid on television and a really bad television personality, he is, underneath that, a really smart guy, a great record producer, and a person who could actually spot talent and promote it and get it out to people and get people enthused about it. As a country we haven't really looked after creating that sort of thing. The television producers and the networks have not really understood popular culture or cared about it, so they haven't really tried to find new Meldrums and they haven't tried to find Australian versions of John Peel or whoever it is. So we've just let it go and we don't really give a fuck.

Most people at one stage discovered music through commercial radio. Now we've got the Triple M network that plays stuff that's 30 years old as if its demographic is kind of stuck in a time warp of some kind. I don't understand their attitude. I can't understand why they don't realise that they're the ones promoting the material rather than saying "this doesn't rate, we tried it once and it doesn't work".

Yeah, I think most of it's bullshit. We've got like three or four stations who are all playing the hits of the 80s. You turn on the car radio and it could be 1985 all over again. It's just insane, and there's no station that has an adult contemporary format, which is one of the most successful formats in the United States. One radio station tried it for 6 months, did it badly, so we're going back to the 80s. It's really bizarre, but I think because it's because the media in this country is a bit of a sheltered workshop for people. It hasn't been that innovative. I think that's probably the problem: there aren't that many people in the pool and it's a very shallow pool.

What about Triple J, as far as radio goes, what's your take on that at this point?

What's my take on Triple J? I don't mind Triple J, it's okay. I think community radio is more interesting than Triple J, but I think Triple J is also very trapped. It's like a goldfish bowl. Popular culture is like a goldfish. Everything sort of swims around and in two seconds it's forgotten what happened to it previously. So you don't find Triple J building a relationship between them and artists. You listen to it, think "that's a good track", and then you move on and you may never think of it ever again. So it's kind of like, "what does it all mean?" Nothing. I find also the other problem is that rock festivals have become such an important part of the way people consume music and I think it's a really terrible way to consume music. It's like you just show up to Big Day Out or Soundwave or whatever the hell it is and there's 25 different bands and they all come on and they do 25 minutes and then they fuck off and you don't ever get a sense of seeing somebody creating a show that's just for you and it's just going to happen that one time and the sound's going to be right and you're actually going to have a unique experience with that band. Instead it's just all about the event, being part of the event, and little bit of music on the side. I just don't think that creates the same kind of relationship that people used to have with artists, that creates a long term relationship with bands.

I've read quite a few articles from your back catalogue while I was researching your career and your writing has a consistent sensibility for the musician. I know you're a keyboard player, you're a musician from the Surfside 6 and whatnot, but there is another approach in music journalism that's really got to do with really loud and almost visceral criticism of artists, personal types of things. There's been a long line of it and probably the loudest line of it in many ways. What do you think of that? What is it, and why is it successful?

Yeah, well I think... criticism is not about, it's not being negative, I don't think. I think the mark of good criticism is something where a writer is kind of engaged, is really well-informed and contextualises the work in a creative way. I think the best criticism isn't about saying whether a piece of work is good or bad; the best criticism is something that illuminates a response to the record. It's important to have an empathy for the aims of the artist. For instance Midnight Oil used to be roundly criticised by Bruce Elder in the pages of the *Sydney Morning Herald*. Every time they did something he would write about how they're terrible because all the fans were suburban bogans and they were singing politics and it was all going over the fans' heads.

But I think he was missing the point. He was looking at the effect of the record and not what the record was trying to do. I think that's a common mistake. Nick Cave is not really aiming for top of the pop charts, you know, and Kylie Minogue isn't aiming to be on top of the alternative charts. There's no point in criticising them for not doing something they didn't intend to do in the first place. I think it's very easy for people to kind of sit around and bag the shit out of things. It doesn't really serve any useful purpose so I've kind of tried to avoid doing that personally. But I think that's the way it's gone. I think the other thing with a lot of internet writing is that it's very easy when you're sitting at the computer to just write negative shit and not really think about it. You just kind of write the first thing that comes into your head and I think that's not a very good way for things to go. My one big criticism about criticism is stars. I really hate when they give something five stars because I think a review should only be one star or it should be five stars. Say something's three stars, what does that mean? Does that mean it's worth $8.50 instead of $16.95? It's either good or it's not good. It's either what happened or not what happened. There's too many three star figures back there.

Coming back to your "grey" thing.

Yeah, it's either good or it's not, you know? Really good or really bad.

But as far as music critics go, the internet's had quite an impact and we've been hearing for a long time the slogan "everyone's a critic".

Yep.

It's based on a few things that have happened: an almost universal availability of music; the decline of the newspaper, especially amongst younger people; and the "prosumer" or "produser" thing which is, you know, that we're all content creators now and everyone's worth listening to. Do you think that music journalism in its printed form is done and dusted or are there viable models? I guess we're

getting back to the curatorial question here, is there something that's going to happen, can you see something emerging from this, say from what Everett True is doing with *Collapse Board*, or some other kind of movement beyond print journalism, is it finished, first of all? Is print journalism finished?

I don't think so. I've had this conversation with Sean Sennett from *Time Off* just a few hours ago and I think that there is going to be a real buzz to print journalism in the future. It may not be mass newspapers, but it may well be smaller, niche things. About a year ago I did this project for the guy who runs the Title stores. He runs this shop which has music and film and he wanted to do a magazine. So we put together this magazine that wasn't current at all, but it had this first-of-the-genre thing where it wasn't going "Oh well, so and so's coming here, this record's coming out, this is released". We said we're not going to do any of those things. What we're going to do is not do anything because it's current, we're going to do stuff because it's good. It doesn't matter when it happened, it doesn't matter if it's on the PR circuit, we're not going to have an exclusive with person x, it doesn't matter. We need to find things to be part of, to get excited about, and let's leave the PR machine, let's turn the PR machine off and get excited about other things and find some other things that are really interesting.

I think that's where the future lies because so much of our culture is wrapped up in this sort of PR monster. Every Friday you'll get five different stories about what's happening on the weekend and they're all the same. The same person who sat down and has given the same interview to 25 different people. It's boring and it's why newspapers are collapsing because you can get stuff from the internet but they're also collapsing because they're really boring. People aren't taking chances with stuff. People aren't finding out new stuff. It's just all the same stuff with different mastheads.

It's the same almost in politics. You can't find any differentiation and the minutest feature of it becomes the differentiating factor rather than the actual substance and effect of the thing. Is it a breakdown in trust? Because curatorial reputation is about trust.

I think the problem is not so much that it's a breakdown in trust, I think it's a breakdown in editing. I think people take the easy way out rather than trying to find new and different things. When I came into the business, even when I started reading newspapers and magazines in the 60s, the magazines that I really went for were things like *Esquire* magazine in America and *Rolling Stone*. The reason I liked them was because the editor was sending people out to find out what the hell was happening in the world and report that back in an interesting way. So you have things like Tom Wolfe with the new journalism stuff where *Esquire* sent him to California and he covered the car culture that was out there, which nobody was writing about. Hunter S. Thompson wrote about The Hell's Angels which no-one was writing about. They were looking for what the hell was going on, looking for what in people's lives wasn't already being covered. You just don't see those kinds of stories any more.

It was a strange kind of anthropological approach, really. At that level it was really in depth: participant-observer Hunter Thompson became a part of it the

group at that point and then those other writers you mentioned also did similar things.

It was kind of like that. I don't really want to lionise the sixties or anything, but look, there was a period where people were changing a lot and people were looking for different ways to be, to find out new ways to talk about what was going on. It was very much about taking chances. But now *everything* is stage managed. And while you can probably still go outside the boundaries, people are disinclined to. They just don't want to do it any more. I don't know why. Maybe it's because the editors are not up to managing it.

People reading *Rolling Stone* were armchairs explorers in cathartic ways to some extent, but has it all been discovered? Where would you go to find a scene that you could actually be engaged in, that people would find interesting now? Where are the outlaws of today if you like? I wouldn't even know where to start looking.

I think a lot of change is going to come not so much from Anglo-western culture but rather from the third world cultures, from what's going on in China. The Australian suburbs are not the same thing that they were in the 70s or 80s, but the stuff in the *Sydney Morning Herald* doesn't go past Balmain. There's three or four million people out past there. There's got to be some stories. There's gotta be stuff happening that we're not being told about because no-one's going to look for it.

For the most part what I've seen is more of a bandits' approach when people do go and do that type of thing now: going to South America or strange parts of India or anywhere and basically take a recording and "thank you very much" and take that with them and put it on a dance track or whatever. That's the extent of the engagement. It seems to me an odd way of doing it, or perhaps it's a prelude to what will happen.

Yeah. Look, I don't know where things are. The one song lyric that's always stayed with me is The Go Betweens song on *Spring Rain*. It's sung by the guitarist: "I want surprises just like spring rain". I think that's what I'm looking for and I'm not seeing any of it.

You're on record more than a few times as having declared an end to youth rebellion. That characterised the rise of rock and roll, and a whole lot of other things—why do you think it's the case that youth have become less rebellious and what's that mean more generally?

I think young people are less rebellious than they have been because there's nothing much to rebel against. When I was young person, sex was not as easily come by and certainly you didn't do it at home. The idea of drugs and getting stoned or all of those kinds of things were not possible. You had to leave home to go to get jobs and live an alternative lifestyle. These things were not acceptable behaviour. But now everything's acceptable. You can tattoo the front of your head and get a job at Macquarie Bank. It's just a different world and there's nothing really to rebel against, which is kind of what I'm saying about the Chinese. When you listen to those people they've got something to rebel against and they're probably going to come up with some of the most angry or exciting stuff. These days we have so much money, everything, so much stuff available, that it really does not offer much to complain about. You don't get good punk rock out of it.

What does that mean for music? Is it just going to be more of the same, is that what you're seeing? Or have we lost it completely?

Look, you're never going to lose music completely. People are always going to want to make music and express themselves, and there's always going to be some good stuff around if you can find it. But at the moment the big thing is groups with animal names and guys mumbling into their beards, and that's what's happening. That's the Bon Ivers and the Fleet Foxes and the Boys and the Bears and what is that about? It's beyond me. So, you know, I think it's a problem.

Australia tends to relegate its artists to history fairly quickly.

Yeah.

The same goes for producers, engineers, A&R staff. To some extent it's understandable for artists and certain music performers, but not for other categories. Do you think there's something unique about our culture that results in this kind of Logan's Run approach to culture?

I've always been really distressed about this whole thing. We pay no respect to the artists that this country's produced. Mike Chapman is a Brisbane boy. He produced Suzie Quatro and a whole lot of artists. It was called the Chin and Chapman sound, the big drum sound that went through a lot of the 70s glam rock and into Blondie's records and a bunch of other stuff like that. Mike Chapman changed the way people heard music and nobody knows about him in this country. Roger Davies managed Sherbet and then he managed Tina Turner, resuscitated her career, and a whole bunch of other people. Robert Stingwood changed music completely. But we don't know who these people are. I think that's really appalling. It's kind of like not knowing who Bradman is. Australians have this sort of thing where we don't really value our indigenous quality stuff. I think it's very sad. It's very annoying and it's at a great cost to the country.

That question sprang out of an interview I read with Mark Moffatt who's now in Nashville. He's from Bundy I think. A great legacy. He made the comment that the Australian pop culture dumped experienced people. Because these people build up a hell of a lot of expertise, something Mark Moffatt would know about. The same with Mike Chapman and the others you mentioned as well. What is it that just says "Nope, we'll get the new one, we'll get the 30 year old rather than the person in their 40s, 50s, or 60s who has the track record". Why do you think that is?

I think it's partly because we don't really care about culture so much. Record companies have a really short horizon. They don't really look backwards much and they don't really look forwards much. It's just whatever they can think of at the time. The one thing that Australians have not been good at that the Americans do really well is to craft a career. They know about this a lot but their whole cultural project of the last couple of years is really interesting in the way management sat down and said "okay we're going to build a demand for this. We're not just going to put it out on the road and sell some tickets and see what happens". They strategically create a lot of interest in something that people have lost interest in. Created a new thing to get excited by, get a bit of a sense of a mystery happening. And it pays off over the long term. Too much stuff in this country is really just short term with no strategic overview.

It's as if it's not recognised elsewhere then it's no good here.

Yeah, I think we still are much more obsessed with things that are really successful overseas and somehow not so many people are successful here.

Another, a lot of the commentary around that issue comes in terms of the so-called small market we have here, twenty plus million. But as you've experienced in Canada there's a lot of people making quite good livings there for sustained periods throughout their lives. I wonder whether it's behind a lot of the commentary we've seen about it being the best thing you can do if you're an Australian is to leave. Australian musician should leave Australia. What do you think of that advice?

One thing that INXS did was always see their career from the beginning as being a global career. They started touring Australia then they started touring around the US and the UK at the same time. They always had a global view and they delivered a global career at the end of it. I think that's a good way to look at it really. And with the internet now it's become much more simple; it really is a village. If you look at something like Gotye's record which has just sold massive numbers, it's ridiculous. So you've got to have that global view and you've got to start early and really believe in yourself.

Nick Cave and The Go-Betweens and those sort of groups had the same kind of view. They would travel the world right from the start. Someone like Nick Cave never really had a huge audience anywhere, just lots of little audiences. He kept that going and eventually it paid off. In the eighties the other problem was that, here, there was so much money to be made in the pub rock scene that everyone talks about. There was fucking ridiculous amounts of cash money and so it was very hard for people to go "okay, well I'm going to turn my back on that and go and risk it". But the ones that did were the ones who had success.

So why have we lost the big gigs? Why have we lost those big money gigs? We used to have numbers of them up here—Bombay Rock, even the Glen Hotel, huge numbers, thousands.

I would say it's partly because the licensing laws changed. I think there's the drink driving thing came in a bit, so you had those sort of changes. I think we went through a period in the late 80s, early 90s of alternative rock where the fashion seemed to be looking at your shoes and mumbling into your beard and so the music wasn't about reaching out to other people; it was more about kind of being unbelievably cool in your own mind or with your friends. So music became less and less a celebration of a public event. The smaller kind of groups that came up in that period, if they only had 55 people that would be preferable to them having 5000 people, so they brought it on themselves. The bands killed it and it's never recovered really. The acts that did really well were the Vines and the Midnight Oils who were putting on a big show. They really went out and tried to win over an audience. That sort of thing went out of favour in the 90s and then grunge and that kind of stuff happened, really. That was sort of it. I think Brisbane was much more lively than Sydney, because Sydney died a long time ago and didn't come back. Brisbane seems to have much more of a positive culture around popular music than Sydney does.

The majors: their back catalogue seems to be carrying them through their business disruptions. There are huge dollars being made in licensing fees paid through services like Spotify. Anyone who wants to stream stuff for free to people are having to stump up massive advances by all accounts. You've written exhaustively on rock history as well, and on the plight of ageing rockers, so I'm fascinated: at the same time as discarding the ageing and the elderly in this business very quickly, there's still a trend towards the past. Is it just profitable nostalgia? Or is it popular music canon becoming like the classical canon?

Yeah, well my girlfriend could tell you my answer to this question because I'm old and past it. But we were in the newsagent today and the magazine covers were The Beatles, Joe Strummer, The Cure. There was one lot of magazines in the newsstand where there was only one modern act. There seems to be more interest in finding out about Joe Strummer than there is about finding out about what's happening now, so I don't think it's just me. I think probably there has been a golden age of popular music. I think every art form has those golden periods and then periods of decline. It was the same for jazz. It was the same thing for music theatre. It was the same thing for cinema. American cinema in the 1970s was possibly the best it's ever been and it's never going to be as good every again. I think the same is true of music. I think it's just had its kind of golden age and we're probably not going to see the likes of that again. We'll see some acts that will still be fantastic and groundbreaking and exciting and wonderful but they'll be fewer and further between.

There's a lot of aspiring artists here tonight, and we can assume that mass media, including print journalism, is going to have a lot to do with their success or otherwise. How would you advise people to go about getting the attention of music writers, and from media in general, apart from going on The X-Factor?

I think if anyone wants a career in music the last place they should go is a TV talent show. It's proven not to be a way of creating careers, with the exception of Jessica Mauboy. It's very good for Simon Cowell's career but it's just not good for musicians. It's good television maybe, but it's not a music career, it's not a way to do that. I think the role that the media can have in the creation of somebody's career is twofold: on the one hand you can send out that information that's important to the act and get the story out there, but I think the other thing is to build the myth. You can't underestimate the value of myth and enigma in the success of an act, because what ultimately is going to keep people long-term interested is unravelling that story. That's why people are still going to see Prince, because there's only one Prince and you kind of want to know what the fuck is going on. And Madonna is the same sort of thing. If something's going on with The Rolling Stones or Bob Dylan, people are still interested in the myth and still interested in working out what singularity there is to that person. So that's part of the role. I think if you can find that, if you can find that original voice, then go for it.

I think music, in terms of a career, music is now probably a better career than it was 20 or 30 years ago. There's more options. I think there's more ways you can make money. The synchronisation fees for publishing are a much bigger thing than they used to be. There's a lot more kind of weird stuff in ads and there's those opportunities. I think it's much more of a global market than it was. There's always been people who've been really successful and then people who haven't been successful at all and I don't think that's changed. The opportunities are still there for people to do really well. Kimbra and Gotye are killing it, the Wolfmothers have been doing really well the last few years, and Luke Steel from Sleepy Jackson has done really well and is still being a really unique artist. So I think the opportunities are still there, probably better than ever, and the structure is there more than it ever was, but I think there's also more opportunity just to be part of the sludge.

In 2005 you said this: "I think the worst thing that happened in music was the CD. Now we're in an age where everything's on shuffle and you can mix it up. You can go from a song from the 1920s to a song that came out 20 minutes ago." Do you still feel the same about CDs given the proliferation of streaming services and everything? Are CDs still the worst thing?

No, probably not. Probably the bottom 500 of the worst things. Yeah, I find that whole streaming thing claiming that they are giving money back to the artist to be absolute bullshit. The artist never gets paid unless they have a really good manager. The other problem with the CD was it was 70 minutes long. The great thing about the album is it's only 40 minutes, so people could spend a year or however long it took just working within that 40 minutes and suddenly you can do 70 minutes and it was just too much stuff. That's when you started to have the decline in the quality of records, when people tried to fill up albums with 70 minutes of stuff, and so that was the problem. If you can do three minutes that's going to blow somebody's head off then that's better than just doing more. More isn't necessarily better. It isn't a volume game. It's a quality game and CDs made it a volume game. And then they stuck all these bonus tracks onto great records which was really annoying. But getting away from that, um, yeah. I think the streaming service is a bit like the music festivals. It all just becomes part of the lifestyle. It becomes part of the wallpaper. It stops being a singular experience.

Michael Smellie was speaking about the downfall of the majors being when they allowed music to become a general commodity available from Woolworths and petrol stations. Would you say that's part of the same trend in your feeling?

Absolutely. I think they also debased their catalogue. I mean you'd have a body of work like Bob Dylan, who is arguably one of the greatest artists of the twentieth century, he's up there with Picasso and Orson Welles and everybody else, and Sony, in the quest to sell their back catalogue, will sell you Bob Dylan records for $5 brand new. It's kind of like saying, the value that they're putting on it is $5, so how much value are you supposed to put on it? It was just stupid trying to create the sort of volume in the game by just saying everything's for sale. It shouldn't be like that. A Bob Dylan record is worth $30. Convince people to pay it and they will pay it.

Music's just the strangest economic beast there is, I think. It's had standardised pricing for so many years and they're still trying to do standardised. Why then isn't a Rolling Stone album, according to the laws of the market, worth $1000 while the latest indie release should be worth only 5 cents?

Quite bizarre.

It's bizarre, and the musician is an even stranger beast than that.

What do you think?

Oh, I think that the musician has the same relationship with the music industry as coal does with the electricity industry.

I think that's true to a large extent, and I think as the music business has become more corporatized that's kind of what's happened. The same thing happened with newspapers. I remember when Fred Hilmer was doing the chairmanship of Fairfax News and he just said "Well, journalists are just the same as widgets". And they stopped investing in journalism. If you can't tell the difference between good and bad then you probably shouldn't be in the business. It became corporatized in that way and it's declined ever since. You can sort of see the whole problem with the internet. It was basically a flaw of capitalism because there was this new delivery system, there was a whole new culture that was developing up around the internet and sharing music, but the guys who were in the offices, and they're all pulling down six figure salaries, their investment is in the business that exists. It's not in their interests to future-proof their business. They're probably not going to be there in three years time anyway, and so they don't really give a fuck. Their only interest is keeping each quarter profitable. So there's no innovation happening and so that's why the internet truck ran them over: because they weren't looking.

But they've been getting run over since the 1920s by new technologies in one way or another.

I think so. But I also think that in the 20s, 30s, 40s and 50s a lot of new people came into the market. Those record companies could come in and challenge the larger companies but didn't change the business in the same way. So, the corporate blunder with the internet was the result of a completely different mindset. From my memory of being in publishing when this all started to happen was that we would just talk to people in the industry and they would say "Oh, well no-one's ever going to get rid of paper" and you go back to the office and there's six people who are 23 years old and they couldn't give a fuck about paper. They were doing everything on the internet from buying Birkenstocks from Germany to publishing. The people in suits just didn't go ask their kids what was going to happen. If they had it would have been a completely different outcome.

I remember doing a review of a research report from UCLA for the New York Times. They were researching the effects of Napster. The majors were suing universities. They found in fact, at that point, and it's been confirmed a number of times since, that the people who share music are twice as likely to buy it than those who don't. So it was kind of a strange journey they've gone on for sure.

Yeah. They should have basically just gone and asked their kids "what do you think?" and the kids would have told them "Dad, forget about that other stuff, this is what's going to happen" and then trusted them. But they didn't want to, there was none of that interest, you know, because it wasn't going to happen for five years and in five years they'd be in the Bahamas or Fiji or whatever.

I want to talk about a couple of your books. *1001 Songs*—first of all you say it was in part a response to the iPad era. I mentioned earlier the 97 million songs in Gracenote which averaged to three minutes a piece will take you

550 something years to listen to non-stop. What's that mean for music journalism? First part, why *1001 Songs* in response to iPods?

Well, because I initially pitched the book to the publishing company as *1001 Albums* and it was just in that time when the iPod was coming out and it seemed like the album was kind of over. So we said "let's do 1001 Songs" and they said "Yeah, let's do that". It was at the point where the album had kind of finished as a way of understanding music and things had just started to become fragmented and come back to songs. So that's why it is *1001 Songs*. The methodology for putting it together was that I just went through all of the main genres that happened, all the major artists and all of the major genres that have happened since about 1955, and looked for the tracks that I thought were the most representative of a particular style of music or of a particular artist, or ones I particularly liked, and ones that had something to say rather than just being a song: Leonard Cohen's *Chelsea Hotel* right through to Janis Joplin. So if it had a good story then that song made it in and a song that didn't have a good story probably didn't.

So given the huge amounts of material, how do you cope with that as a music journalist, what do you do with it? How do you seek it out, how do you approach the curatorial task in this day and age?

Well you have trust in sources, I think. There are some people who I have a lot of respect for, critics being one. I think the best critics are people who are completely immersed in their subject and through that immersion can tell the good things from the bad. Sometimes you can tell just because you know in your gut because you've been doing it for a long time. Sometimes you can tell from all the various objective reasons because something has a ground breaking kind of sound to it, like the first time you heard Nirvana's *Smells Like Teen Spirit* you knew that this was something different. I can still vividly remember the first time I saw that clip on television. And so there are those kinds of moments and there's other times when you just happen to like it and you just trust people's taste. There are critics that I read even though I don't like the same things as they do. But if I read their stuff then I can understand more what the work is and what's interesting about it. And how do you do it? Well you just do it cause you really like listening to music and you can't do anything else.

Music in the 90s was a bit like music in the 70s—the first decade in this century seemed to be a period of fishing around, looking for new directions. Now we've got the new romantic styles coming back from the 80s. It's like there's been nowhere for pop to go in almost 20 years. Why?

I think pop music is the hardest and the most interesting aspect of contemporary music at the moment. I don't listen to it for pleasure, I just like to watch it happen and it's really hard to do. It's really hard to pick. People sit back and they look at something, One Direction, the boy band that's big at the moment, they say "Oh well, it's 4, 5 young boys and they're all cute and of course it works, they have the right producers and all that kind of stuff". But the fact is that all of the record companies all around the world are all the time pushing these things out and with the same producers and the same haircuts and all that stuff. Sometimes it works and sometimes it doesn't. I think there's a mystery there as to why some things catch on. It's just fantastic to watch and it's fantastic to watch it blossom, and how people look after it and how they develop it and keep the things going. It is a challenge. Justin Bieber faces an uphill battle at the moment to try to retain his relevance as his voice drops. And that's going to be a harder trick than Smashing Pumpkins doing their fourth album. It's interesting to watch and it kind of says something about the *zeitgeist* as well. Pop music for the last ten years has been really dominated by girls and it's been really dominated by hip-hop and soul music and it's now taking a different direction. It's about punk and it's about something else. It's quite interesting to watch it, it's really hard to do, and it doesn't happen very often. When it does, it's kind of like the drought breaks and then there's all kind of bands and boy bands just spring up everywhere. They'll have incredibly attractive haircuts and really bad fashion, and all that kind of stuff. It's going to be fun and delightful in 30 years time. When people look back on this era that's what they'll remember. That's what people remember of England in the mid 80s: Boy George and Duran Duran. So it's kind of a good thing. It's a beautiful thing to see.

More Spring Rain.

Exactly!

You could almost say the same about alternative genres as well, that there's a recycling and almost a forgetting of what's gone and presenting something as new and whiz-bang when it sounds like something from Weather Report or something else from the 1970s.

It is kind of weird that the whole thing with alternative is like anything: when something good is discovered that's new and different, then you can make some records like that, then forget about it and all go backwards. It's the same cycles that you find with punk music in particular, that sort of New York punk music from the mid-70s, you know, the CBGB sound: every so often it sort of comes back. The Strokes brought it back but I don't think that's uncommon in any art forms, is it?

No, I don't think so. I just wondered where the breaking point is. How it comes around, how it gets revolutionised.

Well I think everyone just gets sick of things. There are some things happening and there's tons of it around and then suddenly you get sick of guitars and you really want to hear synthesisers again. Or you get sick of lyrics and you want something else. Or you get sick of bland hip-hop bragging and you want to hear something interesting lyrically, and so people will find those people who are doing that at the time. Timing in pop music is absolutely everything. You can be any number of groups who just missed the time and just missed their moment. It didn't happen for them but they were just as good as everybody around them. You've got to be in the right place at the right time.

This is a question I'm asking everybody who's coming along and it's the last question I'll ask before handing you over to the audience. If you were allowed to give only one piece of advice to aspiring artists, what would it be?

I think the most important thing is to find that thing that you can do that no-one else can do as well. That's the most important thing: originality. Originality is worth more than anything else. Originality and application and that's it, basically. That's it from the genesis, that's kind of what it's all about: a unique thing.

Thanks. Okay, I'm going to hand over to the audience: Yes?.

(Audience member): You were talking about the lack of interest in the past and the whole lack of curatorial approach. What do you make of *Long Way to The Top*, stack a whole bunch of residual members of past bands together and put them in stadiums. Do you think that's any kind of reflection of the attitudes that you think might be dying out? Do you think that's a positive sign?

I think the *Long Way to The Top* thing is a positive sign. I think it's really easy to be cynical about that and just go "it's just a bunch of old geezers who are getting up to resume their fame and blah blah blah". Those jokes are all fair enough, but at the same time I went to the last tour and the audience loved that stuff. It was really alive and really vibrant and they really, really cared about it. It's important to remember that and honour it. I think there should be more of it. We don't have that sort of thing where people will build shows around established artists in the way that they do in the United States or the United Kingdom and I think that's really kind of bad.

(Audience member): Just going back to what you were saying at the beginning about how things on the internet are kind of taking over artistically, I suppose, reporting different kinds of art forms and stuff. What are your views on fan-run publications?

I think there's a really important place for fan-run publications. But you know, it's like, I'm misquoting this, but I think it's Orwell who said "Journalism is writing something that somebody doesn't want printed and everything else is PR". I think there's too much of that kind of stuff, there's too much PR going around and not enough people getting to the nitty-gritty of it. And the PR machines now have tightened things up so much so you can't get access, two or three day access with an ad. You can't get that kind of access to get up close and personal with a performer or an artist so people are not getting to know the artist and they're not building that kind of friendship.

Fans are absolutely important and you get a whole different level of stuff from them, but you need to have the other thing as well. But the other thing that occurred to me was, when I was still at school, I used to like to get magazines and I would get up in the middle of the night and I would drive into town and I would go in to buy the latest copy of *Rolling Stone* or *RAM* just to see what's coming out. A lot of the records that you wanted to get in those days you couldn't actually get them, you couldn't buy The Stooges, you couldn't buy The MC5, you couldn't buy The Velvet Underground. They weren't released in Australia. They were impossible to find, and so you spent two or three years just chasing this stuff down and that process gives you an investment in the actual thing. So you'd get the record and you'd spent three years trying to find this fucking thing so you're going to listen to it over and over again, you're going to know the whole thing back to front. Nowadays if you want to get a record you can get it in 25 seconds from iTunes and you can hear something you don't like and you can throw it away. So I think that's why the process is kind of different in a way. There isn't the same level of investment in things.

You started out by saying that we have no respect as a culture for our culture, which is really true. It's terrible to live in a place where Ed Kuepper goes to the shops in Oxley to buy a newspaper and no-one even knows who he is, and how important he is to musical culture. That sort of gets back to this thing

you said which about originality. How does a young person know they're original?

If they don't have an awareness of the culture, they don't have an awareness of the history of where they come from musically or culturally, how do they even know they're original? I had a conversation with Ben Lee once who said to me, because I was complaining about something I'd heard that was so patently obviously a rip-off of something else and he said "It's not important, it's not who did it first, it's who did it last", which I think is bullshit. It kind of ignores everything that is true or honest or rich about things. Is originality the same as authenticity? Is it about hearing somebody sing and actually thinking "this person is being honest with me", is that what real originality is? Is it not about style or genre or, is it actually thinking that you can actually connect with what somebody is saying, and One Direction have nothing to say in that regard. There are people who do have things to say. I don't know what that all meant …

I think One Direction are fantastic, I think they're much better than, um, Boy and Bear because originality—authenticity is overrated I think.

The word is overused. I don't know if the concept is overrated, the word is certainly, I think, badly overused. It's used to kind of cover a lot …

I don't understand what the word means, but like The Monkees for instance were the classic example of the group that people always talk about. They're the 60s something band that a TV station decided to create a TV show like The Beatles and put four people together that didn't know each other. Let's get the best in New York and Los Angeles and get the best writers for their songs, get the best musicians to play their songs, and they did. They made these records that were completely inauthentic by the usual standards of music, but fantastic records. There isn't a better record than *I'm A Believer* or *Last Train to Clarksville* or *Randy Scouse Git*. I could go on. So authenticity is not the big thing. There are a lot of groups from that period that were really authentic and were just singing stuff from the heart. It was music that had never been heard of before or since and they were not perhaps as good. So authenticity I think is not the important thing. I think *originality* is the thing. It's just having that thing that no-one else has done before, and I think the best thing about it is you can't really plan to do it. You can't really make it happen. You have to just keep doing what you're doing and eventually if you're lucky and you work hard enough you'll get that thing and you'll break through.

Would it be part of our job then, though, to make sure that students understand what came before?

Absolutely. I think some of the most original records are actually rewrites of other people's stuff, and that doesn't mean that they're not original. I mean, the fact that *A Hard Rain's a-Going To Fall* is somebody else's composition doesn't negate Dylan's genius in making that song out of that thing. It's what you make out of it that is the final thing.

I remember seeing Billboard Top 10 about a month ago or something, it was actually a top 20 and all but one had a title that had been written before. Every single one of them was not the same song but the same title as another hit. I think there's a big deal of amnesia that comes along with this information and

the greyness of everything else. It's a one-line-at-a-time life and the fragmentation of the consciousness brings a bit of amnesia with it.

It's also with popular culture. I'm 57 years old and I'm still listening to contemporary music, whereas when my parents were 57 years old they weren't listening to the kind of music that I was listening to. So there's this whole generation that's not happened in popular culture before, otherwise we could always just replace the generation.

(Audience Member): What is the difference between Bob Dylan and Woody Guthrie?

What's the difference between Bob Dylan and Woody Guthrie?

Yeah, as far as originality is concerned.

Um, well they both sound completely different from each other and they develop different songs about different things and have different languages.

They're both talked about the same things as far as being somewhat anti-establishment. Bob Dylan clearly was influenced by someone like Woody Guthrie.

Yeah, absolutely, I mean there wouldn't be a Bob Dylan if there wasn't Woody Guthrie. But then, you know, Dylan took it to somewhere else. Dylan created a new sound that no-one had ever heard before, and so that's the difference, I suppose. Different people go in different directions.

How do you feel about that, the older generation holding on.

The older generation—well, it depends. Today I think the older generation should be more listened to. I think, you know, what did you want to know with the question?

Well, as you said your parents when they were your age wouldn't have been listening to your type of music.

No, they wouldn't have. But that was a different art form, really. I was, to be fair, still reading books. They were still reading books that I was reading, so an art form existed that could cross the generation more than rock and roll music perhaps could. We were still reading the same poetry and looking at the same films but music was a different thing. So I guess that's the difference.

(Audience member): You said before that the album is over and I wonder do you think that we're going to continue for some time into this one-song culture and this shuffle culture and there'll be no room for something like a concept album, that you won't be able to make a whole album about one thing any more that's sort of like can be listened right through?

I think that eventually they will, but I think the most exciting stuff in the future is probably not going to be albums; it's probably going to be single songs. I would rather hear like one really great song than seven mediocre ones, and I think more and more you're going to find people are going to be doing that. There isn't the same financial imperative to make albums as there was. The great thing about record companies was that they could sell essentially the same product using the same effort. If it was a single they were selling it for $2 or $1 whereas with an album they could sell it for $12, and there wasn't that much difference in the work involved. With iTunes people are not going to buy albums, they're just going to buy songs that they like, and so the consumer is kind of destroying the album rather than the artist.

But if the artist comes up with a record that is twelve songs that you can't do without, like Frank Sinatra did with Come Fly With Me or In The Wee Small Hours, then people will buy all the songs. But the consumer is going to start cherry-picking, is going to go "I like that one, I like that one, I don't care about that one". So that's kind of what's going to happen with the album. It's not an artistic decision by bands; bands will continue to think people want albums and continue to make them but they won't sell them.

Do you think that's because consumers are just wanting songs.

Yeah.

That this is going to drive record companies and whatnot not to want artists to produce albums, not to do contracts for albums, but to do contracts for songs or something?

There are people who know more than I do but I think that more and more of that's happening. I think the deals are getting shorter and shorter horizons and more and more tight so people are starting to do things more on a record-by-record basis. As the record companies would say: they're doing this because it's greater freedom for the artists but it's just bullshit and they don't give a fuck about the artists.

Is it possible for us as an artist in this musical climate to create a unique product and make it actually noticed by the media?

Well I think in the sense now it's going to be easier, because I think there's going to be fewer and fewer people who are going to be original so if you get it right then it's going to be fantastic. Does that make sense?

Yep.

I mean, there's this big story in *The New Yorker* this week about Bruce Springsteen. I know he's kind of like old and everything, but the whole thing with Bruce Springsteen is that he does these three hour shows, three, four hour shows. At his shows, he sits down and he conceptually speaks about every song and where everybody's going to be in every part of every song and why that song should be in the set and why other songs aren't and so the whole thing is conceived as a complete theatrical piece. Then he goes out and performs it as though he's never going to perform another song, another show ever again. He says that he wants people to come away from his shows feeling that it's a concert they're going to remember for the rest of their lives. And that kind of commitment and that kind of planning and thought that goes into making that show is why at 62 he's still selling out arenas everywhere.

There's a reissue of *Darkness on the Edge of Town*, a documentary that goes with that reissue and in that documentary they go through the thousands, he wrote three or four hundred songs that were not used for that record that he spent two years just making that record because he had a particular thing to say and he wanted to say it. You don't see that much any more. You don't get a sense when you pick up a record that someone is telling you something in the way that people do with novels or films or other art forms. But I think that's kind of why those things last and they've been so strong and other things have not.

(Audience member): I'd like to ask a question from a writer's point of view, and that is: if you're writing about music and entertainment today, what, and obviously as a writer you have something to say, it's not just because you've

been told from PR, you actually want to express your experience and your thoughts and your concepts from your own position. How to go about this effectively because a writer wants to have an audience that's listening and wants to come back and take note, like you said before. Perhaps not really interested in the genre but the writer will be educating their audience and building their audience because of how interesting they are as a writer, what they're noticing and perceiving, and, with that is a tremendous power because you are creating the stories of today. Obviously everything's generating and being recycled or thrown out very quickly but what I wanted to know is what platforms a writer needs to be looking at? We've got things like Facebook and Twitter, we've still got some printed press but what are the platforms that are going to be really effective for having a powerful voice?

Well I think probably it's all about the internet in one sense. That's the main platform. I'm not sure exactly, actually, I don't really know, to tell you the truth. I think there's a place though for printed magazines, I think there's going to be, you're going to start seeing some of them coming back. Not in the way they were before but I think it's something that's really good about that as a means of expression and I think it's going to be a really messy sort of future really. But you know the internet is both good and bad because anybody can be out there, but also everybody can be out there. I think one of the great things about journalism in my career is the editor: behind any great writer is an even better editor and you know, submitting stuff and having people come back and go "that's not very good, fix this, what you need here", that process is really, really, really critical and that's one of the things that's disappearing in the online space.

(Audience member): For those who want to become rich and famous as performers or artists, number one the internet, I agree it's a grey area but it's geometrically proportional to the time you got into it, and the other thing is that the entertainment companies, the multinationals, they're getting their tentacles into absolutely every facet of our lives, even the ABC is running advertorials now on visiting artists and that's an indication of how much these multinational companies are getting their ties. So sooner or later you have to make the deal with the multinationals or a marketing company that's got ties, so that's what people have got to look at if they want to become rich and famous. It's not easy but it's possible.

That's true. They think, people hate the corporate record companies and so forth and I think they do a lot of stupid things but there are a lot of really smart people who are really dedicated at those companies. Almost every great record that's ever been made has actually been made by a multinational record corporation. You can't get around it and I think those people can give you an outside perspective on what you're doing and sometimes they tell you "don't do this" and it's painful to hear it but it's possible it could be the right thing to know. Sometimes. And it depends, some types of record companies are really good for certain types of artists and some are better for other sort of artists. In Australia I would say Sony Music does pop probably better than anybody else. EMI does the best left-field kind of stuff, somebody like Empire of The Sun for example, who sold three or four million copies around the world, massive global hit, that wouldn't have come out of Sony Music Australia I don't think. So it depends where you want to go and what you want to do.

Just to clarify, I don't think that the majors are evil.

No.

That the multinationals are doing this, it's just that, you know, you've got to come to grips with what they're doing and I agree they've done some great things. There's good and bad amongst them.

Yes. It's a capitalist world.

Yeah it is.

We've got time for probably one more question. Yes?

(Audience member): Earlier on you were talking about the artists maintaining a mystery, a myth to keep people interested. On the other hand you've got people like Ariel Hyatt saying to the artists "you've got to share yourself, you've got to let your audience into your personal life, that is how you build a community". And you also lamented the fact that the journalists don't have time to spend with the artists to get to know them any more. Media can be a circus and if an artist starts to make it big a lot of media doesn't have much respect for their privacy. Where do you shut the door and say "this is for me, this is my private stuff, you know, this is as far as I'm going to let you go", how do you set the boundaries? Where is that that the artist has something for themselves as well as sharing with their community, with their fans?

Well that kind of depends, you know, from one person to the next and it depends on all kinds of factors. Somebody who's been around for a long time like David Bowie for instance who is sort of the master of that, he's created this whole persona and then played it out and then five years later he's done it again. You got to know David Bowie in 1973 then 1977 he's a completely different guy and that kept his career interesting and people interested in his career. Sometimes you're in control of it and, you know, sometimes you're not in control of it and it depends on who it is. But I think you know that if you want to be a superstar you can't expect that people aren't going to go through your garbage. It's just unrealistic. So you've just got to put up with it, really. If you make enough money who cares? I don't know, I mean obviously some people do. Success and fame, it's not a pretty sight sometimes. It can really turn nasty. This is what you want; this is what you get.

Chapter 10
Harley Medcalf, Promoter

Abstract This chapter is an interview with Harley Medcalfe. Harley's credits include managing every Elton John tour ever brought to Australia; Barry Humphries' (Dame Edna Everage) producer for over two decades; touring Marlene Dietrich, Frank Sinatra, and Queen to Australia; globally tour-managing Formula One racing; and starting (against all advice and music industry ridicule) the globally successful *Burn The Floor* series of shows after developing an enthusiasm for Ballroom Dancing. Harley is an innovator and an eternal pioneer. Harley's method involves minute attention to detail. It is a lesson learned from costly mistakes, including one small mistake with limousines and airline schedules that unfolded into the spectacular 1974 debacle involving Frank Sinatra, the Australian Journalists Association, some indiscriminate security guards, a national union black ban, and a consequent worldwide media scandal.

Welcome Harley. Some of our most successful industry professionals started out as tour managers. Can you tell us why you think that's the case and how you first moved from that end of the business to become the country's most successful live entertainment producer?

Well back to the beginning: In 1970 I left school. I had no idea what I wanted to do. I went to the beach every day and I was working as a tree lopper earning $47 a week, so I had some money to spend but I had absolutely no idea. But as the summer of 1970 wore on and on and on it became really boring. There was nothing to do. So I came up with this idea of hiring Mona Vale Town Hall—a little town hall in the northern beaches of Sydney—and a couple of local bands. I ran that and made 50 bucks. As I was working 5 days a week starting at 6 am cutting wood for the Cooinda council I thought, "Hmm, there's an easy decision". So I became a dance promoter.

I guess it fuelled this ambition I had. If I could make 50 bucks on Saturday night, why couldn't I make $100 and do a dance on Friday night. So I started a dance at the Cabramatta which made about $10 but that was still pretty good. That was $60 a week. In those days it was well above the average wage. Then I met this guy called Billy Thorpe who would drive up from Melbourne to come and play at my dances. He'd get $400 and then he started complaining: "I'm not driving all this way for $400 you're kidding me. I've got to pay for petrol and pay the guys, so unless you

P. Graham, *Music, Management, Marketing, and Law*, Music Business Research,
https://doi.org/10.1007/978-3-030-02143-6_10

get me more shows I'm not coming". So it ended up that my Billy Thorpe run of dances started in Griffith, NSW and ended in Cairns, and we had about 30 stops by the time we finished.

That's how I discovered a career. My relationship with Billy Thorpe developed and I went from Mona Vale town hall to Sydney town hall and once ran three shows in 1 day with Billy Thorpe at the Capitol Theatre. That's about 6000 people, which is pretty incredible. A guy came back at the last show. His name was Robert Raymond. He was from New Zealand and he said "I'm bringing international acts into New Zealand and I need a tour manager in Australia". I said "What's the act?". He said "I'm bringing BB King". This is late in 1973. Now I didn't know what a tour manager was and I didn't know who BB King was but I said "Absolutely!". So that was where the pathway to my career began—with Robert—and I became a tour manager.

I had learned a lot running my own dances, but in those days the tour manager was it. You did everything: you hired the hall, you did the marketing, you sold the tickets, you swept up afterwards. It was a really good education, and as I graduated into international tours, the logistics, all of those things, you just learned. No-one taught you, you just had to work it out and I've always questioned things. Michael Chugg had a similar path. He was a tour manager. I met Michael probably in the early 70s when he came up from Hobart. He was a tour manager for a long time for Paul Davey and then did similar sort of things. You just did what had to be done and that's how you became a tour manager.

So at what point did you end up with a staff of people? Did you need that for BB King or was it later or was it during the dance promotion stage of things?

I became a freelance tour manager in the 70s and I was just for hire. So if you had a tour you could hire me. And there wasn't many people like me around. I worked for Kerry Packer. That was interesting. I worked for Kevin Jacobson, Pat Condon, and then 1 day I was on tour with a country artist called Hank Snow, a national tour, and Hank and I ran into a guy called Kevin Richie who was touring Suzie Quatro. We met in the waiting area at Adelaide airport and Kevin owned Duet Productions. We were just chatting and he was making fun of Hank Snow and this dreadful rug that he was wearing and I thought it was quite funny. But anyway, he rang me up 2 months later and offered me a job. So I joined Duet as their tour manager in about 1977. I've been there ever since, although Duet's changed a lot in all those years.

You began producing theatre almost at the same time you were a tour manager. From some views they might seem to be completely at odds with each other. How did you manage that transition?

It's an interesting question. I was actually hired by a company that Kerry Packer had called Encore. He hired me as manager—it wasn't called a tour manager—I was the manager of the tour for *Male of the Species*. It starred Edward Woodward and Michelle Dotrice and I knew nothing about theatre. I was a rock and roll person which was noisy with lots of parties—fast paced with everyone in a hurry. I went to the theatre in Sydney, which has since burnt down, the Elizabethan theatre in Newtown. I walked in and it was absolutely quiet. Everyone was speaking very quietly, very formally, and it was just really different. But I really liked it. It was a very different experience. So I always looked for theatre opportunities because I liked the formality and—I guess sanity's not the right word—I just liked the space that theatre was in compared to rock and roll where you're banging your head against a brick wall every day. So I became interested and intrigued by theatre partly because of how well-mannered it was.

So just going back to the previous question, when you said that you've managed 30 stops for Billy Thorpe up and down the coast, was the touring grid in place?

No it didn't exist, absolutely not. There was no touring grid. In fact, unbelievably, I met this guy other day who went to the first show I ever did in Griffith and I couldn't remember where it was. He reminded me that it was in the Woodside Mall. It was in this old, run-down dump of a barn in the Griffith showgrounds. We played in the cinema in Woolongong. We played in Townsville at the racetrack. We just put it together. We were pioneering. You just found places to play and if they weren't there you just made them. We used the showgrounds in Toowoomba. We would just hire somewhere and bring in a semitrailer for the stage and run a power generator or whatever you could to get the power going and away you went. I sold the box office from my car. I parked my car out the front and that was it.

There's a lot of comparisons made between sport and music. We've heard some of them in this series, and some aspects of your career have managed to cross both these areas. Do you think there are similarities between the pursuits?

Well I think there are a lot of similarities. There's no question. If you take rock and roll and theatre, they're opposite, but opposites that attract. Sport, and I mean big sport, like Formula 1 car racing, or the Masters golf, or the Australian Open tennis tournament, they're like rock and roll events. They're brash, they're over-organised, over-merchandised, massive ticket sales, corporate entertainment, hospitality, champagne flowing, the stars walk in and they're like rock stars, they've got their entourage around them and it's just this incredible buzz. So I think big sport, like test cricket, is the same as Rock and Roll. The cricket players strut around like they're rock stars, and they are—they earn a lot of money and develop a fantastic, sort of artistic, ego. There's great similarities between big sport and entertainment, especially in the way they're organised and run.

Do you think it's always been like that?

No, it hasn't always been like that, but everyone looks at each other. It's the rock and roll guys they hire to do these things. There's things at the moment like, pick an example, like the Dinosaurs exhibition that's going around. They're run by big rock and roll production managers. If you take a room with 50 dinosaurs and you've got to pack them in a truck, there are differences in the truck size in Australia and the truck size in America, and the truck size in Europe, so you have to build it to fit all three. Then you have to pack them in the lower deck of a 747 to get to America, or into a 40 foot shipping container. These guys are just wizards. They get down with the computer and design it all. So rock and roll has a huge influence on those big arena productions. Formula 1 is the same. There's a lot of rock and roll people who work in Formula 1 because the way you take all those cars and all those people and move them from Monaco to Singapore in 4 days and set it all up is just a rock and roll approach.

Rock and roll is an incredible discipline full of many talented people and it flows over into sport. In America, if you go to the baseball, it's like going to a rock and roll event. You go to the kerb side and someone's welcoming you and there's an usher to tell you where to go and there's all this stuff going on. There's music playing and people selling programs and peanuts and, yeah, to me that's rock and roll. Usually there's some wizardly looking old guy with long hair out the back calling the shots because he used to be the Rolling Stones' stage director or something. So he knows how to make things happen.

So these days are you still across everything like that? Are you still across all those details when you're doing shows?

I think I'm obsessive compulsive. I'm absolutely obsessive about detail. I learned early on through making mistakes, my mistake, someone else's work. It doesn't matter whose mistake it is. You can't afford mistakes. What I learned really early on was that it's the little things that cause the massive dramas. If there's a huge drama and there's a strike, or the plane's cancelled, or there's a typhoon or SARS—some global problem—all the professionals get together and we work it out. But if you spelled some guy's name wrong in the room list you get absolutely screamed at and it just doesn't help. So you've got to be obsessive about every detail, make sure of where they're sitting on the plane and who's sitting next to them, who's behind them, how they get to the airport, where you park—a thousand details. So check and then check again is kind of the mantra that I learned and I'm obsessive about that in everything. I'm going to check and check and underline things and put sums on pages. You've got to be obsessive otherwise it comes undone. And when it comes undone it's not a lot of fun.

So you're still across the details of any show you're going to tour?

Yeah, I'm lucky these days. In those days it was just me and my wife and slowly we built up staff. And now I have staff and I really check on them and they know me. Most of my staff have worked for me for a long time and they know I'm a pain in the arse and "I'm sorry I'm asking you for the fifth time but you have you done this?". "Yes Harley of course I've done it", "Have you checked this?". They know to check.

What's your philosophy on hiring people? Do you have one?

Not really. I like people who think differently so I really look for someone who—it's a bit of a cliché but—thinks outside the box. "What would you do if this happened?". "Well I don't know" isn't a very good answer. Something that might work is a good answer. You've got to come up with solutions. We run into problems and if someone can't look at you and say "I'll work it out" then they shouldn't be there. They're not going to get it right every time but the positive attitude and saying "I'm going to work it out" is what it's all about.

So you tend to look for people like yourself?

I think if I worked with someone like myself I'd probably shoot them. So no, not really. I just like the people who have different experience but are not afraid to stand up and say "I'll fix this". That's absolutely critical.

You've toured just about everyone who's anyone and it's an incredible list, I'm old enough to remember the chaos around the Frank Sinatra 1974 tour. He seemed to hate it here. The press savaged him as a mobster. He called our female journalists "bums and hookers", sparked all sorts of outrage, the unions

black banned his jet, he was trapped in Sydney in a hotel for 3 days. How did it go so wrong?

I was 24 years old. I tour managed Frank Sinatra in 1974 and I'm actually trying to write all of this down at the moment, to write about that period of my life. I know the quote. He said: "The female journalists are the hookers of the trade. They are bums and parasites". That was the statement that made the Australian Journalists Association take great offense. But it was actually a little thing that caused the first problem and it just got out of hand from there.

Frank Sinatra and his entourage flew from Japan into Sydney and then overnighted there and then flew down the next day to Melbourne in a jet that came for him from Las Vegas. When he got to the airport there was no-one to meet him, including me. We were not there and it was a disaster, basically. We had three Rolls Royces booked and unknown persons decided to take them for a joy ride. They hopped in the Frank Sinatra cars and off they went. One car eventually turned up and I jumped in it and said "Post haste!". As we were going down the road in the very early days of the freeway I saw this scrum of cars go screaming past the other way and thought "Oh shit!". So I got there and Sinatra, who's a time freak, got off the plane with his wife or girlfriend, Barbara Marks, and his security guard, Jilly Rizzo, who's massive. They found a fan waiting outside because they didn't go to the terminal. They were at the gate as you did in those days. The fan guy had a Ferrari. So how the hell the four of them got in the car I'll never know. Sinatra says "Get me to Festival Hall" and the Ferrari guy says "I don't know where it is". Remarkably Sinatra says "I do", and so off they went.

He unfortunately dropped them at the wrong side of festival hall and Sinatra had to run, followed by the press who chased him from the airport. That was where the famous *What made Frankie Run* photograph came from. They came inside while we were coming back from the airport with the rest of the entourage. You can imagine it was hell to pay. Sinatra got his lawyer: "I want more body guards, I need more security". So we hired these guys who were just security guys. They weren't that bright. We did the show. Afterwards, it was off-stage, into the cars, back to the Southern Cross Hotel, into the laneway at the back, with Sinatra followed by the entourage rushing into the hotel. The guys we just hired turned around and whacked a couple of the pursuing press. So it was all over from there. I found out just recently that David Hill—who's gone onto great fame in Fox Sports in America and Channel 9, if anyone watched that series recently about Kerry Packer, he was the camera genius—was a cadet journalist for the ABC in the laneway that night, and I want to write to him asking him what happened from his side. I haven't done that yet. But that's what went wrong.

I learned my lesson. People to this day ask: "Why do you book the cars an hour in advance?". It's because I've got this inbuilt terror that the driver's going to be late. Back in 1974 I probably spent a lot of money on cars, but if I'm meeting someone I want the car there an hour before. I don't care. Just sit there, wait, do not move, do not get out of that car. So that was my lesson from the Frank Sinatra tour: never, ever let the cars not be there.

So when did he make the comments? That was Melbourne wasn't it?

He made it on stage at Festival Hall. He walked out on stage and after about five or six songs he gave this amazing rave from the stage about his life and being pursued by the press and about how they don't leave him alone. And because of the rant he got a standing ovation. I've got to tell you, Frank Sinatra, as you say I've worked with a lot of people, I've been really lucky. How many people I've worked with make the hair on the back of your neck stand up just by walking out onto the stage? Frank Sinatra. The sort of intensity and presence that guy had, he just walked out and it was unbelievable.

So you've worked in about every part of the world and the touring company tends to be a small universe, its own ecosystem that happens wherever it goes. There must be a lot of ways in which different cultures affect how you go about your business when you're there. How hard are the differences to learn to negotiate? I mean you've worked in 180 cities across 6 continents over 40 years. At what point did you start to become fluently multicultural as an entrepreneur?

Well it's actually over 300 cities in ... actually I've stopped counting the countries. I've done shows in over 300 cities, certainly more than 29 countries at last count. It's a real learning process. I think a couple of things that are really important show the sort of cultural difference between three cities. Take China as the first example. The contract that you sign in China is a ceremony. You get to go for a few Mai Tais, lots of toasts, and you sign the contract and the next day the real negotiations begin. What you've signed is just a tea ceremony basically, no-one gives a shit what's on that paper. They start from that day to grind you down. So over a period of time you learn to keep ownership of everything on you aside from the hotels, because you can book them and pay for them. They're not going to grind you down and put you in some flea pit, so that's China.

Japan, on the other hand, is completely different. In Japan you have days and days of incredibly intense negotiations. But once you make an agreement and sign a contract, it's fixed. Don't even think of saying "Can I have one more room?" or "Can I have one more dollar?". You've done the deal and signed the contracts and that's that. It's absolutely terrifying because it can't be changed. So Japan and China are very different.

In the middle is the USA. The famous phrase in this business is "reduce or cancel". You sign a contract in America that's got 70 pages and you initial every page, you do this and do that, and it's all very formal but it's not worth anything. If you're not selling tickets, you get told "Cut your fee, cut your tickets". It's just terrible. But that's what happens. That's America. So there are three examples that are really different. From my point of view, I want to be known as a tough negotiator, so I'll push everything out. I don't want to be seen as soft. But it doesn't become second nature to know how to deal with these things. You just become totally untrusting. You don't trust anybody because all these things are so different and you've got to really think of where you are and what you're saying and what you're signing. So I don't trust anybody any more. That's a bit sad, but that's the way it is, because if you do, you're just going to do it tough at some stage. And seeing as 50% of my business is in the USA it's scary. If you're not right you get sued for these bizarre things. I've made a list of the things that I've been sued for, because I've heard that's an interesting global situation, but I got sued by a lady who got hit by a prop in the Princess Theatre in Melbourne and she got $37,000 from the insurance company. Insurance companies don't want to fight so they'll send you a cheque.

Where did it hit her?

In the face, it knocked her glasses off. I got sued by a guy in Launceston for loss of hearing because the sound of the taps in the PA for Michael Flatley's tap dancing was too loud and damaged his hearing. He got $45,000, I think, from memory. I don't know. It's shocking.

18 months ago I got sued by a patron in a theatre in Portland in the north east of America who was punched by a dancer whilst watching the show. In *Burn the Floor*, my dance show, the dancers enter through the aisles at the beginning of the show and they're a bit wild. When I saw the report I asked the company "Has anyone got a sore hand? Did anyone touch anyone?". "No". You'd think if you'd punched someone you'd know. Anyway, she got $65,000. And then I got sued by Michael Flatley—we'll touch on him more later—but Michael Flatley cancelled. He collapsed in Brisbane on the second tour in 1997 and I remember Michael going out to the ambulance. His last words were "Don't worry Harley, I'll make sure you're looked after". Then he sued me for something like £1.8 million for loss of income and it was just horrible. Fortunately my contract was right with Michael Flatley but I wouldn't say it was settled amicably. You've just got to make sure that your contracts are spot on to protect yourself. My attitude is that I look at a piece of paper—a contract—and ask "What can go wrong?". Find what can go wrong and what can happen and you think of all those things and all the problems that could happen and that's what I worry about. I worry about how are they covered, not what day I'm getting paid or whatever. It's all about what could go wrong and that's my contractual approach.

How do you deal with that? I mean that's a huge question: "what can possibly go wrong?"

Well you can't. You know from experience what can go wrong. You know how many people I've sued? I've sued one person. I sued a theatre owner, an owner of a non-profit organisation in Santa Barbara in California, because in the midst of a *Burn The Floor* tour of USA, the theatre went bankrupt. So we were just told "The theatre's bankrupt, don't come". We were 4 weeks out and that represented hundreds of thousands of dollars loss to us. The theatre went bankrupt and that's just not acceptable. So I sued.

Suing bankrupts is never easy.

Well no, but she had signed a clause that I have in my contract that says either person who signs this agreement takes full personal responsibility. Most people cross it out. She didn't cross it out. Anyway, I didn't win. I got costs, that was it. It went to arbitration, the arbitrator thought it was unreasonable that she should pay a loss. I didn't think it was unreasonable, but arbitration's a weird part of the law in America that you have to deal with.

You've seen a lot of changes in the circumstances surrounding what you do. Has digital media changed your business in any major way? And I don't mean in terms of promotion or communicating with people, I mean the ways in which it's affected recorded music for example. It's completely revolutionised the business model in that area.

No, I don't think it has in terms of live entertainment and I don't know how it could change it. I mean marketing and publicity absolutely. Communications, totally. But entertainment is about the live experience. A lot of times people go to a venue just to be able to say "I was there when so and so performed at ANZ Stadium and it was a great event". You were 350 m away but you were there with 50,000 other people. So I don't think—well perhaps this is where my career will come to an end and this is a very bold statement—I cannot see where the digital age will change live entertainment in the traditional sense that someone buys a ticket to see a band, other than how they buy the ticket, how you tell them about the ticket, or the atmosphere that you inevitably create with digital toys. I don't see that it can change any of that. Perhaps I've become a dinosaur. Someone else might work it out, but I can't see it. Am I right, am I wrong? Let's look at that again in 20 years time.

So not forgeries or other such?

Not really. We had forgeries in tickets before we had digital printing, so not really. You pick up forgeries usually because you check every ticket. You check the seats, and we're talking about that happening very early on. We found that out in the old days. I think live entertainment's about the experience. "I was there", "he did this", "she did that", "I loved it", "I went with my friends", "I went with these people", "we had a great time". If you can continue to provide a quality experience then you know you'll make money. I can still hear the words of my father, bless his heart, ringing in my ears: "This is fun what you're doing, and I'm sure you enjoy doing it, but you should get a trade because it will end". Well it hasn't, and I don't think it will. I love going to shows, I love going to the theatre. So do lots of other people.

When you're into promotion I've noticed probably over the last 5 years or so it seems to be really pronounced but there's almost no mass-media promotion for large touring shows any more, you hardly ever see it. Why is that?

Well the whole business is different. If I wanted to do something with someone in 1974 I wrote them a letter: "Dear Mr So and So, I'd like to work with your artist. Will you think about coming to Australia?". About a month later you got a reply saying "Dear Mr Medcalf, thank you for enquiring, unfortunately we're not interested in touring, should we change our mind we'll write you a letter". And that's how you did business.

It seems prehistoric. It moved so slowly. And then along came the telex. So you'd come in in the morning and there's rolls of paper all over the place. So you could actually write to someone, they weren't particularly responsive, in a week you might get an answer on what you wanted. But going from a month to a week was great, because in those days if you rang someone up, which was a really foreign and impolite thing to do, they'd say: "Send me a letter, write to me!". So then along came the fax machine, which Australia adapted to really quickly but the rest of the world didn't. But all of a sudden you could get an answer within the day. Then came the mobile phone. The Motorola brick, this huge thing that was the only thing you could fit in your briefcase, and people could actually find you all the time. And then the dreaded email. You can't escape any more.

I said to you earlier, I just had a couple of days off with my wife because it's our 30th wedding anniversary. I turned my phone off for the first time ever in my life. I've never turned it off before. I've never said "You can't find me, I'll see you on Friday the 21st, I'm not answering emails or taking calls". I've never done that. But that's the impact that digital has had on life in this business. If you take today, when I get back to the office tomorrow, I have *Burn the Floor* going, they start a promotional tour in Hong Kong tomorrow. We've got shows this year in Singapore, Hong Kong, five cities in Korea, two cities in Japan, and we open in the West End for a long run on the 6th of March. I'm doing the marketing for all that stuff now and I can see it all in front of my eyes in 1 day: "What does this look like? What's happening? Who's doing that?" and it's full speed ahead.

Plus I've got all this other stuff going on. You just do so much in a day that once upon a time you just couldn't do. Say you wanted a piece of artwork, you'd send a courier off to your advertising agency and they'd work on it for a couple of days. You'd send it back by courier if you didn't like it and eventually you'd get it back with corrections. Now you ring them up and sit there on the screen and say "No, the type there on the left hand side, that should be a little bit larger. Why don't you put it in italics? The second word, why don't you make that jump out. Okay that's it, send it to the paper". The digital life is totally different. You can see a TV ad made in front of your eyes and you don't even have to leave the office. It's really just so different from where I began. Sometimes it's a little overwhelming but you can be so much more productive.

Have you changed your outlook on promotion? Say *Burn the Floor* had never been heard of before and you didn't have that wonderful hook up with *So You Think You Can Dance* and all that sort of thing and all of a sudden had to put a show on in Brisbane, what would you do?

You see it's interesting, it's really interesting. I mean we obviously do a lot on the internet. We have all the usual tools: the website, Twitter, Facebook, and we put all that together. We have a philosophy that with Facebook you don't sell tickets but you do on Twitter. We don't do press ads. I love television. I love moving images. But if you're speaking to someone in Louisville, Kentucky and you try and tell them that putting a press ad won't sell tickets, they won't believe you. So you go on this philosophical battle about what you should or shouldn't do.

An example: I toured Billy Connolly 18 months ago and we launched the tour on Facebook. We spent no money on advertising. We came to Brisbane and did three or four shows at the convention centre. I didn't do any advertising because we put the word out that Billy Connolly is coming. The ticketing companies use EDMs (Electronic Direct Mailouts) with images to the people on their subscribers list and the tickets sell, thank you very much. You don't advertise; you just put it out there and it happens. I mean it's very different in that regard, very different.

You've produced shows for Barry Humphries all over the world including a Dame Edna tour in the middle east. I can't imagine what that would have been like or how it even happened, and that's sort of underlying the question: what is it about him that seems to translate across cultures? His work's really parochial in terms of its grounding but he's made it work almost everywhere. Why do you think he's so translatable?

There was a quote that Michael Edgley, wonderful Australian presenter particularly in circus over the years, and really fantastic entertainment family, talking about Torville and Dean, the ice show, which was massive in Australia and Europe but never did anything in America. He said "Some things work in some places for some reason". That kind of sums it up. Why did Barry Humphries get two runs on Broadway? Why did he run for 9 months in San Francisco? How did we do 50 cities in America that sold out? I'll use good old Louisville Kentucky because it's the middle of nowhere. How the hell did we go to Louisville Kentucky and sell out? Well Barry of course had the Broadway branding, which is incredible to have in America.

What kind of people came, what were the fans like?

Just normal people, theatre people. You know, America has this incredible model in theatre called subscription theatre where you buy five shows and you get the same seats every year, year after year. It's a really fantastic model, a bit broken at the moment, but really "How did Barry do it?" is probably the better question. Well the moment we got into the city, someone would meet us in the airport and Barry was at it straight away—"Who's the most famous gay icon in Louisville or Atlanta or Cleveland or Columbus?" And "Is there a really famous woman who's a bit overweight and a celebrity in this town, what's her name? Where would you live if you lived in a trailer park, what's the name of that suburb? And he would just start asking the guy carrying the bags and the person serving breakfast. He would just ask all these questions and he's got an incredible memory. So he'd walk out on stage the next day and it would be localised, and people would say: "Oh my god, how did he know that's where the trailer parks are?". He's just clever and I think that's the real hidden secret: he's got a camera in the stage manager's console there's a little joystick and it controls a camera that can go out and it can zoom in up there and "are you wearing a wedding ring?" Or "what sort of jewellery have you got on?", or "are you fidgeting?" And he can go around and the stage manager can say "three rows up two seats in they're holding hands, she's got a wedding ring on, there's your married couple." Fantastic stuff. That's a dreadful secret, but he's smart.

So how did you go with him? He's known for being quite the obsessive over detail.

I think I'm obsessive over detail. No, not really. I mean he just fired me but we had a fantastic 20 year relationship which just ended. That's a whole other story, I'm not even going to go there. But shit happens. He's the hardest working person that I've ever, ever worked with and he just works and he works and he does the publicity and, sure, he complains, but you just say "Barry, this is selling tickets" or "We need to sell tickets, you've got to do this".

What was the main point of contention?

He was tired. In those days we did eight shows a week and the day off was the travel day which in America is 12 hours really. It doesn't matter whether you travel in the front of a plane, it's hell on wheels. By the time you've settled into your hotel and you've finished drilling the room service guy about who does what, it's a long day. So he's got incredible energy for someone who's done it for so long and an amazing memory. He's driven and really smart.

Given the list of people you've worked with, it seems you ought to have gotten danger money at times. You worked with the likes of Billy Connolly and

Elton John when they were at their wildest. Have you ever had to worry about your health and safety through all of this?

No, because you don't have time to think about your health and safety. You've just got to get the job done. On a big tour you get a few hours' sleep. That's the worst part: you get a few hours' sleep a night and that's it. By the time the business of the day is done and dusted, it might be 3 o'clock and you're up at 6—day after day after day. Perhaps that's the hardest thing and I'm not as good as I used to be, but over the years that's what would wear you down. Eventually you just get really tired and want to sleep for 24 hours to catch up. So in terms of health and safety, not really. I mean some pretty bizarre things happened to me in my life. Sometimes I think I'm lucky I'm still alive, but you certainly don't think about it or dwell on it.

This is a really good story. I guess it would have been late 80s, it would have to have been when Alan Bond was around. When did he go down the toilet, early 80s, mid 80s, something like that? I was touring with Elton John and I'd come up with this idea for Elton because he had 85 pieces of luggage and moving from city to city was an absolute ordeal. So I said "Why don't we just stay in Melbourne and we'll hire a jet and just fly to Brisbane and fly to Sydney and fly to Adelaide. No need to unpack". He thought that was a great idea. So we were based in Melbourne. In fact first show we had to fly to Brisbane and Elton's a time freak—most people of that calibre are—time is everything. If you're leaving at 3 o'clock, you're leaving at 3 o'clock, so you'd cut things tight. What time's the show in Brisbane? You're on show at 8 o'clock. I want to be there at 7:15. So you back it out from there: an hour 15 to fly, leave the hotel 4 o'clock, bang, police escort into the venue, you know, quick relax then on stage. Everything's timed to a tee. So on this particular day we get in the cars out of the Hilton hotel, get on the freeway. We're barely there I get a call on my Motorola brick—imagine if there hadn't been Motorola bricks. I get the message that Alan Bond's plane has been repossessed. "What are you talking about Alan Bond's plane has been repossessed? It's wheels up in 30 minutes!". "No, it's already gone, it's been repossessed". "Okay, thank you". So out with the black book, which is something you build up over the years, and start calling people.

"I need a plane, tell them we're there in 30 minutes time. What have you got?" "Nothing. Oh just let me have a look. Oh the ANZ plane, it's an HSV 7, takes 11 people, just came out of service, you know, x thousand dollars and it'll be waiting for you. I've got pilots, we'll be there, 30 minutes". So you pull out as if nothing's happened. Your shirt's a bit wet through, but in you get. You pile in the plane and Elton's on a high. This is great, off to Brissie, do a little show, door gets closed you start taxiing away and we had a friend travel with us who actually worked for QANTAS. We're just sitting there. "I've got to have a leak". He goes into the toilet, opens the door and there's just a hole in the floor. They hadn't reinstalled the toilet after the service. So "We need it out here now!". They just pushed it out and didn't double check. If we'd have taken off we'd be dead. We were 5 minutes away from a complete nightmare.

So what did you do?

Well the plane turned around and the door comes down and these people ceremoniously carry out the toilet, they fit in a new one, You can physically see the steam starting to come out of Elton's ears and our old friend from QANTAS Ken Groves, he's one of the funniest people in the world, the most delightful man, he can see we're right on it. He calls up to Elton on the back of the plane, "Wouldn't have happened if you'd travelled on QANTAS, Dear!". So Elton thought that was funny and the moment passed and off we went.

Did you make it on time?

We made it on time, absolutely. But you know, if you think about the things that can go wrong you have absolutely no control because you're moving at that pace. It's a bit scary. There's no margin for error.

So when you're doing that, are you with Billy Connolly all the time, with Elton John all the time, or do you consciously separate yourself from the goings on in order that you can function?

I've gone from this self-obsessed person who thought that the show couldn't happen unless I was there to one that says "Maybe I can just ring up six times and find out what's happening", which is kind of where I'm at today. I can't always be there because I'm more productive in the office. I can't always be there because I might have three or four things going on at the same time. At one stage I had Billy Connolly touring Australia about 8 years ago, 2004 maybe. He was touring here exactly the same time as I had Barry Humphries touring in America. Now I could say with Billy—because Billy's just the coolest, nicest, best person in the whole world—I can say to Billy "Hey, I've got to go to the US for a month, you'll be fine, I'll see you when I get back, off you go". Billy's happy, plays the banjo, does his shows. Kevin Richie, who is the founder of Duet who'd retired came back, and Billy loves him. He went on the road and spent time with Billy.

So I can say that to Billy but when it came to, say, Barry, "I've just got to go back Australia for a week". He'd ask why. "Well I've got to go see Billy Connolly". I wouldn't be out the door before the phone was ringing with "What's going to happen with this, what's going to happen with that". So, it's just different, and Barry would terrorise me on the telephone. He'd ring me at 3 o'clock in the morning: "My music director's sick, what am I going to do?". "I'm in Adelaide Barry, I'll call someone". Or at 4 o'clock in the morning "What time is it?" "What time is it where, Barry?" It's good in one way because I think I'm missed, he needs me. But why is he calling me in Australia to ask what time it is? Because he can and he knows how much it pisses me off.

So do you think that's part of why you've succeeded at what you've done, because you've been like you are with people?

I don't know, I've always figured I over-service. You create a rod for your own back doing that. Why do I have breakfast with him every morning, lunch with him every day, and dinner with him, and then walk him home after the show? Why do I do that? Because it means he's comfortable, and it means he does a good show. The philosophy I developed really early, which is why I never talk about myself and you never read about me, is because my job is not about me, it's about the artist. My job is to get the artist on stage in the best possible frame of mind I can. If that means I'm having breakfast with him 30 times in the next 6 weeks, whatever. That's my job: to make the artist happy, make sure the theatre is full, make sure he's got what he wants, and that he's got no reason to feel uncomfortable. I can't imagine what some artists go through to get themselves on stage. I can't imagine what hell they put themselves through to get out there and put themselves at risk every night. I couldn't do it. Not many people can.

Who has the most trouble with that in your experience, and how does that manifest?

It manifests in screaming terror, getting abused, getting yelled at: "Get me out of this hotel!", "I don't like him", "I don't want them tomorrow, get rid of them!". Okay. "I hate this dressing room, I'm not coming back here tomorrow!". I mean you go through all that stuff. It's not the end of the world, you just do it. Some of them really suffer. It was really interesting, on the last tour Billy Connolly had become very introspective. He told me "I get so nervous before I go on stage, I really don't like it. Maybe I just shouldn't do it any more". I'm like "God forbid! It's like it's your old friend, you know. Here's your old friend. Hello old friend. It must be show time". He looked at me and said "Not a good answer". And then he asked me "How does Barry Humphries do it, what does he do?". I told him that Barry's a really great example because he can arrive at a theatre in absolutely the worst mood you could ever imagine: doesn't want to be there, doesn't want to see anybody, doesn't want to do a show, goes into the dressing room, slams the door, awful. Anyway, he gets in there, starts doing the makeup and somewhere in the next half an hour the makeup goes on, the wig goes on, someone else takes over.

Suddenly that bad mood is just not his problem any more, it's Edna's, and I've got tell you, I've done thousands of shows with Humphries and he's been in some absolute stinkers. But he's never once in his life come off stage in a bad mood. He gets it all out, the adrenaline cuts in, he loves adrenaline, he always came off in a great mood. What happened before didn't really matter, it's just gone.

So when you compare a high maintenance artist versus a Billy Connolly type, do you think they are better off being one or the other in terms of what you do? Does the squeaky wheel really get more oil?

No, I don't think so. It's whatever it takes that person to get him or her in a state to go and perform, to do what they have to do, to go on there for 2 hours and be the impossible person, to do an incredible show and make everybody happy. I think everyone's different, even Billy. I've toured with Billy for over 30 years and I've only been in the situation once when he was upset and, as usual, it was just one of the little things. We were staying in the Hyatt Regency Hotel in Melbourne and the day sheet from the hotel—the list of activities that are on for today—comes under the door. It says "This is on and you can still buy tickets for Billy Connolly at the Arts Centre. Call this number". Well, Billy's shows had been sold out for 3 months and it didn't really matter apart from the fact that the Dire Straits were in the same hotel. So he felt like I had let him down in front of his friends by putting it around that his show hadn't sold out. Well I hadn't let him down, but maybe I should have spoken to the hotel knowing that the day sheet comes and said "Whatever you do, don't put Billy Connolly's name on that."

How would you guess to do that?

I know, but someone might. But they're the sort of things that happen, that make your day a little unpleasant.

Which is the artist you've worked with that stands out as being the smartest and why? I'm not talking about the most talented—intelligence and talent have different names for very good reason. I mean most intelligent in terms of making and managing their career.

The truth of the matter is that it's really hard to split it and I think you have to split it to get to a result. The most talented—Freddie Mercury, just radiated like a laser beam, charisma, talent, I mean he was unbelievable. I was lucky to see him live on stage, lucky to see him in the flesh. He's an unbelievable talent and no-one, I don't think, will ever come near the fierce intensity that he had on stage. So most talented: Freddie Mercury.

Most intelligent: Elton John. Elton John could have six shows in Sydney lined up and say "Well, day one invite the cricket team. Day two invite the tennis players. On day three, the soccer players. On day four bring in some fashion people". He'd invite a different set of people every night. Now when the cricket players came in he knew everything. He knew who was in form, who was out of form, who was getting the runs, taking the wickets, who was dropped, who was out there waiting to be discovered—he knew the lot. And next, tennis players come. So and so had just won the Open and it was 4 all in the fifth set and "what a great finish it was", and the drop shot he did, and "he's going to win Wimbledon next year" because he's done this and he would have these amazing conversations. And then someone from the music business would come in and Elton would start: "What about that new release? You had that kid from so-and-so, but if you'd done that a little differently", and at a 100 miles an hour rattles off these different statistics and names. His mind was just unbelievable.

How did he keep up with that sort of detailed knowledge?

Sometimes he'd be talking to you and you'd be playing cards and he'd have the phone and he's listening to his team play soccer and I mean, unbelievable. I don't know how he kept up. He just goes at a 1000 miles an hour cracking jokes left right and centre. Everyone's rolling around laughing and he's just amazing. The most intelligent.

But if you take the career decision, the person who really had it together both as talent and as someone who totally controlled his own career and knew exactly what he wanted that was Michael Flatley, *Lord of the Dance*. This was a guy with Mensa level intelligence combined with a ditch-digger street smarts from Chicago—I mean street fighter professional, and roll them all into one. He's an incredible guy, a visionary. Michael visualised. He'd go for a walk, come back, and say "I want this. I want to see that". He'd see it in his mind and then he wants it. His intensity, his ambition: "I want to be the most successful show ever", which it was. He lives in a castle in Scotland worth £100 million. But he was the most ruthless guy I've ever encountered. He chewed through producers, managers, production managers, and staff like you've never seen. He challenged them every day. You might say "Michael, what an incredible show", and he'd grumble and say "It'll be better tomorrow". He wasn't being silly, he actually meant it. And it always was better the next time. So the gong for the combination of most talented and most intelligent was Michael Flatley. But the result there was that he's got a lot of money. What's he got inside? I don't really know. What else has it given him? I don't know.

Did he burn out do you think?

He got really ill. I mean he collapsed in a heap in Australia because he was burning the candle at 65 ends. A few years ago he got really ill, some mysterious auto-immune disease, and nearly died. But he toured and actually performed again last year. Michael always had it worked out. He had a two hour show that he danced 13 minutes in and you never knew it was 13 minutes unless you had your stopwatch. He's a very interesting guy. Should he be your role model? I guess he should be. I certainly based *Burn the Floor* on the model of *Lord of the Dance*, taking dance to the masses, but yeah, an interesting character.

I have to ask you about Marlene Dietrich. I mean you worked with Marlene Dietrich. Who can say that? There are few people in entertainment who've achieved her status, maybe Elvis, maybe Bogart and Marilyn. What was she like and what stands out about her in your memory?

Well that was back in 1975. I have a quote from Marlene that kind of sums her up for me: "Darling, the legs aren't so beautiful, I just know what to do with them". When I met her she was not really saying how old she was but was well into her seventies. I was 25. I have a picture of me and Marlene together, which is a famous picture that appeared in Time magazine. It very much depicted me in that age with my turtle neck jumper and suede pants.

You were the toy boy?

Absolutely. Well that's what was portrayed in the magazine. And there she was looking at the camera as if to say "I'm going to kill you" but looking beautiful as we came off the plane in Melbourne. She was incredibly formal. Everything was Mr. and Mrs. and spoken, as I said about the theatre, in hushed tones. The letters—she was a routine freak, an absolute routine freak. Everything had to be planned to the absolute tee. When you get to her hotel room all the windows were sealed, not because of the paparazzi but to keep the light out. So all the curtains were completely tight so no light would come in. Every night I'd lie in my bed at 2 o'clock waiting to hear the "whoosh" as the letter came under the door and they contained my instructions for the next day: what time she wanted to go to the theatre, where she wanted to have lunch, what she wanted to have for lunch, what she wanted to do after then, what time she wanted to leave the theatre, what she wanted to drink in the dressing room. It went on and on and on, with a few strange requests—someone was coming to the show. Where are their seats? How will they collect them? Will you call them up?. On and on and on, all beautifully typewritten, and I had to answer. I had to answer that night so that when she woke up in the morning at 7 am each day to have her breakfast my letter was there. So picture me, I'm still not a very good typist, in the basement of the hotel with an old-fashioned typewriter with Tipp-Ex and carbon paper: "Dear Marlene" . . . it was just hell on wheels. So I'd have to go and stick the letter under her door at half past 3 and then I'd go to sleep.

But I think the one thing that typified Marlene Dietrich, sadly, that was her last ever tour. She broke her hip as she was about to go on stage in Sydney in rather sad circumstances. She was getting pretty frail but, and I don't say this as a funny story, but she was holding onto the curtain as it went up and when it got two feet off the ground she realised what she was doing and let it go and broke her hip in the fall. The curtain comes down. Everybody's asking what's going on. We call an ambulance because she was obviously in extreme pain. She asked me whether there were people waiting at the door. "Yes there will be people". "How many people?". I said I'd go and check. "Marlene, there's 50, 60 people at least waiting for you". She asks "How are you taking me to the hospital?". "I've called an ambulance". "No", she said, "I will not. I will go in the Rolls Royce". I said "Well we're going to have to carry you and . . ." . "I will go in the Rolls Royce". So we had to pick her up, carry her, and put her in the back seat of the car so she could pull up to where the people were and wave through the window and be the Hollywood star.

So, for me, that typifies everything about her. Whatever pain she was in must have been unbelievably extreme. But she would not be seen to be carried on a stretcher to leave. Extraordinary stuff. That's a real star, you know, the public, what they think of them is all that mattered. It was the end of an era with her, no question.

This keeps coming back as a theme: these people's control of detail, the "time freaks", you've used that term a number of times. Is it something that's common?

I think it is in a lot of cases. I figure actors and performers are addicted to adrenaline. They love it. They know "at 8:15, I'm going to be happy". They want to know what the time is, "what time are you doing this, what time are you doing that?"—time runs everything. You don't want to be late. So I think that has a bit to do with it. But they know once they're up there, everything will be okay. But if you're talking about characteristics, charisma has to be a theme for successful people in show business. You can find businessmen boring as bat shit. I'm pretty boring. But performers have charisma. They have star power. They own the room, so to speak.

I've often wondered whether they're born with that or whether they manage to shape their environment so that's how it is when they walk in: so they're the centre of attention.

I don't think people are born with an artistic ego; I think they discover it. It's like, "Oh my god, I can do that, I moved all those people". Other than Freddie Mercury who was probably born with it, I don't think there's that many people. I think a lot of performers have an inner demon that they are escaping. Poverty, abusive parents, bad relationship, extreme stage fright—a lot of them seem to have an inner terror, a fear of failure, that makes up this really complex personality. They're all different at the end of the day.

It's just interesting that each person we've talked about has been an example of somebody driven by time.

I think if you're going to go on a world tour that has 57 cities and 170 shows, you want to know. You want to pick up a book that says "I'm going to be doing this at that time" and so you want to feel comfortable that it's organised and it's all flowing along. You don't want to have other things to add to your insecurity such as "Why the hell are we always late?" "Where's the car?". Thank god the car was booked an hour early.

We all get a bit more retrospective as we get older. I wonder if you've thought recently about how much things have changed since your early days in Mona Vale at the dance. Have you considered whether someone among our

young folk here today could achieve what you've done during your life, or have things changed and the days of the global entertainment entrepreneur are over with?

Well first off it's just a business now. It's just a business about money. There's no loyalty.

For you, you mean?

No, for everyone. For the areas I work in, that's what it's about. Business, brand, money. That's it. Nothing else counts. Can't compute that? Forget it, goodbye. Maybe there's the person sitting out here who's worked out what I can't work out, which is how the digital will change live entertainment. But I think how I began, a guy sitting at a telephone in a little room in Sydney, to a good network of people who do big things on a global basis, that can only get better. So I think the future is incredible. Anything you can do today I reckon in 10 years time will be easier, faster, quicker, and present greater opportunities. All the things out there that I haven't worked out are the things that people are now discovering or have discovered. I just haven't seen them, or other things that are on the way. They've got an incredible opportunity. The way business is done today tells me there's no question that there is greater opportunity on a global basis for the future, absolutely no question.

So how could someone learn to do what you do, other than 40 years of hard work?

Well how can I explain that? I took all these things I learned in different areas: rock and roll taught me to think big picture, think big, think fast. Theatre taught me to think of everything, think of every little detail. Because, whereas in rock and roll selling tickets was easy, in theatre it's really hard. You've got to really think and work every little bit. Experience has taught me to think differently. So I kind of mix the role of "think big" and "think of everything" and that's how I push my operation.

I've always thought of myself as a lucky person. I've been so lucky to do what I've done. But you make your own luck. You know, there's that old saying: "the harder I work the luckier I get". But you know, luck for me has always been important. I've been prepared to grasp opportunities by doing the work, and I've been lucky enough to be in the right place at the right time to meet someone, see something, do something. So today it's just a greater opportunity to go places, meet people, do things, see things, find things, discover things. In fact you don't even have to leave home. You just turn on your computer and the whole world's at your fingertips. So I think there's huge opportunity. I think it's about building a network of people from scratch, people that you can talk to, ask questions, go to an experience, you've got to, if you're interested in theatre, go to Broadway. See every show you can. You like rock and roll? While you're in New York go to Madison Square Garden, go to Jones Beach. There's shows on all the time in Europe. Go to shows. Work out how they do it. Watch them and see what they do. Ask how it all comes together.

I think travelling, experience, meeting people, talking is educational in this business. In this country you ring someone up: "Can I speak to Mike Edgeley?". "What does he want? Does he know why you're calling?". Even I can't get onto Michael and I've known him since 1972. But you go to New York and it's much more open. I was in New York recently and I've been working with a young girl called Greta Bradman, a soprano, and I wanted to find out who was the person who broke Andre Bocceli internationally. So I rang a friend who said "Yeah, I know them, this is the number, call them up". So I call: "Hi, I'm Harley Medcalf from Australia. I'm interested in your story, can I come and talk to you?". "Yeah, absolutely! I live in such and such, come around Saturday at 11:30". It's really different. In Australia I think everyone is afraid—"What do you want?" or "Why would I tell you that?". But especially in New York, and to a degree in London, but particularly in New York, which is the centre of the entertainment business, you can ring anybody up and say "Can I come and talk to you? I'm so and so", and I guarantee you that 9 times out of 10 they'll say "Yeah, okay, I can see you Friday week for half an hour or an hour, or send me what you want to talk about". It's different and that's such an asset. I do it all the time. I ring people: "Can I talk to you? I need to find out about this". Because there's so much still to discover.

You've done wonderful things for dance over recent years, I mean from Michael Flatley onwards. I think the So You Think You Can Dance and various Dancing with the Stars have all fed into a popularity that dance hasn't experienced since maybe 1950-something. What drew you to dance and why do you think it's become such a force again in entertainment after so many decades in the dark?

That's a really broad question. In the late 90s I was so frustrated by this business. It had gone from being a business that you could get emotional reward from to a business that was simply about money. Nothing else mattered. And it was really difficult to get through some days where all you did from the moment you got up in the morning until the moment you went to bed is argue with someone about money. It just grinds you down and I thought "I can do more than this, there's got to be something I can own". And ownership really is everything in this business and certainly will be in the future. So by coincidence I'd just finished the tour with Michael Flatley and I was thinking "Why can't I do something like that?" and I came across a group of ballroom dancers in London who were 18, 19 year old kids. I got into a conversation with them and I thought "Oh my god, you're really incredible". These kids, you know, living, sleeping on a friend's floor, three jobs waiting tables, washing dishes, washing cars to earn money, to get coaches to improve their performance in competitions, to become ballroom dancers, and they had this incredible work ethic.

What was the payoff for them?

Well it was shit. They'd go to a competition with 600 people and one person wins $2000 and everyone else would go home unhappy. Perchance I saw these young kids dance at Elton John's 50th birthday party, which was a circus in fancy dress that was totally out of control, and in the middle of it out come 16 ballroom dancers and I thought "This is going to be interesting", and they just blew this room away. Everyone was transfixed with the energy and this was not ballroom dancing; these kids came out and went "Bang!". I was like "Oh my god". So I went and spoke to these kids and they said "Come and see us dance. We're at the Albert Hall next week". So I went to the Albert Hall and there's these same inspirational kids and the music's about two beats off and the follow spot was 6 feet behind and I realised that at Elton's party they were in rock and roll mode. So I thought that ballroom dancing and rock and roll could put it together, and that's how it began.

It was a nightmare because my greatest weakness is that I think I can do anything, like making ballroom dancing successful. It was pretty tough for a couple of years but slowly we started to build up an audience and we started with little tours that lasted three or 4 weeks and became four and 5 weeks. Then we'd go home for a couple of months and go somewhere else. Slowly we started to build momentum. Then suddenly we had a huge breakthrough in Japan. We sold 100,000 tickets in 2 days and I'm thinking "there's something here". So we started this thing off and it went on and on and we had these great days and we had disasters, like our first American tour opening on September 11, 2001. So I thought "Jesus, I've kicked the black cat". We've been through SARS and all this other stuff that's gone around the world, but we kept at it. In 2005 television discovered ballroom dance. *Strictly Dancing* became *Dancing with the Stars* in America. *Dancing with the Stars* is now the most successful television franchise ever. *So You Think You Can Dance* and all these other dance shows started, and all of a sudden all these people are talking about dance and there was me with my dance show going "Oh, I wish I could sell more tickets" and it just started a groundswell. Now the show has just entered its 14th year and we've just finished a two and a half month tour of South Africa. We've played 193 shows on Broadway. We're going back to the West End for the second time for 6 weeks, and we're really just hitting our straps.

Is it easier than theatre and rock and roll?

No, it's both. It's rock and roll and theatre. It's everything. Everything rolled into one, which is why I love it. I deeply love the show. I also love the fact that, although the dancers have changed, some dancers have been in the company for 10 or 12 years. Others have married, had kids, and moved on, and so we have a totally new young company, average age 22 years old at the moment, who are just as incredible as the first dancers I met. We're trying to talk the BBC into doing a television show about dancers who've gone from *Burn the Floor* to *Dancing with the Stars*. Kim Johnson, for example, danced in my first workshop as 19 year old girl in London. It was the first workshop I did for *Burn the Floor*. She joined *Dancing with the Stars* in Australia. I was devastated when she left. She did *Dancing with the Stars* in Australia, *Dancing with the Stars in America*, won the mirror ball trophy, came and danced with us on Broadway. She was a major dance celebrity and, unbelievably, the girl who replaced her—I hired this 17 year old kid from Perth called Peta Murgatroyd—she won the ballroom trophy last year in *Dancing with the Stars in America*. So there's about 40 kids who've gone through our show into greater pursuits like the *Dancing with the Stars* franchise, which is something I'm really proud of.

Are you connected with that franchise?

Well up until about 6 months ago we weren't even talking because what would happen was that Jason Gilkerson, who's my choreographer, who's just the most wonderful person, we scout out these young kids that were 17 or 18 years old and sign them up to *Burn the Floor*. We'd work on them and train them and style them and teach them everything that we knew about dance and life and shows and talking to media. But after a couple of years they'd get offered $10,000 a week for *Dancing with the Stars* and they'd leave. So I tried to figure out if I could do anything? No, I can't do anything about this but I can manage the process. So I've tried to say to *Dancing with the Stars* "If you want one of my people, absolutely fine, but talk to me about it, let's plan it". "Oh, no, we have no interest in talking to you". So I toughened up my contracts and I started getting legal letters from *Dancing with the Stars* and it got really messy. About 6 months ago the head of the franchise in London rang me up and asked "Why don't we have a very good relationship?". I resisted the temptation to say "Because you're assholes". I just bit my tongue and said "Yeah, we should, we're a resource for you". He said "Let's talk". And we've now been talking for 6 months and I think what's going to happen is we're going to produce a show together which will take the best of what *Burn the Floor* has, which is ensemble dance and passion and love and all these beautiful fluffy things, and combine it with what they've got, which is money, power, and television. I'm meeting with them in October in London, so that'll be interesting.

We've almost run out of time Harley, I've got a couple of other questions I'd love to ask you so I hope we get time afterwards. But I've got two questions that are sort of opposite sides of each other—what's one mistake you'll never make again?

I haven't slept over this question. It tortured me. There are all these things where I'm thinking "Why the hell did I do that? Is that the worst mistake I've ever made?" I've been tossing and turning all night. The truth is the thing that I absolutely try to avoid to do is not listen to my instincts. If my gut tells me to do this I should do it. But maybe I'm like a tortured artist. I ask myself: "Should I? Would I? Can I? What if?

I should just cut all that crap and say "that's a really great idea" and back myself. So to anyone wanting to be in this career, it's an instinct business. Back yourself 100%. I could simplify my life by following my own advice. It's really difficult because you question all these things that happen. But at the end of the day when I've really stuffed up, I already know I've stuffed up. But you've done it and you know you shouldn't have done it, so that's the one thing. If I was able to roll back time and fix a few things it would be because my instinct said "You're an idiot". But what's made me do it? Maybe pride's made me do it or you know, sort of desire to do a particular thing has made me do it. At the end of the day my instincts are pretty good and I should trust them.

And final question before we hand over to the audience for a couple. Lots of our audience are hoping for a career in music and I ask all our guests this question: If you were only allowed to give them one piece of advice, what would it be?

I didn't sleep on Thursday night last week because of this one. I think the truth in that really is there's no one piece of advice. There's a number of pieces of advice that might make sense. You could take the pragmatic approach—in a very pragmatic, business-like way—and that is never rush. It's easy to get into a deal and really hard to get out of it, so never rush. Think about it, take your time, get it right. Because once you're in, getting out's not going to be easy, so make sure. That's kind of the pragmatic part. Then there's the romantic "follow your dream" part. I think that's a great piece of advice. I don't want to be dismissive of following your dream. If you have a dream absolutely follow it, no matter how hard the road is, or how tough, or how many people say "You can't do that". Just follow it. That's the romantic advice. The realistic advice is "just do it". No-one else is going to do it for you. If you've got an idea don't sit there waiting for a manager or an agent. Just do it. I think that is, at the end of the day, what it's all about.

(Audience member): You talked about tickets and how especially with the ballroom concerts you were doing in Japan it really took off. Have you ever had an instance coming up to the event or a touring show where ticket sales haven't been large enough, and if that has happened how have you recovered?

Empty seats are like tombstones to me. I mean truly. You have a show and you peek through the curtains and you think "Oh my god". How do you fix it? Well the first thing is, if you can't sell the tickets, you can't give them away. If people aren't interested, you know, two for one, 10 bucks, here's a free one. If you can't sell them you can't give them away. So you do a show with a few people in it for a particular reason because you're trying to build or start something. So you take it on the chin. You talk to the players. I've done it with the dancers over the years: "Guys, there's 150 people there tonight in a 2000 seat auditorium, but we're going to send that 150 people away happy as can be thinking we're the greatest show they've ever seen because when we come back in a year's time there's going to be 300". So you take the philosophical approach, but it's heartbreaking. I hate being in empty rooms and the thing is you can't change momentum. You take an advertising campaign, usually in theatre it sets into a rhythm—300, 400 bucks a day you can spend a lot of money and still sell 300, 400 tickets a day in that rhythm, you open and it might pick up, word of mouth cuts in and it grows, it's not easy to change the rhythm. If you're not selling tickets you're in the shit, and that's it. So get out, maybe, cancel it, don't do it. Unless you've got a real reason, cut your losses and run. So you know, it's something that's very much at the heart of this industry, ticket sales. Good ones and bad.

(Audience member): What you said before about being sued, obviously you would recommend professional indemnity insurance for people who are engaged in management or promotion. If you wanted to do a tour of somebody, how much money would you have to have upfront to make a decent tour? Can you make a tour on making the bookings and what you're going to get back? Or do you have to have a substantial amount of money to start off with?

Well there's two sides to that question. The first part is find the best advisor that you can in every area. If it's insurance, find a broker who's got unbelievable amounts of experience in insurance because the basic principle of insurance is "thank you for your money, I'm never going to give you anything". Insurance is a ruthless business. I have a public liability policy worldwide that I pay varying amounts territory by territory, but the average is I pay 25c per ticket sold to my insurance broker for my liability and that way I've got complete cover wherever I go. So I pay a premium advance for the year and at the end of the year I send a report, that details all the tickets I sold and they send me a bill. So that's fairly advanced, but public liability policies in entertainment are fairly okay. Indemnity is easy to get. Cancellation is very complicated but easy to get, hard to claim. But you've got to find a really, really great broker.

In terms of funding, the basic principle is you don't get any money from the box office until after the show is over, so you have to fund it from outside sources. It's not the same in every country in the world. It's certainly the same here thanks to Harry Miller who went bankrupt in 1978 and the rules changed. Prior to '78 you could use ticket sales money to fund your operation. Since '78 the venues and ticket offices hold that money. The producer or promoter does not get it until the show is actually complete and sometimes 7 days after that. So you've got to be able to fund your cash flow, your advertising, flights. So if you book a flight you pay for it. There's no credit any more so you've got to be able to fund flights, immigration, sometimes deposits for hotels, various other deposits—so it can take up quite a bit of money. And then if you're hiring an artist they want, as an average, 50% of the fee 30 days in advance. So you're constantly fronting a lot of cash. That's what I like about *Burn the Floor*. Because I'm the artist, people have to pay me. I prefer that.

Chapter 11
Kate Miller-Heidke and Keir Nuttall

Abstract This chapter is an interview with Kate Miller-Heidke and Keir Nuttall. They represent "ground zero" of the music industry for the series: the artists, the creative labourers who make the music that makes money for them and everybody else in the business. Kate and Keir are partners in life and music, and in that sense they are a rare combination. Kate's creative repertoire spans indie-alternative, pop, heavy metal, musical theatre, and Opera. The couple is quite obviously on a journey of continual renewal at every level: as artists, musicians, and business people. The interview makes clear, I think, that Kate and Keir are new kinds of artists who are emblematic of successful charting a way through the music business's digital interregnum. Shortly after the interview, Kate parted company with her label to become entirely independent, with both her and Keir beginning solo ventures in areas as diverse as comedy, musical theatre, and opera, as well as continuing their professional collaborations.

Welcome Kate and Keir. Kate, you're reported as saying that you wrote 60 or 70 songs for the *Nightflight* Album. How did you manage to cut that down to 11? At what stage did you know that there were 50 songs that weren't right?

KMH: There was nearly 4 years between the album before and this one. So 60 or 70 songs sounds like a lot but in 4 years it's not that staggering. It was a ruthless process cutting it down to the final 11. I think what happened was there was this thread that started to become really apparent and noticeable—the thematic thread of the record—themes of mortality and death and this kind of dark, creepy thing that started to give the album some cohesion. So any songs that didn't fit with that theme were jettisoned and that's how I made sense of it to myself.

Did your record company have a lot to do with that?

KMH: No, in fact my record company were pretty much entirely absent from the whole process, which was good.

KN: At the end of every week we'd send them the work that we'd done. Sometimes it was a finished track and sometimes an acoustic treatment of a track and we would hear almost nothing back, which I guess is a freedom that a lot of people would appreciate. But after about 9 months of that it became somewhat nerve wracking.

P. Graham, *Music, Management, Marketing, and Law*, Music Business Research,
https://doi.org/10.1007/978-3-030-02143-6_11

How did that happen?

KMH: I think our A&R just got busy. Anyway, it was good.

KN: Yes, we're very happy.

So at what stage can you decide that a song doesn't make it?

KN: There was culling going on right from the start. When we first started the final tracking we actually had too many songs to track in the time we had. We knew that we weren't going to make it and it simply became the case, with the last 20, anyway, the songs that we got bored with and we'd come back to and say "that's not good enough". As Kate said, the theme guided the choices. And we were both ruthless about each other's writing too, sometimes.

KMH: And our own.

KN: And our own of course. But sometimes we would cut a song really early.

KMH: We took the new songs out on the road as well, just on an acoustic tour, playing in smaller places where the pressure wasn't on to have a highly polished show. So we road-tested a lot of the new material and the songs that went down well had more of a chance of making the record.

And how important has that been for you in the past, road-testing material, working it out in a live situation, before you actually decide to record it?

KMH: Well it hasn't been something that we've really had the luxury of doing time-wise before, except for the first record which was a culmination of 5 years work or so.

KN: The songs on the first record were all the songs we'd written up until that point. Whereas for this latest record, it was the first time we actually had the luxury of having a writing window where we could say, "Okay, next three months we're going to just sit in this house and write songs". Up until that point, we'd never had that opportunity. We were too busy touring or whatever. With how well the record before went, we were able to actually allocate that time, so it was a luxury in a way, and we wanted to not squander that luxury. We actually had a pretty fierce work ethic during that time. We'd get up every morning and write all day, and that's part of the reason we ended up with so many songs.

Being ruthless with each other's writing sounds difficult for a married couple. One of the hardest things to do is to work with anybody with whom you have a relationship. I think it's even harder in music. How do you manage to do it? You write together, you tour together, you're signed to the same label. How do you do it?

KMH: Well Keir's not signed. It's good that he's not signed because it means he still gets paid.

KN: That was a decision we made early on, actually, that I would not be signed to anybody, including publishing. It's largely because that means we're able to have a bit of freedom in the way we charge for things. If I co-produce a record I can actually charge, whereas if we were both signed, that'd just be expected of me.

KMH: The question: I think that for a big portion of the last 5 years we have treated the music as a band. So I don't think of myself as a solo artist with backing musicians or whatever. It truly has been a collaboration and, yeah, Keir has started to feel more ownership of it. But it's not always easy and we have to work sometimes at getting that delineation about who we are as a couple and who we are as musicians collaborating.

KN: Part of it is we're really lucky that we're very, very compatible as a couple, I think. And when we clash in the working relationship, it means we've got a bit of room to play with because we're really good friends. But it's tough at times, especially the writing I think. But the touring's pretty cool.

So do you have any specific strategies? Any sort of no-go areas, any things you can and can't say? Or is all that more a worked-out, organic thing?

KMH: Keir? (laughs) we need a safe word.

KN: Yeah, we need a safe word.

KMH: I think it's just, well for me it's a matter of protecting myself because sometimes because I look to Keir for moral support and creative encouragement and stuff. Sometimes I'm tempted to show him a song before it's actually ready, or share an idea while it's still developing. Sometimes I think that's where both of us look out for our own interests. If I'm following a thread of a new song, it's not something I can share with him all the time until I'm happy with it and I feel confident enough with it. That's something I learned the hard way.

KN: Yeah we both did. That's one of the things we were talking about today. Going into the next record we're going to hold off. Because we trust each other so much and respect each other's opinion, if you're just starting work on something and you show it to the other person and they just go—and I know Kate so well she doesn't even have to say anything—I can just tell by how her eyebrow raises. Then that means I just can't work on that song any more. It's stillborn in that moment. So that's a process we're still working on.

Well congratulations for getting it this far, really. Kate, you've worked in West End of London, you've been offered a lead in the Australian Opera, you've recorded just about every style—pop, rock, indie, electro and even metal with Double Dragon. I think within the context of a major record label contract, a career like yours would have been almost impossible even 15 years ago, maybe even 10 years ago. How have you managed to maintain such a diverse portfolio and not get slotted into a genre or stylistic thing?

KMH: Well I think that's been the key to whatever success that I might have enjoyed up to this point. I've built this niche for myself because I don't fit into the pop singer mould. I've briefly dabbled in it but I just don't think that's sustainable for me in the long term. I remember Laurie Anderson spoke about how she chooses which projects to be involved in. She said "It either has to be creatively challenging, a lot of fun, or really good money". If two or more of those criteria can be filled then she'll do it. I think that's a pretty good rule for me as well. I find that doing this as seasons makes sense. Already you go through seasons of not writing and seasons of writing, seasons of being on the road, or recording, or doing the theatrical stuff that I've done, or dabbling in other things I find really inspiring. Actually, it's always an opportunity to restock the pond and just leave all of my own bullshit behind for a while and sing other people's music: be a character.

And have you had to fight your company in creative decisions about what you do on a record?

KMH: No, never. Well actually on this record it's been kind of weird. They just sort of checked out of the project, which I'm not going to complain about. On the last record we had some feedback on certain songs about what should be the outro, what should change in this lyric, or whatever. But we just diplomatically fielded those.

KN: Yeah, one of them was this song called *Can't Shake It*. It was an ironic pop record. We knowingly made a pop record but we were being ironic about it. I don't know if you remember a band called Ratcat but they were a sort of ironic pop band and we had that as one of our references when we were making that record. A lot of the tracks are ironic—they're winking—and one of those songs was *Can't Shake It*. It's a dance song about not being able to dance. Someone who's no longer at Sony was saying "Now that song's great, but you just need to change Can't Shake It to I'm Just Going to Shake It because no-one's going to believe that Kate Miller-Heidke can't shake it".

KMH: They haven't seen me dancing.

KN: That was one piece of feedback I can remember.

Everything in the recording industry's changed. The nature of deals has changed as the majors have gotten less money from record sales and such. The companies have been reaching out for tour money and publishing money and sync money and just about everything else. And so they've come up with the 360° deal. We've had a bit of discussion in previous talks here about that. What are your thoughts on it?

KMH: I just think those deals stink. I wouldn't go near it. I wouldn't sign a regular deal with a major label at the moment either.

Why?

KMH: Recording is so cheap now that you can get something which sounds great for not much money. So it doesn't make sense not to own your own recordings. If you want to use a label to distribute it then licensing makes sense. But I think the traditional deal is kind of obsolete now, let alone the 360 one. That sounds like being a slave.

KN: Yeah, unless you're somebody who's on TV or something—an actor, a soap star or something—I can't see that it would make any sense either. There's so many good independent publicists and people like that now, you can outsource the stuff that you need. The biggest part of it is the amount of money that it takes to do the publicity and the marketing rather than the actual recording, but it does seem a little antiquated.

It seems to me that the entire strength of the majors now is around marketing and distribution. Are you clear on what benefit you receive from your deal?

KMH: Yeah, definitely. It's this hugely powerful machine that, when it kicks into action, can make a huge impact—their relationships with radio and record stores and iTunes and everything.

So on that basis, how would you structure a deal?

KMH: You still get that with the licensing deal, just the Publicity and Distribution deal, and that way you hold onto your own masters forever.

And is that what you do now?

KMH: No, I'm still under contract. I signed just before all of this awareness started happening. In 2006 people were still buying CDs and so it was a slightly different era. I have two more albums to go on this deal, not that I'm counting.

I'm always surprised at the diversity you manage to bring. I look at the last album and the difference between *Sarah*, for example, and *Last Day on Earth*, seems to me anyway to be quite a distance in stylistic approach: one being a really classic ballad form, the other one being, I don't know how you'd describe it other than as a report of a profound dream, so can you tell us about how you went about writing those things? Is the process the same?

KMH: It's pretty much the same. I know what you mean that stylistically the songs are different but I still use a pop structure when I write. I still think it's the best structure for a pop song. It's extremely simple, the verse, chorus, pre-chorus, post-chorus, and outro are the elements and it's just getting the right amounts of each. Sarah was more of a story song. That was influenced by Nick Cave's *Murder Ballads* and, I suppose, it's a lot more dramatic. It's got dramatic impetus. But I don't see those two songs as that different, really, they're just pop songs.

You just have one way of writing then?

KN: *Last Day on Earth* was around for a long time and it went through several drafts. I remember it started with the main hook, which is a little instrumental thing (sings). It started with that and we just kept trying to find parts that went with that and that were equal to it . . .

KMH: and Keir had the title which was ripped off the chapter of a Tom Wolfe book, *Last Day on Earth*. I can't remember which book. Books are a good place to get titles, actually. Just look at the chapter heads.

KN: And then we had another chorus with different words but then Kate re-wrote the chorus to that title. One thing we do try and do is amass titles. That came from one of those lists, so did another song off that record called *Caught in the Crowd* and I think *Can't Shake It* did too.

KMH: And also *Sarah*. It started with a concept. *Last Day on Earth* started with the concept of a love song set during the apocalypse. For *Sarah*, I had this story fully-formed in my mind. I find those are the kind of songs that come out easiest and stick around longest, when you actually have something to write about rather than just "Aww feelings, I feel this, or blah blah blah". I like having something to say.

Can you talk to the role of drama in how you write? When you write are you thinking about how you're going to deliver this or what? Is it a live concept? does that have a role in the writing process?

Yeah, I think that's an interesting question and a big question because some songs don't need the drama. I feel the more reflective songs that are just about a particular feeling or a sadness and I also am drawn to story songs or character songs, songs with a narrative arc like *Sarah*. Part of the reason for that is my background in opera and a love of musical theatre. I like characters and stories. Stories are a huge part of music and art for me. I think a lot of pop songs—take *Somebody That I Used To Know*—it sounds to me like that song could be in a musical as well. It has characters and a reveal at the end. A lot of great pop songs have that innate theatrical sense to them. I like the theatre of using my classical voice, judiciously and tastefully, hopefully, but there's something very theatrical about the sound of opera singing that can really heighten things. I remember having lots of long discussions with Andy Arthurs when I was studying music here about how I put my opera voice into my pop songs. That's something that's a continual process, but it's something that adds drama as well.

Are we going to see more from Fatty Gets a Stylist? I love that album.

KN: I doubt it.

KMH: It wasn't really a mainstream success.

KN: No.

KMH: It's interesting. It's a side project, an electronic side project, that we did a couple of years ago and I'm putting on a different voice in it to the point where my voice is unrecognisable. We played it in the van to my band and none of them knew it was me and that was fun. The disguise was a big part of the appeal of that project, but it didn't go anywhere really. Although the first track has been used heavily in advertising in the US. It's a song called *Are You Ready* and it's been the theme song for the New York Lottery for the past year. They're about to start a nationwide Target ad using that song.

Gold.

KMH: Yeah. I don't know if we'll do more.

KN: It'd be nice to do more. I'd like to do more.

KMH: The thing is no-one liked it except you.

KN: No-one likes it.

Obviously the lottery did.

KMH: Yeah.

Your roots are in the Brisbane music scene. People have talked about the Brisbane sound for years. Do you think there is one, and if so why?

KMH: I think it's about the people. People I met when I studied here, I'm still really good friends with. It's having that network of supportive people in the music business. Just looking at the names of people on the local scene and half of them are friends of mine. You go down to Melbourne and Sydney and it's not the same, for different reasons. Sydney is very competitive and they often say "I can't believe how many musician friends you have, we don't sort of hang out with the other bands in Sydney, it's every man for himself kind of a thing". That's a broad generalisation, and Melbourne's very much kind of, it's got this "scenester" thing. It's all about the aesthetic of something: being cool, being timely, having a sound that's very current. Whereas I think in Brisbane you're so far away from anything that's important in the Australian music industry that you actually have more time and space to nurture your craft and write good pop songs. I think, Hungry Kids of Hungary, Ball Park Music, The Boat People, there's no-one, there aren't any bands in Australia writing pop songs like those.

KN: And that's a sound, those three bands, that sounds like a, that's a specific Brisbane sound I reckon.

You think?

KN: I reckon, yeah. I mean those three bands feel like they're part of the same movement to me. It's really canny, intelligent pop.

Would you tell us a little bit about how you approach the recording process? Where does it start? Do you make your own material as you go along?

KMH: More and more it is at home. We've got a home studio now and often you can create something at home that's got a certain feeling or atmosphere that's impossible to recreate even if you're at a lavish, expensive studio. So I think that down the track, more and more, we'll just expand what we're doing at home. It's important to have an amazing mixer. I think that's still something that you can't really fake.

KN: And great sound engineers are really good. As my engineering chops get better we've been able to transfer more of the demo stuff into the actual sessions that we do when we make the record. But still a lot of my stuff's really sloppy. I can't record guitars, and you need a drum room to make good drum sounds and other things. But that whole aspect of being able to do it at home is really becoming important. We do all the pre-production demos that are very detailed, almost good enough to release. The *Fatty* record is basically the pre-production demo without a couple of things that just aren't acceptable. Then we went and tracked it in a very short amount of time. But with Kate's records, as we go on, the pre-production demos have become more and more polished; more and more close to what the end product sounds like.

Do the home recordings become part of it naturally?

KMH: Yeah.

KN: We lift whole guitar solos or backing vocal parts. We tend to re-record all the main vocal parts, but a lot of the little parts we've kept and transferred across. We were lucky enough, for the Fatty record and the new Kate record, to work with a mixer called Cenzo Townsend who's based in England. He's one of the new breed of mixer who will take your demos into account and really will just do his best to match your vision. I know that in a lot of times the producer might mix and they have a specific idea of how they want to construct a mix. Whereas for us we're actually putting that together in pre-production a lot of the time now. Whether or not we do the next record like that, though, we don't know yet. We don't want to set that in stone so early.

How do you find people to work with and choose them? Is your record company involved in that, finding new mix engineers and studios to work in and so forth?

KMH: Yeah, they're involved to the extent that we get a big list of names. We also look at the credits of albums that we've loved the sound of and get in touch with those people. I remember with *Curiouser* I was on the phone to about 20 different guys all from America and eventually you'd just have a conversation with someone that you think, yeah, that you click with. I think it can be a bit dangerous to do it that way though.

It's like eHarmony for producers.

KMH: And just because you get along with someone doesn't mean they have anything to add to your music. But also there's the whole "arse has fallen out of that business" in America. So there are all these dudes that have amazing credits, like you know, they've recorded U2's album or whatever, and their child support's due so they say yes to doing this little hokey band from Australia that they don't give a shit about that they can just do a half-arsed job and take the money.

Has that happened to you?

KMH: No, it hasn't happened to us. It was going to happen to us but then our producer started to like us and he was like "Aw, you guys, I guess I will do a proper job then".

KN: He didn't admit that.

KMH: It was obvious.

Are you allowed to name names?

KN: No! He's our friend now.

KMH: I've spoken to a lot of mid-level bands, the same level as us, and it has happened to them. They've gone to the States to work with some guy that's got these incredible credits and they get over there and just realise that the person could not give less of a shit about their band or their music.

So how do you protect against that?

KMH: The latest record we did in Melbourne with Lindsay Gravina who is just an incredibly passionate person. I think that's a problem you encounter more overseas, in Australia it's . . .

KN: In Australia a lot of the producers are struggling because people, as soon as they have a budget of a certain amount, the record company will encourage them to go to LA for one thing because they're kind of superstitious that something coming from Hollywood must be incredible. Also they get stars in their eyes about "Oh this guy worked on this record. I loved that record, it was a huge record, this record, this record".

When we worked with Lindsay we worked midday until midnight with a one-hour break for dinner every night. It was him and his engineer and we got them for an amount that was probably two thirds of what it would have cost to just go to have the producer in America. They did an incredible job and the two of them together are such good engineers and, you know, incredibly creative people who are down there in a studio in Melbourne... I can't speak highly enough of Lindsay Gravina and Rob Long, his engineer.

So in a relationship with the producer there's a couple of extreme schools of thought. One is that the producer's there to realise the artist's vision. The other one is an expectation that the producer will bring their own vision to it and then you enter into a conversation about that. Which is your favoured approach?

KMH: I really think that's less and less the case nowadays in my experience. I've never sought out a producer to bring their vision to my music. I want someone to who I can say "This is how I want this song to sound" and for them to be able to recreate it. But I guess to that degree we've self-produced and Keir co-produced my last two records. But basically what I want from a producer is a great engineer with their own studio.

So you want an engineer?

KMH: Yeah, with the studio. That's key. And someone that you trust to give an objective opinion when asked, but not someone to try to shoehorn their musical sensibilities into my work.

So you're self-produced in that respect?

KMH: Well yeah, I guess.

So apart from producers, how do you maintain your ecology? I mean, how big of an enterprise is Kate Miller-Heidke Proprietary Limited?

KMH: What do you mean?

Well, there's merch, there's publishing, there's distribution, there's other potential business things going on, there's booking, there's all of these areas. How do you keep that going, or is that something you don't get involved with or is it just all through your management?

KMH: Yeah, there's a team of people. I have a manager in Australia, a manager in America, an agent in America, an agent here, and my manager has six or seven staff—that plus the label.

KN: You manage it all. You spend a lot of time on it. You get up every morning and read emails and make sure everybody's coordinated.

KMH: Yeah, I guess I'm a bit of a control freak in that way but I don't . . .

KN: Kate started off managing herself. In fact that's one of the reasons that I think Kate is so successful: she was actually doing a manager's job before she ever had a manager.

KMH: But everyone is doing that nowadays.

KN: Yeah, but some people are really bad at it.

KMH: (laughs) I guess. I've definitely learned the hard way that everything that comes out, like in terms of photos and bio and ads, videos, all that is really important. I have everything to do with the creative process and read everything that goes out because if I don't there's going to be something wrong or bad in there that I don't agree with or approve of. So that does take a fair bit of time.

So how much time a day do you spend?

KMH: Doing emails?

Making sure everything's right.

KMH: Probably two or three hours.

That's huge, really, for an artist.

KMH: I take some time off but it's not something you can ever truly detach yourself from because it's ongoing. I can't ever really just have a holiday.

I'm assuming your manager's wonderful of course but, would you ever be able to find a manager that you could delegate all that stuff to?

KMH: No, I don't think so. I think people recognise what's authentic in an artist and what's not. It's like the Twitter and Facebook thing: it's very obvious if someone's not writing their own posts, especially me. I do see myself as a niche artist and I'll be the one to suffer for it if something goes out that I don't agree with. For example: I hate the artwork on my first album and it's just a regret that I'll carry with me forever. I just don't want that to happen again.

All of that marks you as a really different kind of artist, part of a new generation of artist-entrepreneurs I think.

KMH: I think yeah, everyone I know is the same. All my friends that do this are the same. Yep.

The management thing is really, really interesting and you've kind of answered the question to some degree, self-producing, largely self-managing with people sort of executing stuff. Is that it?

KMH: No, no no no. I don't do anywhere near as much work as they do.

But no I mean, they're sort of acting on your strict instructions I guess, no?

KMH: No, they're not. All I know is how to proofread something and choose a photo and choose on the best creative people to make videos and things like that. But they're doing all sorts of things that I never even hear about. I think being a manager is mostly about connections: being friends with the people who promote festivals and maintaining networks and all the stuff that I'm never going to do.

It's been a recurring theme in the talks here that the artist's manager is the most important in the whole mix. Do you think so?

KMH: Definitely.

So at what stage did you hand all that over? And how did that happen?

KMH: Well when I was desperate for a manager in Brisbane, and there's a dearth of them here. I needed someone to help me with all of the boring shit that goes along with being a musician. I didn't want to spend all of my days booking flights and all that stuff. I tried about three or four different people in Brisbane. I remember one guy, he was my manager. One day I just couldn't call him anymore. He just stopped answering his phone. Six months later I saw a mutual friend of ours and she was just like "Oh yeah, he's just been living in his garage for the last six months, he hasn't come out". So anyway, I went through a few and I got Leanne de Souza. I don't know if that was because of my career or whatever. Leanne was my first proper manager. She's Brisbane-based. Some of you might know her. Since that contract finished I'm now managed by One Louder in Sydney. They managed Paul Kelly and Sarah Blasko and so they really good. They know their shit. They're amazing. Good people. I think the most important thing is to find people who you, on a basic level, share the same values. I think that's what's most important in a manager.

And how did it come about that you got a first good manager? Did you wait for someone to approach you?

KMH: Yeah, I think it comes back to what Keir was saying before, that if you put in a lot of the work then in the end they'll come to you or you can at least persuade them to come to you.

KN: They're simply looking, or in the early stages, simply looking to see that they can make money out of the whole thing. It's a hell of a lot of effort to be a manager and they're not going to do it for free. I'm not saying it's a bad thing—you need someone who was good and they will want to be paid for their time. And the other model is that I think people who are starting out as managers like a friend of ours Briese Abbott who manages a band called Pivot. That's an example of someone who was early on in the management and she spotted Pivot who she thought had incredible potential and then works really hard to help them and it has been a mutually beneficial thing. But trying to land a manager is hard. Kate had to pursue Leanne for a while.

KMH: Yeah, I pretty much had to beg.

KN: And she held off for a long time. In the end she saw that she could do well out of it, I think. Not in a bad way. And she was awesome. But it's one of those things where I know that in the bands I was in before I worked with Kate we always just thought that someone would turn up to a gig and give us a management deal. Or we'd write a stupid letter to John Watson: "John Watson, will you be our manager?". "Why would I be your manager? You're not pulling anyone to your shows". That was us.

KMH: But it is a courtship process. You have to woo them, definitely.

Speaking of your past bands, Keir, Transport was one that was a band of great expectations.

KN: Thank you.

And are we going to see them back?

KN: I think it's unlikely. Because we were all in our early 30s when we started that band I think it was our last shot at being in a band. We all got band tattoos and we said "Okay guys, pact: we'll all quit our jobs or quit our current jobs to make room for jobs that only fit in being in the band". And then we toured on our drummer's credit card for a long time. He was the only one who had a credit card. He was the most organised guy and we did that for a long time around in circles and I just think that our music wasn't very likeable.

I know a couple of people really like it but I think on the whole it repelled people, and I mean that. I've thought about it a lot because when that band broke up it was very traumatic. Not really broke up but we stopped working largely because I was too busy doing Kate's stuff. It was one of those things where I think now if I went back and I was in bands again I would do every band for 1 year and if you weren't seeing that generally people were really into what you were doing I wouldn't waste my energy on it any more. I would go "Okay, cool, time for another band". I know it's really hard to find people. Maybe the same people would make a different style of music and for me that's more fun than to just drive something into the ground where you want to kill each other and you owe a credit card thousands and thousands of dollars. Anyway, we're going to do a gig in November for better or worse.

KMH: So come along and be repelled!

I'm glad you're doing a gig in November. We had The Veronicas along recently, and they're just about to release a new album. They were great. They've released their own fashion line, they've been doing all kinds of endorsements and such. Can you see that in your future? Anything like that? Diversification in your portfolio?

KMH: No, I can't, I don't think so. I'm just not hot enough to do that.

KN: Yes you are sweetie.

KMH: Thanks, and also, I'm not interested really enough in fashion. I can't think of what other products I might launch. Nope. Handbags? No.

Makeup line? For sure.

KMH: Yeah, to be honest I think I've got enough going on without that.

Okay. It's a question. What professional mistakes will you never make again?

KMH: Well, what I mentioned before: making sure that no photos or artwork goes out without me approving it. Sometimes people can kind of bully you with time constraints: "If you don't approve this by 5pm today we're going to miss the deadline and your album's going to have to be delayed for three weeks", that kind of thing. I'd be more strong, stand up against that. Professional mistakes? Oh, I'm never going to go on Q&A again, definitely. Keir, do you have anything to add?

KN: I have so many professional mistakes that I've made it would be impossible for me to sum them up. But I would never spend any time with a band that didn't have a great singer. I think that any time I've ever been a band and, yeah, I was the singer in the last band. The singer is the lens between the music and the audience, if you're a band that has songs that aren't instrumentals. That would be one of the big ones. I'd just spend the time looking for the right singer because I think it was a big professional mistake to have me sing.

We recently got news that musicians in Australia are making an average of $7500 a year. That's after last year's reports from APRA and Arts Vic that artists were making on average $12–15,000 a year. So it's going down really, really quickly now. We're seeing bands go out on a bill of five for $10 a head and so forth. Can you see any break in the future of this? Can you see where it's changing?

KMH: I don't know, I mean it's always going to be hard. There's just such a huge pool of people and bands and musicians. Some of them, through a combination of luck and talent and perseverance, will manage to make a go of it and a lot of others possibly just as deserving won't. Some of my dear friends, some of the most amazing musicians I know, are still working in car garages and stuff.

KN: And hard working musicians too, some are, some are not. There's two types of musicians. There's musicians who are in it for a laugh. That's totally cool and you get really great bands out of that as well. But there's a lot of people who earnestly really work very hard for years.

KMH: I am a fan of this whole crowd sourcing, crowd funding model that seems to be coming up. I think possibly the industry will be able to support more medium-level artists through that sort of thing. People that have a really strong group of fans, amazing people that might have otherwise, in the major-label days, fallen off the radar and been forgotten, with the internet and with funding things directly through your fans you could possibly sustain a career that way.

Surely the venues should be paying people. If that's their stock-in-trade and the way they pull in people to drink booze or whatever, surely they should be paying. Why is it that musicians are allowed to work for nothing when everyone else is on minimum wage which is $35,000 I think.

KMH: I think if someone were to draft up a new regulation then I'd sign on the line, but I don't know what else to say except that if someone there, someone's going to do it for free and other people demand payment then maybe a union, I've always wanted a proper musicians union.

There was one.

KN: Was there?

Oh yeah, I'll tell you the story of that later.

KN: It's because it's so fiercely competitive that people will always just do it for nothing and we did it for nothing for a long time. And I don't know, though. Then there's originals and covers too, and so is that statistic covers musicians as well?

I think it's everybody out there who's playing music, I think even the cover opportunities, I know for a fact they've dropped off markedly over the years. Anyway, back to the question I was going to ask you which is what's next, what happens next with you two?

KMH: Well next week we're going back to the US to open for Ben Folds Five for a month. After that we're touring Germany as the opening act for an artist called Katie Melua. Then I'm going back to London to work with the English National Opera on a new opera. Then back to Australia over summer. We'll do some festivals and stuff, I think we've got Woodford Folk Festival which is one of my favourites.

That's all between now and Woodford? Wow, spectacular. I've asked this of all our guests—many of our audience here tonight hope to make a living in music. If you're only allowed to give them one piece of advice each what would it be? Kate?

KMH: Depends on what kind of music they want to make, I guess, so I don't really want to narrow it down to one. But don't underestimate the importance of Triple J is something I'd say. It's really the core of most Australian musicians' careers and it's easy to get them offside, so be wary of that, make sure you've caught them as well.

KN: And I said it before but I do mean it that if you're in a band and you don't have the right singer it's a waste of time. If you listen to most of the music that sinks, you just listen to it and I bet you that the person singing isn't good enough. If you can get that singer, the right singer, and there's only about ten of them. That's not true, but you know when someone's the right singer. You know when someone has that voice. I firmly believe that. I think that's really good advice.

Thank you. Well that's my questions, I'm going to invite the audience now to throw some curly ones at you, who's got questions?

(Audience member): Talking about self-management and stuff, I'm really interested in self-marketing, and we're talking more about how you take photos of the audience and they respond and get likes on Facebook and I was just wondering if you'd found any other ways to draw significant attention online?

KMH: I guess the thing online that's really worked for me was a novelty song about Facebook. Three years ago it was filmed at a live gig and it's been the star. I played at Coachella because of that song. It's ridiculous and it's got I think 1.5 million views now or something. But I guess not everyone wants to write a novelty song.

It's the Facebook song.

KMH: Yeah. I don't think there are any tricks but just to be sort of interested in engaging with people on Twitter and Facebook and Instagram or whatever. Something I've found Twitter really useful for is connecting with other musicians just as much as connecting with fans—my peer group or people that I admire, writers, people in the arts—Twitter gives you an instant line to all of these people that I was fans of and now I can actually have conversations with them on Twitter. It's pretty amazing.

Audience member: Do you think that it's naïve or stupid to not use Facebook if you want to be a popular musician?

KMH: Well, do you have like a stance against it? A conscientious objection?

I don't have a stance against it. I just don't have it and I'm getting to the stage where I've got original songs and I guess I have to have it. I don't have anything against it, I just don't have it.

KMH: Well, if you don't have any fans yet then you probably don't need it. But once you get to the point where people want to be able to see where you're next playing it's useful. Daniel Kitson's my favourite comedian. He's an objector. He refuses to go on Twitter and Facebook and that's like his thing. The only way he connects with his fans is through his newsletter direct to their email. He's not attempting to reach a wide group of people.

KN: And there is that thing with people where you're constantly being hassled by them to like their page but it doesn't necessarily translate into anything. It's like the MySpace hits when people would just collect MySpace friends. Like Kate said, they don't necessarily translate into anybody coming to a gig. I have friends that just hassle me all the time to like their page.

KMH: Yeah, that's annoying spamming.

KN: Yeah, I think that has the opposite effect to what's intended.

KMH: So maybe don't go down that line.

KN: But YouTube is definitely the thing, right? YouTube is where people can actually watch music. So many things take off on there just because they're good. It's easy to share and it's quick and you can reply to big videos.

KMH: I'm pretty sure I've read that YouTube is the first place that people go to hear a song.

You were saying you don't see the money from the records selling, aren't you sort of entitled to those royalties as a performer and writer?

KMH: Well as a writer, yes, I maybe should have made that clear, I mean record sales, sales of the actual record. So apart from songwriting royalties there's a few different royalty streams. But no-one can take your APRA royalties from you, no, that's sacred.

Kate, what did you do after studying before your success? Did you have a job or did you just start on your musical career.

KMH: Yeah I had a job. I taught singing from home for quite a while, and piano. That's how I paid the bills. I was also in the chorus with Opera Queensland, so that was like a regular job and then I just did one-off gigs.

So it was all music based?

KMH: Yeah, it was always music-based, but you know, I did the teaching thing which I hated and was bad at, all of my students just got worse, so.

In your credits there's a songwriting competition that you won. How do you know which competitions are good? There's just so many of these competitions going around, and things like *The Voice* and *Australia's Got Talent* and stuff like that. Some people say it's a death knell to go on programs like that. How do you know what's good competition that's worthwhile for you to enter?

KMH: Well I'd say the TV talent quest, that's a separate issue. There are people out there running competitions that are just a rort. They make up these competitions and it's $50 to enter or whatever and they just keep all the money—definitely. Certain competitions just have a profile, they're respected. There aren't too many of them either. The International Song Writing Competition, The Vanda and Young Competition . . .

KN: We knew the International Song Writing Competition was good because Tom Waits was one of the judges and Neil Finn, I think.

KMH: So you look at who's attached themselves to it, like John Butler and the JB Seed. There are some good ones, but there aren't very many. It seems dodgy that your prize is to get to play on a stage . . . that's not really a prize. Keir and I met at a band competition at The Regatta Hotel. It was an unplugged night and the prize was four jugs of VB.

And a guitar player.

KMH: Well, that came later, but.

KN: I won.

KMH: Yeah, Keir won, but it was a faulty judging mechanism because it was judged using a clap-o-meter and I think the batteries were running low.

KN: It was a scientific instrument.

KMH: Yeah, right.

Audience member: What advice would you give to someone who wants to be successful in Opera.

KMH: Well I think there's a pretty well-trodden path down that route. It's more like a normal job in that way. I think if you've got a good teacher, study at the right place, and go to the right auditions, as far as I can tell opera is a lot more merit-based than pop music. Although they are starting to get fixated on image and, you know, buff men and hot women and stuff, but that's new.

Audience member: Why would you not do Q&A again?

KMH: (laughs) Because I think that people don't want to see their favourite musician talking about politics. I think it dilutes the essence of their music.

Is it not important for you to talk about politics?

KMH: It's not important for me to talk in public about my political views. I'm involved with several charity things that have a political message and I'm happy to put my name to that, but Q & A's too unregulated and I don't want to sort of restrict the people that like my music. I don't want to alienate people on the political right if they want to buy the album come to a gig. I want everyone to feel welcome. I don't want them to think "Oh that's that fucking pinko chick that . . ." . People have said to me on Twitter: "Shame you're such a lefty". I feel that is a shame, it's a shame because people listen to a song and they create this whole persona around who's singing that and I don't want to disturb that for anyone.

That's very nice of you.

KMH: Thanks, yeah.

Following on from what you were saying in terms of connecting with your audience: How important do you think it is for us to have a manifesto or to stand up for something as an artist?

KMH: Do you mean, like, on a worldwide kind of basis?

Well that as well, but political in general. If you have something you have to say, do you think an artist should have a manifesto?

KMH: For me just making art is in itself quite a political statement. When you look at how society works and how the vast majority of people live their lives, making art is a radical thing. I see normal people with normal jobs and I feel like an outsider. But having said that, I don't see myself as a politician. But when there's something that's blatantly wrong with society like, for example, the inequality around gay marriage, that's something I feel strongly about and I attach myself to various causes to do with that. It's a balancing act I guess.

Okay.

I read an article in a newspaper where a woman complained about you swearing on stage in front of her child. Do you refrain from using the f-bomb depending on who is in the audience?

KN: She doesn't, she just drops it. And we just did a gig 2 weeks ago in Darwin in the amphitheatre there and I looked into the front row and there were all these tiny little kids and I was just going over to Kate and saying (whispers "there's kids") and she just stands up and says "fuck!"

That's an exaggeration, but it's basically what happened though. She doesn't censor herself, except when we're in China.

KMH: Yeah, we were literally censored in China. I think that parents that bring young kids to a gig that's on at like 9, 10 pm at night can't complain. If it's in the afternoon then, yep, I definitely won't do the rude songs and fair enough. But if it's a night time gig . . . .

What kind of stories like that can you tell us about?

KMH: Well yep, if you're talking about the Powerhouse show, that's a 9:30 pm start and if I didn't do that rude stuff some people would be disappointed. So you're always going to disappoint someone. But I think most of the people that come to my shows are quite worldly and they educate their kids well and they realise that their kids have probably heard worse already. Or it's an opportunity to start the dialogue.

Audience member: You mentioned earlier about maybe about mass listing song titles. I was wondering if there was anything on your three albums or from your three albums that made the cut from the list of song titles?

KMH: What just because the title was so good?

Where it inspired you to write something really good from the song title.

KMH: Oh yeah. Well, we were talking about Last Day on Earth.

KN: *Caught In a Crowd* was the title of one, yeah. I think *The Devil Wears a Suit* started as a title off the new one.

KMH: *God's Gift to Women* was a title. I think it, yeah, you can't underestimate the importance of that, like whether it's often the tagline to the end of the chorus but if you look at the charts—that's not something I do often—you're not going to find some wordy, non-catchy title in there. It's very important I think.

Do you do this regularly, like?

KMH: Probably not regularly enough.

KN: I keep the list on my phone of stuff.

I have a question about Triple J: just wondering if you had any suggestions on how you would approach the DJs, or whether you need to have that mid-level support on unearthed or approach them directly?

KMH: No. If you're on Twitter you can follow them all individually. You can see that they really love it when you send your EP with some sort of gimmick. One of them posted a photo the other day. Someone had sent them their record in a giant balloon or something like that. It sounds ridiculous but actually that kind of shit sticks out for them and they like it. They're just like any normal people. I'm sure they like it if you suck up to them on Twitter as well.

At what point did you make an impression on the station?

KN: BigSound, wasn't it?

KMH: Actually yeah. It was BigSound. They had this thing at what was then called The Troubador, Black Bear Lodge now, where they played like 12 different tracks from Brisbane artists and they had a panel of people who then said what they thought about each song. One of my songs came up and Richard Kingsmill was on the panel and that's how it happened. So go to BigSound, it's good.

Chapter 12
Retrospective Conclusions and Predictions

Abstract This chapter summarises the themes of the interviews and contextualises them in the current environment. Five years after the interviews, indications are that we were talking at a genuine point of settlement in both music business and music industry. The characteristics of the uneasy digital "bargain" that developed between 2000 and 2012 seems to have changed very little since other than in quantitative terms. Among the more significant changes since the interviews were held is the decline of Apple Music's dominance as a point of online sales for music and, with that decline, the general withering of sales in relation to streaming as an overall source of music revenues. The role of television, or more precisely "screen media", in the entertainment landscape has also changed substantially since 2012; most notable is the absence of any mention of Netflix in the interviews, which that year had just started to produce its own content with an audience of just over 2 million subscribers. The major record companies have enjoyed a financial renaissance in the interime, collectively reaping billions from streaming services for access to their catalogues, including the multi-billion dollar capitalisation windfall from Spotify's IPO in April, 2018.

As I said in the introduction, as individual contributions, the interviews require little discussion or explanation. As a collection, the common themes are evident, especially where advice for aspiring future professionals is concerned. Five years after the series, indications are that we were talking at a genuine point of settlement in both music business and industry. That is to say, not much has changed in the meantime and the characteristics of the uneasy digital "settlement" that developed between 2000 and 2012 seems to have changed very little since, other than in quantitative terms. Among the more significant changes since the interviews were held is the decline of Apple Music's dominance as a point of online sales for music and, with that decline, the general withering of sales in relation to streaming as an overall source of music revenues. The role of television, or more precisely "screen media", in the entertainment landscape has also changed substantially since 2012; most notable is the absence of any mention of Netflix in the interviews, which that year had just started to produce its own content with an audience of just over 2 million subscribers. In respect of streaming services, their ongoing dominance,

P. Graham, *Music, Management, Marketing, and Law*, Music Business Research,
https://doi.org/10.1007/978-3-030-02143-6_12

and the relatively woeful implications of streaming revenues for working musicians, there have been few improvements. If anything, and despite the optimism of our industry veterans who assumed in 2012 that they could only get better, things seem to have gotten worse, at least for musicians' revenues. On the other hand, the major record companies have enjoyed a financial renaissance, collectively reaping billions from streaming services for access to their catalogues, including a multi-billion dollar capitalisation windfall from Spotify's IPO in April, 2018 (cf Graham, 2015; Rushe, 2018).

The fortunes and failures of Spotify are emblematic of the way the industry has developed in the meantime. The company's long-anticipated market capitalisation, consummated in May, 2018, had been held back by a series of individual and class actions aimed at claiming higher revenues from streaming for composers and performers. The eventual windfall from Spotify's (2018) IPO was an historic revenue highpoint for the majors. In 2017, the paper value of Spotify was said to be worth more than twice the entire North American music market at $16 billion, and twice its estimated paper value in 2015 (Sassard, Soderpalm, & Swahnberg, 2017). By the time it floated on the share market on April 4, 2018, Spotify achieved a paper value of $29.5 billion (Rushe, 2018). If there were ever to be an indication of such a financial event as a "music bubble", the Spotify IPO is it. Despite the valuation, the company has never made a profit and in fact loses increasing amounts of money in inverse proportion to the number of its paying customers and overall revenues, with a record loss in 2017 of $1.5 billion (Castillo, 2018). Musicians are also earning less per stream as the number of paying customers increases. All of this suggests imminent change, whether driven by market success or revenue sharing failures.

When we look across the value chain of music, as evidenced by the interviews, we see that the work of composing, producing, and performing musicians has long supported significant numbers of allied personnel: managers, agents, lawyers, record company executives from all departments; publishers, radio and playlist pluggers, road crew, tour managers, recording studio personnel, music supervisors, venue owners, royalty collection agencies—the list is seemingly endless. Add to those the new array of intermediaries who have established themselves, thanks to the centralising technical affordances of new media, and the digital value chain becomes diabolically complex, very long, and very expensive. It is as if the relationship between music as an industry (the domains in which the goods of music are made for audiences) and music as a business (those parts of the ecology dedicated to making money from those goods) is symbolic of current political economic circumstances more broadly. In organisational terms, the further away one is from the "factory floor", where the "things" of music are made, the more one is likely to get paid. While Spotify, Google, YouTube and other streaming platforms are notorious for paying musicians poorly, Spotify, for example, pays its employees 'an average of 172,000 euros ($180,000) per employee annually, versus the 164,000 Euros ($171,000) on average it paid to employees in 2015' (Christman, 2017). Over the same period the company increased its losses by 48% while increasing its revenues by 52% (Christman, 2017).

What will be glaringly obvious to the contemporary reader about the makeup of interviewees in this book is the overwhelming representation of males among them. It was not an oversight in programming; it reflects a male-dominated music business that our guests were engaged in recounting. It was, as the song goes, "a man's world". In another 20 years time, such a recount of the early digital era will look very different in terms of gender representation. It will also look different in terms of occupational and corporate composition. The major labels continue to hold a powerful position in the business at a global level, with access to their catalogues still being *sine qua non* for any would-be viable streaming startup. However, thanks to the accumulated force of close to four decades of digital upheaval in the realm of production, independents are closer to taking a majority share of global sales, accounting for 38.4% of worldwide recorded music revenues in 2016 with a collective revenue of $6 billion as compared with the majors' combined revenues of $9 billion (World Independent Network (WIN), 2017, p. 8). More importantly, and contributing greatly to the changes that are to come, independents are producing and releasing by far the greatest proportion of new music (IFPI, 2014; WIN, 2017, p. 7).

What that means for the future of revenues for recorded music is unclear in the short term, but further into the future it is a fairly safe bet to assume that increasing dominance of the independent sector must weaken the majors' position in respect of barriers to entry where new digital distribution platforms are concerned. The financial success of Spotify's float practically guarantees a proliferation of new entrants into the streaming market, all of them attempting to be the 'neo-Spotify' that Peter Colby predicted during his interview. As the fans of recording artists whose heyday came between the 1960s and 1990s grow old and pass into history, and the catalogues of independent artists like Adele, Taylor Swift, and Ed Sheeran become the new *de rigeur* for streaming services success, the "rules of the road" are likely to change in favour of independent artists and labels where distribution of revenues are concerned. The sheer size of the windfall for Spotify shareholders has already generated questions about the rights of artists in the float itself. The majors are again front and centre of attention because, as well as being beneficiaries of Spotify "revenue guarantees", they are all shareholders in Spotify, with Sony the fifth largest of all shareholders, with 10 million Spotify shares, 5.7% of Spotify equity, worth $1.5 billion. Warner and Universal are rumoured to own 4% each, with each 4% being today worth about $1 billion (Fuscaldo, 2018). Add to that the $1 billion or so per year that Spotify has paid out to the majors and the returns are impressive, especially because they are almost pure profit thanks to the 'black-box' status of the income (Tschmuck, 2012, p. 184). Spotify is around half of the global streaming market by volume of tracks (47.78%) and income (51.51%) (The Trichordist, 2018).[1] That means we can assume around $2 billion per year streaming income to the majors in the form of obscurely named 'revenue guarantees' which are publicly called 'advances' (Graham, 2015).

[1]The Trichordist lists the ten most influential and successful streaming services in the following order based on marketshare for revenue and quantities of streams: Spotify, iTunes, Pandora, Google, Amazon, Deezer, Tidal, Rhapsody, YouTube, and Xbox Music (2018).

All of this new wealth (or financial puffery, depending on how you view things) draws attention to the fact that musicians stand to gain next to nothing from the Spotify float, despite Spotify's entire fortune being built on a foundation of composing and recording artists' effort without which the service would be worth nothing. It seems unlikely that musicians will see much without some kind of major legal upset. Zack O'Malley Greenburg (2018) remarks that on the issue of paying artists any share of their post-float windfall, the majors are 'long on promises and short on details':

> A rep from Warner Music Group referred me to a 2-year old quote from its CEO affirming the company's intention to compensate acts, while a Sony spokesperson also sent a previously-released statement.
>
> "Sony Music and The Orchard are committed to sharing with their artists and distributed labels any net gain they may realize from a sale of Sony Music's equity stake in Spotify," reads Sony's explanation. "This is consistent with our previously announced policy of sharing breakage and equity proceeds from digital catalog licenses with our artists and distributed labels."
>
> Representatives from Universal Music Group, the third and largest major label, did not immediately return a request for comment; a Spotify spokesperson referred me back to the record companies. Beyond the statements offered, none of the majors would elaborate on the record about their plans. (Greenburg, 2018)

Paul Resnikoff is even less hopeful for the fortunes of artists: 'if Enrique Iglesias can't get paid on some aging downloads, then very few others have a shot. And don't forget, Spotify's valuation was falling by the Monday bell. This isn't a profitable company' (Resnikoff, 2018). Resnikoff makes the moral point that there is 'just something wrong with lavish Spotify billionaires powered by starving artists' (Resnikoff, 2018).

So its IPO emphasised the already obvious revenue disparities between Spotify and the musicians on whose backs its fortunes have been made. Of course it is nothing new for musicians to get a raw deal from businesses that make money selling their music; it is simply that the scale of the IPO is so large that the unfairness seems so much more pronounced. Also, Spotify's distance from the industry of music making is unlike that era of the major label system our interviewees have been largely concerned with throughout this book. That is to say, throughout the corporate history of the major labels, they have been involved in what was very much a vertically integrated business model in which personal relationships were key at every level: the majors "discovered" artists, composers, and small labels; funded the production of music, often with direct input into artistic matters; they packaged, promoted, and distributed the music; and they quite often held the publishing rights to the music being recorded, albeit at arms-length, as with Warner-Chappell, Sony ATV, BMG, and Universal Music Publishing Group. Even though some musicians fared poorly through that system, with many more being excluded from its benefits for one reason or another, the majors could at least be seen to play a major part in funding the writing and recording—the industry—of new music. Also, as Michael Smellie points out, the global industry was a lot smaller up to the advent of CD and the subsequent financialisation of the major labels, so the people affected by poor payment regimes seemed not to be so numerous or ubiquitous. Finally, Spotify is the digital equivalent of an analogue era retailer. It is the point at which mass audiences "get" their music from. But it also functions much like radio did for the analogue era as a discovery: that is, through its playlist system, Spotify facilitates a tastemaking function, something that commercial radio has long since abandoned across much of the world for much "safer", demographically-driven market research approach to playlisting music, as noted by a multiple interviewees.

All of that implies imminent and significant change, or at least a significant range of potential motivations for it. Kate Miller-Heidke and Keir Nuttall give us the most insight into how historical and future forces are most likely to influence changes to the ways in which music industries and businesses interact. Kate goes to the essence of one change that is most often sidelined in discussions of music business futures when she says: "Recording is so cheap now that you can get something which sounds great for not much money. So it doesn't make sense not to own your own recordings. If you want to use a label to distribute it then licensing makes sense. But I think the traditional deal is kind of obsolete now, let alone the 360 one." Almost three decades of digitally driven change in the plant and equipment required to make records has had numerous effects. Today, given a skilled enough engineer and producer, a recording made in someone's bedroom on a laptop is indistinguishable from one made in a large-format, multi-million dollar professional recording facility, even to the most discerning ears (Goold, & Graham, in press). That has meant a logarithmic increase in the numbers of people with access to what would once have been called "broadcast quality" recording equipment, a related increase in the number of individual rights holders, and in the number of new songs being released daily. All of those were aspects of industry that, by and large, were controlled by the major labels for most of the last century. But as motivating issues for change, they are not so nearly as well aired forces as the rapid "democratisation" of the facility for high-fidelity infinite replication of recorded music and global distribution facilitated by digital communication technologies and broadband internet.

Thus to the paradox at the heart of changes that must shape the future: a proliferating number of unorganised and diffuse rights holders within systems of national and global legal rights designed largely for the expedience of a few centralised and massive rights holders. As Shane Simpson said,

> I think that the corporate investment in copyright is so enormous that I don't see any threat to copyright itself as an economic construct. Almost every major corporation on the planet has on its books a huge investment in IP, intellectual property. So I don't think copyright's going to go away any time soon. But of course how money is made out of copyright, what those copyrights protect, who owns those copyrights, those are continually changing. They've been changing since Gutenberg and the printing press.

The only constant beside such changes, he said, was that 'you must always assume the technology's going to change', and that laws to govern those changes would and in fact *should* lag somewhat. In his view the system must necessarily get fixed. The ways in which people use the centrifugal forces of ever cheapening production technologies and how that interacts against the centripetal forces of vested interests with global market power and a legal system designed largely in their favour are the motivating features of the age.

Then there is the obvious centralising tendency of the internet. What was once touted as a new frontier in freedom, an untrammeled benefit to humanity, has shown characteristic tendencies towards monopoly, for-profit mass surveillance, and political economic centralisation enough times for its message to be clear. Google, YouTube, Facebook, Apple, Twitter, Instagram, Netflix, and of course Spotify, all exemplify the different kinds of 'knowledge monopolies' that one might be tempted to identify in the field of internet culture (Innis, 1951). But they do not have the qualities of knowledge monopolies so much as they do the qualities of a massive mobilisation of 'audience labour' on a global scale (Smythe, 1981). Most successful in harnessing the labour of millions is YouTube, with 300 hours of video being uploaded every minute, almost ten times the amount of footage noted during the interviews. Facebook is the leader in terms of numbers engaged in their platform (2.1 billion users at the time of writing), with its business model being a mixture of advertising and sales of personal data to advertisers, as revealed in recent outrages involving Cambridge Analytica, Brexit, and Donald Trump's election to the US Presidency (Solon, 2018).

The currently turbulent world of global politics may seem tangential to our subject of music industry and business, except that many millions of Spotify users have joined Spotify using Facebook since 2011. In 2017, Spotify began letting users know it would soon be mandatory for them to have a Facebook account if they wished to continue using Spotify, an eventually failed extension a policy begun in 2011 requiring all new accounts to be activated through Facebook (Humphries, 2011). In an even more invasive move related to its partnership with Spotify, 'Facebook Messenger's intelligent assistant now delivers Spotify suggestions when music is brought up in conversation. The prompts are triggered by a variety of phrases and specific words' (Deahl, 2017).

> Spotify's integration with Facebook Messenger began in March, with an implementation that (clumsily) allowed people to choose songs and playlists and send them to others. At the time, Spotify told The Verge that "users can expect further enhancements," and in April, the Spotify Messenger bot launched along with a chat extension. In June, Group Playlists for Messenger arrived, which allowed users to collaborate on shared playlists by picking and adding songs in Spotify through Messenger itself. (Deahl, 2017)

In other words, Spotify is now implicated in the same set of public interest issues that surround the Cambridge Analytica scandal through close technical integration with Facebook and enthusiastic onselling of user data. The degree to which Spotify's data is entangled with Facebook's is unclear, yet detail must come to the fore at some time fairly soon, if only because of the level of detail it holds about about its users' listening preferences:

> Today, in Spotify's SEC filing to go public through an unusual direct listing, the company writes that "a key differentiating factor between Spotify and other music content providers is our ability to predict music that our Users will enjoy. Our system for predicting User music preferences and selecting music tailored to our Users' individual music tastes is based on advanced data analytics systems and our proprietary algorithms."
>
> That data came from The Echo Nest—200 petabytes of user behavior data to be exact. That's compared to the 60 petabytes Netflix had in 2016. Spotify logs 150 billion plays, shares, skips, follows and other signals per day that tune its recommendations. (Constine, 2018)

Such deep and detailed access to users' listening data can only be a boon to those interested in influencing public opinion given music's well-researched links with individual and social identity, emotion, affect, group belonging, attitude, age, perception, cognition, and the many other aspects of human decision making that music choice can tell the analytically minded (Peretz, Gagnon, & Bouchard, 1998; Thompson, Graham, & Russo, 2005). Its intimate links with Facebook implicate Spotify in mainstream politics and political economy through the many potentials for persuasion linked to people's music listening habits.

The strange and ever-changing business models around music will without doubt continue to change with time, and the new rights complex involved in streaming technologies is without doubt subject to change at any time, whether legally, technically, or in response to popular opinion. Whether streaming-based business models will have the longevity of the vinyl-radio nexus that held sway between the mid-1950s and the late-1980s, or whether they will be like CD whose heyday lasted little more than a decade, or cassette tapes with their brief year of global market dominance as a distribution format in 1989, remains to be seen. The movement of music seems to be in all directions at once, like that of technology more generally. That is to say, people seem to want their music everywhere, all the time, with everything ever recorded being available on demand in one place. That is another strange characteristic of the global music market; whereas streaming services focused on movie and television offerings, and even distribution of something as technically generic as access to converted print offerings (e-books and such), have hundreds of points of online distribution, retail, and other forms of access, music audiences seem to tend towards services that are centralised, comprehensive, and ubiquitous.

The equally strange attitudes of streaming music companies—namely that audiences *should* have everything ever recorded available everywhere, for free if necessary—is only possible in a world where musicians' rights are at such a distant remove from the point at which their audiences interact with those rights commercially in the act of listening. It is also a requirement that musicians ultimately agree to allow their music to be used in such a way. In effect, Spotify, along with many other social media companies, have extended the 'audience labour' model, first identified by Humphrey McQueen (1977) and later elaborated by Dallas Smythe (1981), into the most intimate aspects of human activity (Graham, 2006). Smythe notes that in broadcast media economies, the dominant business model is that media companies produce audiences for sale to advertisers, developing what Smythe calls the 'audience commodity' (1981). In 2016, Spotify fused new and old media models by both charging subscriptions, running advertisements, and added the digital boon: offering its users' data for sale 'globally across Spotify's 59 markets. Buyers can target audiences by age, gender, genres and playlists—all in real time' (Wycislik-Wilson, 2016). Spotify (2018) gives a sly wink in its pitch to "buyers" (advertisers) when they describe the potential level of influence one can have once armed with intimate knowledge of their audiences' music listening habits:

> Playlists are no longer just simple collections of songs. They've grown to become cultural epicenters, complete with their own communities. On RapCaviar, more than 8 million hyper-engaged fans keep up with the hip-hop world. Viva Latino! has 6 million passionate listeners

> of its own. And hundreds of millions of listeners streamed Your Time Capsule, a personalized playlist that took them back to the music they loved as a teenager.
>
> When people follow these playlists, they put Spotify at the center of their lives. The more they listen, the more we're able to reflect today's culture—and sometimes even shape it.
>
> [. . .] All of these insights fuel our streaming intelligence—psychographic and behavioral audience insights that go way beyond traditional demographics. By pairing our first-party data with third-party research, we're connecting these streaming behaviors to real-world behaviors. (Spotify, 2018)

It can only be a matter of time before Spotify finds itself in the crosshairs of regulatory scrutiny into treatment of its users' data. It is also a potential flashpoint for a "MySpace moment" that could leave its users feeling betrayed or misused. Add to that the fast-growing awareness of the degree to which many musicians and composers are disadvantaged by current arrangements, the constant flow of new entrants into streaming media, and the lack of apparent profitability in streaming's underlying business model, the lightning-fast proliferation of independent and individual rights holders, and Spotify's dominance seems likely to be a relatively brief phenomenon, somewhere between cassette and CD.

When it happens that the current streaming becomes an historical phenomenon, it will model bring to a close the digital "settlement" we have seen documented in this series of interviews. Or perhaps it is more of an "interregnum", a brief détente between the age of mass coordinated copyrights held by global corporations, alongside the literal financialisation of music business which might well have begun with Michael Smellie's lease-back deal on the Little River Band's catalogue, and the age in which millions of independent copyright owners, which currently makes up at least 30% of Spotify's streamed music, asserts itself collectively through some yet-to-be-formed institution or platform.

Whatever happens, we can be sure that the current situation is not the end of change for music business or industry, as indicated by all of our interviewees. Michael Taylor's insightful commentary about the tensions between art and commerce point to the main motivating dynamic of "the business". While the machinations of distribution and the many related outrages associated with those play out, the more fundamental movement will continue: the proliferation of "small" rights holders, individuals who own and control their own recordings, compositions, and copyrights, and whose sense of music business is equal to their mastery of music making.

Coming full circle back to Veblen (1923), we might understand what is happening as a fast-emerging 'handicraft' era for recorded music. Veblen is convinced that, historically, 'the modern era begins with the rise of handicraft', an era in which industry and business were in the same hands:

> The craftsman was an artificer engaged in mechanical operations, working with tools of which he had the mastery, and employing mechanical processes the mysteries of which were familiar to his everyday habits of thought; but from the beginning of the era of handicraft and throughout his industrial life he was also more or less of a trader. He stood in close relation with some form of market, and his proficiency as a craftsman was brought to a daily practical test in the sale of his wares or services, no less than in the workmanlike fashioning of them. (Veblen, 1923, pp. 209–210)

Now it is a given that a pre-capitalist craftsman selling shoes, pots, *carillon*, or whatever they might have made, is a vastly different phenomenon than a contemporary musician recording music for sale to the world. But in principle they are alike to the degree they must embrace and merge industry and business principles; they must face the practical test of their wares in a global market amidst millions of others doing the "same" thing. The future of any future musical career for artists will depend on their ability to do both. As Keir Nuttall said of his partner: 'Kate started off managing herself. In fact that's one of the reasons that I think Kate is so successful: she was actually doing a manager's job before she ever had a manager'. The lone woman in our series is perhaps the clearest harbinger of major change, an artist emblematic of the future, someone in possession of their rights and in touch with all areas of their business, bound neither by genre nor contract.

In recounting the past, the interviews given by our guests all pointed toward an exciting future, one that is far from likely settled. As Shane Simpson said, nobody has the answers and people who say they do are 'just snake oil salesmen'. I count myself very fortunate to have had the opportunity to spend time and speak with such a group. They are people who are as much a part of world cultural history as they are of Australia's music industry and business. The series will, I hope, continue to stand the test of time. It describes how things got to be the way they are, both explicitly and implicitly, by people whose job it has been to figure out how to respond to culture, technology, aesthetics, law, management, and political economy on a daily basis and in real-time, for global audiences. It shows the mistakes, triumphs, and, miserable failures endemic to music as an ongoing and constantly groundbreaking experiment in selling commercialised cultural goods. It gives often surprising reasons for famous events that were failed, mistaken, genius, or, however coincidentally, momentously successful. It gives insight into the most foundational assumptions of copyright, in all its forms. It shows the almost irreconcilable differences between issues of quality, quantity, and price. Most of all the series showed, in so may ways, the productive dynamism generated by the inherent conflicts built into the relationships between art and commerce; production and distribution; industry and business; and culture, technology, and the law.

References

Castillo, M. (2018, February 28). Music streaming service Spotify files to go public, lost $1.5 billion last year. *CNBC News*. Retrieved from https://www.cnbc.com/2018/02/28/spotify-files-for-ipo.html

Christman, E. (2017, June 15). Spotify's losses more than double to $581M, revenues rise to $3B. *Billboard*. Retrieved from https://www.billboard.com/articles/business/7833686/spotify-2016-losses-financial-results-revenue

Constine, J. (2018, March 1). Going public pits Spotify's suggestions against everyone. *Techcrunch*. Retrieved from https://techcrunch.com/2018/02/28/the-worlds-dj/

Deahl, D. (2017, August 14). Facebook Messenger now makes Spotify suggestions based on your conversations. *The Verge*. Retrieved from https://www.theverge.com/2017/8/14/16143354/facebook-messenger-spotify-recommendations-find-music

Fuscaldo, D. (2018). Top 6 Spotify shareholders. *Investopedia*. Retrieved from https://www.investopedia.com/news/top-3-spotify-shareholders/

Goold, L., & Graham, P. (in press, June 23). The uncertain future of the large-format recording studio. In *Proceedings of the 2017 12th Art of Record Production Conference*. Royal College of Music (Stockholm)/Journal on the Art of Record Production.

Graham, P. (2006). Monopoly, monopsony, and the value of culture in a digital age: An axiology of two multimedia resource repositories. In C. Kapitzke & B. C. Bruce (Eds.), *Libr@ries: Changing information space and practice* (pp. 253–270). New Jersey: Lawrence Erlbaum.

Graham, P. (2015). Issues facing fair compensation for musicians in the era of streaming. *Music Australia News*. Retrieved from http://musicaustralia.org.au/2015/06/issues-facing-fair-compensation-for-musicians-in-the-era-of-streaming/

Greenburg, Z. (2018). Spotify goes public at $30 billion; when will artists see any of that? *Forbes*. Retrieved from https://www.forbes.com/sites/zackomalleygreenburg/2018/04/03/spotify-ipo-goes-public-at-30-billion-when-will-artists-see-any-of-that/#521b43b337b0

Humphries, M. (2011). Spotify now requires a Facebook login for new accounts. *Geek.Com*. Retrieved from https://www.geek.com/news/spotify-now-requires-a-facebook-login-for-new-accounts-1424177/

IFPI. (2014). *IFPI digital music report 2014: Lighting up new markets*. Available at: https://www.ifpi.org/downloads/Digital-Music-Report-2014.pdf

Innis, H. A. (1951). *The bias of communication*. Toronto: Toronto University Press.

McQueen, H. (1977). *Australia's media monopolies*. Melbourne: Widescope.

Peretz, I., Gagnon, L., & Bouchard, B. (1998). Music and emotion: Perceptual determinants, immediacy, and isolation after brain damage. *Cognition, 68*(2), 111–141.

Resnikoff, P. (2018, April 3). Spotify wins. Artists lose. Any questions? *Digital Music News*. Retrieved from https://www.digitalmusicnews.com/2018/04/03/spotify-wins-artists-lose-questions/

Rushe, D. (2018, April 4). Spotify goes public with a bang after flag snafu to mark first day of trading. *The Guardian*. Retrieved from https://www.theguardian.com/technology/2018/apr/03/spotify-ipo-flag-error-swiss-sweden-first-day-trading

Sassard, S., Soderpalm, H., & Swahnberg, O. (2017). Spotify's valuation turned up to $16 billion in private trades. *Reuters*. Retrieved from https://www.reuters.com/article/us-spotify-listing-exclusive/exclusive-spotifys-valuation-turned-up-to-16-billion-in-private-trades-sources-idUSKCN1C226W

Smythe, D. (1981). *Dependency road: Communications, capitalism, consciousness, and Canada*. New Jersey: Ablex.

Solon, O. (2018, April 5). Facebook says Cambridge Analytica may have gained 37m more users' data. *The Guardian*. Retrieved from https://www.theguardian.com/technology/2018/apr/04/facebook-cambridge-analytica-user-data-latest-more-than-thought

Spotify. (2018). *Obsession and nostalgia: What streaming habits reveal about your audience*. Stockholm: Spotify. Available at: https://spotifyforbrands.com/en-US/news/obsession-and-nostalgia-what-streaming-habits-reveal-about-your-audience/

The Trichordist. (2018). 2017 Streaming Price Bible! Spotify per stream rates drop 9%, Apple Music gains marketshare of both plays and overall revenue. *The Trichordist*. Retrieved from https://thetrichordist.com/2018/01/15/2017-streaming-price-bible-spotify-per-stream-rates-drop-9-apple-music-gains-marketshare-of-both-plays-and-overall-revenue/

Thompson, W. F., Graham, P., & Russo, F. A. (2005). Seeing music performance: Visual influences on perception and experience. *Semiotica, 2005*(156), 203–227.

Tschmuck, P. (2012). *Creativity and innovation in the music industry* (2nd ed.). Berlin: Springer.

Veblen, T. (1923). *Absentee ownership and business enterprise in recent times: The case of America*. New York: B. W. Huebsch.

World Independent Network. (2017). *Wintel worldwide independent market report 2017*. Warwick: Warwick University. Retrieved from http://winformusic.org/files/WINTEL%202017/WINTEL%202017.pdf

Wycislik-Wilson, M. (2016). Spotify sells your personal and playlist data to advertisers making you the product. *Betanews*. Retrieved from https://betanews.com/2016/07/22/spotify-sells-user-data-to-advertisers/

MIX
Papier aus verantwortungsvollen Quellen
Paper from responsible sources
FSC® C105338

If you have any concerns about our products,
you can contact us on
ProductSafety@springernature.com

In case Publisher is established outside the EU,
the EU authorized representative is:
Springer Nature Customer Service Center GmbH
Europaplatz 3, 69115 Heidelberg, Germany

Printed by Libri Plureos GmbH
in Hamburg, Germany